109

181

279

Venice

Editorial

Editor Anne Hanley
Copy editor Ros Sales
Proofreader Marion Moisy
Indexer Rebecca Knott

Editorial Director Sarah Guy
Management Accountant Margaret Wright

Design

Senior Designer Kei Ishimaru
Designer Thomas Havell
Group Commercial Senior Designer Jason Tansley

Picture Desk

Picture Editor Jael Marschner
Deputy Picture Editor Ben Rowe
Freelance Picture Researcher Lizzy Owen

Advertising

Managing Director of Advertising St John Betteridge
Advertising Jinga Media Ltd (www.jingamedia.com)

Marketing

Senior Publishing Brand Manager Luthfa Begum
Head of Circulation Dan Collins

Production

Production Controller Katie Mulhern-Bhudia

Time Out Group

Chairman & Founder Tony Elliott
Chief Executive Officer Tim Arthur
Chief Commercial Officer Kim O'Hara
Publisher Alex Batho
Group IT Director Simon Chappell
Group Marketing Director Carolyn Sims

Contributors

Venice Today Anne Hanley. **Diary** Anne Hanley. **Explore** Gregory Dowling, Anne Hanley, Lee Marshall, Michela Scibilia, Jo-Ann Titmarsh, Jill Weinreich. **Children** Patrizia Lerco. **Film** Jo-Ann Titmarsh. **Gay & Lesbian** Salvatore Mele. **Nightlife** Kate Davies. **Performing Arts** Anne Hanley. **Escapes & Excursions** Jill Weinreich, Anne Hanley. **History** Anne Hanley. **Architecture** Anne Hanley. **Venetian Painting** Frederick Ilchman. **Hotels** Anne Hanley, Nicky Swallow. **Essential Information** Jill Weinreich, Anne Hanley.

Maps LS International Cartography, via Decemviri 8, 20138 Milan, Italy. www.geomaker.it

Cover and pull-out map photography F. Lukasseck/Masterfile

Back cover photography Clockwise from top left: SoWhat/Shutterstock.com; Michele Gamberinini; Nikolas Koenig; Phant/Shutterstock.com; Olivia Rutherford

Photography Pages 2/3 Dudarev Mikhail/Shutterstock.com; 4 (top), 38 Paul Prescott/Shutterstock.com; 4 (bottom), 7, 23, 32/33 (bottom), 34/35, 82, 83, 94, 98, 116, 142, 183, 292 Olivia Rutherford; 5 (top), 10, 11, 14 (middle), 16 (top and middle), 22, 22/23 (top), 24, 24/25 (top), 25, 53, 60, 61, 63, 72, 74, 75, 84, 86, 90, 92, 101, 103, 106, 109, 110, 111, 112, 121, 124, 132/133, 139, 140, 145, 168, 169 (bottom), 172, 186, 187, 194 (top), 197, 261, 264, 266, 269, 271, 273, 274, 276 Olivia Rutherford; 5 (bottom right), 279 Nikolas Koenig; 10/11 Deborah McCague/Shutterstock.com; 13 (top left) VanderWolf Images/Shutterstock.com; 13 (bottom) Michele Crosera; 14 (top) Adrian Zenz/Shutterstock.com; 14 (bottom), 141 Adriano Castelli/Shutterstock.com; 15 (top), 149 © ORCH orsenigo_chemollo; 15 (bottom) Deborah Lynn Guber; 16/17 (bottom), 22/23 (bottom), 147 Andrea Sarti/CAST1466/Peggy Guggenheim Collection; 17 (top) Dave Bramhall; 17 (middle) Motordigitaal/Shutterstock.com; 18/19 Luciano Mortula/Shutterstock.com; 24/25 (bottom), 69, 88, 255 Renata Sedmakova/Shutterstock.com; 26/27 ©Vogalonga; 28 (top) Gian Giacomo Stiffoni; 28 (bottom) Captblack76/Shutterstock.com; 29 (bottom) National Geographic/Getty Images; 30 (top) cheyennezj/Shutterstock.com; 30 (bottom) Rolf_52/Shutterstock.com; 32/33 (top) Kiev.Victor/Shutterstock.com; 35 Vito Poma; 36/37 andras_csontos/Shutterstock.com; 38/39 JLR Photography/Shutterstock.com; 40 (top) posztos/Shutterstock.com; 40 (middle), 175 Ki Zel/Shutterstock.com; 40 (bottom), 176 (bottom) federicocandonifoto/Shutterstock.com; 41 Mariusz Niedzwiedzki/Shutterstock.com; 42, 65 Brendan Howard/Shutterstock.com; 43 (top) Jake Foster/Shutterstock.com; 43 (bottom) maigi/Shutterstock.com; 44 Circumnavigation/Shutterstock.com; 45 pseudolongino/Shutterstock.com; 46 (top), 66, 243 Tupungato/Shutterstock.com; 46 (bottom) Sergey Novikov/Shutterstock.com; 47 (top) Roman Sigaev/Shutterstock.com; 47 (bottom) Federico Rostagno/Shutterstock.com; 48 Kiril Stanchev/Shutterstock.com; 48/49 Iakov Kalinin/Shutterstock.com; 52 Andreas Zerndl/Shutterstock.com; 54 SoWhat/Shutterstock.com; 58 Marina99/Shutterstock.com; 72/73 Irina Mos/Shutterstock.com; 78, 91 (top), 150, 236 wjarek/Shutterstock.com; 79 Tamara Kulikova/Shutterstock.com; 81 Paul Brown; 87 Jorge Sanchez/Shutterstock.com; 91 (bottom) eldeiv/Shutterstock.com; 92/93 Serg Zastavkin/Shutterstock.com; 95 (top) Crisferra/Shutterstock.com; 95 (bottom) S-F/Shutterstock.com; 99 ZRyzner/Shutterstock.com; 102 Boris-B/Shutterstock.com; 105 Bildagentur Zoonar GmbH/Shutterstock.com; 108 ChinellatoPhoto/Shutterstock.com; 113 pica82/Shutterstock.com; 117 Giovanni Dall'Orto; 118 baldovina/Shutterstock.com; 123 naten/Shutterstock.com; 127 grafalex/Shutterstock.com; 129 (left) Deea/Shutterstock.com; 129 (right) Frank11/Shutterstock.com; 132, 213 meunierd/Shutterstock.com; 134, 160/161 BasPhoto/Shutterstock.com; 152 Taiftin/Shutterstock.com; 152/153 S.Borisov/Shutterstock.com; 154 Luisa Fumi/Shutterstock.com; 155 (top and bottom right) Angela Colonna; 158 Vladislav Proshkin/Shutterstock.com; 159 Vision; 160, 164 LYSVIK PHOTOS/Shutterstock.com; 162, 176 (top) Angelo Giampiccolo/Shutterstock.com; 163 Victoria Gopka/Shutterstock.com; 169 (top) StockCube/Shutterstock.com; 170, 252/253 Phant/Shutterstock.com; 171 Ilko Iliev/Shutterstock.com; 173 catalunyastock/Shutterstock.com; 177 starman963/Shutterstock.com ; 184 la Biennale di Venezia; 185 iriselmo/Shutterstock.com; 189 Michele Gamberinini; 192 Matteo De Fina; 193 ChinellatoPhoto/Shutterstock.com; 198/199 A.Sampino/Getty Images/Flickr RM; 200 gkuna/Shutterstock.com; 202 LianeM/Shutterstock.com; 203 Pietro Basilico/Shutterstock.com; 204, 206 (bottom), 207 (bottom) vvoe/Shutterstock.com; 206 (top) s74/Shutterstock.com; 210 Tomasz Kozal/Shutterstock.com; 211 mary416/Shutterstock.com; 212 (top) meunierd/Shutterstock.com; 212 (bottom) dimbar76/Shutterstock.com; 214 strenghtofframeITA/Shutterstock.com; 215 (top) Flegere/Shutterstock.com; 215 (bottom) Steve Heap/Shutterstock.com; 218 AJE/Shutterstock.com; 219 (top) Tom Roche/Shutterstock.com; 219 (bottom) cristalvi/Shutterstock.com; 220, 221 Blaz Kure/Shutterstock.com; 222 Dmitri Ometsinsky/Shutterstock.com; 224 Claudio Giovanni Colombo/Shutterstock.com; 225 dreadek/Shutterstock.com; 226 Maria Veras/Shutterstock.com; 227 Renata Sedmakova/Shutterstock.com; 228 Jorg Hackemann/Shutterstock.com; 229 Nicola Dal Zotto/Shutterstock.com; 230/231 Lledo/Shutterstock.com; 232/233 Imagno/Getty Images; 235 Leemage/UIG/Getty Images; 238 Bridgeman Art Library; 241 Tertman/Shutterstock.com; 244/245 Getty Images/The Bridgeman Art Library; 247 ©The Frick Collection; 254 Baloncici/Shutterstock.com; 256 Georgios Kollidas/Shutterstock.com; 257 onixxino/Shutterstock.com; 258 Myroslava/Shutterstock.com; 259 txIlxt/Panoramio; 260 Thomas Winwood; 265 Jan S./Shutterstock.com; 272 (top) Pascal Benard; 292 (bottom left) Anibal Trejo/Shutterstock.com; 295 Moviestore Collection/Rex Features; 302/303 StevanZZ/Shutterstock.com.

The following images were supplied by the featured establishments: pages 5 (bottom left), 13 (top right), 29 (top), 57, 155 (left), 166, 178/179, 180, 181, 190, 191, 194 (bottom), 196, 262/263, 272 (bottom), 292 (bottom right)

About the Guide

GETTING AROUND

Each sightseeing chapter contains a street map of the area marked with the locations of sights and museums (**①**), restaurants (**①**), cafés and bars (**①**), and shops (**①**). There are also street maps of Venice at the back of the book, along with an overview map of the city and vaporetto map. In addition, there is now a detachable fold-out street and vaporetto map inside the back cover.

THE ESSENTIALS

For practical information, including visas, disabled access, emergency numbers, lost property, websites and local transport, see the Essential Information section. It begins on page 262.

THE LISTINGS

Addresses, phone numbers, websites, transport information, hours and prices are all included in our listings, as are selected other facilities. All were checked and correct at press time. However, business owners can alter their arrangements at any time, and fluctuating economic conditions can cause prices to change rapidly.

The very best venues, the must-sees and must-dos in every category, have been marked with a red star (★). In the sightseeing chapters, we've also marked venues with free admission with a FREE symbol.

THE LANGUAGE

Many Venetians speak a little English, but a few basic Italian phrases go a long way. You'll find a primer on page 293, along with some help with restaurants on page 292.

PHONE NUMBERS

The area code for Venice and its province is 041; for Padua it's 049, for Verona 045 and for Vicenza 0444. You must use the code, whether you're calling from inside or outside the area.

From outside Italy, dial your country's international access code (00 from the UK, 011 from the US) or a + symbol, followed by the Italy country code (39), 041 for Venice (without dropping the initial zero) and the rest of the number as listed in the guide. So to reach the Palazzo Ducale, dial + 39 041 271 5911. For more on phones, *see p288*.

FEEDBACK

We welcome feedback on this guide, both on the venues we've included and on any other locations that you'd like to see featured in future editions. Please email us at guides@timeout.com.

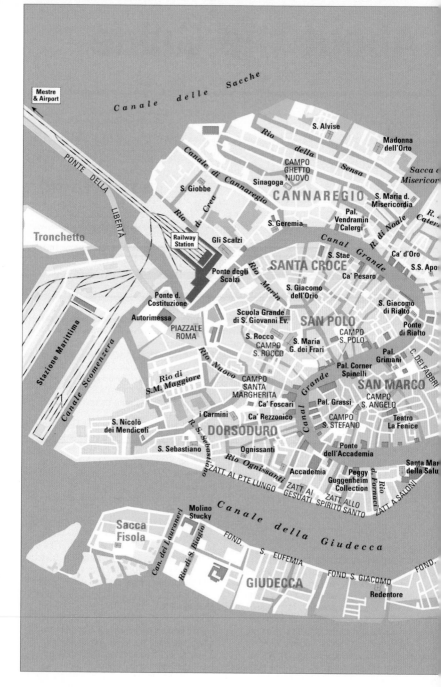

Contents

38

32

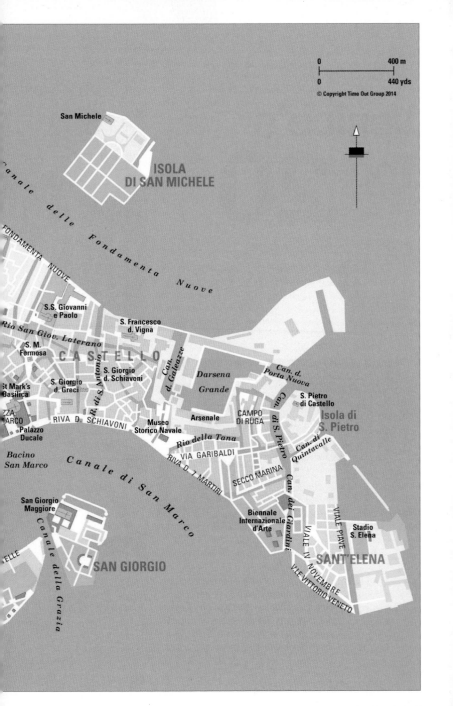

0   400 m

0   440 yds

© Copyright Time Out Group 2014

San Michele

ISOLA DI SAN MICHELE

Canale delle Fondamenta Nuove

FONDAMENTA NUOVE

S.S. Giovanni e Paolo

S. Francesco d. Vigna

Rio San Giov. Laterano

S. M. Formosa

CASTELLO

S. Giorgio d. Schiavoni

Can. d. Galeazze

Darsena Grande

Can. d. Porta Nuova

St Mark's Basilica

S. Giorgio d. Greci

R. di S. Antonio

S. Pietro di Castello

Isola di S. Pietro

ZZA MARCO

Palazzo Ducale

RIVA D. SCHIAVONI

Museo Storico Navale

Arsenale

CAMPO DI RUGA

Can. di S. Pietro

Can. di Quintavalle

Bacino San Marco

Rio della Tana

VIA GARIBALDI

RIVA D. 7 MARTIRI

SECCO MARINA

Can. dei Giardini

Canale di San Marco

San Giorgio Maggiore

Biennale Internazionale d'Arte

VIALE IV NOVEMBRE

VIALE PIAVE

Stadio S. Elena

SAN GIORGIO

SANT'ELENA

V.LE VITTORIO VENETO

Canale della Grazia

ELLE

Venice's
Top 20

*Art, churches, palaces, gondolas,
markets and more.*

1 I Frari
(page 126)

A remarkable repository of fine art, this
huge hangar-like church is dominated
by Titian's glorious *Assumption of the
Virgin*, swirling heavenwards wrapped
in her scarlet gown and blue cape. Also
here is a *Madonna and Child with saints*
by Giovanni Bellini, arguably one of his
greatest works, and Titian's magnificent
Madonna di Ca' Pesaro.

2 Basilica di San Marco
(page 50)

A heart-stopping sight lording it over piazza San Marco, the basilica of St Mark is equally magical inside where acres – literally – of glistening golden mosaic follow the sinuous curves of its domes. From the upstairs museum, where the four bronze horses are displayed, to the gem-encrusted Pala d'Oro, it's all wondrous.

3 Rialto Markets
(pages 112-118)

Venetians stock up each morning (Mon-Sat) at the north-west foot of the Rialto bridge, where stalls are piled high with fruit and vegetables, and – in the Pescaria – slimy, slithering creatures of the deep, many of which you'll be hard-pressed to identify. With its Grand Canal frontage, this must surely count as one of the world's most atmospheric shopping venues.

4 La Fenice
(pages 69, 195)

Venice's opera house is a gem – and one with a long season of top-rate operas and concerts. If you can't catch a performance, there are guided tours of the building, offering a chance to see the gilded, stuccoed extravaganza of the auditorium and the state-of-the-art backstage areas.

5 Gallerie dell'Accademia
(page 145)

One of the world's great galleries, the Accademia has recently expanded into neighbouring premises, giving curators a chance to pull some forgotten treasures out of storage, and arrange familiar masterpieces in a more effective way. From the stiff icon-like first stirrings of Venetian art to the greats of the Renaissance, they're all here, in all their glory.

6 Gondola
(page 282)

Eight varieties of tree, 280 pieces of wood, one expensive ride – but gliding beneath Venice's bridges, along its quiet canals, with just the splash of the single oar as it propels you through the labyrinth in this oh-so-Venetian craft is certainly a unique experience.

7 La Biennale
(page 31)

Officially the name of Venice's massive arts umbrella organisation, 'La Biennale' is used to refer to unmissable contemporary art (odd years) and architecture (even years) bonanzas that draw the world's finest practitioners, and its *cognoscenti*, for shows that last through the summer months – offering a chance to get inside the otherwise-shut Arsenale and the Biennale gardens (for both, *see p85*).

8 Palazo Ducale (Doge's Palace)
(page 56)

This iconic building was where Venice wielded its power and displayed its might, in public rooms designed to instil shock and awe, and with artworks to drive the Serene Republic's self-important message home. Meeting halls, private apartments, torture rooms and prison cells – they're all here in the fulcrum of power.

⑧

9 Torcello
(pages 173-174)

'Mother and daughter, you behold them both in their widowhood: Torcello and Venice,' wrote John Ruskin. A powerful player well before Venice proper, the island of Torcello today is picturesquely forlorn and almost uninhabited. Only a cathedral with remarkable mosaics, a little museum and a pretty round church remain as testimonies to its more important former self.

⑨

10 Venice Film Festival
(page 184)

Movie world A-listers, razzmatazz, hordes of paparazzi and furious bustle: you'd barely recognise Venice's sleepy seaside Lido island for those ten days in August-September when the Film Festival comes to town. The world's oldest – though no longer its most cutting edge – the Venice event (unlike many others) still offers the public a good chance to see the films on show.

⑩

11 **Punta della Dogana**
(page 147)

The stunning makeover by Japanese archi-star Tadao Ando of the Serene Republic's bonded customs warehouse at the southern end of the Grand Canal, facing across the water to St Mark's square, is worth a visit simply for the spaces. But there's also a chance to see a selection from French tycoon Francois Pinault's contemporary art collection too.

12 **Vogalonga**
(page 29)

Unquestionably the jolliest of Venice's many annual rowing competitions, the Vogalonga brings a multicoloured jumble of craft and rowers from all over Europe (and further afield) for a madcap scramble around the lagoon and down the Grand Canal.

13 **Santi Giovanni e Paolo**
(page 79)

Once the final resting place for Venice's rulers, there are 25 doges buried in this huge church. But there are also artworks by Giovanni Bellini, Lorenzo Lotto and Paolo Veronese, as well as some very fine sculpture by the Lombardo family.

14 **Mascari**
(page 117)

Dry-goods stores like Mascari are a rarity these days, which makes a visit to this old-fashioned emporium, overflowing with Venetian goodies (*bigoli* pasta, *buranei* biscuits) and with teas, coffees, herbs and spices from all over the world – a reminder that Venice was once a major centre of international trade.

15 Galleria Cini
(page 146)

Tiny, well hidden Galleria Cini glows with calm Madonnas on gilded backgrounds, and unsettles you as the eyes of its beautiful portraits follow you around the room. It's low-key by Venetian standards, but displays some wonderful art from Ferrara and Florence.

16 Carnevale
(page 28)

It may be a 1970s reincarnation of long-dead Venetian merry-making but it's no less exceptional for all that: for two weeks in the run-up to Lent, Venice shrugs off its winter lethargy and fills with masked-and-costumed revellers who flock for a programme of events that grows by the year.

17 San Giorgio Maggiore
(page 159)

Occupying a piece of prime real estate directly across the water from the Doge's Palace, this most elegant of churches was designed by the great Renaissance architect Palladio. There are artworks to admire, by Tintoretto *et al*, but San Giorgio's biggest draw is its belltower, with spectacular views over Venice and far beyond.

18 Regata storica
(page 30)

Venice rolls out all its love of pomp and circumstance on the first Sunday of September for the Regata storica – a series of rowing races along the Grand Canal. There are wigs and sumptuous costumes a-plenty, and you'll have to book very early if you want to see the action from a canal-side stand. But for Venetians, it's the rowing that counts: these races are taken very seriously.

19 Peggy Guggenheim Collection

(page 147)

Charmingly unfinished Grand Canal-side Palazzo Venier dei Leoni was the home of eccentric millionairess Peggy Guggenheim who brought her extraordinary collection of modern art (and artists) with her to the lagoon city in 1949. With garden, café and fascinating artworks, it's little wonder this is Venice's third-most-visited sight.

20 Da Lele

(page 131)

This hole-in-the-wall bar sums up so much of what workaday Venice is about. It opens at dawn but there's no coffee machine: just alcohol. It makes some very good snacks but when the day's batch finishes, that's it: latecomers go hungry. Unadorned and always busy, it's the epitome of hard-working, salt-of-the-earth Venice – the flip side of the city's finery and pomp.

Venice Today

Unique city, unique issues.

TEXT: ANNE HANLEY

There's no doubt that Venice faces some distressing natural challenges. Prey to rising waters caused by winds and tidal surges, the city seems to be at the mercy of the waves. *Acqua alta* (high water: more than 80cm at the Punta della Salute) lapped over pavements 155 times in 2013, as against 80 times in 2008 and 66 in 2003.The MoSE moveable flood barrier scheme for the three exits from the lagoon to the sea was three-quarters complete as this guide went to press but continued to draw fierce criticism, both for its immense costs and for damage it might – ecologists maintain – cause to the lagoon's fragile ecosystem. Moreover MoSE, many argue, is absorbing vital funds that would otherwise go to Insula, the publicly owned company responsible for dredging canals, repairing and raising pavements and ensuring that the very foundations of this waterlogged city remain sufficiently intact to keep the miracle of urban planning well above the waves.

BESET BY PROBLEMS, OR CREATING ITS OWN?

Yet for the visitor who turns up when Venice is going through a dry patch, these forces of nature are not necessarily obvious. Between wondering at the artistic and architectural marvels of this dazzling and unique city, you might find yourself asking why a place that survives on tourism can't provide easy-access public transport information for your smartphone. Or a one-stop city-provided virtual noticeboard for sights information, both factual and practical. Or even a few benches here and there on which to rest bones wearied by endless sightseeing. For a tourist hub, Venice doesn't go out of its way to make visitors' lives easy.

In June 2006, British economist John Kay provoked outrage among Venetians when he argued that 'Venice is already a theme park... The economics of the city are the economics of Yosemite and Disneyland, not the economics of Bologna or Los Angeles.'

This is, to some extent, a gross over-simplification. But lose yourself in the St Mark's square maelstrom, or wander across the Rialto bridge. You may find yourself wondering if there's a single Venetian left, and asking what *are* these mounds of the tackiest possible souvenirs doing in one of the world's most perfectly preserved treasure troves?

Is it inertia, or are the city fathers actively encouraging the kind of hit-and-run tourism in which droves of day-trippers are herded into the most heavily touristed spots in the *centro storico*, never ploughing any more back into the local economy than the price of a plastic gondola? Even those visitors who choose to bed down in *La Serenissima* stay for an average 2.5 nights, against a considerably healthier average in Rome of 3.5 nights.

Cynics might say that this state of affairs suits Venetians, for whom St Mark's square is a no-go area, and who know alternative routes to just about everywhere: predictable madding crowds confined to easily avoidable areas means they can get on with life.

Venice lives on tourism but considers its visitors annoying obstacles; its beauty is unimaginable but quality control is lacking. It's a theme park without the irony and a museum without sufficient true conoisseurs. Over 1,000 years as one of Europe's great powers has left it unable to face up to handling its insignificance.

MEANWHILE, ON TERRA FERMA

Beyond island Venice is another world again, that of the Veneto region. While *La Serenissima* continues to hold the world in her thrall, the *terra ferma* side of the lagoon has come quietly but steadily into its own. Besides being one of Italy's biggest economic success stories, it now has a burgeoning tourist industry as well. In a region that ranks among Italy's most-visited, almost 16 million people, including 10.2 million non-Italians, checked into a hotel here in 2012, spending a total of 62.3 million nights; admittedly, 4.5 million of these people (including 3.8 million non-Italians) headed for Venice and its province, but Verona clocked up a healthy 1.3 million.

Any success that Venice and the Veneto have experienced has been recent. Venice had slipped far into decline before the city capitulated to Napoleon's troops in 1797. Under Austrian rule (1815-66) it was relegated to the status of a picturesque, inconsequential backwater. But if the city suffered, the fate of its former mainland territories was even worse: with no industry to speak of, and agriculturally backwards, the Veneto ran the semi-feudal south a close race for the title of Italy's own Third World. Between 1876 and 1901, almost 35 per cent of the 5.2 million desperate Italians who sought a better life abroad fled from the crushing poverty of the Veneto and the neighbouring Friuli region.

Industrialisation in Venice's mainland Porto Marghera between and after the wars shifted the more impoverished sectors of the population from agricultural to urban areas. But poverty remained. In 1961, 48 per cent of homes in the north-east had no running water, 72 per cent were without a bathroom and 86 per cent had no central heating.

What the people of the Veneto did have, however, was a deep-rooted attachment to their traditional crafts, and a cussedness of character unmatched anywhere else in Italy. In the past, both had proved detrimental: when captains of heavy industry sought meek vassals to man the furnaces, many of the natives of the Veneto who protested were forcibly deported to populate Fascist new towns in the malarial swamps south of Rome.

THINGS CAN ONLY GET BETTER

It was not, in fact, until the 1970s that north-eastern determination came into its own. With industrial downscaling all the rage, those family-run workshops that had ridden out the bad times gradually became viable business concerns. Giuliana Benetton's knitting machine gave birth to a global clothing empire centred in Treviso; Leonardo del Vecchio's metalworking lessons in an orphanage spawned Luxottica, the world's biggest spectacle frame-maker, based in Belluno; and Ivano Beggio progressed from tinkering with bikes in his father's cycle shop in Noale to running Aprilia, one of Europe's largest manufacturers of motorcycles and scooters. Through the mid to late 1990s a third of the country's huge balance of trade surplus was generated in the north-east. In 1997, local industrialists boasted that the unemployment rate had fallen to zero; in 2007, it stood at 3.3 per cent, well below the national average of 6.1 per cent. By mid-2013, unemployment in the Veneto region had leapt to 7.5 per cent – still well below the national average of 12.7 per cent.

The 21st century has seen a tarnishing of the Veneto's Midas touch. The competitive edge for exports created by a weak lira was lost with the introduction of the euro. Crippling labour costs have forced many businesses to relocate eastwards; a manpower shortfall was bridged by hiring immigrant workers, resulting in an unprecedented ethnic potpourri: learning to live with social and cultural differences is one of the biggest challenges the famously insular Veneto must face today.

The post-war parabola experienced by island Venice was, if anything, bleaker. As *terra ferma* became industrialised, workers looked across the water for employment. Realising that housing on the mainland was cheaper, drier and easier to park in front of, they moved out in an exodus that brought the resident population of island Venice plunging from around 175,000 in 1951 to little more than 56,000 today.

For an area of 5.17 square kilometres (3.2 square miles), however, that's still a respectable figure. Few such small cities, moreover, can lay claim to a population comprising gondoliers, mask-makers, glass-blowers, fishermen, monks, nuns, musicians, artists, writers, architects, historians, academics, restoration experts and many of Italy's rich and famous. Add to that a sizeable student population, a dedicated group of expats and part-time residents and the result is a solid base of 'locals' that gives Venice its distinct flavour. Because there *is* a 'real' city where dogged residents are prepared to persevere – despite exorbitant prices, grocers' turning into mask shops, and the chance that *acqua alta* may cause irreparable damage to their carpets.

And there *are* initiatives under way to keep Venice above water – both literally and figuratively – in the 21st century. For every headline-grabbing problem project – such as the 'tower of light' (www.palaislumiere.eu) skyscraper project on the mainland planned by Venetian exile Pierre Cardin, but thankfully shelved in 2013 – others carry on with no fanfare and much success. Take Insula (www.insula.it), for example: a consortium that has worked its way around Venice since 1997, dredging clogged canals, removing hundreds of thousands of cubic metres of mud, and rebuilding footpaths in a quiet but vital maintenance programme.

On the mainland, too, things are on the move. Among the high-tech businesses attracted to the rapidly developing Science and Technology Park at the northern end of Porto Marghera is a nanotechnologies laboratory that makes Venice a world leader in the field.

THE HIDDEN CITY

Dazzled, disorientated and besieged by pigeons, the average visitor to *La Serenissima* may not even realise that a traipse from St Mark's to the Rialto tells them as much about the city as a guided tour of the Tower of London or a lift to the top of the Empire State Building tell about London and New York. Much of Venetian life takes place behind closed doors, concealed from the casual observer.

An isolated culture, hedged about by water, one that remained an independent republic for over a millennium, one that once lorded it over the entire Mediterranean, cannot be easily penetrated by an outsider, although everyone and anyone is welcome to try. Otherwise, feel free to simply sit back and enjoy the show.

Itineraries

Don comfortable shoes and dive into Venice.

Day 1

10AM Get to grips with what makes Venice splendid by dedicating one day to getting some of the city's major sights under your belt. You might like to gird yourself with a fine cappuccino and pastry at **Da Bonifacio** (*p83*) before starting at the heart, with a visit to **St Mark's basilica** (*p50*). Don't forget to climb up to the museum in the loggia to see the famous bronze horses, and enjoy the sweeping view over St Mark's square from the balcony. If you're not culturally overwhelmed already, tour the **Doge's Palace** (*p56*) next door. Alternatively, take the lift to the top of the **campanile** (*p55*) for a bird's-eye view of the city.

12:30PM Get your breath back by fleeing culture for an hour or so. From the San Zaccaria stop, hop on a vaporetto to the Palanca stop on the Giudecca, and grab a canalside table for a quick plate of pasta at **Alla Palanca** (*p156*). Enjoy the sight of Palladio's magnificent church of **San Giorgio Maggiore** (*p159*) as you steam past.

6PM

Clockwise from top left: **St Mark's basilica; Alla Palanca; Sbarlefo; Peggy Guggenheim Collection**.

2PM Sail back to Zattere, and head for the **Gallerie dell'Accademia** (*p145*), Venice's foremost treasure trove for the grand masters of classical art. If, on the other hand, your preference is for something more up-to-date, you can choose between modern art at the charming **Peggy Guggenheim Collection** (*p147*), or very contemporary works at the **Punta della Dogana** (*p147*).

4:30PM Take the route through campo San Barnaba to campo **Santa Margherita** (p138) and refresh yourself in one of the many café-bars in this lively square, before heading on to **I Frari** (*p126*) for another art feast... but don't linger too long over your *caffè*: the church closes at 6pm and there's a lot to see in here.

6PM No Venetian evening has really begun without a couple of stopovers for *aperitivi*. You'll be

backtracking slightly to get to **Sbarlefo** (*p143*) but it's worth the detour for a great choice of wine in slick surroundings, in an area that has become quietly trendy. The bars in the market area at the north-western foot of the Rialto, on the other hand, are tried-and-tested favourites for the city's creative types: make your way there and grab a *spritz* at **Al Mercà** (*p113*) or **Alla Ciurma** (*p116*).

8PM You're all set now to stroll through to the Rialto and climb to the top of the bridge. It's clichéd, of course, and more than likely to be packed. But the view along the Grand Canal is romantically memorable. Savour the memory as you cross the bridge, then bear left, heading for **La Bottega dei Promessi Sposi** (*p100*) for dinner – but make sure you've booked or you'll never get a place in this popular osteria.

9:30AM

11AM

Day 2

9:30AM Explore further afield today, starting off at the **Museo Storico Navale** (*p86*), which charts Venice's magnificent maritime past with model ships, naval charts and depictions of furious ship-building activity in the nearby Arsenale. The **Arsenale** (*p85*) itself is just north of here. Generally, you can only admire this massive complex from outside, but if there are **Biennale** (*p31*) events going on inside, make sure to take advantage and visit: whether or not you're interested in what's on show, the buildings are worth a look.

11AM The city's north-eastern reaches are echoing, little-visited areas, with the occasional gem such as **San Francesco della Vigna** (*p78*), with its facade by Palladio. Further west, don't miss **Santi Giovanni e Paolo** (*p79*) and – right next door – the freshly restored **Scuola Grande di San Marco** (*p81*). Before you start in on these sights, boost your flagging energy levels with a cappuccino in the branch of **Rosa Salva** (*p63*) alongside the church.

1PM By this time, you'll be dropping from hunger, so continue tacking west and try not to get too lost looking for **Trattoria Storica** (*p109*), where the fixed-price menu will set you up for the rest of the day.

2:30PM The route from here to the **Madonna dell'Orto** (p104) is walkable but round-about: you might prefer to take a vaporetto from Fondamenta Nove for one stop to Orto to enjoy Tintoretto's huge works inside the church. Now wend your way south into the **Ghetto** (*pp102-104*) where the **Museo Ebraico** (*p104*) charts the history of Venice's Jewish community.

5PM Had enough walking? At the Guglie stop, take the 4.1 for a long trip, up the final reaches of the Grand Canal, under the new

Clockwise from top left:
**Museo Storico Navale;
Rosa Salva; Ponte della
Costituzione; Piazza San
Marco; Madonna dell'Orto.**

5PM

2:30PM

Ponte della Costituzione
(aka ponte di Calatrava,
p261), past what counts as
Venice's industrial wasteland
and the cruise ship terminal,
and on across the Giudecca
canal to Palanca. There are
few finer places in the world
to watch the sun set than
the **Skyline Bar** (*p157*)
on the roof of the Molino
Stucky Hilton.

7PM From Palanca (or
indeed any of the stops
along the Giudecca, if
you feel like a stroll along
that fondamenta) the 4.1

continues on to San Marco.
Nearby, the **Osteria San
Marco** (*p69*) serves gourmet
bar snacks, and excellent sit-
down meals – but you'll need
to book to get a table.

10PM You've seen **piazza
San Marco** (*p50*) during
the day, but it's quite a
different place at night. An
after-dinner stroll through
this magical square, with
the tinkling of palm court
orchestras from surrounding
cafés accompanying you on
your way, is a hopelessly
romantic end to any day.

10PM

Diary

The Venetian year.

Venice has never shied away from merry-making: saints' days, military victories, even the arrival in town of a foreign diplomat – they were all good excuses for a party. The arrival of Napoleon's troops in 1797 ended this state of affairs. By that time, Venice's celebrations had become frantic and excessive, the tawdry death-throes of a city in terminal decline. It wasn't until well into the 20th century that the city's traditional revelries began to be resuscitated – this time by officials with an eye firmly on tourist revenue. The most famous example is Carnevale, dusted off in 1979 and now a tourist draw so immense that new spaces for events are being opened up. The Regata Storica, too, is something of a historical pastiche, though in this case one that dates from 1899 when it was hoped it would lend the Biennale a little Venetian colour.

Vogalonga. *See p29*.

Local tradition

Despite the tourist focus of Venice's big events, the locals haven't lost the knack of enjoying themselves, and residents enter enthusiastically into these revamped shindigs, especially if they take place on the water. There are more than 120 regattas in the lagoon each year. The **Regata Storica** (*see p30*) may look like it's funded by the tourist board, but Venetians get seriously involved in the races; the **Vogalonga** (*see p29*) is a remarkable display of the Venetian love of messing about in boats.

For a full list of events, see the Venice city council website: www.comune.venezia.it, or download the free Venezia Unica app.

PUBLIC HOLIDAYS

New Year's Day (Capodanno)
1 Jan

Epiphany (Befana)
6 Jan

Easter Monday (Pasquetta)
varies

Liberation Day (Festa della Liberazione) and patron saint's day (San Marco)
25 Apr

Labour Day (Festa del Lavoro)
1 May

Assumption (Ferragosto)
15 Aug

All Saints' Day (Ognissanti)
1 Nov

Festa della Salute (Venice only)
21 Nov

Immaculate Conception (L'Immacolata)
8 Dec

Christmas Day (Natale)
25 Dec

Boxing Day (Santo Stefano)
26 Dec

CARNEVALE
Masked madness.

Venice's pre-Lenten **Carnevale** had existed since the Middle Ages, but it came into its own in the 18th century. As the Venetian Republic slipped into terminal decline, the city's pagan side began to emerge. Carnevale became an outlet for all that had been prohibited for centuries by the strong and sober arm of the doge. Elaborate structures would be set up in piazza San Marco as stages for acrobats, tumblers, wrestlers and other performers. Masks served not only as an escape from the drabness of everyday life but to conceal the wearer's identity – a useful ploy for nuns on the lam or slumming patricians.

The Napoleonic invasion in 1797 brought an end to the fun and games, and Carnevale was not resuscitated until the late 1970s. When it was reintroduced, it was with money-earning in mind: the city authorities and hoteliers' association saw the potential, and today the heavily subsidised celebrations draw revellers from all over the world.

But if Carnevale fills Venetian hotels and coffers, it also gives the locals a chance for fun and games. Visitors flock to piazza San Marco, where professional *poseurs* in ornate costumes occupy prime spots and wait for the world's press photographers to immortalise them. From 2014, organisers sought to relieve the pressure of numbers in St Mark's by moving some events into the Arsenale. Venetians, on the other hand, organise private masked and costumed celebrations, or gather in smaller squares.

The party starts two weekends before *martedì grasso* (Shrove Tuesday). The www.carnevale.venezia.it site has a full programme of events.

Spring

★ Carnevale
Date 2wks ending on Shrove Tuesday.
See left **Carnevale**.
▶ *For Carnevale costume hire, see p120* **Atelier Pietro Longhi**, *p90* **Banco Lotto N°10**.

Su e Zo per i Ponti
Information: 041 590 4717, www.suezo.it.
Date Sun in Mar or Apr.
Literally 'Up and Down the Bridges', this excursion is inspired by the traditional *bacarada* (bar crawl). It's an orienteering event in which you are given a map and a list of checkpoints to tick off. Old hands take their time checking out the *bacari* along the way. Individuals can register at the starting line in piazza San Marco on the morning of the event. Costumes, music and dancing liven up the route.

Benedizione del Fuoco
Basilica di San Marco. Vaporetto San Marco Vallaresso or San Zaccaria. **Date** Maundy Thursday.
At around dusk on the eve of Good Friday, all the lights are turned off inside St Mark's basilica (*see p50*) and a fire is lit in the narthex (entrance porch). Communion is celebrated and the four elements are blessed: earth is represented by the faithful masses, fire by the large altar candle, water at the baptismal font and air by the surrounding environment.

Festa di San Marco
Bacino di San Marco. Vaporetto San Marco Vallaresso or San Zaccaria. **Date** 25 Apr.
The feast day of Venice's patron saint is a surprisingly low-key affair. In the morning, there is a solemn Mass in the basilica, followed by a gondola regatta between the island of Sant'Elena (*see p87*) and the Punta della Dogana (*see p147*) at the entrance to the Grand Canal. The day is also known as *La Festa del boccolo* ('bud'): red rosebuds are given to wives and lovers.

Clockwise from left: **Venezia Jazz Festival**; Italy's Biennale pavilion; Regata della Sensa.

Venezia Jazz Festival

Information: via Corriva 10, Cavasagra di Vedelago (0423 452 069, www.venetojazz.com). **Box office** at venues before performances. **Date** July-Aug.
Keith Jarrett and Chick Corea were among headlining giants of the jazz scene who in 2013 performed alongside lesser-known talents in various venues around Venice and in the Veneto. This annual event draws serious jazz-heads for great music in fantastic venues.
▶ *For more annual music events, see p188 Festivals.*

Summer

★ Biennale d'Arte Contemporanea & Architettura

Headquarters: Ca' Giustinian, San Marco 1364A, calle Ridotto. Vaporetto San Marco-Vallaresso (041 521 8711, www.labiennale.org).
Exhibition: Arsenale & Giardini della Biennale. Vaporetto Arsenale or Giardini. **Date** *Art* (odd years). *Architecture* (even years) June-Nov.
See p31 **La Biennale**.

Palio delle Antiche Repubbliche Marinare

Bacino di San Marco. Vaporetto San Marco Vallaresso or San Zaccaria. **Date** June or July.
This competition takes place in Venice once every four years (next scheduled for 2015; other years it's in Amalfi, Genoa or Pisa). The 2,000m race starts at the island of Sant'Elena and finishes at the Doge's Palace. Beforehand, 400-odd boats carrying costumed representatives of the four Marine Republics parade along the riva dei Sette Martiri and the riva degli Schiavoni.

Festa di San Pietro

San Pietro in Castello. Vaporetto Giardini.
Date week ending 29 June. **Map** p326 Q8.
The most lively and villagey of Venice's many local festivals in celebration of San Pietro Martire. A week

Festa e Regata della Sensa

San Nicolò del Lido & Bacino di San Marco (www.sensavenezia.it). **Date** Weekend following Ascension Day (5th Thur after Easter).
In the days of the Venetian Republic, the doge would board the glorious state barge, the Bucintoro, and be rowed out to the island of Sant'Andrea. Once there, he would throw a gold ring overboard, to symbolise *lo sposalizio del mare* – Venice's marriage with the sea. Today, the mayor does the honours, the Bucintoro looks like a glorified fruit boat and the ring is a laurel wreath. The ceremony is now performed at San Nicolò, on the Lido, and is followed by a regatta. If it rains, local lore says it'll tip down for the next 40 days.
▶ *There's a model of the Bucintoro in the Museo Storico Navale; see p86.*

★ Vogalonga

Information: 041 521 0544/www.vogalonga.com.
Date Sun in May or early June.
For one chaotically colourful day, Venetians (or at least those with strength enough to complete the 33km/20.5 mile route) protest against motorboats and the damage they do by boarding any kind of rowing craft and making their way through the lagoon and the city's two main canals in this annual free-for-all on the water. They are joined by a host of out-of-towners and foreigners. Boats set off from in front of the Doge's Palace at 8.30am. *Photo p26.*

of events centres on the church green of San Pietro (*see p88*): there are competitions, concerts, food stands and bouncy castles.

Festa di San Giacomo dell'Orio

Campo San Giacomo dell'Orio. Vaporetto Rivadi Biasio or San Stae. **Date** 10 days in late July. Concerts, a barbecue and a charity raffle make up this local fair: it provides a great occasion to 'do as the Venetians do' in a truly beautiful campo.

★ Arena di Campo San Polo

Campo San Polo (information: 041 524 1320, www.venicemoviebook.it). Vaporetto San Silvestro or San Tomà. **Date** late July-early Sept.
A huge outdoor theatre is set up in campo San Polo to show current films, usually dubbed into Italian, occasionally with English subtitles. When the Venice Film Fest (*see p184*) swings into action across on the Lido in late August, a selection of festival offerings is screened here in an event entitled Esterno Notte (nights outside).

★ Festa del Redentore

Bacino di San Marco, Canale della Giudecca (www. redentorevenezia.it). **Date** 3rd weekend of July.
The Redentore is the oldest continuously celebrated date on the Venetian calendar. At the end of a plague epidemic in 1576, the city commissioned Andrea Palladio to build a church on the Giudecca – Il Redentore (the Redeemer). Every July, a pontoon bridge is built across the canal that separates the Giudecca from Venice proper, so people can make the pilgrimage to the church. While the religious part of the festival falls on Sunday, what makes this weekend so special are the festivities on Saturday night. Boats of every shape and size gather in the lagoon between St Mark's, San Giorgio, the Punta della Dogana and the Giudecca, each holding merry-makers supplied with food and drink. This party culminates in an amazing fireworks display, from 11.30pm.

Ferragosto – Festa dell'Assunta

Date 15 Aug.
If you want Venice without Venetians, this is the time to come, as everyone who can leaves the city. Practically everything shuts down and people head to the beach. There is usually a free concert in the cathedral of Santa Maria Assunta (*see p174*), on the island of Torcello, on the evening of the 15th. Tourist offices (*see p289*) have more information.

★ Regata Storica

Grand Canal. **Date** 1st Sun in Sept.
This event begins with a procession of ornate boats down the Grand Canal (*see pp38-47*), rowed by locals in 16th-century costume. Once this is over, the races start – which is what most locals have come to see. There are four: one for young rowers, one for women, one for rowers of *caorline* – long canoe-like boats in which the prow and the stern are identical – and

Right:
**Festa del
Redentore**;
Below:
**Venice
Marathon**

theFlast, the most eagerly awaited, featuring two-man sporting *gondolini*. The finish is at the sharp curve of the Grand Canal between Palazzo Barbi and Ca' Foscari: here, the judges sit in an ornate raft known as the *machina*, where the prize-giving takes place.

★ Mostra Internazionale D'Arte Cinematografica (Venice International Film Festival)

For listings and review, *see p184*.

Autumn

Sagra del Pesce

Burano. Vaporetto 12. **Date** 3rd Sun in Sept.
Fried fish and lots of white wine are consumed in this feast, in the *calli* between Burano's brightly painted houses. Those rowers who are not legless then take part in the last regatta of the season.

Sagra del Mosto

Island of Sant'Erasmo. Vaporetto 13 to Chiesa. **Date** 1st weekend in Oct.
This festival is a great excuse for Venetians to spend a day 'in the country' on the island of Sant'Erasmo (*see p182*), getting light-headed on the first pressing of wine – which is why it's best to down a glass before the stuff has had much chance to ferment. Sideshows, grilled sausage aromas and red-faced locals abound.

Venice Marathon

Information: 041 532 1871,
www.venicemarathon.it. **Date** 4th Sun in Oct.
The marathon starts in the town of Stra, east of
Padua, follows the Brenta Canal, and then winds
through Venice to end on the riva Sette Martiri.

Winter

Festa di San Martino

Date 11 Nov.
Kids armed with *mamma*'s pots and spoons raise a
ruckus around the city, chanting the saint's praises
and demanding trick-or-treat style tokens in return
for taking their noise elsewhere. Horse-and-rider
shaped San Martino cakes, with coloured icing
dotted with silver balls, proliferate in cake shops.

Festa della Madonna della Salute

Church of Madonna della Salute. Vaporetto Salute.
Date 21 Nov.
In 1630-31, Venice was 'miraculously' delivered from
the plague, which claimed almost 100,000 lives – one
in three Venetians. The Republic commissioned a
church from Baldassare Longhena, and his Madonna
della Salute (literally, 'good health') was completed in
1687. On this feast day, a pontoon bridge is strung
across the Grand Canal from campo Santa Maria del
Giglio to La Salute so that a procession led by the
patriarch (archbishop) of Venice can make its way on
foot from San Marco. Along the way, stalls sell cakes
and candles for pilgrims to light inside the church.
Then everybody eats *castradina* – cabbage and
mutton stew – which tastes nicer than it sounds.

Christmas, New Year & Epiphany (La Befana)

Venice's Yuletide festivities are low-key affairs. There
are two events: the New Year's Day swim off the Lido
(www.lidovenezia.it), and the Regata delle Befane on
6 January, a rowing race along the Grand Canal in
which the competitors, all aged over 50, are dressed
up as *La Befana* – the ugly witch who gives sweets
to good children and pieces of coal to bad ones.

LA BIENNALE
Art and architecture.

Officially known as l'Esposizione
internazionale d'arte della Biennale
di Venezia, Venice's **Biennale** (*see p29*)
was responsible for putting the city on the
map of international contemporary art back
in 1895. Since then this massive exhibition
has been 'invading' Venice throughout the
summer of every odd year.

It was the first (its closest rival Sao
Paolo didn't start until 1951), and to this
day it remains one of the few to include
national exhibits as part of a wider-ranging
collective event.

In 1980, Biennale organisers decided
to fill in even years with an architecture
equivalent – a far lower-profile event to
start off with but now as extravagant,
sprawling and (almost as) well-attended
as its arty sister.

From the start, the Biennale spread
over the leafy Giardini del Biennale park
in eastern Castello, where some 30 small
national pavilions cluster around the far
larger central pavilion – previously Italy's
Biennale home but now renovated and
called the Palazzo delle Esposizioni,
housing the Biennale archive (*see p85*)
and part of the themed event.

Much more of the curated section
of the Biennale now straggles into the
glorious spaces of Venice's Arsenale (*see
p85*), where each year an internationally
renowned artist, architect, critic or expert
selects exhibits around a theme of his
or her choosing. And all over town, shows
mounted by nations with no foothold in the
Giardini and no space in the Arsenale occupy
palazzi, galleries, gardens and other settings,
opening up rarely glimpsed spaces to a
curious public in a three-month art jamboree.

Unusually for Italy, the Biennale has a
US-style financial model mixing sponsorship,
public funds, and income generated by
ticket sales and merchandising. With
money from sources other than the public
purse, this organisation enjoys an autonomy
from political manoeuvring envied by many.
It also boasts figures that leave others
standing: in 2012, 178,000 people turned
up for the Architecture event curated by
Britain's David Chipperfield; 475,000
visitors and over 7,000 journalists – two
thirds of them from outside Italy – attended
2013's art Biennale.

Venice's Best

Check off the essentials with our list of hand-picked highlights.

Sightseeing

VIEWS

Campanile, piazza San Marco (p55)
A commanding view over the heart of the city.

Campanile, San Giorgio Maggiore (p159)
Across the city and into the mountains: the widest possible view.

Campanile, Santa Maria Assunta (p174)
Across the wild and lonely lagoon to Venice.

Hotel Molino Stucky – Skyline bar (p157)
Relax, imbibe and admire: all of Venice is laid out at your feet.

ART: OLD MASTERS

Gallerie dell'Accademia (p145)
Venice's one-stop shop for all that's magnificent in art.

Galleria Cini (p146)
Quietly wonderful collection of Florentine and Ferrarese masterpieces.

Museo della Fondazione Querini Stampalia (p75)
A gorgeous Bellini and documentary works.

ART: IN CHURCHES

I Frari (p126)
Two superb Titians in a Gothic barn of a church.

Santi Giovanni e Paolo (p79)
A Bellini and some exquisite sculpted tombs.

View from Campanile, piazza San Marco.

San Zaccaria (p80)
Bellini's magnificent *Madonna and Saints*.
Madonna dell'Orto (p104)
Tintoretto let rip in this northern church.
Santa Maria dei Miracoli (p107)
Wonderful delicate sculptures by the Lombardo family.
San Sebastiano (p135)
Arguably Venice's most colourful church, thanks to works by Paolo Veronese.
Santa Maria della Salute (p148)
Tintoretto's *Marriage at Canaan*: 'perfect,' said Ruskin.
Santa Maria Assunta (p174)
A *Last Judgment* mosaic to take your breath away.

ART: MODERN & CONTEMPORARY
Peggy Guggenheim Collection (p147)
Superlative selection of modern art in a Grand Canal-side palazzo.
Punta della Dogana (p147)
Cutting-edge contemporary; striking architectural setting.
Biennale dell'Arte (p31)
Bi-annual binge of all that's happening on the international art scene.

ART: IN SCUOLE
Scuola di San Giorgio degli Schiavoni (p88)
A series of enchanting scenes by Vittore Carpaccio.
Scuola di San Rocco (p129)
Enough Tintorettos to make you dizzy.

History

Palazzo Ducale (Doge's Palace; p56)
Splendour, pomp, circumstance and prisons in Venice's centre of power.

Scuola Grande di San Marco.

Museo Correr (p55)
Portraits of doges, early globes, model ships, and the apartments of Princess Sissi.
Museo Storico Navale (p86)
Everything there is to know about Venetian shipbuilding.
Palazzo Mocenigo (p122)
A history of Venetian costume, plus a sidebar on perfumery.
Palazzo Grimani (p78)
Beautiful interiors in an historic palazzo.
Scuola Grande di San Marco (p81)
Arguably the finest hospital entrance anywhere.
Museo del Merletto (p172)
Exquisite lace through the ages, plus some ladies showing how it's done.
Museo dell'Arte Vetrario (p166)
A history of glass making: Murano's trademark craft.

Eating & drinking

BLOW-OUT
Gran Caffè Quadri (p69)
Michelin-starred pyrotechnics from the chef Max Alajmo.
Venissa (p172)
Home-grown and zero-kilometre gourmet surprises in a rural island setting.
Il Ridotto (p89)
Venetian-classic-inspired experiments in a hot-house for young cooking talent.
Osteria San Marco (p69)
Seriously good inventive fare, served throughout the day.
Alle Testiere (p82)
Tiny, excellent, mainly seafood – and with a fantastic wine list.
Osteria di Santa Marina (p83)
Attention to detail is the trademark of this upmarket seafood eaterie.

CLASSIC VENETIAN FARE

La Bottega ai Promessi Sposi (p100)
Book ahead for great Venetian classics in pared-back simplicity.
Antiche Carampane (p119)
Difficult to find, but worth it for recherché specialities.
Vecio Fritolin (p125)
Seasonally changing menu with some light touches.
Alla Palanca (p156)
Perfect seafood simplicity with a fantastic water view.

SOMETHING COMPLETELY DIFFERENT

Gam Gam Kosher Restaurant (p104)
Latkes, matzo balls, gefilte fish and falafel, Venetian-style.
Algiubagiò (p108)
Angus steak is the very un-Venetian speciality here.

TO FEED A SWEET TOOTH

Marchini Time (p66)
A baking dynasty produces Venice's best breakfast *cornetti* – and much more.
Da Bonifacio (p83)
Well hidden but never empty; delicious pastries keep regulars faithful.
Alaska Gelateria-Sorbetteria (p125)
Intriguing flavours from an eccentric ice-cream maker.

BACAROS FOR SNACKING

Al Portego (p82)
Particularly tasty *cicheti* from the overloaded counter.
Alla Ciurma (p116)
Rowdy, packed and with excellent bar snacks beneath a suspended boat.
All'Arco (p116)
Standing room only for delicious *cicheti* and an *ombra*.

Al Prosecco (p125)
Pair your prosecco with some great snacky options.

PIZZA BREAKS

Dai Tosi (p89)
Decent pizza in a salt-of-the-earth neighbourhood.
Birraria la Corte (p120)
Filling pizzas served in a former brewery.

APERITIVO STOPOVERS

Muro Rialto (p113)
Deep within the markets, locals crowd here for evening drinks.
Al Mercà (p113)
Spot the *spritz*-swilling crowds outside this market hole-in-the-wall.
Da Lele (p131)
It's wine or (very cheap) wine in this standing-only Venetian classic.
Cantinone (già Schiavi) (p150)
Much *spritz* and prosecco is consumed on the canal-side walk outside.

CAFFE CLASSICS

Caffè Florian (p61)
Mirrors, stucco and orchestra on piazza San Marco – all at a price.
Gran Caffè Quadri (p60)
Stendhal, Wagner and Balzac frequented this piazza San Marco café.
Rosa Salva (p63)
Great coffee, excellent cakes.

HIP SIPPING

L'Ombra del Leone (p70)
The Grand Canal-side terrace is a very good place to enjoy an aperitivo.
El Sbarlefo (p143)
Great wines in a chic and sophisticated locale.
Skyline Bar (p157)
The best perch in town for a cocktail-with-a-view.

Shopping

GIFTS & SOUVENIRS

Davide Penso (p168)
Limited-edition glass jewellery inspired by patterns in nature.
Fortuny Tessuti Artistici (p157)
A treasure trove of gorgeous (and very expensive) fabrics.
Signor Blum (p144)
Wooden puzzles of *palazzi*.
Attombri (p117)
Unique jewellery incorporating antique beads and cameos.
Gilberto Penzo (p121)
Model gondolas, *vaporetti* and more to take home and stick together.
Vittorio Costantini (p109)
Intricate lamp-blown glass animals and insects.
Papier Mâché (p84)
Masks inspired by Klimt, Tiepolo and Carpaccio.
Perle e Dintorni (p68)
Lovely jewellery plus a vast array of glass beads to create your own.

Skyline Bar.

Al Portego.

L'Isola – Carlo Moretti (p67)
Contemporary bowls, glasses, light fittings and more made in glass.
Ebrú (p67)
Hand-made marbled paper, scarves and ties.

FOOD & DRINK
Drogheria Mascari (p117)
A marvellous old-fashioned dry-goods grocery store.
Rialto Biocenter (p126)
For wholegrain, macrobiotic and gluten- and dairy-free.
VizioVirtù (p131)
Exquisite chocolate concoctions in a chocolate box of a shop.
Rialto markets (pp112-118)
An exuberant, rowdy and colouful slice of everyday Venetian life.

DESIGN & DESIGNERS
Madera (p144)
Sleek housewares and jewellery in natural materials.

Banco Lotto N°10 (p90)
Fashions with a retro touch, made in Venice's prison.
Kalimala (p84)
Handmade shoes in a range of wonderful colours.
Araba Fenice (p63)
Classic yet original line of women's clothing.

Nightlife

LATE BARS
Café Rosso (p142)
The classic hangout for Venice's boho-chic denizens.
Orange (p143)
Locals down cocktails here until the wee hours.
Naranzaria (p116)
Superbly located venue with Grand Canal views and good wines.
Santo Bevitore (p100)
Packed café-pub popular with locals and visitors.
Paradiso Perduto (p189)
With frequent live jazz and salsa, this bar attracts the city's arty types.

CLUBS
Piccolo Mondo (p189)
Still going strong, Venice's one and only true nightclub.

Arts

THEATRE
Teatro la Fenice (p195)
One of Europe's leading opera houses.
Teatro Fondamenta Nove (p195)
Avant-garde theatre and dance, plus symposiums and exhibitions.

MUSIC
Interpreti Veneziani (p195)
Nightly concerts of Baroque favourites in the church of San Vidal.
La Pietà (p196)
I Virtuosi Italiani ensemble play Vivaldi in the church where the composer taught and worked.
Venice Jazz Club (p189)
A lively, friendly venue for some serious jazz.

FESTIVALS
La Biennale (p31)
Two world-renowned extravaganzas – of contemporary art and architecture.
Venice Film Festival (p184)
International A-listers flock to Venice for this end-of-summer filmfest.

Explore

The Grand Canal

The Grand Canal is Venice's high street, and although the craft caught up in today's waterborne traffic jams carry more tourists than exotic luxury goods arriving from around the Mediterrean and beyond, this mighty thoroughfare still provides a superb introduction to the city, telling you more about the way Venice works – and has always worked – than any historical tome.

Every family of note had to have a palazzo along the three and a half kilometre (two-mile) sweep from the railway station to San Marco, and this was not just for social cachet. The *palazzi* are undeniably splendid but they were first and foremost solid commercial enterprises, and their designs are as practical as they are eye-catching.

EXPLORE

Ponte della Costituzione.

Don't Miss

1 **Ca' d'Oro** Gloriously ornate Gothic (p43).

2 **Ponte della Costituzione** (Ponte Calatrava) The newest bridge (p42).

3 **Ponte di Rialto** Simple, effective and very mercantile (p44).

4 **Palazzo Venier dei Leoni** Charmingly incomplete (p46).

5 **Santa Maria della Salute** Queening it over the Grand Canal (p47).

Vaporetti.

Motoscafo.

Motonave.

HISTORY & ARCHITECTURE

Most of the notable buildings on the canal were built between the 12th and 18th centuries. When a family decided to rebuild a palazzo, they usually maintained the same basic structure – for the good reason that they could use the same foundations. This resulted in some interesting style hybrids: the Grand Canal offers many examples of palazzi in which Veneto-Byzantine or Gothic features are incorporated into the Renaissance or Baroque.

Each palazzo typically had a main water-entrance opening on to a large hall with storage space on either side; a *mezzanino* with offices; a *piano nobile* (main floor – sometimes two in grander buildings) consisting of a spacious reception hall lit by large central windows and flanked on both sides by residential rooms; and a land entrance at the back. Over the centuries, architectural frills and trimmings were added, but the underlying form was stable – and, as always in Venice, it is form that follows function.

In the following description of the most notable *palazzi*, many names recur, for the simple reason that families expanded, younger sons inheriting as well as older ones. Compound names indicate that the palazzo passed through various hands over time. Originally the term 'palazzo' was reserved for the Doge's Palace. Other *palazzi* were known as Casa ('house') or Ca' for short: this is still true of some of the older ones, such as **Ca' d'Oro** (*see p94*).

This chapter deals mainly with canal-side *palazzi*. Churches and museums facing on to the canal are covered elsewhere in the guide (cross references are given). The itinerary on these next pages is best followed from the rear deck of a vaporetto, looking backwards as you make your way from piazzale Roma or the train station (Ferrovia) towards St Mark's square.

IN THE KNOW
KNOW YOUR VAPORETTI

Though even the locals tend to lump them together, not all Venetian passenger ferries are, strictly speaking, *vaporetti*. A **vaporetto** is a larger, slower and more rounded 230-passenger boat; older models have much sought-after outside seats at the front. It plies routes along the Grand Canal. The 160-passenger **motoscafo** is sleeker, smaller and faster, with outside seats only at the back. It's used on routes encircling the island. **Motonave** are larger (600-1,200 people) double-decker steamers that cross the lagoon regally to the Lido.

EXPLORE

Ca' d'Oro.

MUD HOUSES

The challenges of building on a lagoon.

If you absolutely must build a city on a squishy base of a hundred-odd marshy islets in an inhospitable lagoon, it's clear you're going to have to think about foundations. Especially if, in time, you want this city to grow into more than a collection of wooden huts on stilts, to become a flourishing trade empire, acquiring some stunning marble-clad churches and *palazzi* in the process.

Beneath the Venetian lagoon is a layer of compacted clay called caranto, the remains of the ancient Venetian plain that subsided aeons ago. On top of this firm base are silt deposits that vary in depth – from very shallow by the mainland to many metres deep out by the Adriatic.

As the builders of this most unlikely of cities were soon to realise, nothing of any size would stay vertical unless it was standing firmly on the caranto. So great trunks of larch and oak trees were driven down through the mud, to bear the weight of what would then be built above. Lack of oxygen in the clay saved the wood from decomposition, turning the stakes as hard as rock. As you walk through Venice's *calli*, you are, in effect, striding over a petrified forest.

The solution is a good one, but it's certainly not perfect. As the sea level inexorably rises and the caranto level subsides – at an estimated one millimetre per year – there's no way that the trunks can be stretched to keep the floor above water.

And occasionally the wood rots, especially if the piles are shaken – with the risk of oxygen sneaking in – by passing motorised water traffic. At which point, those wooden piles will need to be replaced, at a substantial cost – and it's no fun having a forest dragged through your living room floor either.

There are photos of uncovered wooden piles on www.venicebackstage.org.

Vaporetto stop Piazzale Roma

The first notable sight is the new bridge over the Grand Canal, linking the car park to the train station. Officially named the **Ponte della Costituzione**, it is still known to most Venetians as Ponte Calatrava, after its designer, the Spanish architect-superstar Santiago Calatrava. Its single, elegantly curving arch is constructed of steel, and the pavement is in the traditional Venetian materials of glass and Istrian stone.

Before the Scalzi bridge is the church of **San Simeone Piccolo**, with its high green dome and Corinthian portico. For those arriving in Venice it's a picturesque introduction to the city.

The **Ponte degli Scalzi**, which leads across to the station, was built in stone by Eugenio Miozzi in 1934.

Vaporetto stop Riva di Biasio

Just before the rio del Megio stands the **Fondaco dei Turchi**, a 19th-century reconstruction of the original Veneto-Byzantine building, which was leased to Turkish traders in the 17th century as a residence and warehouse. Some of the original material was used but the effect as a whole is one of pastiche. Once lived in by the poet Torquato Tasso, it's now the **Museo di Storia Naturale** (*see p122*).

The **Depositi del Megio** (state granaries) have a battlemented, plain-brick façade. The sculpted lion is a modern replacement of the original, destroyed at the fall of the Republic. The church of **San Stae** (*see p124*) has a Baroque façade by Domenico Rossi, with exuberant sculpture.

Ferrovia vaporetto stop.

Vaporetto stop Ferrovia

At the foot of the Ponte degli Scalzi is the fine Baroque façade of the **Scalzi** church (*see p98*).

Unusually narrow **Palazzo Flangini** is a 17th-century building by Giuseppe Sardi. It owes its shape to the simple fact that the family's money ran out. Just before the wide Cannaregio Canal is the church of **San Geremia**; from the Grand Canal, the apse of the chapel of **Santa Lucia** is visible.

Standing with its main façade on the Cannaregio Canal is **Palazzo Labia**, the 18th-century home of the seriously rich Labia family. The story goes that parties ended with the host throwing his gold dinner plates into the canal to demonstrate his wealth; the servants would then be ordered to fish them out again. The building is now the regional headquarters of the RAI (the Italian state broadcaster). It contains suitably sumptuous frescoes by Tiepolo, which are opened very occasionally to the public.

Ponte della Costituzione

Ponte degli Scalzi

Ca' da Mosto.

Vaporetto stop San Marcuola

The next building of note is **Palazzo Vendramin Calergi**, an impressive Renaissance palazzo designed by Mauro Codussi in the first decade of the 16th century. It uses his characteristic arched windows incorporating twin smaller arches; porphyry insets decorate the façade. Wagner died here in 1883. It now houses the Venice **Casinò**.

A fairly uneventful stretch ends at the **Ca' d'Oro** (*see p94*), the most gorgeously ornate Gothic building on the Grand Canal. Yet it is now sober compared with its original appearance, when its decorative features were gilded or painted in ultramarine blue and cinnabar red. It has an open loggia on the *piano nobile*, like the Doge's Palace, but unlike any other post-Byzantine palazzo.

Vaporetto stop Ca' d'Oro

Just before the rio dei Santi Apostoli is **Palazzo Mangilli Valmarana**, built in 1751 for Joseph Smith, the British consul, who amassed the huge collection of Canaletto paintings that now belongs to the Queen. It now houses the Argentinian Consulate.

Beyond the rio dei Santissimi Apostoli stands the **Ca' da Mosto**, once the site of the Leon Bianco (white lion) Hotel. This is one of the earliest Veneto-Byzantine *palazzi* on the Grand Canal. It still has three of the original five arches of its water-entrance and a long array of Byzantine arches on the first floor.

At the foot of the Rialto bridge is the **Fondaco dei Tedeschi**, a huge residence-cum-warehouse leased to the German community from the 13th century onwards. The present building was designed by Spavento and Scarpagnino in 1505-08 after a fire. The façade once had glorious frescoes by Titian and Giorgione – now in a sad state of repair in the Ca' d'Oro gallery (*see p94*). The Fondaco – for the time being, still the main post office – was bought by the Benetton group in 2008 and was, at the time of writing, swathed in scaffolding as

---

San Stae.

Vaporetto stop San Stae

On the rio di Ca' Pesaro, and with a magnificent side wall curving along the canal in gleaming marble, is **Ca' Pesaro** (*see p122*), a splendid example of Venetian Baroque by Longhena.

After two smaller *palazzi* stands the **Palazzo Corner della Regina**, with a rusticated ground floor featuring grotesque masks, some just above water level. It was built for a branch of the Corner family, who were descended from Caterina Cornaro, Queen of Cyprus; Caterina was born in an earlier house on the site. The present palazzo dates from the 1720s.

The covered fish market, or **Pescaria**, has occupied a site here since the 14th century. The current neo-Gothic construction was built in 1907, replacing an iron one. Beyond this is a building with a parade of arches along the canal; this is the longest façade on the Grand Canal and belongs to Sansovino's **Fabbriche Nuove**, built in 1554-56 for Venice's financial judiciary; it now houses the Court of Assizes.

Just beyond this stands the **Fabbriche Vecchie** by Scarpagnino, built after a fire in the early 16th century.

Vaporetto stop Rialto Mercato

Before the Rialto bridge, the **Palazzo dei Camerlenghi** (1523-25) is built around the curve of the canal; the walls lean noticeably. It was the headquarters of the Venetian Exchequer, with a debtors' prison on the ground floor.

RIGHT BANK

The **Ponte di Rialto** was built in 1588-92, to a design by aptly named Antonio Da Ponte. Until the 19th century, it was the only bridge over the Grand Canal. It replaced a wooden one, which can be seen in Carpaccio's painting of *The Miracle of the True Cross* in the Accademia (*p145*). After the decision was taken to build it, 60 years passed, during the course of which designs by Michelangelo, Vignola, Sansovino and Palladio were rejected. Da Ponte's simple but effective project eventually went ahead, probably because it kept the utilitarian features of the previous structure, with its double row of shops. The bridge thus acts as a continuation of the market at its foot. Palladio's design was more beautiful, but made no provision for the sale of plastic gondolas.

Vaporetto stop San Silvestro

Beyond the San Silvestro vaporetto stop are a few houses with Veneto-Byzantine windows and decorations, including **Ca' Barzizza**, one of the earliest Byzantine houses in Venice. Before the rio San Polo is the 16th-century **Palazzo Cappello Layard**, once the home of Sir Henry Austen Layard, archaeologist and British ambassador to Constantinople. A little way before the San Tomà stop is the **Palazzo Pisani Moretta**, a large Gothic palazzo of the 15th century, often hired out for parties.

Palazzo Pisani.

LEFT BANK

it is turned into a vast shopping complex. Between the bridge and the Rialto vaporetto stop is **Palazzo Manin Dolfin**, with a portico straddling the *fondamenta*. The façade is by Sansovino (late 1530s); the rest was rebuilt by Ludovico Manin, the forlorn last doge of Venice (*see p243*). It now belongs to the Bank of Italy.

Vaporetto stop Rialto

Palazzetto Dandolo is a Gothic building that appears to have been squeezed tight by its neighbours. Enrico Dandolo, the blind doge who led the ferocious assault on Constantinople in 1204 (*see p238*) was born in an earlier palazzo that stood on this site. **Palazzo Farsetti** and **Palazzo Loredan** are Veneto-Byzantine buildings that now house the city hall and various municipal offices. Though heavily restored, these two adjoining *palazzi* are among the few surviving examples of the 12th-century Venetian house, with its first-floor polyforate window.

Palazzo Grimani is one of the largest *palazzi* on the Grand Canal. Its creator, Michele Sanmicheli, was famous for his military architecture, and this building is characteristically massive and assertive. The Grimani family were nouveaux riches, and wanted each one of their windows to be larger than the front door of the palazzo that used to stand opposite.

Seven *palazzi* further on, before the rio Michiel, stands the pink **Palazzo Benzon**, home of Countess Marina Querini-Benzon, a great society figure at the end of the 18th century. Byron was charmed by her when she was already in her sixties. She inspired a popular song, '*La biondina in gondoleta*', which the gondoliers used to sing before international tourism imposed the Neapolitan 'O' Sole Mio'.

Before the Sant'Angelo vaporetto stop is the small-scale **Palazzo Corner**, built in the last decade of the 15th century by Mauro Codussi. It is one of the most beautiful early Renaissance buildings in Venice, with a rusticated ground floor, elegant balconies and the characteristic double-arched windows.

Ponte di Rialto

Vaporetto stop Sant'Angelo

A little beyond the traghetto (*see p50*) station for San Tomà stand the four **Palazzi Mocenigo**, with blue and white poles in the water. The central double palazzo (16th century) was where Byron and his menagerie of foxes, monkeys and dogs lived in 1818-19; he wrote to a friend: 'Venice is not an expensive residence… I have my gondola and about 14 servants… and I reside in one of the Mocenigo palaces on the Grand Canal; the rent… is two hundred a year (and I gave more than I need have done).'

Just before the San Samuele vaporetto stop is heavy, grey-white **Palazzo Grassi** (*see p65*), designed by Giorgio Massari. This was the last of the great patrician *palazzi*, built in 1748-72 when the city was already in terminal decline. Acquired by Fiat in the 1980s, it was sold again in 2005 to French magnate Francois Pinault and functions as a gallery.

Palazzo Grimani

Vaporetto stop San Tomà

Palazzo Balbi (1582-90), whose obelisks are an indication that an admiral lived here, is the seat of the Veneto Regional Council.

Looking down the rio Ca' Foscari, you can see the archways of the city's fire station. (Further away, rio Novo, a canal dug in the 1930s to provide a short cut to the car park and station; traffic rocked the foundations of the buildings along the canal, so public transport stopped using the rio Novo in the 1980s.) Between the fire station and Palazzo Balbi is a minor building, on a site once scheduled to hold Frank Lloyd Wright's Centre for Foreign Architectural Students. In the end, his designs were judged too radical for so conspicuous a spot.

Just beyond the rio Ca' Foscari come three magnificent mid 15th-century Gothic *palazzi*. The first and largest is **Ca' Foscari**. It was here that Henry III of France was lavishly entertained in 1574 – so lavishly that his reason seems to have been knocked permanently askew. Doge Francesco Foscari died here of a broken heart after being ousted from office. The palazzo is now the headquarters of Venice's Università Ca' Foscari. The next two buildings are the **Palazzi Giustinian**; Wagner stayed in one of them in the winter of 1858-59, composing part of *Tristan und Isolde*. The horn prelude to the third act was inspired by the mournful cries of the gondoliers.

Ca' Rezzonico (*see p139*) is a Baroque masterpiece by Longhena, begun in 1667 for the Bon family, then sold to the Rezzonico family. Robert Browning died here, while staying with his profitably married but otherwise talentless son Pen, who bought the palazzo with his wife's money. Later guests included Whistler and Cole Porter. The building now contains the museum of 18th-century Venice.

Vaporetto stop Ca' Rezzonico

Just after the Ca' Rezzonico stop is the 15th-century **Palazzo Loredan**. The **Gallerie dell'Accademia**, once the church and monastery of Santa Maria della Carità, now holds an unrivalled collection of Venetian art (*see p145*).

RIGHT BANK

Ponte dell'Accademia.

Vaporetto stop Accademia

In 1932, the iron **Ponte dell'Accademia** that had been built by the Austrians was replaced by a 'temporary' wooden one. When this was discovered to be on the point of collapse in 1984, the Venetians had grown too fond of it to imagine anything else spanning the canal, so it was rebuilt exactly as before.

After the Accademia four fine Renaissance *palazzi* comes campo San Vio, one of the few *campi* on the Grand Canal. In the corner is the Anglican church of **St George** (*see p287*). To one side of the campo is the 16th-century **Palazzo Barbarigo**, with eye-catching but tacky 19th-century mosaics. Next is the pretty Gothic **Palazzo da' Mula**.

A little beyond that is the single-storey **Palazzo Venier dei Leoni**. Work ground to a halt in 1749 when the family opposite objected to their light being blocked by such a huge pile. Art collector Peggy Guggenheim lived here from 1949 to 1979; she was the last person in Venice to have her own private gondola. The building now contains the **Peggy Guggenheim Collection** (*see p147*).

Next-but-one comes the pure, lopsided charm of the Renaissance **Ca' Dario**, built in the 1470s, perhaps by Pietro Lombardo, with decorative use of coloured marbles and chimney pots. Venetians say the palazzo is cursed; certainly the list of former owners who have met sticky ends is impressive. **Palazzo Salviati** is a 19th-century building with gaudy mosaics advertising the products of the Salviati glass works.

LEFT BANK

Vaporetto stop San Samuele

A short way beyond the stop, the **Ca' del Duca** incorporates, in one corner, a part of the rusticated base and columns of a palace that Bartolomeo Bon was going to build for the Cornaro family. In 1461, the site was bought by Francesco Sforza, Duke of Milan; Bon's project was never completed.

San Samuele vaporetto stop.

Immediately beyond this are two **Palazzi Barbaro**, which have literary associations. The first one – 15th-century Gothic, with a fine but battered Renaissance water-entrance – still partly belongs to the Curtis family, who played host to Henry James at intervals between 1870 and 1875. The building was the model for Milly Theale's palazzo in *The Wings of the Dove*.

Just before one of the few Grand Canal gardens comes the bashful **Casetta delle Rose**, set back behind its own small trellised garden. Canova had a studio here; novelist Gabriele D'Annunzio once stayed in the house.

The massive rusticated ground floor of the **Palazzo Corner della Ca' Grande** (now the Prefecture) influenced Longhena's Baroque *palazzi*. The highest of High Renaissance, the imposing pile was commissioned in 1537 from Sansovino for Giacomo Cornaro, and built after 1545. Never one to mince words, Ruskin called it 'one of the worst and coldest buildings of the central Renaissance'.

Ponte dell' Accademia

Ponte dell' Accademia

Vaporetto stop Giglio

After campo Santa Maria del Giglio comes the 15th-century Gothic façade of **Palazzo Gritti**, now one of Venice's poshest hotels (*see p265*). Three *palazzi* further on is the narrow Gothic **Palazzo Contarini Fasan**, traditionally, but quite arbitrarily, known as Desdemona's house. It has beautiful balconies with wheel tracery.

The **Europa & Regina** hotel was once the home of Kay Bronson, an American society hostess whose hospitality was much appreciated by Henry James.

The last notable building is **Ca' Giustinian**, built in the late Gothic style of the 1470s, and once a hotel where Verdi, Gautier, Ruskin and Proust stayed. George Eliot's honeymoon here was ruined when her husband fell (or threw himself) off the balcony into the Grand Canal. Recently restored, it houses the offices of the Biennale (*see p31*).

At the corner of calle Vallaresso is **Harry's Bar** (*see p69*), the near-legendary Venetian watering hole, founded by Arrigo Cipriani senior in the 1930s.

Vaporetto stop San Marco Vallaresso

Just beyond the vaporetto stop lie the pretty **Giardinetti Reali** (*see p50*) and **piazza San Marco** (*see p50*).

San Marco
vaporetto stop.

The former abbey of **San Gregorio** – now a luxury hotel – is the last building before the Salute stop, with a fine 14th-century relief of St Gregory over a Gothic doorway. (Beyond can be seen the apse of the former church of the same name.)

Vaporetto stop Salute

In a triumphant position, at the opening of the Grand Canal, stands the wonderfully curvy church of **Santa Maria della Salute** (*see p148*). Baldassare Longhena's audacious Baroque creation (1671) took 50 years to build. Every year on 21 November (*see p31*) a procession from the basilica di San Marco makes its way across a specially-erected pontoon bridge to the church. Beyond the church is the Patriarchal Seminary.

The right bank ends at Punta della Dogana (Customs Point) with its complex of customs-related buildings: the extensive warehouses, which date from the 19th century and are now a major new contemporary art gallery (*see p147*); and the **Dogana di Mare** (Customs House, 1677), with its tower, gilded ball, weathervane figure of Fortune and spectacular view out across the Bacino di San Marco towards the Lido. Ships wanting to enter Venice would have their cargoes examined here by customs officials.

Dogana di Mare.

San Marco

Piazza San Marco, Napoleon said, is the 'drawing room of Europe' – an acute observation. It may not be homely, but it is a supremely civilised meeting place. At times it appears that much of Europe's population is crammed into this great square, and the pulsating shopping streets packed with big-name labels leading out of it, making the narrow *calli* that wind their way off the beaten track very enticing.

Three main thoroughfares link the key points of this neighbourhood: one runs from piazza San Marco to the Rialto bridge, one from the Rialto to the Accademia bridge, and one from the Accademia back to piazza San Marco. For a respite from the jostling crowds, wander off these routes; even in this most tourist-packed *sestiere* you can always find little havens of purely Venetian calm.

EXPLORE

Palazzo Ducale.

Don't Miss

1 Basilica di San Marco Arguably one of the greatest churches in Christendom (p50).

2 Campanile The view from the bell-tower in piazza San Marco is peerless (p55).

3 Gran Caffè Quadri The ultimate gourmet blow-out (p60).

4 Palazzo Ducale The hub of Venetian power and magnificence (p56).

5 Calle delle Botteghe Galleries and a jumble of fascinating shops (p65).

PIAZZA SAN MARCO & AROUND

Vaporetto San Marco Vallaresso or San Zaccaria.

In magnificent piazza San Marco, Byzantine rubs shoulders with Gothic, late Renaissance and neoclassical. The Venetians have always kept the square clear of monuments (on occasion stooping to mendacity to do so – as with the monument to Bartolomeo Colleoni; *see p75*). This is typical of Venice, where individual glory always plays second fiddle to the common weal.

The north side of the square dates from the early 16th century. Its arches repeat a motif suggested by an earlier Byzantine structure (seen in Gentile Bellini's painting *Translation of the Relics of the Cross* in the Accademia; *see p145*). Here resided the procurators of St Mark's, who were in charge of maintaining the basilica – hence the name of this whole wing, the Procuratie Vecchie. At its eastern end is the **Torre dell'Orologio** (*see p60*).

Construction of the Procuratie Nuove, opposite, went on for most of the first half of the 17th century, to designs by Vincenzo Scamozzi. Napoleon joined the two wings at the far end – not for the sake of symmetry, but in order to create the ballroom that was lacking in the Procuratie Nuove, which had become the imperial residence. So, in 1807, down came Sansovino's church of San Geminiano and up went the Ala Napoleonica, which now houses the **Museo Correr** (*see p55*).

The **Campanile** (*see p55*) and **Basilica di San Marco** (*see p50*) close off the square in all its splendour to the east.

North of the basilica lies the **piazza dei Leoncini**, a small square named after two small marble lions rubbed smooth by generations of children's bottoms. The large palazzo at the far end of the square is the 19th-century residence of the patriarch (cardinal) of Venice.

IN THE KNOW HONOURING NAPOLEON

Ever self-effacing, Napoleon intended to embellish **piazza San Marco** with a statue of himself. In fact, the emperor's likeness spent the brief period of French reign in front of the Doge's palace, then was hastily removed. In 2002, the statue – now in the **Museo Correr** (*see p55*) – was donated to the city by the *Comité français pour la Sauvegarde de Venise*. Furious letters were written to the local press suggesting that Venice should respond by donating a statue of Hitler to Paris.

Between the basilica and the lagoon, the **Piazzetta** is the real entrance to Venice, defined by two free-standing columns of granite. What appears to be a winged lion on top of the eastern column is in fact a chimera from Persia, Syria or maybe China; the wings and book are Venetian additions. St Theodore, who tops the other column, was Venice's first patron saint. The man who erected the columns in the 12th century asked for the right to set up gambling tables between them. The authorities agreed, but soon put a damper on the jollity by using the pillars to string up criminals. Superstitious locals still avoid walking between them.

Foreign visitors used to disembark here, and were dazzled by the pomp and magnificence. The area directly in front of the **Palazzo Ducale** (Doge's Palace; *see p56*) corresponded to a modern-day parliamentary lobby. Known as the *broglio*, it was the place where councillors conferred and connived (hence the term 'imbroglio'). Opposite the palace stands the **Biblioteca Marciana** (*see p56*), now the main city library.

West of the Piazzetta are the **Giardinetti Reali** (Royal Gardens), created by the French. The dainty neoclassical coffee house by Gustavo Selva is now a tourist information office. By the San Marco Vallaresso vaporetto stop is **Harry's Bar** (*see p69*), the city's most famous watering hole, founded in the 1920s and made legendary by Ernest Hemingway, Orson Welles and a bevvy of other famous drinkers.

Heading east from the Piazzetta, you will cross the **ponte della Paglia** (Bridge of Straw). If you can elbow your way to the side of the bridge, there is a photo-op view of the **ponte dei Sospiri** (Bridge of Sighs). From the Bridge of Straw there is also a superb view of the Renaissance façade of the Palazzo Ducale.

Sights & Museums

★ FREE **Basilica di San Marco**

San Marco, piazza San Marco (041 522 5205, www.basilicasanmarco.it). Vaporetto San Marco Vallaresso or San Zaccaria. **Open** *Basilica, Chancel & Pala d'Oro, Treasury* 9.45am-5pm Mon-Sat; 2-5pm Sun. *Loggia & Museo Marciano* 9.45am-3.45pm daily. **Admission** *Basilica* free. *Chancel & Pala d'Oro* €2. *Treasury* €3. *Loggia & Museo Marciano* €5. **No credit cards**. **Map** p51 C6 ➊
Note: To skip the huge queues that form at the basilica entrance at busy times, you can book your visit (€2 fee) through www.venetoinside.com. Large bags or rucksacks can be deposited (free) in a building in calle San Basso, off the piazzetta dei Leoncini. The basilica is open for mass and private prayer from 7am to 9.45am, with entrance from the piazzetta dei Leoncini door.

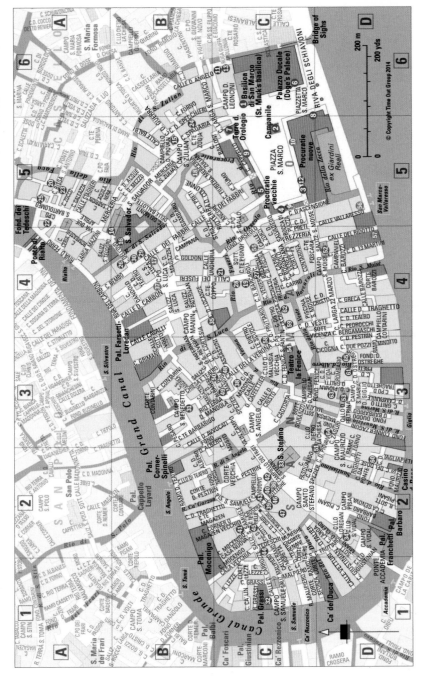

EXPLORE

Basilica di San Marco.

Often seen as the living testimony of Venice's links with Byzantium, St Mark's basilica is also an expression of the city's independence. In the Middle Ages any self-respecting city state had to have a truly important holy relic. So when two Venetian merchants swiped the body of St Mark (though some historians believe they got Alexander the Great's remains by mistake, a theme developed by Steve Berry in his 2007 novel *The Venetian Betrayal*) from Alexandria in 828, concealed from prying Muslim eyes under a protective layer of pork, they were going for the very best – an Evangelist, and an entire body at that. Fortunately, there was a legend (or one was quickly cooked up) that the saint had once been caught in the lagoon in a storm, and so it was fitting that this should be his final resting place.

The Venetians were traders, but they never looked askance at a bit of straightforward looting as well. The basilica – like the city as a whole – is encrusted with trophies brought back from Venice's greatest spoliatory exploit, the Sack of Constantinople in 1204, during the free-for-all that went under the name of the Fourth Crusade.

The present basilica is the third on the site. It was built mainly between 1063 and 1094, although the work of decoration continued until the 16th century. The church became Venice's cathedral only in 1807, ten years after the fall of the Republic; until then the bishop exerted his authority from San Pietro in Castello (*see p88*).

Being next door to the Palazzo Ducale, Venice's most important church was associated with political as much as spiritual power. Venetians who came to worship here were very aware that they were guests of the doge, not the pope.

Exterior

The first view of the basilica from the western end of piazza San Marco is an unforgettable experience. It is particularly impressive in the evening, when the mosaics on the façade glow in the light of the setting sun (as they are mostly 17th- and 18th-century replacements, the distance improves them). The façade consists of two orders of five arches, with clusters of columns in the lower order; the upper arches are topped by fantastic Gothic tracery.

The only original mosaic (c1260) is the one over the northernmost door, *The Translation of the Body of St Mark to the Basilica*, which is the earliest known representation of the church. Of curiosity value is the 17th-century mosaic over the southernmost door, which shows the body of St Mark being filched from Alexandria and the Muslims reeling back in disgust from its pork wrapping.

The real treasures on show are the sculptures, particularly the group of three carved arches around the central portal, a Romanesque masterpiece. The inner curve of the outer arch is the liveliest, with its detailed portrayals of Venetian trades, arts, crafts and pastimes. The upper order, with fine 14th-century Gothic sculpture by the Dalle Masegne brothers and later Tuscan and Lombard sculptors, can be seen from the Loggia.

Visible through the doors, the narthex (covered porch) has an opus sectile marble floor; a small lozenge of porphyry by the central door is said to mark the spot where the Emperor Barbarossa paid homage to Pope Alexander III in 1177. The influence of Islamic art comes through in the few remaining grilles that cover the wall niches where early doges were buried. Above, a series of 13th-century mosaics in the Byzantine style shows Old Testament scenes.

12th and 13th centuries, are the work of Venetian craftsmen influenced by Byzantine art but developing their own independent style. The chapels and Baptistry were decorated in the 14th and 15th centuries; a century later, replacements of earlier mosaics were made using cartoons by such artists as Titian and Tintoretto. However, most of these later mosaics are flawed by the attempt to achieve the three-dimensional effects of Renaissance painting.

In the apse, *Christ Pantocrator* is a 16th-century reproduction of a Byzantine original. Beneath, in what may be the oldest mosaics in the church, are four saint-protectors of Venice: Nicholas, Peter, Mark and Hermagoras. The central dome of the Ascension, with its splendidly poised angels and apostles, dates from the early 13th century. The Passion scenes on the west vault (12th century) are a striking blend of Romanesque and Byzantine styles. The Pentecost dome (near the entrance) was probably the first to be decorated; it shows the *Descent of the Holy Spirit*. Four magnificent angels hover in the pendentives.

In the right transept is the *Miraculous Rediscovery of the Body of St Mark*: this refers to an episode that occurred after the second basilica was destroyed by fire, when the secret of the whereabouts of the body was lost. The Evangelist obligingly opened up the pillar where his sarcophagus had been hidden (it's just opposite and is marked by an inlaid marble panel). Notice, too, the gorgeous 12th-century marble, porphyry and glass mosaics on the floor.

Baptistry & Zen Chapel

The Baptistry contains the Gothic tomb of Doge Andrea Dandolo and some interesting mosaics, including an image of Salome dancing. In the adjoining Zen Chapel is the bronze 16th-century tomb of Cardinal Zen (a common Venetian surname). The baptistry and chapel are very rarely open.

Chancel & Pala d'Oro

The Chancel is separated from the body of the church by the iconostasis – a red marble rood screen by the Gothic sculptors Jacobello and Pier Paolo Dalle Masegne, with fine statues of the Madonna, the apostles and St George. Access to the Chancel is via the San Clemente chapel to the right, with a mosaic showing merchants Rustico di Torcello and

The south façade, towards the Palazzo Ducale, was the first side seen by visitors arriving by sea and is thus richly encrusted with trophies proclaiming *La Serenissima*'s might. There was a ceremonial entrance to the basilica here as well, but this was blocked by the construction of the Zen Chapel (*see right*) in the 16th century. At the corner by the Doge's Palace stand the Tetrarchs, a fourth-century porphyry group of four conspiratorial-looking kings. These come from Constantinople and are usually accepted as representing Diocletian and his Imperial colleagues. However, popular lore has it that they are four Saracens turned to stone after an attempt to burgle the Treasury.

The two free-standing pillars in front of the Baptistry door, with Syrian carvings from the fifth century, come from Acre in modern-day Israel, as does the stumpy porphyry column on the corner, known as the Pietra del Bando, where official decrees were read.

The north façade, facing piazzetta dei Leoncini, is also studded with loot, including the carving of 12 sheep on either side of a throne bearing a cross, a seventh-century Byzantine work. Note the beautiful 13th-century Moorish arches of the Porta dei Fiori, which enclose a Nativity scene.

Interior

A lifetime would hardly suffice to see everything contained in this cave of wonders. The lambent interior exudes splendour and mystery, even when bursting with tourists. The basilica is Greek cross in form, surmounted by five great 11th-century domes. The surfaces are totally covered by more than four square kilometres (1.5sq miles) of mosaics, the result of 600 years of labour. The finest pieces, dating from the

---

**IN THE KNOW
MUSEUM PASSES**

The museums around piazza San Marco (but not the paying parts of the basilica) can only be visited with a multi-entrance ticket. These can be bought at the sights themselves, by phone or online. For details of the tickets available and how to buy them, *see p289* **Tourist Information**.

Buono di Malamocco, apparently about to FedEx the body of St Mark to Venice. St Mark's sarcophagus is visible through the grate underneath the altar. It was moved here from the 11th-century crypt in 1835; the crypt remains a popular venue for society weddings, though it's closed to the rest of us.

The indigestibly opulent *Pala d'Oro* (Gold Altarpiece) is a Byzantine work and, for a change, was acquired honestly. It was made in Constantinople in 976 on the orders of Doge Pietro Orseolo I and further enriched in later years with amethysts, emeralds, pearls, rubies, sapphires and topaz, topped off with a Gothic frame and resetting in 1345. It's a worldly corner of the church, this. Set in the frame of the curving sacristy door are bronze busts of its maker, Sansovino, and his friends, Titian and Aretino, who helped to get him out of prison in 1545. Aretino was a poet and playwright who moved to Venice in 1527 after scandalising Rome with his *Lewd Sonnets*. A great satirist and hedonist, he is said to have died laughing at a filthy joke about his sister.

The left transept contains the chapel of the Madonna Nicopeia (the Victory Bringer), named after the tenth-century icon on the altar, another Fourth Crusade acquisition. The St Isidore chapel beyond, with its 14th-century mosaics of the life of the saint, is reserved for private prayer and confessions, as is the adjacent Mascoli chapel. The altarpiece in this chapel, featuring Saints Mark and John the Evangelist with the Virgin between them, is a striking piece of Gothic statuary. The chapel's mosaics, dating from 1430-50, have a definite Renaissance look to them. They are mostly by Michele Giambono, although some of the figures have been attributed to Jacopo Bellini and to the Florentine Andrea del Castagno, who was in Venice in 1432.

Loggia & Museo Marciano

Of all the pay-to-enter sections of the basilica, this is definitely the most worthwhile – and it's the only part of the church you can visit on Sunday morning. Up a narrow stairway from the narthex are the bronze horses that vie with the lion of St Mark as the city's symbol; here, too, is Paolo Veneziano's exquisite *Pala Feriale*, a painted panel that was used to cover the *Pala d'Oro* on weekdays. The Loggia also provides a marvellous view over the square.

The original bronze horses are now kept indoors. They were among the many treasures brought back from the Sack of Constantinople, where they had stood above the city's Hippodrome. For many years they were attributed to a Greek sculptor of the fourth century BC, but the idea that they may be a Roman work of the second century AD has recently come into favour: the half-moon shape of their eyes is said to have been a Roman characteristic. They were at first placed in front of the Arsenale (*see p85*), but in around 1250 were moved to the terrace of the basilica.

In 1797 it was Napoleon's turn to play looter; the horses did not return to Venice from Paris until after his defeat at Waterloo. Apart from the parentheses of the two World Wars, when they were put away in safe storage, they remained on the terrace until 1974, when they were removed for restoration. Since 1982 they have been on display inside the basilica, with exact but soulless copies replacing them outside.

Treasury

This contains a hoard of exquisite Byzantine gold and silver plunder – reliquaries, chalices, candelabras. If you can stand the glitter, the highlights are

Piazza San Marco. *See p50.*

a silver perfume censer in the form of a church and two 11th-century icons of the Archangel Michael.

★ Campanile

San Marco, piazza San Marco. Vaporetto San Marco Vallaresso or San Zaccaria. **Open** *Nov-Mar* 9.30am-3.45pm daily. *Mar-June, Oct* 9am-7pm daily. *July-Sept* 9am-9pm daily. **Admission** €8. **No credit cards. Map** p51 C5 ❷

At almost 99m (325ft), the Campanile is the city's tallest building, originally built between 888 and 912. Its present appearance, with the stone spire and the gilded angel on top, dates from 1514. In July 1902 it collapsed, imploding in a neat pyramid of rubble; the only victim was the custodian's cat. It was rebuilt exactly 'as it was, where it was', as the town council of the day promised.

The Campanile served both as a watchtower and a bell tower. It provided a site for public humiliations: people of 'scandalous behaviour' were hung in a cage from the top. More wholesome fun was provided by the *volo dell'anzolo*, when an *arsenalotto* (shipwright) would slide down a rope strung between the Campanile and the Palazzo Ducale at the end of Carnevale. The flight is still re-enacted today.

Holy Roman Emperor Frederick III rode a horse to the top of the original in 1451; these days visitors take the lift. The view is superb, taking in the Lido, the whole lagoon and (on a clear day) the Dolomites in the distance. Sansovino's little Loggetta at the foot of the tower, which echoes the shape of a Roman triumphal arch, was also rebuilt using bits and pieces found in the rubble.

▶ *For an eye-to-eye view of the Campanile, climb up the Torre dell'Orologio; see p60.*

Fondazione Bevilacqua la Masa

Exhibition space *San Marco 71C, piazza San Marco (041 523 7819/www.bevilacqualamasa.it). Vaporetto San Marco Vallaresso.* **Open** (during exhibitions only) 10.30am-5.30pm Mon, Wed-Sun. **Map** p51 C5 ❸

Offices & exhibition space *Dorsoduro 2826, fondamenta Gherardini (041 520 7797). Vaporetto Ca' Rezzonico.* **Open** *Office* 10am-6pm Mon-Fri. *Exhibition space* days and times vary. **Map** p322 C8.

The Fondazione Bevilacqua la Masa was founded more than a century ago by Duchess Felicita Bevilacqua La Masa, who left her palace of Ca' Pesaro (*see p122*) to the city in order to give local artists a space in which to explore new trends.

This institution is very active in organising exhibitions, collaborating with the Arts and Design faculty of the IUAV (architecture university), and with other organisations working to foster new art in Italy. There are talks, performances, an archive and an artist-in-residence programme. The annual *esposizione collettiva* is dedicated to artists based in the Veneto area under the age of 30. The address given above is the main exhibition space; offices are at Dorsoduro 2826, fondamenta Gherardini (041 520 7797).

Museo Correr, Biblioteca Marciana & Museo Archeologico

San Marco 52, piazza San Marco/sottoportego San Geminian (041 240 5211, www.visitmuve.it). Vaporetto San Marco Vallaresso. **Open** 10am-5pm daily. **Admission** *see p53* **Museum Passes Map** p51 C5 ❹

These three adjoining museums are all entered by the same doorway, which is situated beneath the Ala Napoleonica at the western end of piazza San Marco.

Museo Correr

The Museo Correr is dedicated to the history of the Republic. Based on the private collection of Venetian nobleman Teodoro Correr (1750-1830), it has gems – including some very fine artworks – enough to elevate it well beyond mere curiosity.

The museum is housed in the Ala Napoleonica, the wing that closes off the narrow western end of the piazza, and in a constantly expanding area of the Procuratie Nuove. Napoleon demolished the church of San Geminiano, which faced off across the piazza to the basilica, in order to make way for his exercise in neoclassical regularity, complete with that essential imperial accessory, a ballroom. It is through this ballroom that you enter the Museo Correr today. At the far end, in a secluded niche, stands an unlabelled statue (1811). This is the city's hated conqueror, Napoleon (*see p50* **In the Know**).

The route now leads through nine recently opened rooms that made up the suite occupied by Sissi, aka Empress Elizabeth of Austria, wife of Franz Joseph I. In fact the beautiful, tragedy-prone Sissi spent no more than a few months here, in 1861-62, but the stuccos and fittings – including beautiful textile reproductions by Rubelli (*see p57* **Material Makers**) – faithfully reflect the decor of the period.

Passing through the pretty oval 'everyday dining room', the spirit of these same years continues in Rooms 4 and 5, dedicated to the beautiful if icy sculpture of Antonio Canova, whose first Venetian commission – the statue of *Daedalus and Icarus* displayed here – brought him immediate acclaim. Some of the works on display are Canova's plaster models rather than his finished marble statues.

From Room 6, the historical collection – which occupies most of the first floor of the Procuratie Nuove building – documents Venetian history and social life in the 16th and 17th centuries through displays of globes, lutes, coins and robes. Room 6 is devoted to the figure of the doge. Room 11 has a collection of Venetian coins, plus Tintoretto's fine *St Justine and the Treasurers*. Beyond are rooms dedicated to the Arsenale (*see p85*), a display of weaponry and some occasionally charming miniature bronzes.

Beyond Room 15 lies the Correr's most recent addition: the nine-room Wunderkammer, charmingly laid out in a style inspired by the 18th-century passion for eclectic collecting. Curators went

EXPLORE

through the Museo Correr's store rooms, dusting off and restoring a few real gems, including a couple of early works by Vittore Carpaccio, and a remarkable portrait of dashing 16th-century mercenary Ferrante d'Avalos, formerly attributed to Leonardo da Vinci – an attribution once rubbished but now being reconsidered. Other rooms contain exquisite painted china produced for the Correr family, Renaissance bronzes and ivory carvings.

In the final room of the Wunderkammer at the time of writing is the first-ever print of Jacopo de' Barbari's 1500 intricate bird's-eye view map of Venice, along with the original matrices in pear wood. This extraordinary woodcut is so finely detailed that every single church, palazzo and well-head in the city is clearly portrayed.

Stairs from the next room lead up to the Quadreria picture gallery – one of the best places to get a grip on the development of Venetian painting between the Byzantine stirrings of Paolo Veneziano and the full-blown Renaissance story-telling of Carpaccio. Rooms 25 to 29 are dedicated to Byzantine and Gothic painters; note Veneziano's fine *St John the Baptist* in Room 25 and the rare allegorical fresco fragments from a 14th-century private house in Room 27. Room 30 fast-forwards abruptly with the macabre, proto-Mannerist *Pietà* (c.1460) of Cosmè Tura.

The Renaissance gets into full swing in Room 34 with Antonello da Messina's *Pietà with Three Angels*, haunting despite the fact that the faces have nearly been erased by cack-handed restoration. The Bellinis get Room 36 to themselves.

The gallery's most fascinating work, though, must be Vittore Carpaccio's *Two Venetian Noblewomen* – long known erroneously as *The Courtesans* – in Room 38. These two bored women are not angling for trade: they're waiting for their husbands to return from a hunt. This was confirmed when *A Hunt in the Valley* (in the Getty Museum in Los Angeles) was shown to be this painting's other half.

Back downstairs, the historical collection continues with rooms dedicated to the Bucintoro (state barge), festivities, trade guilds and fairground trials of strength. The atmosphere gets neoclassical again along the corridor to the exit, café and giftshop which is lined with reliefs by Canova.

Museo Archeologico

This collection of Greek and Roman art and artefacts is interesting not so much for the individual pieces as for the light they cast on the history of collecting. Assembled mainly by Cardinal Domenico Grimani and his nephew Giovanni, the collection is a discerning 16th-century humanist's attempt to surround himself with the classical ideal of beauty. Highlights are the original fifth-century BC Greek statues of goddesses in Room 4, the Grimani Altar in Room 6, and the intricate cameos and intaglios in Room 7. Room 9 contains a fine head of the Emperor Vespasian. Room 20 has a couple of Egyptian mummies.

Biblioteca Marciana/Libreria Sansoviniana

In 1468, the great humanist scholar Cardinal Bessarion of Trebizond left his collection of Greek and Latin manuscripts to the state. Venice didn't get round to constructing a proper home for them until 1537. Jacopo Sansovino, a Florentine architect who had settled in Venice after fleeing from the Sack of Rome in 1527, was appointed to create the library, a splendid building right opposite the Doge's Palace. With this building, Sansovino brought the ambitious new ideas of the Roman Renaissance to Venice. He also appealed to the Venetian love of surface decoration by endowing his creation with an abundance of statuary. His original plan included a barrel-vault ceiling. This collapsed shortly after construction, however, and the architect was immediately clapped into prison. His rowdy friends Titian and Aretino had to lobby hard to have him released.

The working part of Venice's main library is now housed inside La Zecca (*see p60*) and contains approximately 750,000 volumes and around 13,500 manuscripts, most of them Greek.

The main room has a magnificent ceiling, with seven rows of allegorical medallion paintings, produced by a number of Venetian Mannerist artists as part of a competition. Veronese's *Music* (sixth row from the main entrance) was awarded the gold chain by Titian. Beyond this is the anteroom, in which a partial reconstruction has been made of Cardinal Grimani's collection of classical statues, as arranged by Scamozzi (1596). On the ceiling is *Wisdom*, a late work by Titian. Don't miss Fra Mauro's map of the world (1459), a fascinating testimony to the great precision of Venice's geographical knowledge, with surprisingly accurate depictions of China and India.

There are occasional free guided tours in English; call 041 240 7241 for information.

▶ *For information on use of the library, see p286.*

Negozio Olivetti

San Marco 101, piazza San Marco (041 522 8387, www.negozioolivetti.it). Vaporetto San Marco Vallaresso or San Zaccaria. **Open** 11am-4.30pm Tue-Sun. **Admission** €5; €2.50 reductions. **No credit cards. Map** p51 C5 ❺

Snatched back from neglect by the admirable FAI – Italy's equivalent of the UK's National Trust – this former showroom for the Olivetti business machines company was given a modernist makeover in the mid 1950s by architect Carlo Scarpa. Clean and linear, and dramatically lit by hidden natural light sources, the showroom is a gem. The floor in particular, with its inlaid coloured glass tessera, is superb. *See also p261* **Scarpa in Venice.**

★ Palazzo Ducale (Doge's Palace)

San Marco 1, piazzetta San Marco (041 271 5911, bookings 041 4273 0892, www.visit muve.it). Vaporetto San Marco Vallaresso or San Zaccaria. **Open** 8.30am-5.30pm daily. **Tours** (book at least two days in advance)

MATERIAL MAKERS

How sumptuous fabrics became and remained a hallmark of the city.

Gritti Palace.

The fact that rich-hued brocades – from luscious silks to sad nylon rip-offs – adorn thousands of Venetian hotel rooms does not signal lack of imagination on the part of local interior designers. The choice, in fact, reflects a traditional craft that dates back to the 13th century, or perhaps earlier.

It was *La Serenissima*'s privileged trading position with the Orient and its close links with Byzantium that provided the initial impetus. Venetian merchants filled the holds of their ships with the raw materials – cotton and silk – on their return to Venice from the great trading centres of the eastern Mediterrean. It may have been weavers from Byzantium who first showed the Venetians how to make fabric. But craftsmen brought from Lucca, an earlier Italian centre of textile excellence, also played a part. By the 14th century, Venice's fabrics – from cheap low-grade cottons to the most luxurious of heavy silks – had become highly sought-after commodities around Europe and the Levant. If Venice had become an international byword for unimaginable richness, it was in large part due to its textiles.

Today, the lagoon city is more commonly associated with lace, but this is misleading: far more fabric is now produced in and around Venice than lace. Manufacturers of the very finest materials are household names with top designers everywhere. **Rubelli** (Palazzo Corner Spinelli, San Marco 3877, Campiello del Teatro, 041 241 7329, www.rubelli.com) has been weaving in the Veneto since 1835: its fabrics grace the La Fenice opera house (*see p69*) and all rooms of the Gritti Palace hotel (*see p265*). Its magnificent textile archive goes back far further than the company's own history, however, with examples of Venetian and many other fabrics dating from the 15th century onwards. It can be visited by appointment.

The **Bevilacqua** dynasty has operated in Venice for more than two centuries and some of its output is still produced on the original looms in its workshop in the Santa Croce district (Santa Croce 1320, campiello de la Comare, 041 721 566, www.luigi-bevilacqua.com). The shop at the same location sells fabric, household and apparel accessories and textile-related books, as well as holding the company's huge archive. There's more Bevilacqua fabrics, and homewares made with it, at the Bevilacqua shops near San Marco (*see p61*).

Spanish fashion designer-cum-polymath Mario **Fortuny** (*see p157*) opened his textile factory in a former convent on the Giudecca island in 1921, installing machinery specially designed by him that is still in use and remains a closely guarded secret. The factory's showroom can be visited, however: it positively glows with the colours emanating from the massive bolts of glorious fabrics that line the walls.

Fortuny.

Palazzo Ducale (Doge's Palace).

9.55am, 10.45am, 11.35am daily. **Admission** see p289 **Tourist Information**. **Tours** €20, €14 reductions. **Map** p51 C6

An unobtrusive side door halfway down the right wall of the nave in San Marco leads straight into the courtyard of the Palazzo Ducale (Doge's Palace). Today's visitors take a more roundabout route, but that door is a potent symbol of the entwinement of Church and state in the glory days of *La Serenissima*. If the basilica was the Venetian Republic's spiritual nerve centre, the Doge's Palace was its political and judicial hub. The present site was the seat of ducal power from the ninth century onwards, though most of what we see today dates from the mid 15th century. Devastating fires in 1574 and 1577 took their toll, but after much heated debate it was decided to restore rather than replace – an enlightened policy for the time.

The palace is the great Gothic building of the city, but is also curiously eastern in style, achieving a marvellous combination of lightness and strength. The ground floor was open to the public; the work of government went on above. This arrangement resulted in a curious reversal of the natural order. The building gets heavier as it rises: the first level has an open arcade of simple Gothic arches, the second a closed loggia of rich, ornate arcading. The top floor is a solid wall broken by a sequence of Gothic windows. Yet somehow it doesn't seem awkward.

The façade on the Piazzetta side was built in the 15th century as a continuation of the 14th-century waterfront façade. On the corner by the ponte di Paglia (Bridge of Straw) is an exquisite marble relief carving, the *Drunkenness of Noah* from the early 15th century, while on the Piazzetta corner is

a statue of Adam and Eve from the late 14th century. The capitals of the pillars below date from the 14th to the 15th centuries, although many of them are 19th-century copies (some of the originals are on display inside the palace).

The Porta della Carta (Paper Gate – so called because this was where permits were checked), between the palace and the basilica, is a grand piece of florid Gothic architecture and sculpture (1438-42) by Bartolomeo and Giovanni Bon. The statue of Doge Francesco Foscari and the lion is a copy dating from 1885; French troops smashed the original when they occupied the city in 1797.

Behind the palace's fairy-tale exterior the complex machinery of empire whirred away with assembly-line efficiency. Anyone really interested in the inner workings of the Venetian state should take the 90-minute *Itinerari Segreti* tour. This takes you into those parts of the palace that the official route does not touch: the cramped wooden administrative offices; the stark chambers of the Cancelleria Segreta, where all official documents were written up in triplicate by a team of 24 clerks; the chamber of the three heads of the Council of Ten, connected by a secret door in the wooden panelling to the Sala del Consiglio dei Dieci, and the torture chambers beyond. The tour ends up in the leads – the sweltering prison cells beneath the roof from which Casanova staged his famous escape (probably by bribing the guard, though his own account was far more action hero) – and among the extraordinary beams and rafters above the Sala del Maggior Consiglio (see p59).

Following reorganisation, the main visit – for which an audio guide is recommended – now begins at the Porta del Frumento on the lagoon side

EXPLORE

of the palace. The Museo dell'Opera, just to the left of the ticket barrier, has the best of the 14th-century capitals from the external loggia; the ones you see outside are mostly copies.

In the main courtyard stands the Arco dei Foscari – another fine late-Gothic work, commissioned by Doge Francesco Foscari in 1438, when Venice was at the height of its territorial influence. It was built by Antonio Bregno and Antonio Rizzo. Rizzo also sculpted the figures of Adam and Eve (these too are copies; the originals are in the first-floor *liagò*), which earned him gushing accolades and led to his appointment as official architect in 1483, after one of those disastrous fires. Rizzo had time to oversee the building of the overblown Scala dei Giganti (where doges were crowned) and some of the interior before he was found to have embezzled 12,000 ducats; he promptly fled, and died soon after.

The official route now leads up the ornate Scala d'Oro staircase by Jacopo Sansovino, with stuccoes by Vittoria outlined in 24-carat gold leaf.

First floor: Doge's apartments
The doge's private life was entirely at the service of *La Serenissima* and even his bedroom had to keep up the PR effort. These rooms are occasionally closed or used for temporary exhibitions; when open, the Sala delle Mappe (also known as the Sala dello Scudo) merits scrutiny. Here, in a series of 16th-century maps, is the known world as it radiated from Venice. Just to the right of the entrance is a detailed map of the New World with Bofton (Boston) and Isola Longa (Long Island) clearly marked. Further on, seek out Titian's well-hidden fresco of St Christopher (above a doorway giving on to a staircase): it took the artist a mere three days to complete.

Second floor: State rooms
This grandiose series of halls provided steady work for all the great 16th-century Venetian artists. Titian, Tintoretto, Veronese, Palma il Vecchio and Jacopo Bassano all left their mark, though the sheer acreage that had to be covered, and the subjects of the canvases – either allegories or documentary records of the city's pomp and glory – did not always spur them to artistic heights.

The Sala delle Quattro Porte was where the Collegio – the inner cabinet of the Republic – met before the 1574 fire. After substantial renovation it became an ambassadorial waiting room, where humble envoys could gaze enviously at Andrea Vicentino's portrayal of the magnificent reception given to the young King Henry III of France in 1574. The Anticollegio, restored in part by Palladio, has a spectacular gilded stucco ceiling, four Tintorettos and Veronese's blowsy *Rape of Europa*.

Beyond here is the Sala del Collegio, where the inner cabinet convened. The propaganda paintings on the ceiling are by Veronese; note the equal scale of the civic and divine players, and the way both Justice and Peace are mere handmaidens to Venice

herself. But for real hubris, stroll into the Sala del Senato, where Tintoretto's ceiling centrepiece shows *The Triumph of Venice*. Here the Senate debated questions of foreign policy, war and commerce, and heard the reports of Venetian ambassadors. Beyond again are the Sala del Consiglio dei Dieci and the Sala della Bussola, where the arcane body set up to act as a check on the doge considered matters of national security. In the former, note Veronese's ceiling panel, *Juno Offering Gifts to Venice*. By the time this was painted in 1553, the classical gods had started to replace St Mark in Venice's self-aggrandising pantheon. The itinerary continues through an armoury.

First floor: State rooms
The Sala dei Censori leads down to a *liagò* (covered, L-shaped loggia), which gives on to the Sala della Quarantia Civil Vecchia (the civil court) and the Sala del Guariento. The latter's faded 14th-century fresco of *The Coronation of the Virgin* by Guariento (for centuries hidden behind Tintoretto's *Paradiso* in the Sala del Maggior Consiglio) looks strangely innocent amid all this worldly propaganda. The shorter arm of the *liagò* has the originals of Antonio Rizzo's stylised marble sculptures of Adam and Eve from the Arco dei Foscari.

Next comes the Sala del Maggior Consiglio – the largest room in the palace. This was in effect the Republic's lower house, though this council of noblemen had fairly limited powers. Before the fire of 1577 the hall had been decorated with paintings by Bellini, Titian, Carpaccio and Veronese. When these works went up in smoke, they were replaced by less exalted ones, with one or two exceptions. Tintoretto's *Paradise*, on the far wall, sketched out by the 70-year-old artist but completed after his death in 1594 by his son Domenico, is liable to induce vertigo, as much for its theological complexity as its huge scale. In the ceiling panels are works by Veronese and Palma il Giovane; note too the frieze of ducal portraits carried out by Domenico Tintoretto and assistants; the black veil marks where Marin Falier's face would have appeared had he not unwisely conspired against the state in 1356.

On the left side of the hall, a balcony gives a fine view over the southern side of the lagoon. A door leads from the back of the hall into the Sala della Quarantia Civil Nuova and the large Sala dello Scrutinio, where the votes of the *maggior consiglio* were counted; the latter is flanked by vast paintings of victorious naval battles, including a dramatic *Conquest of Zara* by Jacopo Tintoretto and *Battle of Lepanto* by Andrea Vicentino.

Criminal courts & prigioni
Backtracking through the Sala del Maggior Consiglio, a small door on the left leads past the Scala dei Censori to the Sala della Quarantia Criminale – the criminal court. The room next door retains some of the original red and gold leather wall coverings. Beyond this is a

EXPLORE

small room that has been arranged as a gallery, with Flemish paintings from Cardinal Grimani's collection.

The route now leads over the Bridge of Sighs to the Prigioni Nuove, where petty criminals were kept. Lifers were sent down to the waterlogged *pozzi* (wells) in the basement of the palazzo itself. By the 19th century most visitors were falling for the tour-guide legend that, once over the Bridge of Sighs, prisoners would 'descend into the dungeon which none entered and hoped to see the sun again', as Mark Twain put it. But when this new prison wing was built in 1589, it was acclaimed as a paragon of comfort; in 1608 the English traveller Thomas Coryat remarked, 'I think there is not a fairer prison in all Christendom.'

Some of the cells have their number and capacity painted over the door; one has a trompe l'œil window, drawn in charcoal by an inmate. On the lowest level is a small exercise yard, site of an unofficial tavern. Up the stairs beyond is a display of Venetian ceramics found during excavations, and more cells, one with cartoons and caricatures left by 19th-century internees. Back across the Bridge of Sighs, the tour ends on the lower floor in the Avogaria – the offices of the clerks of court. Next to this a bookshop has been set up, with a good selection of works on Venice.

▶ *For a primer on Venice's convoluted system of government, see p71 Machinery of State.*

Torre dell'Orologio.

Torre dell'Orologio

San Marco 147, piazza San Marco (bookings 041 4273 0892, www.visitmuve.it). Vaporetto San Marco Vallaresso or San Zaccaria. **Open** Guided tours in English 10am, 11am Mon-Wed; 2pm, 3pm Thur-Sun. **Admission** €12; €7 reductions. **Map** p51 C5 ➐

Note that there is no lift and the stairs are steep and narrow. The clock tower can *only* be visited on a tour, which can be booked at the Museo Correr (*see p55*), online, or by calling the number given above.

The clock tower, designed by Maurizio Codussi, was built between 1496 and 1506; the wings were an addition, perhaps by Pietro Lombardo. Above the clock face is the Madonna. During Ascension week and at Epiphany, the Magi come out and bow to her every hour, in an angel-led procession. At other times of year the hours and minutes are indicated in Roman and Arabic numerals on either side of the Madonna; this feature dates from 1858 – one of the earliest examples of a digital clock. On the roof, statues of two burly Moors, made of gunmetal and cast in 1497, strike the hour. Another Moore (Roger) sent a villain flying through the clock face in the film *Moonraker*.

After lengthy restoration, the tower reopened in 2007. The tour reveals the workings of the clock, which dates from 1753 and was a remake of the original of 1499. Until 1998 the clock was wound manually by a *temperatore* who lived in the tower. Amid controversy the last incumbent was replaced by an electrical mechanism. The tour concludes on the roof of the tower with a fine view over piazza San Marco, the basilica and the palace.

FREE La Zecca

San Marco 7, piazzetta San Marco (041 520 8788). Vaporetto San Marco Vallaresso or San Zaccaria. **Open** 8.10am-7pm Mon-Fri; 8.10am-1.30pm Sat. **Admission** free. **Map** p51 C6 ➑

The Mint, designed by Sansovino, was completed by 1547. It coined Venice's gold ducats – later referred to as *zecchini*, whence comes the English word 'sequins'. It is more impregnable in appearance than the neighbouring Biblioteca Marciana (*see p56*), though the façade had to accommodate large windows on the piano nobile (for relief from the heat) and open arches on the ground floor, where the procurators of St Mark's operated a number of cheese shops. It now houses most of the contents of the civic library.

Restaurants

Gran Caffè Quadri

San Marco 120, piazza San Marco (041 522 2105, www.quadrivenice.com, www.alajmo.it). Vaporetto San Marco Vallaresso or San Zaccaria. **Open** *Café* 9am-midnight daily. *Bistrot* noon-3pm, 7-10.30pm daily. *Restaurant* 12.30-2.30pm, 7.30-10.30pm Tue-Sun. **Average** €180. **Map** p51 C5 ➒

Marcel Proust used to bring his *maman* to eat in this Venetian classic that has been operating since 1638, and you can still imagine the couple in the plush red upper dining room with its spectacular view across St Mark's square. But the food – the exquisite, sometimes surprising creations of star chef Massimiliano Alajmo – might surprise them (as might the bill). Since the advent of the Alajmos (brother Raffaele runs the house) in 2011, everything here is *recherché*, from the extraordinary coffee specially toasted for the café at piazza level, through the club sandwiches and deceptively simple pasta plates served (at slightly lower prices than the restaurant) in the ABC Bistrot, to the marvels cooked up (prawn and curried clam cappuccino, wild duck risotto with truffle and foie gras drops, seabass with olive, caper and chicory pesto) for what is arguably the city's finest eating experience, recognised with a Michelin star in 2012. There are taster menus at €170, €235 and €300.

Originally called Il Rimedio, the café takes its name from Giorgio Quadri, who was among the first to bring Turkish-style coffee to Venice when he took the place over in the late 18th century. Stendhal, Wagner and Balzac were habitués. In the evening, a palm court orchestra competes out in the square with the one at Florian's (*see below*) opposite, and romantics pay small fortunes to sip cocktails under the stars.

Cafés, Bars & Gelaterie

See also p60 **Gran Caffè Quadri**.

Caffè Florian
San Marco 56, piazza San Marco (041 520 5641, www.caffeflorian.com). Vaporetto San Marco Vallaresso. **Open** 9am-midnight daily. **Map** p51 C5 ⑩
Florian sweeps you back to 18th-century Venice with its mirrored, stuccoed and frescoed interior. Founded in 1720 as 'Venezia Trionfante', Florian's present appearance dates from an 1859 remodelling. Rousseau,

Goethe and Byron hung out here – the last in sympathy with those loyal Venetians who boycotted the Quadri (*see p60*) across the square, where Austrian officers used to meet. These days, having a drink at Florian is more bank statement than political statement, especially if you sit at one of the outside tables, where not even a humble *caffè* costs less than €10.

Shops & Services

★ Bevilacqua
San Marco 337B, ponte della Canonica (041 528 7581, www.bevilacquatessuti.com). Vaporetto San Zaccaria. **Open** 10am-7pm Mon-Sat; 10am-5pm Sun. **Map** p51 C6 ⑪ **Fabric**

EXPLORE

Caffè Florian

This diminutive shop offers exquisite examples of hand- and machine-woven silk brocades, damasks and velvets. *See also p57* **Material Makers**. **Other location** San Marco 2520, campo Santa Maria del Giglio (041 241 0662).

Martinuzzi
San Marco 67A, piazza San Marco (041 522 5068). Vaporetto San Marco Vallaresso. **Open** 9am-7pm Mon-Sat. **Map** p51 C5 ❷ **Homewares**
The oldest lace shop in Venice, Martinuzzi has exclusive designs for bobbin lace items such as place mats, tablecloths and linens. If you have an odd-sized bed, not to worry – Martinuzzi will create a sheet set especially for you. Also open Sunday in summer.

Studium
San Marco 337C, calle Canonica (041 522 2382). Vaporetto San Zaccaria. **Open** 9am-7.30pm Mon-Sat; 9.30am-6pm Sun. **Map** p51 C6 ❸ **Books & music**
This shop stocks a wide selection of works on Venice, as well as travel books and novels in English. The shop's true speciality is revealed as you step into the back room, which is filled with theology studies, icons and prayer books.

PIAZZA SAN MARCO TO THE RIALTO

Vaporetto Rialto, San Marco Vallaresso or San Zaccaria.

Piazza San Marco is linked to the Rialto by the busiest, richest and narrowest of shopping streets: the Mercerie. The name is plural, since it is divided into five parts: the Merceria dell'Orologio; di **San Zulian** (on which stands the church of the same name; *see p62*); del Capitello; di **San Salvador** (with its church of the same name; *see p62*) and del 2 Aprile.

Mercerie means 'haberdashers', but we know from John Evelyn's 1645 account of 'one of the most delicious streets in the world' that in among the textile emporia were shops selling perfumes and medicines too. Most of the big-name fashion designers are to be found here now. The ponte dei Baretteri (Hatmakers' Bridge), in the middle of the Mercerie, is a record holder in Venice: six roads lead directly off the bridge.

The Mercerie emerge near campo San Bartolomeo, the square at the foot of the Rialto, with the statue of playwright Carlo Goldoni looking amusedly down at the milling crowds.

Sights & Museums

★ FREE San Salvador
San Marco, campo San Salvador (041 270 2464). Vaporetto Rialto. **Open** 9am-noon, 4-6.15pm Mon-Sat; 4-6pm Sun. **Map** p51 B4 ❹

If you can't make it to Florence on this trip, come to San Salvador instead. Begun by Giorgio Spavento in 1506, it was continued by Tullio Lombardo and completed by Sansovino in 1534. But even though the geometrical sense of space and the use of soft-toned greys and whites exude Tuscan elegance, the key to the church's structure is in fact a combination of three domed Greek crosses, which look back to the Byzantine tradition of St Mark's. The church contains two great Titians, the *Annunciation* at the end of the right-hand aisle (with the signature *'Tizianus fecit, fecit'* – 'Titian made this, made this'; the repetition was intended either to emphasise the wonder of the artist's creativity, or is a simple mistake) and the *Transfiguration* on the high altar; note the exquisite glass water jug in the lower right hand corner of the the former painting; the latter conceals a silver reredos, revealed at Christmas, Easter and 6 August (the feast of San Salvador).

There's also some splendid Veneto-Tuscan sculpture, including Sansovino's monument to Doge Francesco Venier, situated between the second and third altars on the right. At the end of the right transept is the tomb of Cristina Cornaro, the hapless Queen of Cyprus (d.1510), a pawn in a game of Mediterranean strategy that ended with her being forced into abdicating the island to Venetian rule. In the left aisle, the third altar belonged to the school of the Luganagheri (sausage makers), and has vibrant figures of San Rocco and San Sebastiano by Alessandro Vittoria, influenced by Michelangelo's *Slaves*. The sacristy (rarely accessible) contains delightful 16th-century frescoes of birds and leafage.

FREE San Zulian
San Marco, mercerie San Zulian (041 523 5383). Vaporetto San Marco Vallaresso or San Zaccaria. **Open** 9am-7pm daily. **Map** p51 B5 ❺
The classical simplicity of Sansovino's façade (1553-55) for San Zulian is offset by a grand monument to Tommaso Rangone, a wealthy and far from self-effacing showman-scholar from Ravenna, whose fortune was made by a treatment for syphilis, and who wrote a book on how to live to 120 (he only made it to 80). He unilaterally declared his library to be one of the seven wonders of the world, and had himself prominently portrayed in all three of Tintoretto's paintings for the Scuola Grande di San Marco (now housed in the Gallerie dell' Accademia; *see p145*).

The interior of San Zulian has a ceiling painting of *The Apotheosis of St Julian* by Palma il Giovane, and a Titianesque *Assumption* by the same painter on the second altar on the right, which also has good statues of St Catherine of Alexandria and Daniel by Alessandro Vittoria. The first altar on the right has a *Pietà* by Veronese.

▶ *Mass is said here in English at 10.30am on Sundays. Anglicans head across the Grand Canal to St George's (Dorsoduro 870, campo San Vio) for sung service at 10.30am on Sundays.*

IN THE KNOW THE MAIN DRAG

The **Mercerie** (*see p62*) – the maze of crowded, narrow alleyways leading from piazza San Marco to the Rialto – and the streets known collectively as the **Frezzeria**, which wind between La Fenice (*see p69*) and piazza San Marco, have been the main retail areas in this city for the past 600 years or so.

The densest concentration of big-name fashion outlets can be found around calle larga XXII Marzo, just west of the piazza, where top names such as Prada, Fendi, Versace and Gucci have all staked territory for their boutiques.

FREE Telecom Italia Future Centre

San Marco 4826, campo San Salvador (041 521 3200, www.telecomfuturecentre.it). Vaporetto Rialto. **Open** 10am-6pm Tue-Sun. **Admission** free. **Map** p51 B4 ⑯

The 16th-century cloisters of the monastery of San Salvador underwent a thorough restoration in the 1980s to provide a showcase for the latest offerings of the building's owner, Telecom Italia. The cloisters are now host occasional exhibitions and conferences. If it happens to be open for an event, be certain not to miss the splendid refectory with its 16th-century frescoed ceiling.

Cafés, Bars & Gelaterie

Caffetteria Doria

San Marco 4578C, calle dei Fabbri (329 351 7367 mobile). Vaporetto Rialto. **Open** 6am-8.30pm Mon-Sat; 1-8.30pm Sun. **No credit cards**. **Map** p51 B4 ⑰

Take a page out of the locals' book and squeeze into this popular, standing-room-only bar for a delicious cup of coffee, mid-afternoon snack or one of the best *spritz* in town. Service is always friendly and welcoming. Knowledgeable owners Andrea and Riccardo stock a huge selection of wine and spirits.

★ Rosa Salva

San Marco 950, calle Fiubera (041 521 0544, www.rosasalva.it). Vaporetto Rialto or San Marco Vallaresso. **Open** 8am-8.30pm daily. **No credit cards**. **Map** p51 B5 ⑱

This long-established family-owned café and *pasticciere* makes one of the smoothest *cappuccini* in town, and some very delicious cakes to go with it. If it's ice-cream you fancy, all the flavours are made on the premises. There's a good lunch spread, with interesting sandwiches and filled rolls, as well as pastas and simple salads. The candied fruit in intriguing jars and piles of sugared rose buds and violet leaves are delightful.

Other location Castello 6778, campo Santi Giovanni e Paolo (041 522 7949).

Shopping & Services

Araba Fenice

San Marco 1822, Frezzeria (041 522 0664). Vaporetto Giglio or San Marco Vallaresso. **Open** 9.30am-7.30pm Mon-Sat. **Map** p51 C4 ⑲ Fashion/accessories

A classic yet original line of women's clothing made exclusively for this boutique, plus jewellery in ebony and mother-of-pearl.

Carteria Tassotti

San Marco 5472, calle de la Bissa (041 528 1881). Vaporetto Rialto. **Open** 10am-1pm, 2-7pm daily. **Map** p51 A5 ⑳ Stationery

A charming selection of greeting cards, decorative paper, diaries and notebooks. Wedding invitations and business cards can also be ordered.

★ Daniela Ghezzo Segalin Venezia

San Marco 4365, calle dei Fuseri (041 522 2115, www.danielaghezzo.it). Vaporetto Rialto or San Marco Vallaresso. **Open** 10am-1pm, 3-7pm Mon-Fri; 10am-1pm Sat. **Map** p51 C4 ㉑ Accessories

The shoemaking tradition that was established by 'the Cobbler of Venice', Rolando Segalin, continues through his talented former apprentice Daniela Ghezzo. Check out the footwear in the window, including an extraordinary pair of gondola shoes. A pair of Ghezzo's creations will set you back anything between €650 and €1,800. Repairs are done as well.

Daniela Ghezzo Segalin Venezia.

Diesel

San Marco 5315-6, salizada Pio X (041 241 1937, www.diesel.com). Vaporetto Rialto. **Open** 10am-7.30pm Mon-Sat; 11am-7pm Sun. **Map** p51 A5 @ **Fashion**

This well-known Veneto-based company's kooky, club-wise, lifestyle-based styles have invaded Europe and North America; its hipper-than-hip store is a landmark on the Venetian shopping scene.

Dolceamaro

San Marco 5415, sottoportego de la Bissa (041 241 3045). Vaporetto Rialto. **Open** 10.30am-7.30pm daily. **Map** p51 A5 @ **Food & drink**

Dolceamaro ('bitter-sweet') has choc delights ranging from 100 per cent cocoa chocolate slabs for fundamentalists to a beautifully tailored man's shirt made entirely from milk chocolate. In colder weather, the hot chocolate is a must: get an espresso-sized shot of this dark gloopy delight.

Marchini Pasticceria

San Marco 676, calle Spadaria (041 522 9109). Vaporetto Rialto or San Zaccaria. **Open** 9am-8pm daily. **Map** p51 B5 @ **Food & drink**

Probably Venice's most famous sweet shop, and certainly the most expensive, Marchini has exquisite chocolate, including *Le Baute Veneziane* – small chocolates in the form of Carnevale masks. Cakes can be ordered.

Nalesso

San Marco 5537, salizada fontego dei Tedeschi (041 522 1343). Vaporetto Rialto. **Open** 10am-7.30pm Mon-Sat; 11am-7pm Sun. **No credit cards**. **Map** p51 A5 @ **Books & music**

Specialising in classical Venetian music, Nalesso also sells concert tickets for the Fenice and Malibran theatres as well as for concerts in various churches.

★ L'O.FT

San Marco 4773, calle dell'Ovo (041 522 5263, www.otticofabbricatore.com). Vaporetto Rialto. **Open** 9am-12.30pm, 3.30-7.30pm Mon-Sat; 11am-7pm Sun. **Map** p51 B4 @ **Accessories**

Aka L'Ottico Fabbricatore, this ultra-modern shop specialises in designer eyewear – the kind you won't find anywhere else, with extraordinary frames in anything from buffalo horn to titanium. Pop in for a pair of sunglasses, or bring along your prescription and treat yourself to glasses the likes of which chainstore opticians can only dream. The boutique also sells gossamer-like cashmere and sensual silk apparel, plus a selection of luxurious bags in materials ranging from calfskin to ostrich.

Paropàmiso

San Marco 1701, Frezzeria (041 522 7120). Vaporetto San Marco Vallaresso or Rialto. **Open** 10.30am-7.30pm Mon-Sat; 11am-7pm Sun. **Map** p51 C4 @ **Accessories/homewares**

An overwhelming mix of beads in minerals, glass, coral and metal makes this wholesale emporium a true delight. As well as Venetian wares, Paropàmiso has imports from Africa and the Far East. You can buy ready-made jewellery or put together your own: clasps and materials for stringing are also available. There's a selection of other ethnic goods here too, including fabrics, rugs, masks and small items of furniture.

Pot-Pourrì

San Marco 1810, ramo dei Fuseri (041 241 0990, www.potpourri.it). Vaporetto San Marco Vallaresso. **Open** 3.30-7.30pm Mon; 10am-1pm, 3.30-7.30pm Tue-Sat. **Map** p51 C4 @ **Fashion/accessories/homewares**

Walking into this shop is like stepping into an elegant friend's bedroom. Clothes are draped over armchairs or hang from wardrobe doors while charming knick-knacks cover the dressing table. This faux-boudoir houses designers such as Cristina Effe and Marzi as well as homewares.

Rizzo Regali

San Marco 4739, calle dei Fabbri (041 522 5811). Vaporetto Rialto. **Open** 9am-8pm Mon-Sat. **Map** p51 B4 @ **Food & drink**

This old-fashioned shop sells traditional cakes, sweets and chocolates. For *pesce d'aprile* (April Fool's Day), you can buy bags of foil-wrapped chocolate goldfish. If you can't find the *torrone* (nougat) you're looking for here, then it doesn't exist.

Testolini

San Marco 4744-6, calle dei Fabbri (041 522 3085, www.testolini.it). Vaporetto Rialto. **Open** 9am-7.30pm Mon-Sat. **Map** p51 B4 @ **Accessories/stationery**

Testolini carries stationery, backpacks, briefcases, calendars and supplies for both art and office. The staff can be on the cool side but the choice is huge... by Venetian standards.

FROM THE RIALTO TO THE ACCADEMIA BRIDGE

Vaporetto Accademia, Rialto, San Samuele or Sant'Angelo.

The route from the Rialto to the Accademia passes through a series of ever-larger squares. From cosily cramped campo San Bartolomeo, the well-marked path leads to campo San Luca, then campo Manin with its 19th-century statue of Daniele Manin, leader of the 1848 uprising against the Austrians (*see p243*). An alley to the left of this campo will lead you to the **Scala del Bòvolo** (*see p66*), a striking Renaissance spiral staircase. Back on the main drag, the calle della Mandola leads to broad campo Sant'Angelo with its dramatic view

Campo Santo Stefano.

of **Santo Stefano**'s leaning tower (*see p65*); off calle della Mandola to the right is the Gothic **Palazzo Fortuny** (*see p65*), once home to the Spanish fashion designer Mariano Fortuny.

Just before the Accademia bridge (*see p68*), **campo Santo Stefano** is second in size only to piazza San Marco in the *sestiere*. The tables of several bars scarcely encroach on the space where children play on their bikes or kick balls around the statue of Risorgimento ideologue Nicolò Tommaseo. (Poor Tommaseo is known locally as *il cagalibri*, 'the bookshitter', for reasons which become clear when the statue is viewed from the rear.) At the Accademia bridge end of the square is the 18th-century church of **San Vidal** (*see p66*).

On the Grand Canal to the north-west of campo Santo Stefano is campo San Samuele, with a deconsecrated 11th-century church and the massive **Palazzo Grassi** exhibition centre (*see p65*). Leading there from the campo, **calle delle Botteghe** is a hotch-potch of fascinating shops. Nearby, in calle Malipiero, the 18th-century love machine, Giacomo Casanova, was born (though in which house exactly is not known). The neighbourhood is full of Casanova associations, including the site of the theatre where his mother performed (corte Teatro).

Palazzo Fortuny

San Marco 3958, campo San Beneto (041 520 0995). Vaporetto Sant'Angelo. **Open** hours vary. **Admission** varies. **No credit cards**. **Map** p51 B3 ③①

This charming 15th-century palazzo, which belonged to Spanish fashion designer Mariano Fortuny (1871-1949), should not be missed on the occasions when it opens for temporary exhibitions. These are often photographic, photography being one of Fortuny's interests, alongside theatrical set design, cloth dyes and some elegant silk dresses. Also on display are some of Fortuny's paintings of Middle Eastern views.

Palazzo Grassi

San Marco 3231, campo San Samuele (041 523 1680, www.palazzograssi.it). Vaporetto San Samuele. **Open** during exhibitions 10am-7pm Mon, Wed-Sun. **Admission** €15 (€20 Palazzo Grassi & Punta della Dogana; *see p147*); €10 (€15 both) reductions. **Map** p51 C1 ③②

This superbly – though boringly – regular 18th-century palazzo on the Grand Canal was bought in 2005 by French billionaire businessman François-Henri Pinault. Pinault brought in Japanese superstar-architect Tadao Ando for an expensive overhaul, which increased the exhibition space by 2,000sq m (21,000sq ft). Most of the palazzo's shows centre on Pinault's own massive contemporary art collection. Next door at no.3260, the Teatrino Grassi – another Ando makeover – shows art videos and hosts events.

▶ *François-Henri Pinault's new mega-gallery in the Punta della Dogana is even more impressive; see p147.*

Santo Stefano

San Marco, campo Santo Stefano (041 522 5061, www.chorusvenezia.org). Vaporetto Accademia or San Samuele. **Open** 10am-5pm Mon-Sat. **Admission** €3 (or Chorus; *see p89*). **Map** p51 C2 ③③

EXPLORE

Santo Stefano is an Augustinian church, built in the 14th century and altered in the 15th. The façade has a magnificent portal in the florid Gothic style. The large interior, with its splendid ship's-keel roof, is a multicoloured treat, with different marbles used for the columns, capitals, altars and intarsia, and diamond-patterned walls. On the floor is a huge plaque to Doge Morosini (best known for blowing up the Parthenon) and a more modest one to composer Giovanni Gabrieli. On the interior façade to the left of the door is a Renaissance monument by Pietro Lombardo and his sons, decorated with skulls and festoons. In the sacristy are two tenebrous late works by Tintoretto, *The Washing of the Feet* and *The Agony in the Garden* (*The Last Supper* is by the great man's assistants), and three imaginative works by Gaspare Diziani (*Adoration of the Magi, Flight into Egypt, Massacre of the Innocents*).

FREE San Vidal

*San Marco, campo San Vidal (041 277 0561).
Vaporetto Accademia.* **Open** *9.30am-6pm daily.*
Map p51 D2 ③④
This early 18th-century church, with a façade derived from Palladio, was for years used as an art gallery. It has now been restored and hosts concerts. Over the high altar is a splendid Carpaccio painting (1514) of St Vitalis riding what appears to be one of the bronze horses of San Marco. The third altar on the right has a painting by Piazzetta, *Archangel Raphael and Saints Anthony and Louis.*
▶ *Classical music concerts by the Interpreti Veneziani are held here most days, beginning at 8.30pm. For information, see p194.*

Scala Contarini del Bòvolo

*San Marco 4299, corte dei Risi (041 260 1974,
www.scalabovolo.org). Vaporetto Rialto.* **Closed** for restoration. **Map** p51 B4 ③⑤
Follow the signs for the Scala del Bòvolo from campo Manin and you will emerge in a narrow courtyard entirely dominated by this elegant Renaissance spiral staircase, built sometime around 1499 by Giovanni Candi. Spiral staircases are called *scale a chiocciola* (snail staircases) in Italian; *bòvolo* is Venetian dialect for snail. It was beautifully restored in 1986 but has been closed again for further restoration – a shame, as the view from the top is charming.

Cafés, Bars & Gelaterie

Bar all'Angolo

*San Marco 3464, campo Santo Stefano (041 522
0710). Vaporetto Sant'Angelo.* **Open** *6.30am-9pm
Mon-Sat. Closed Jan.* **No credit cards. Map** p51
C2 ③⑥
Secure a table outside and watch the locals saunter through the campo as you enjoy a coffee or *spritz*. Inside, you have your choice of standing at the usually crowded bar or relaxing in one of the comfy seats in the back where you'll find locals and tourists being served good *tramezzini*, panini and salads by friendly, if hurried, staff. There are certainly bigger bars in this busy campo, but none match the quality here.

Marchini Time

*San Marco 4598, campo San Luca (041 241
3087, www.marchinitime.it). Vaporetto Rialto.*
Open *7.30am-8.30pm Mon-Sat; 9am-8.30 Sun.*
No credit cards. Map p51 B4 ③⑦

San Vidal.

The Marchini pastry empire is the oldest in *La Serenissima*. This space lights up campo San Luca with its colourful windows displaying the latest cakes, cookies and chocolates. There's a dizzying array of *cornetti* to enjoy with your breakfast coffee – the raspberry jam-filled one is mouth-watering.

Shops & Services

See also p155 **Gardens of Marvels**.

Alberto Bertoni – Libreria
San Marco 3637B, rio terà degli Assassini (041 522 9583, www.bertonilibri.com). Vaporetto Sant'Angelo. **Open** 9am-1pm, 3-7.30pm Mon-Sat. **Map** p51 C3 ㊳ **Books & music**
Just off calle de la Mandola (look for the display case marking the turn-off), this well-hidden cavern is home to art books, exhibition catalogues and the like, all with significant reductions off cover prices.
Other location San Marco 4718, calle dei Fabbri (041 522 4615).

Antiquus
San Marco 2973, calle delle Botteghe (041 520 6395). Vaporetto Sant'Angelo. **Open** 10am-noon, 3-7.30pm Mon-Sat. **Map** p51 C2 ㊴ **Gallery/ antiques**
This charming shop has a beautiful collection of Old Master paintings, furniture, silver and antique jewellery, including Moors' heads brooches and earrings.
Other location Dorsoduro 873A, calle Nuova Sant'Agnese (041 241 3725).

Arcobaleno
San Marco 3457, calle delle Botteghe (041 523 6818). Vaporetto Sant'Angelo. **Open** 9am-12.30pm, 4-7.30pm Mon-Fri; 9am-12.30pm Sat. **No credit cards. Map** p51 C2 ㊵ **Artists' materials**
Arcobaleno stocks a vast assortment of artists' pigments. As well as art supplies, it carries all the basics in hardware, light bulbs and detergents.

Chiarastella Cattana
San Marco 3357, salizada San Samuele (041 522 4369, www.chiarastellacattana.it). Vaporetto Sant' Angelo or San Samuele. **Open** 10am-1pm, 3-7pm Mon-Sat. **Map** p51 C2 ㊶ **Homewares**

Chiarastella Cattana's elegantly stylish tablecovers, duvet and sheet covers, bathrobes and accessories are crafted from natural hand-loomed textiles in gorgeously muted colours with botanical motifs.

★ Ebrû
San Marco 3471, campo Santo Stefano (041 523 8830, www.albertovallese-ebru.com). Vaporetto Accademia or Sant'Angelo. **Open** 10am-1.30pm, 2.30-7pm Mon-Wed; 10am-1pm, 2.30-7pm Thur-Sat; 11am-6pm Sun. **Map** p51 C2 ㊷ **Accessories/stationery**
Beautiful, marbled handcrafted paper, scarves and ties. These are Venetian originals, whose imitators can be found in other shops around town.

★ Gaggio
San Marco 3441-51, calle delle Botteghe (041 522 8574, www.gaggio.it). Vaporetto San Samuele or Sant'Angelo. **Open** 10.30am-1pm, 4-6.30pm Mon-Fri; 10.30am-1pm Sat. **Map** p51 C2 ㊸ **Accessories/homewares**
Emma Gaggio is a legend among seamstresses, and her sumptuous handprinted silk velvets are used to make cushions and wall hangings as well as bags, hats, scarves and jackets.

Galleria Marina Barovier
San Marco 3216, salizada San Samuele (041 523 6748, www.barovier.it). Vaporetto San Samuele. **Open** (by appointment) 10am-12.30pm, 3.30-7.30pm Mon-Sat. **No credit cards. Map** p51 C2 ㊹ **Gallery**
Marina Barovier hosts a collection of masterpieces of Venetian 20th-century works in glass and represents numerous renowned artists (local and international) working in glass. It stages a few shows a year.

Galleria Venice Design
San Marco 3146, salizada San Samuele (041 520 7915, www.venicedesignartgallery.com). Vaporetto San Samuele. **Open** 10am-1pm, 3-7pm daily. **Map** p51 C2 ㊺ **Gallery**
As one of the historical landmarks of contemporary art in Venice, this gallery deals especially in sculpture by established artists, both Italian and international. It also focuses on artists' jewellery pieces and interior design.
Other location San Marco 1310, calle Vallaresso (041 523 9082).

L'Isola – Carlo Moretti
San Marco 2970, calle delle Botteghe (041 5233 1973, www.carlomoretti.com). Vaporetto Sant'Angelo or San Samuele. **Open** 10am-7.30pm daily. **Map** p51 C2 ㊻ **Homewares**
This long-established family firm produces exquisitely coloured contemporary glasses, bowls, vases, light fixtures and much else. Each piece is hand-crafted, some are limited editions and many find their way into important glass collections. The

EXPLORE

showroom closes some Sundays in August and all Sundays from January to March.

Laura Crovato

San Marco 2995, calle delle Botteghe (041 520 4170). Vaporetto Sant'Angelo. **Open** 4-7.30pm Mon; 11am-1pm, 4-7.30pm Tue-Sat. **Map** p51 C2 **⏺ Fashion**

Nestling between expensive galleries and antique shops, Laura Crovato offers a selection of used clothes and a sprinkling of new items, including raw-silk shirts and scarves, costume jewellery and sunglasses.

Ottica Carraro Alessandro

San Marco 3706, calle della Mandola (041 520 4258, www.otticacarraro.it). Vaporetto Sant'Angelo. **Open** 9.30am-1pm, 3-7.30pm Mon-Sat. **Map** p51 C3 **⏺ Accessories**

Get yourself some unique and funky eyewear – the frames are exclusively produced and guaranteed for life. Ottica Carraro Alessandro offers extraordinary quality at reasonable prices.

★ Perle e Dintorni

San Marco 3740, calle della Mandola (346 588 1618). Vaporetto Sant'Angelo. **Open** 9.30am-7.30pm Mon-Sat; noon-7pm Sun. **Map** p51 C3 **⏺ Beads**

Here you can buy bead jewellery or assemble your own unique pieces, choosing from a vast assortment of glass beads, most of which are new versions based on antique designs.

Wellington BooKs

San Marco 4000, calle della Mandola (041 523 4964, 331 712 9641, www.wellington books.weebly.com). Vaporetto Sant'Angelo. **Open** 10.30am-8.30pm Mon-Sat; 2-8pm Sun. **Map** p51 B3 **⏺ Books & music**

IN THE KNOW
COFFEE VARIATIONS

Don't even think of ordering a Frappuccino in Venice (at the time of writing, there were no Starbucks here anyway). Instead, go for a **cappuccino**, **caffè latte**, or try one of these:

caffè espresso
caffè americano espresso diluted with hot water, served in a larger cup
caffè corretto espresso with a shot of alcohol (usually grappa)
caffè doppio double espresso
caffè lungo espresso made with slightly more water
caffè macchiato espresso with just a dash of milk
decaffeinato any of the above drinks but without the buzz

Opened in 2013 in a bid to reverse the trend of failing bookstores in Venice, Wellington BooKs (the capital is intentional, the reference is to *acqua alta* and rubber boots) offers an intelligent choice of titles in English, many of them in pretty cloth-bound editions, to visitors, students and lovers of the printed word. Check the Facebook page (wellingtonbooks.venice) for the occasional literary event and/or book club meeting.

THE ACCADEMIA BRIDGE TO PIAZZA SAN MARCO

Vaporetto Accademia, Giglio or San Marco Vallaresso.

The route from Santo Stefano back to piazza San Marco zigzags at first, passing through small squares, including campo San Maurizio, with its 19th-century church now transformed into the **Museo della Musica** (*see p68*), and campo **Santa Maria del Giglio** (aka Santa Maria Zobenigo; *see p69*). It winds past banks, hotels and top-dollar antique shops, to end in wide via XXII Marzo, with an intimidating view of the Baroque statuary of **San Moisè** (*see p68*). Off to the left as you make your way towards San Marco is the opera house, **La Fenice** (*see p69*), and more streets of supersmart shops, in the Frezzeria district (*see p63* **The Main Drag**).

Press on and you will be ready for what is arguably the greatest view anywhere in the world: piazza San Marco from the west side.

Sights & Museums

⏺FREE Museo della Musica

San Marco 2601, campo San Maurizio (041 2411 840, www.interpretiveneziani.it). Vaporetto Giglio. **Open** 9.30am-7.30pm daily. **Admission** free. **Map** p51 D2 **⏺**

This small private museum, set up in the former church of San Maurizio, is run by the Interpreti Veneziani concert concern (*see p196*). Serving partly as a sales and promotion outlet, the museum contains an interesting collection of period instruments. But it also presents an opportunity to appreciate the neoclassical interior of the church, designed by Giannantonio Selva, the architect of the Fenice theatre (*see p69*). The museum puts on concerts, mainly Vivaldi and other baroque favourites, at the church of San Vidal (*see p66*); tickets can be bought at the museum.

⏺FREE San Moisè

San Marco, campo San Moisè (041 528 5840). Vaporetto San Marco Vallaresso. **Open** 9.30am-12.30pm daily. **Map** p51 D4 **⏺**

The Baroque façade of San Moisè has been lambasted by just about everybody as one of Venice's truly ugly pieces of architecture. Inside, an extravagant Baroque sculpture occupies the high altar,

Teatro La Fenice.

representing not only Moses receiving the stone tablets but also Mount Sinai itself. Near the entrance is the grave of John Law, author of the disastrous Mississippi Bubble scheme that almost sank the French central bank in 1720.

Santa Maria del Giglio

San Marco, campo Santa Maria Zobenigo (041 275 0462, www.chorusvenezia.org). Vaporetto Giglio. **Open** 10am-5pm Mon-Sat. **Admission** €3 (or Chorus; *see p89*). **No credit cards. Map** p51 D3 ⑤

This church's façade totally lacks any Christian symbols (give or take a token angel or two). Built between 1678 and 1683, it's a huge exercise in defiant self-glorification by Admiral Antonio Barbaro, who was dismissed by Doge Francesco Morosini for incompetence in the War of Candia (Crete). On the plinths of the columns are relief plans of towns where he served; his own statue (in the centre) is flanked by representations of Honour, Virtue, Fame and Wisdom.

The interior is more devotional. You may not have heard of the painter Antonio Zanchi (1631-1722), but this is his church. Particularly interesting is *Abraham Teaching the Egyptians Astrology* in the sacristy, while the Cappella Molin has *Ulysses Recognised by his Dog* (an odd subject for a church). The chapel also contains a *Madonna and Child*, which is proudly but erroneously attributed to Rubens. Behind the altar there are two paintings of the Evangelists by Tintoretto, formerly organ doors.

★ Teatro La Fenice

San Marco 1983, campo San Fantin (041 2424, 041 786 511, www.teatrolafenice.it). Vaporetto Giglio. **Open** 9.30am-6pm daily. **Admission** €9; €6.50 reductions. **No credit cards. Map** p51 C3 ⑤

Venice's principal opera house – aptly named 'the phoenix' – has a long history of fiery destruction and rebirth. The theatre (1792) designed by Giannantonio

Selva replaced the Teatro San Benedetto, which burnt down in 1774. Selva's building was destroyed in 1836, and was rebuilt by the Meduna brothers, recreating the style of Selva. In 1996, a massive blaze broke out, courtesy of two electricians. After years of legal wrangling, the theatre was rebuilt and inaugurated in December 2003. Hidden away from view behind the ornate gilding and faux-Baroque plush are state-of-the-art technological innovations. The tour with audio guide lasts roughly 45 minutes.

▶ *For information on performances at La Fenice, see p195.*

Restaurants

Osteria San Marco

San Marco 1610, Frezzeria (041 528 5242, www.osteriasanmarco.it). Vaporetto San Marco Vallaresso. **Meals served** 12.30-11pm Mon-Sat. Closed 2wks Jan. **Average** €60. **Map** p51 C4 ⑤

This smart, modern *osteria* on a busy shopping street is a breath of fresh air in this touristy area. The guys behind the operation are serious about food and wine, and their attention to detail shows through both in the selection of bar snacks and wines by the glass, and in the sit-down menu, based on the freshest of local produce. Prices are high, but you're paying for the area as well as the quality. This is one of the few places in Venice where you can eat a proper meal throughout the day.

Cafés, Bars & Gelaterie

Harry's Bar

San Marco 1323, calle Vallaresso (041 528 5777, www.cipriani.com). Vaporetto San Marco Vallaresso. **Open** 10.30am-11pm daily. **Map** p51 D5 ⑤

This historic watering hole, founded by Giuseppe Cipriani in 1931, has changed little since the days when Ernest Hemingway came here to work on his

EXPLORE

next hangover… except for the prices and the numbers of tourists. But despite the crush, a Bellini (peach juice and sparkling wine) at the bar is as much a part of the Venetian experience as a gondola ride. At mealtimes, diners enjoy Venetian-themed international comfort food at steep prices (€140-plus for three courses). Stick with a Bellini, and don't even think of coming in here wearing shorts or ordering a *spritz*.

L'Ombra del Leone
Ca' Giustinian, San Marco 1364, calle del Ridotto (041 241 3519). Vaporetto San Marco Vallaresso. **Open** 9am-9pm daily. **Map** p51 D4 ⑤
Located inside the Grand Canal-side Ca' Giustinian, the headquarters of the Biennale (*see p181*), this sleek modern café-restaurant offers a superb panorama from its terrace on the water as well as good (and reasonably affordable) light lunches and a hopping evening aperitivo scene, especially in the warmer months. Incongruously for this hyper-cool venue, the Kids' Space (*see p181* **Tips for Tinies**) right next to the café has small children's playthings, along with nappy-changing and breast-feeding areas.

Shops & Services

Antichità Marciana
San Marco 1864, campo San Fantin (041 523 5666, www.antichitamarciana.it). Vaporetto San Marco Vallaresso. **Open** 3.30-7.30pm Mon; 9.30am-1pm, 3.30-7pm Tue-Sat. **Map** p51 C3 ⑤ **Gallery/homewares**
Primarily a purveyor of (minor) Old Master paintings, this shop also has a tasteful selection of antique baubles and a range of soft furnishing made from richly painted velvets created by the owner in her workshop. A favourite among interior designers.

Bugno Art Gallery
San Marco 1996D, campo San Fantin (041 523 1305, www.bugnoartgallery.it). Vaporetto San Marco Vallaresso. **Open** 4-7.30pm Mon, Sun; 10.30am-7.30pm Tue-Sat. **Map** p51 C4 ⑤ **Gallery**
Large windows overlooking the Fenice opera house reveal a space devoted to artists working in all types of media. Well-known local artists are also included in the gallery's collection. So packed is the exhibition calendar that shows often spill over into a smaller exhibition space nearby.

Caterina Tognon
San Marco 2746, Palazzo da Ponte, calle del Dose (041 520 7859, www.caterinatognon.com). Vaporetto Giglio. **Open** 10am-1pm, 3-7pm Tue-Sat. **Map** p51 D2 ⑥ **Gallery**
Following the success of her first gallery, which she opened in Bergamo in 1992, renowned curator Caterina Tognon created this Venetian showcase

for contemporary art in glass in 1998. In 2004, the gallery expanded on to the first floor of the palazzo it occupies. Various shows take place each year by emerging and renowned artists.

Cristina Linassi
San Marco 2434, ponte delle Ostreghe (041 241 7532, www.cristinalinassi.it). Vaporetto Giglio. **Open** 9.30am-1pm, 2.30-7.30pm Mon-Sat; 9.30am-1pm, 2.30-7pm Sun. **Map** p51 D3 ⑤ **Homewares**
This boutique sells gorgeous hand-embroidered nightgowns, towels and sheets made in its own workshop. The catalogue has designs for made-to-order items.

Galerie Bordas
San Marco 1994B, calle dietro la Chiesa (041 522 4812, www.galerie-bordas.com). Vaporetto San Marco Vallaresso. **Open** 11am-1pm, 4.30-7.30pm Mon-Sat. **Map** p51 C4 ⑤ **Gallery**
The only gallery dealing in serious graphics by internationally renowned masters. The space is small but the collection of artists' books held here is huge.

Galleria Traghetto
San Marco 2543, campo Santa Maria del Giglio (041 522 1188, www.galleriatraghetto.it). Vaporetto Giglio. **Open** 3-7pm Mon-Sat. **Map** p51 D3 ⑤ **Gallery**
This gallery with a 30-year history of dealing with Venetian 20th-century abstracts is a point of reference for established artists and for contemporary emerging artists working in all media.

Trois
San Marco 2666, campo San Maurizio (041 522 2905). Vaporetto Giglio. **Open** 4-7.30pm Mon; 10am-1pm, 4-7.30pm Tue-Sat. **No credit cards**. **Map** p51 D3 ⑤ **Fabric**
This is one of the best places in *La Serenissima* to buy original Fortuny fabrics – and at considerable savings on the prices you'd find in the UK and the US (though this still doesn't make them particularly cheap). Made-to-order bead-work, masks and accessories are also available.

Venetia Studium
San Marco 2425, calle delle Ostreghe (041 523 6953, www.venetiastudium.com). Vaporetto Giglio. **Open** 9.30am-7.40pm Mon-Sat; 10.30am-6pm Sun. **Map** p51 D3 ⑤ **Accessories/homewares**
Venetia Studium is the sole authorised manufacturer of the distinctive Fortuny lamps. It also stocks splendid silk pillows, scarves, handbags and other accessories in a marvellous range of colours. They're certainly not cheap, but they do make perfect gifts.
Other location San Marco, Torre dell'Orologio (041 522 6791)

MACHINERY OF STATE

Navigating the corridors of power.

The longevity of the Venetian republic was due, to a large extent, to a finely honed system of checks and balances that kept the powerful merchant aristocracy closely involved in the machinery of state without allowing any one person or dynasty to lord it over the others. Rules, numbers and duties changed. At the end of the 13th century, what had started out as something close to a democracy became an oligarchy, with only the members of the 200-odd powerful clans included in the Libro d'oro (Golden Book) eligible for office. Later, anyone with the necessary funds could buy into the machinery of state. The main ruling bodies were:

Il Doge.

COLLEGIO DEI SAVI
College of Wise Men – a group of experts, elected by the senato, who staffed special committees to oversee all aspects of internal, marine and war policy.

CONSIGLIO DEI DIECI
Council of Ten – appointed by the senato, the council's extensive network of spies brought any would-be subversives to a closed-door trial, in which defence lawyers were forbidden. In time, the increasingly powerful consiglio dei dieci would have the Inquisition to assist it in its task.

IL DOGE
The Duke – elected for life in a complicated, cheat-proof system of multiple ballots, the sumptuously robed Duke of Venice was glorious to behold. He could not, however, indulge in business of his own, receive foreign ambassadors alone, leave Venice without permission, or accept personal gifts. If his city state tired of him, he could be deposed. With the doge's extended family banned from high office for the term of his reign, many doges hailed from less politically adept clans. Most were very old by the time they donned the biretta, the distinctive horned hat – the average age of doges between 1400 and 1570 was 72. However, the doge was the only official privy to all state secrets and eligible to attend all meetings of state organs; he could, if he played his cards right, have a determining effect on Venetian policy.

MAGGIOR CONSIGLIO
Great Council – the Republic's parliament – made up of all voting-age males from the clans that were included in the Libro d'oro – which elected (and provided the candidates for) most other state offices, including that of the doge.

MINOR CONSIGLIO
Lesser Council – elected by and from the maggior consiglio, this six-man team advised – or kept tabs on – the doge.

PIEN COLLEGIO
Full College – made up of the minor consiglio and the collegio dei savi, this became Venice's real government, eventually supplanting the senato.

QUARANTIE
The three supreme courts; the 40 members were chosen by the senato.

SENATO
Senate – known until the late 14th century as the pregadi, the senato was the upper house of the Venetian parliament; by the 16th century it had some 300 members.

SERENISSIMA SIGNORIA
Most Serene Lordships – the minor consiglio, the heads of the three quarantie courts and the doge; this body was vested with ultimate executive power.

EXPLORE

Castello

Castello is not only Venice's largest *sestiere*. It's also the most remarkably varied, stretching from the bustle and splendour in the north-west around Santa Maria Formosa and Santi Giovanni e Paolo, to the homely, washing-festooned stretches around and beyond wide via Garibaldi.

To this mix add the immense Arsenale complex – Venice's former shipbuilding centre and great military powerhouse, currently awaiting a comprehensive development project – plus the giardini della Biennale, where the world's contemporary art and architecture aficionados flock for extraordinary shows through the summer, a slew of remarkable churches, a football pitch whose days may be numbered and some seriously good restaurants. Castello really is a Venice unto itself.

San Francesco della Vigna.

Don't Miss

1 Arsenale Any chance to enter this fascinating complex should be seized (p85).

2 Fondazione Querini Stampalia Superb art collection, urbane café (p75).

3 Scuola di San Giorgio degli Schiavoni Enchanting works by Carpaccio (p88).

4 Papier Mâché If you need a mask, these are the real deal (p84).

5 San Francesco della Vigna Palladio and Bellini in a deserted corner of the city (p78).

Monument to Bartolomeo Colleoni.

NORTHERN & WESTERN CASTELLO

Vaporetto Bacini, Celestia, Fondamente Nove, Ospedale, Rialto or San Zaccaria.

The canal dividing the Doge's Palace (*see p56*) from the prison marks the end of the *sestiere* of San Marco. This means that the **Museo Diocesano di Arte Sacra** (*see p75*) and stately **San Zaccaria** (*see p80*), although closely associated with San Marco, actually belong to Castello. But the heart of northern and western Castello lies inland: **campo Santa Maria Formosa** (literally, 'Shapely St Mary'; *see p80*), a large, bustling, irregular-shaped square on the road to just about everywhere.

This square has all you could possibly need: a fine church, a market, a couple of bars and an undertaker. Nearby is the museum-cum-library of the **Fondazione Querini Stampalia** (*see p75*). Buzzing with locals and tourists, the campo is surrounded by *palazzi* that range in style from the very grand to the very homely. It is, in effect, Castello in miniature.

You'll have to trek west from here, to hard up against the border with the *sestiere* of San Marco, to visit the church of **Santa Maria della Fava** (*see p80*).

Southward from Santa Maria Formosa runs the busy shopping street of **ruga Giuffa,** named after either a community of Armenian merchants from Julfa, or a band of thugs – *gagiuffos* in 13th-century dialect – who used to terrorise the area. The first turn to the left off this street leads to the grandiose 16th-century **Palazzo Grimani** (*see p78*).

For more grandeur, head north to **campo Santi Giovanni e Paolo**. The Gothic red brick of the Dominican church (*see p79*) is beautifully set off by the glistening marble on the trompe l'œil façade of the **Scuola Grande di San Marco** (*see p81*) – now housing the civic hospital, but with a series of magnificent rooms of the historic *scuola* now open to the public – and the bronze of the equestrian **monument to Bartolomeo Colleoni** (*see p75*) gazing contemptuously down.

It's a short walk through narrow *calli* from Santi Giovanni e Paolo to the fondamenta Nuove, where the northern lagoon comes into view. The cemetery island of San Michele (*see p164*) is always in sight, acting as a grim *memento mori* for patients in the hospital.

Eastwards from Santi Giovanni e Paolo, a road called Barbaria delle Tole (the meaning of the name is shrouded in mystery: *tole* – *tavole* in Italian – are planks; *barbaria*, on the other hand, could refer to the wild appearance of the area, the presence of numerous barbers' shops, the barbaric behaviour of local carpenters, or the fact that the planks were destined mainly for the Barbary Coast) passes the Baroque church of **Santa Maria dei Derelitti** (*see p80*) by Baldassare Longhena, with its teetering façade adorned with leering faces. The church now belongs to an old people's home, which contains an exquisite 18th-century music room. Barbaria delle Tole leads into one of the least touristy areas of the city. Here, beyond the old gasworks, is austere **San Francesco della Vigna** (*see p78*).

Sights & Museums

★ Monument to Bartolomeo Colleoni
Castello, campo Santi Giovanni e Paolo. Vaporetto Ospedale or Fondamente Nove. **Map** p76 B2 **❶**
Bartolomeo Colleoni was a famous *condottiere* (mercenary soldier) who left a legacy to the Republic on the condition that a statue be erected to him in front of St Mark's. Not wishing to clutter up St Mark's square with the statue, but loath to miss out on the money, Venice's wily rulers in 1479 gave him a space in front of the Scuola di San Marco. Geddit? To make up for this flagrant deception, the Republic did Colleoni proud, commissioning the Florentine artist Andrea Verrocchio to create this fine equestrian statue. On Verrocchio's death it was completed, together with the pedestal, by Alessandro Leopardi (1488-96). It is not a portrait, but a stylised representation of military pride and might. Colleoni's coat of arms (on the pedestal) includes three fig-like objects, a reference to his name, which in Italian sounds very similar to *coglioni* – testicles, of which this soldier was said to possess three.

Museo Diocesano di Arte Sacra
Castello 4312, ponte della Canonica (041 522 9166, www.veneziaubt.org). Vaporetto San Zaccaria. **Open** 10am-5.30pm Tue-Sun. **Admission** €5, €2.50 reductions. **No credit cards. Map** p76 B4 **❷**
This museum is situated in the ex-monastery of Sant'Apollonia, whose Romanesque cloisters are unique in Venice (you're meant to have a ticket to view the cloisters but staff will probably let you take a peek). The museum contains a number of works of art and clerical artefacts (reliquaries, chalices, missals, crucifixes) from suppressed churches and monasteries. The *quadreria* is notable for two energetic paintings by Luca Giordano (*Christ and the Money-Lenders, Massacre of the Innocents*) and for three recently acquired works by Venice's great colourist Tintoretto. From the church of San Donato there is a fine altarpiece by Paolo Veneziano, *San Donato e Devoti*, with the saint in relief, in gilded and painted wood.

Museo della Fondazione Querini Stampalia
Castello 5252, campo Santa Maria Formosa (041 271 1411, www.querinistampalia.it). Vaporetto Rialto. **Open** *Museum* 10am-8pm Tue-Sun. **Admission** €10; €8 reductions. **Map** p76 B3 **❸**
This Renaissance palazzo and its art collection were bequeathed to Venice by Giovanni Querini, a 19th-century scientist, man of letters and silk producer from one of the city's most ancient families. Querini specified in his will that a library should be created here that would open 'particularly in the evenings for the convenience of scholars', and that the foundation should promote 'evening assemblies of scholars and scientists'. Today, the Querini Stampalia still exudes something of its founder's spirit: the first-floor library is a great place to study.

The ground floor and gardens, redesigned in the 1960s by Carlo Scarpa, offer one of Venice's few successful examples of modern architecture (*see also p261* **Scarpa in Venice**). On the second floor, the gallery contains some important paintings, including Palma il Vecchio's portraits of Francesco and Paola Querini (for whom the palace was built in the 16th century), as well as a marvellous

EXPLORE

Museo della Fondazione Querini Stampalia.

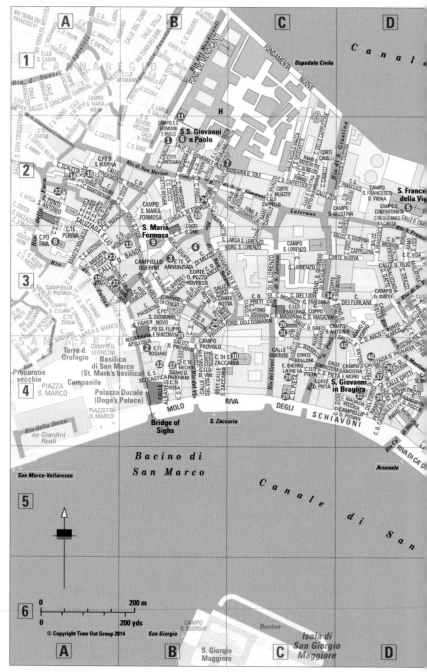

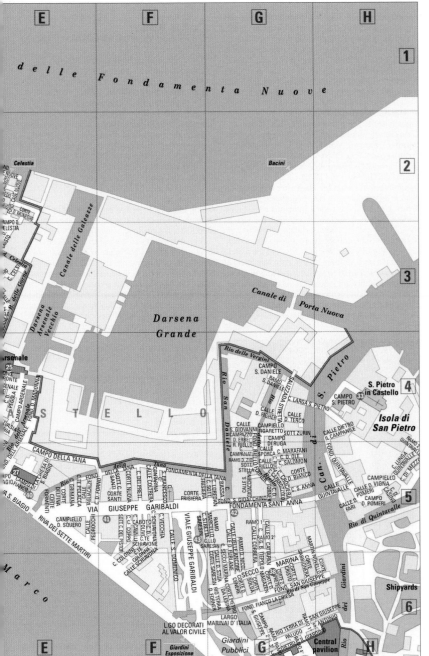

Presentation in the Temple by Giovanni Bellini, and a striking *Judith and Holofernes* by Vincenzo Catena. It also has a fascinating series of minor works, such as Gabriele Bella's 67 paintings of Venetian festivals, and a selection of Pietro Longhi's scenes of bourgeois life in 18th-century Venice. On the top floor is a gallery designed by Mario Botta, which hosts exhibitions of contemporary art. For library hours, *see p185*.

★ Palazzo Grimani

Castello 4858, ramo Grimani (041 520 0345, www.palazzogrimani.org). Vaporetto San Zaccaria. **Open** 8.15am-2pm Mon; 8.15am-7.15pm Tue-Sun. **Admission** €8.50; €6.50 & €4.50 reductions (*see also right* **Grimani & Accademia**). **No credit cards. Map** p76 B3 ❹

Inaugurated in December 2008 after a restoration process lasting 27 years, this magnificent palazzo in a tiny street off the ruga Giuffa has an original nucleus built by Antonio Grimani, doge of Venice, in the 1520s. However, it is most closely associated with his nephew Giovanni Grimani, cardinal and collector of antiquities. He enlarged and extended the palace, imposing a style of Roman classicism that is especially noticeable in the courtyard, and calling artists from central Italy, including Francesco Salviati and Federico Zuccari, to decorate it. The palazzo was conceived as a grand showcase for his fine collection of antiquities. Its fame was such that it was one of the buildings that Henry III of France insisted on seeing

Santi Giovanni e Paolo.

IN THE KNOW
GRIMANI & ACCADEMIA

If you're planning to visit both Palazzo Grimani (*see left*) and the Accademia Gallery (*see p145*), save money with a cumulative ticket, which costs €10.50 (€7.50 reductions). There may be a surcharge if either or both places are staging special exhibitions. If you purchase your ticket *in situ*, you must pay cash; if you book them beforehand (through the call centre 041 520 0345 or the websites of either) you can pay with most major credit cards.

during his visit to Venice in 1574. Film buffs may remember the palace as the setting for the final gory scenes of Nicholas Roeg's film, *Don't Look Now*.

A grand staircase, modelled on the Scala d'Oro of the Doge's palace, leads up to the *piano nobile*. Highlights of the tour are the Michelangelo-esque Sala della Tribuna, with its multicoloured marbles, where the most important pieces of statuary were once exhibited (a Ganymede being borne off by Jupiter hangs from the ceiling as an example), and the *Sala ai Fogliami*, the ceiling of which is decorated with foliage and birds painted with scrupulous naturalistic accuracy.

▶ *Cardinal Grimani's collection of antiquities is now mostly in the Museo Archeologico; see p56.*

FREE San Francesco della Vigna

Castello, campo San Francesco della Vigna (041 520 6102). Vaporetto Celestia. **Open** 8am-12.30pm, 3-7pm Mon-Sat; 3-6.30pm Sun. **Map** p76 D2 ❺

San Francesco may be off the beaten track, but the long trek over to the down-at-heel area beyond the gasworks is worth it. In 1534, Jacopo Sansovino was asked by his friend Doge Andrea Gritti to design this church for the Observant Franciscan order. The Tuscan architect opted for a deliberately simple style to match the monastic rule of its inhabitants. The façade (1568-72) was a later addition by Andrea Palladio; it is the first example of his system of superimposed temple fronts.

The dignified, solemn interior consists of a single broad nave with side chapels. The Cappella Giustiniani on the left of the chancel holds a marvellous cycle of bas-reliefs by Pietro Lombardo and school, moved here from an earlier church on the same site. In the nave, the fourth chapel on the right has a *Resurrection* attributed to Paolo Veronese. In the right transept is a fruity, flowery *Madonna and Child Enthroned* (c1450), a signed work by the Greek artist Antonio da Negroponte.

From the left transept, a door leads into the Cappella Santa, which contains a *Madonna and*

Saints (1507) by Giovanni Bellini (perhaps assisted by Girolamo da Santacroce). From here, it is possible to make a detour and visit two of the church's peaceful Renaissance cloisters.

Back in the church, the fifth chapel on the left is home to Paolo Veronese's first Venetian commission, the stunning *Holy Family with Saints John the Baptist, Anthony the Abbot and Catherine* (c1551). The third chapel has trompe l'œil frescoes in chiaroscuro by GB Tiepolo (1743, recently restored). The second chapel has three powerful statues of saints Roch, Anthony the Abbot and Sebastian (1565) by Alessandro Vittoria.

★ Santi Giovanni e Paolo (San Zanipolo)

Castello, campo Santi Giovanni e Paolo (041 523 5913, www.basilicasantigiovanniepaolo.it).
Vaporetto Ospedale or Fondamente Nove.
Open 9am-6pm Mon-Sat; noon-6pm Sun.
Admission €2.50, €1.25 reductions.
No credit cards. Map p76 B2 ❻

Santi Giovanni e Paolo was founded by the Dominican order in 1246 but not finished until 1430. Between 1248 and 1778, 25 doges were buried here. The vast interior – 101m (331ft) long – is a single spatial unit; the monks' choir was removed in the 17th century, leaving nothing to impede the view. Santi Giovanni e Paolo is packed with monuments to Venetian heroes as well as doges.

The entrance wall is dedicated to a series of funerary tributes to the Mocenigo family. The grandest – a masterpiece by Pietro, Tullio and Antonio Lombardo – belongs to Pietro Mocenigo, who died in 1476: the doge stands on his own sarcophagus, supported by three warriors representing the three ages of man. The religious reference above – the three Marys at the sepulchre – seems almost an afterthought.

The second altar on the right features an early polyptych by Giovanni Bellini (1465) in its original frame. Continuing down the right side of the church, the huge Baroque mausoleum by Andrea Tirali (1708) has two Valier doges and a *dogaressa* taking a bow before a marble curtain. Tirali also designed the Chapel of St Dominic, notable for its splendid ceiling painting by Giovani Battista Piazzetta of *St Dominic in Glory* (c1727). The right transept has a painting of *St Antonine Distributing Alms* (1542) by Lorenzo Lotto. Above are splendid stained-glass windows, to designs by such Renaissance artists as Bartolomeo Vivarini and Cima da Conegliano (1470-1520).

On the right side of the chancel, with its Baroque high altar, is the Gothic tomb of Michele Morosini; opposite is the tomb of Doge Andrea Vendramin, by the Lombardo family.

The rosary chapel, off the left transept, was gutted by fire in 1867, just after two masterpieces by Titian and Bellini had been placed here for safe keeping. It now contains paintings and furnishings from suppressed churches. The ceiling paintings,

RUNNING IN VENICE

Giving the city the runaround.

Venice's bridges and narrow alleys make it a difficult holiday venue for those that need to pound pavements to get their daily fix of oxygen. But choose your time (best hour for '*footing*' is early morning) and your location, and you'll find that there are others who share your passion for running. Popular spots include the *fondamenta* by the Giardini vaporetto stop, further east under the shady pineta of Sant'Elena and the wider pavements on the Zattere.

For something more competitive, the **Venice Marathon** (*see p31*) takes place in October. The starting line is at the Villa Pisani at Strà; the race passes along the **Brenta Canal** (*see p206*), over the bridge to Venice, then by a specially erected pontoon over the lagoon to the finishing line on the riva degli Schiavoni. The less competitive **Su e Zo per i Ponti** (*see p28*) takes place in March.

Venice Marathon.

EXPLORE

The Annunciation, Assumption and *Adoration of the Shepherds*, are by Paolo Veronese, as is another *Adoration* to the left of the door.

FREE Santa Maria dei Derelitti (Ospedaletto)

Castello 6691, barbarie delle Tole (041 271 9012). Vaporetto Fondamente Nove. **Open** *Church* 3.30-6.30pm Thur-Sun. *Hospice* by appointment. **Admission** (incl guided tour) €2. **No credit cards. Map** p76 C2 ●

The church was built in 1575 within the complex of the Ospedaletto, a hospice for the poor and aged. There is still an old people's home here. Between 1668 and 1674 Baldassare Longhena gave the church its staggering façade, complete with bulging telamons (architectural supports in the shape of male figures) and leering faces. The interior contains interesting 18th-century paintings, including one of Giambattista Tiepolo's earliest works, *The Sacrifice of Isaac* (fourth painting over the arch on the right). The hospice contains an elegant music room with charming frescoes by Jacopo Guarana (1776), depicting girl musicians performing for Apollo; the scene is stolen by a dog in the foreground being tempted with a doughnut. There is also a spiral staircase, apparently unsupported, designed by Sardi and completed by Longhena.

FREE Santa Maria della Fava

Castello, campo della Fava (041 522 4601). Vaporetto Rialto. **Open** 9.30-11.30am, 4.30-7pm Mon-Sat; 4.30-7pm Sun. **Map** p76 A3 ●

St Mary of the Bean – the name is said to refer to a popular bean cake produced by a bakery that stood nearby – is on one of the quieter routes between the Rialto and San Marco. This 18th-century church is worth visiting for two paintings by the city's greatest artists of that period, which neatly illustrate their contrasting temperaments. Tiepolo's *Education of the Virgin* (first altar on the right) is an early work, painted when he was still under the influence of Giovanni Battista Piazzetta; but the bright colours and touchingly human relationships of the figures are nonetheless in contrast with the sombre browns and reds of the latter's *Virgin and Child with St Philip Neri* (second altar on the left). In Piazzetta's

more earnest painting, which still bears traces of Counter-Reformation gravity, the lily, bishop's mitre and cardinals' hats show the worldly honours rejected by the saint.

Santa Maria Formosa

Castello, campo Santa Maria Formosa (041 275 0462, www.chorusvenezia.org). Vaporetto San Zaccaria or Rialto. **Open** 10am-5pm Mon-Sat. **Admission** €3 (or Chorus; *see p89*). **No credit cards. Map** p76 B3 ●

In the pre-Freudian seventh century, St Magnus, Bishop of Oderzo, had a vision in which the Virgin appeared as a buxom (*formosa*) matron, and a church was built in this bustling square to commemorate the fact. The present church was designed by Mauro Codussi in 1492 and has something fittingly bulgy about it. Codussi retained the Greek cross plan of the original in his Renaissance design. It has two façades, one on the canal (1542), the other on the campo (1604). The Baroque campanile has a grotesque mask, now recognised as a portrait of a victim of the disfiguring Von Recklinghausen's disease.

The first chapel in the right aisle has a triptych painted by Bartolomeo Vivarini, *Madonna of the Misericordia* (1473), which includes a realistic *Birth of the Virgin*. The altar in the right transept was the chapel of the Scuola dei Bombardieri, with an altarpiece of St Barbara, patron saint of gunners (a heaven-sent lightning bolt saved Barbara's life when it struck her father as he prepared to kill her) by Palma il Vecchio. Half-hidden by the elaborate high altar is one of the few works on show in Venice by a woman artist: an 18th-century *Allegory of the Foundation of the Church, with Venice, St Magnus and St Maria Formosa* by Giulia Lama.

FREE San Zaccaria

Castello, campo San Zaccaria (041 522 1257). Vaporetto San Zaccaria. **Open** 10am-noon, 4-6pm Mon-Sat; 4-6pm Sun. **Map** p76 C4 ●

Founded in the ninth century, this church has always had close ties with the Doge's Palace. Eight Venetian rulers were buried in the first church on the site, one was killed outside and another died while seeking sanctuary inside. The body of St Zacharias, the father of John the Baptist, was brought to Venice in the ninth century; it still lies under the second altar on the right.

The current church was begun in 1444 but took decades to complete, making it a curious combination of Gothic and Renaissance. The interior is built on a Gothic plan – the apse, with its ambulatory and radiating cluster of tall-windowed chapels, is unique in Venice – but the architectural decoration is predominantly Renaissance. The façade is a happy mixture of the two styles.

Inside, every inch is covered with paintings, though of varying quality. Giovanni Bellini's magnificent *Madonna and Four Saints* (1505), on the second altar on the left, leaps out of the confusion.

In the right aisle is the entrance to the Chapel of St Athanasius (admission €1), which contains carved 15th-century wooden stalls and *The Birth of St John the Baptist*, an early work by Tintoretto, and a striking *Flight into Egypt* by Giandomenico Tiepolo. The adjoining Chapel of St Tarasius was the apse of an earlier church that occupied this site; it has three altarpieces (1443) by Antonio Vivarini and Giovanni d'Alemagna – stiff, iconic works in elaborate Gothic frames.

The frescoed saints in the fan vault are by the Florentine artist Andrea del Castagno. Though painted a year before the altarpieces, they have a realistic vitality that is wholly Renaissance in spirit. In front of the altar are remains of the mosaic floor from the early Romanesque church; the tenth-century crypt below is usually flooded.

FREE Scuola Grande di San Marco

Castello, campo Santi Giovanni e Paolo (041 529 4111, www.scuolagrandesanmarco.it). Vaporetto Ospedale or Fondamente Nove. **Open** 9.30am-1pm, 2-7pm Tue-Sun. **Admission** free. **Map** p76 B2 ⓫
Once home to one of the six *scuole grandi* – the confraternities of Venice (*see p129* **Scuole Stories**) – this is now occupied mainly by the city hospital. But late in 2013 some of the finest of the *scuola* rooms were opened to the public, beautifully restored.

The *scuola*'s façade by Pietro Lombardo and Giovanni Buora (1487-90) was completed by Mauro Codussi (1495). It features magnificent trompe l'œil panels by Tullio and Antonio Lombardo representing two episodes from the life of St Mark and his faithful lion. Over the doorway is a lunette of *St Mark with the Brethren of the School* attributed to Bartolomeo Bon.

STADIUM CONTROVERSY

Plans to replace a decrepit but distinctive ground have hit problems.

As you round the easternmost point of Venice proper, a strange sight heaves into view. The dark, square belltower (a 1950s reconstruction of a 16th-century structure) of the church of Sant'Elena peers down at banks of arc lights and what looks like a pile of rusting scaffolding. This is the Stadio Pierluigi Penzo, home to Football Club Unione Venezia. And yes, when it comes down to it... it's a pile of scaffolding.

Poor Unione Venezia is a bit down on its luck. Since its one glorious recenti-ish season in Serie A (1998/9) its grip on the higher rungs of Italian football has slipped: at the time of writing it was floundering in the Lega Pro Divisione 1 (a much-expanded version of what used to be Serie C). But its owner, Russian businessman Yuri Korablin, has stuck with his on-a-whim purchase since 2011. Everything now hangs on the stadium.

If the Stadio Penzo seems picturesquely, forlornly Venetian to those few intrepid visitors who make it this far (Japanese fans arrived by the dozen for matches in Venezia's Serie A season when Hidetosha Nakata was on loan to the lagoon side) it is merely an inconvenience for jaded mainlanders who would rather drive their cars up to the *stadio* entrance. Korablin agrees.

His blueprint for the state-of-the-art, eco-friendly, 30,000-seater Green Venice Arena was fully drawn up at the time of writing, and his consortium had pledged to foot the bill for the €150 million project.

But attempts to agree with local authorities on construction of the grounds in Tessera, near Venice airport, had run up against a solid wall of local politicking.

Until such time – and it may be a long time – as the new ground is ready, fans will continue to board the dedicated *vaporetti* and chug across the lagoon to Sant'Elena for home matches. To join them, you must purchase tickets in advance: in person at the *tabaccheria* (cigarette shop) at Castello 3544, salizada Sant'Antonin, open 8.30am-1pm, 3.30-7.30pm Mon-Sat; or online on the team's website (www.fbcunionevenezia.com). Note that tickets are personal: you must present a valid ID document **for each match goer** when purchasing (or fill in ID details when buying online). Take the same ID with you to the stadium: the details on your ticket will be checked against your document as you enter.

EXPLORE

Inside, the immense column-punctuated entrance to the *scuola* is also the entrance to the hospital: surely one of the grandest hospital entrances in the world. At the top of a staircase designed by Mauro Codussi, the chapter house has a magnificent gilded coffered ceiling. Cases here contain ancient manuscripts pertaining to medical practice, and historical records of the Venetian hospital. On the walls are excellent reproductions of works done for the *scuola* but carried off over the centuries: Palma il Giovane's *Christ in Glory with St Mark* hangs over the altar, and around the walls are four magnificent scenes from the life of St Mark by the Tintoretto clan. The Sala dell'Albergo, which contains the hospital's ancient library, is dominated by a reproduction of *St Mark Preaching in Alessandria* by Giovanni and Gentile Bellini. Originals of some of the scuola's art works can be seen in the Accademia gallery (*see p145*).

Restaurants

See also *p83* **Ai Tre Mercanti**.

Alla Basilica
Castello 4255, calle degli Albanesi (041 522 0524, www.allabasilicavenezia.it). Vaporetto San Zaccaria. **Meals served** noon-3pm Tue-Sun. **Average** €14. **Map** p76 B4 ⑫
Run by the diocese of Venice, Alla Basilica has all the charm of a company canteen, and the solid home cooking will win no prizes. But at a fixed price of €14 for a full meal (wine is extra), it's a cheap way to fill an empty space, and it's brilliantly central, located (as the name implies) right behind

St Mark's basilica. Groups can eat here in the evenings too if they book ahead.

Alle Testiere
Castello 5801, calle del Mondo Novo (041 522 7220, www.osterialletestiere.it). Vaporetto Rialto. **Meals served** noon-2pm, 7-10.30pm Tue-Sat. Closed late Dec-mid Jan & late July-Aug. **Average** €60. **Map** p76 B3 ⑬
This tiny restaurant is today one of the hottest culinary tickets in Venice. There are so few seats that staff do two sittings each evening; booking for the later one (at 9pm) will ensure a more relaxed meal. Bruno, the chef, offers creative variations on Venetian seafood; *caparossoli* (local clams) sautéed in ginger and John Dory fillet sprinkled with aromatic herbs in citrus sauce are two mouth-watering examples. Sommelier Luca guides diners around a small but well-chosen wine list. The desserts, too, are spectacular.

Al Portego
Castello 6015, calle Malvasia (041 522 9038). Vaporetto Rialto. **Open** 10.30am-3pm, 5.30-10pm daily. **Average** €30. **No credit cards. Map** p76 A2 ⑭
With its wooden decor and happy drinkers in the calle outside, this rustic *osteria* is every inch the traditional Venetian *bacaro*. Alongside a big barrel of wine, the bar is loaded down with a selection of *cicheti*, from meatballs and stuffed squid to *nervetti* stewed with onions. In a second room, simple pasta dishes and soups and *secondi*, such as *fegato alla veneziana*, are served up for early lunch and dinner. A glass and a plateful of *cicheti* at the bar should cost around €10-€15, sitting down more than double that.

Scuola Grande di San Marco. *See p81.*

Osteria di Santa Marina

Castello 5911, campo Santa Marina (041 528 5239, www.osteriasantamarina.com). Vaporetto Rialto. **Meals served** 7.30-9.30pm Mon; 12.30-2.30pm, 7.30-9.30pm Tue-Sat. Closed 2wks Jan. **Average** €60. **Map** p76 A2 ⓯

This upmarket *osteria* in pretty campo Santa Marina has the kind of professional service and standards that are too often lacking in Venice, and the ambience and the high level of the seafood-oriented cuisine justify the price tag. Raw fish features strongly among the *antipasti*; *primi* give local tradition a creative twist in dishes such as the turbot- and mussel-filled ravioli in celery sauce. The joy of this place is in the detail: the bread is all home-made, a taster course turns up just when you were about to ask what happened to the *branzino* (sea bass). Book ahead.

Cafés, Bars & Gelaterie

★ Boutique del Gelato

Castello 5727, salizzada San Lio (041 522 3283). Vaporetto Rialto. **Open** Feb-May, Oct, Nov 10am-8.30pm daily. *June-Sept* 10am-11.30pm daily. Closed Dec-Jan. **No credit cards. Map** p76 A2 ⓰

Be prepared to be patient at this tiny outlet on busy salizzada San Lio because there's always a huge crowd waiting to be served. The choice of flavours is limited but the quality is high. And though the staff at peak times are not always charming, it's worth the wait.

★ Da Bonifacio

Castello 4237, calle degli Albanesi (041 522 7507). Vaporetto San Zaccaria. **Open** 6.30am-7.30pm Mon-Wed, Fri; 7.30am-7.30pm Sat, Sun. **No credit cards. Map** p76 B4 ⓱

In a narrow calle behind the Danieli Hotel, this is a firm favourite with Venetians, whom you'll find outside the entrance in great numbers, waiting to squeeze inside for a coffee, drink and something from the cake cabinet. As well as a tempting array of snacks and traditional cakes such as *mammalucchi* (deep-fried batter cakes with candied fruit), Da Bonifacio is famous for its creative *fritelle* (with wild berry, chocolate, almond or apple fillings), which appear in January and remain through Carnevale.

La Mascareta

Castello 5183, calle lunga Santa Maria Formosa (041 523 0744/www.ostemaurolorenzon.it). **Open** 7pm-2am daily. **Map** p76 B2 ⓲

Genial, bow-tied Mauro Lorenzon keeps hundreds of wines – including some rare vintages – in his cellars, serving them up by the bottle or glass along with plates of cheeses, seafood, cold meats or *crostini*. His current kick is natural unfiltered wine – but you might prefer to insist on the more traditional stuff. At mealtimes, the pressure will be on to sit down and eat a proper meal, but though the food here is good, it's not exceptional and prices are

Al Portego.

high: it's better to stick with the drink and the personality-led Lorenzon experience.

Shops & Services

Ai Tre Mercanti

Castello 5364, ponte alla Guerra (041 522 2901, www.itremercati.it). Vaporetto Rialto. **Open** 11am-7.30pm daily. **Map** p76 A3 ⓳ **Food & drink**

There's an interesting selection here of seriously good Italian food and wine, much of it from local producers but some from further afield. Stock includes excellent olive oils, preserved vegetables, pastas and rices – none of them cheap but all of them chosen with an eye to quality. At a street-side window, passersby can pick up sandwiches and rolls: a choice of locally made breads with 30-odd fillings. And there are gourmet variations on *tiramisù* to go as well. (A couple of perching-tables inside mean you can consume on the premises if you prefer.)

**IN THE KNOW
NUNS BEHAVING BADLY**

Attached to the church of **San Zaccaria** (*see p80*) was a convent where aristocrats with more titles than cash dumped female offspring to avoid having to rake together a dowry. The nuns were not best known for their piety. While the tales of rampant licentiousness may have been exaggerated, a painting in **Ca' Rezzonico** (*see p139*) shows that such convents were more worldly salon than place of contemplation.

Anticlea Antiquariato

Castello 4719A, calle San Provolo (041 528 6946). Vaporetto San Zaccaria. **Open** 10am-1.30pm, 2-7pm Mon-Sat. **Map** p76 B3 ⑳
Antiques

Packed with curious antique treasures, as well as an outstanding selection of Venetian glass beads.

★ Filippi Editore Venezia

Castello 5284, calle Casseleria (041 523 6916, www.libreriaeditricefilippi.com). Vaporetto San Zaccaria. **Open** 9am-12.30pm, 3-7.30pm Mon-Sat. **Map** p76 A3 ㉑ Books & music

Venice's longest-running publishing house has over 400 titles on Venetian history and folklore – all limited editions in Italian. The beautiful tomes can also be ordered online.

Giovanna Zanella

Castello 5641, calle Carminati (041 523 5500, www.giovannazanella.it). Vaporetto Rialto. **Open** 9.30am-1pm, 3-7pm Mon-Sat. **Map** p76 A2 ㉒
Accessories

Venetian designer-cobbler Giovanna Zanella creates a fantastic line of handmade shoes in an extraordinary variety of styles and colours. A pair of shoes costs €450 to €1,000. There are bags and other accessories too.

Filippi Editore Venezia.

Kalimala

Castello 5387, salizada San Lio (041 528 3596, www.kalimala.it). Vaporetto Rialto. **Open** 9.30am-7.30pm Mon-Sat. **Map** p76 A3 ㉓ Accessories

Unlike Giovanna Zanella (*see left*) and Daniela Ghezzo (*see p63*), Kalimala is a Venetian cobbler whose shoes are stylish without being quirky, and the prices are less idiosyncratic too (from about €80 upwards). Handmade in beautiful Tuscan leather, in a wonderful range of colours, Kalimala's range covers boots, loafers and sandals, plus bags and tablet holders.

★ Papier Mâché

Castello 5174B, calle lunga Santa Maria Formosa (041 522 9995, www.papiermache.it). Vaporetto Rialto. **Open** 9am-7.30pm Mon-Sat; 10am-7pm Sun. **Map** p76 B2 ㉔ Gifts & souvenirs

This workshop uses traditional techniques to create contemporary masks inspired by the works of Klimt, Kandinsky, Tiepolo and Carpaccio. It stocks ceramics and painted mirrors too.

SOUTHERN & EASTERN CASTELLO

Vaporetto Arsenale, Giardini, San Pietro, San Zaccaria or Sant'Elena.

The low-rise, clustered buildings of working-class eastern Castello housed the employees of the **Arsenale** (*see p85*) – Venice's docklands. Also here were Venice's foreign communities, as local churches testify: there's **San Giorgio dei Greci** (Greeks; *see p87*), with its adjoining **Museo dell'Istituto Ellenico** (*see p86*) icon museum; and there's also the **Scuola di San Giorgio degli Schiavoni** (Slavs; *see p88*), with its captivating cycle of paintings by Vittorio Carpaccio. The great promenade along the lagoon – the riva degli Schiavoni – was named after the same community.

Inland from the *riva* is the quaint Gothic church of **San Giovanni in Bragora** (*see p87*) in the square of the same name. Antonio Vivaldi was born on this *campo* on 4 March 1678, though it's not known in which house. Further back in the warren of streets is the church of **Sant'Antonin** – undoubtedly the only church in Venice in which an elephant has been shot. The unfortunate animal escaped from a circus on the *riva* in 1819 and took refuge in the church, only to be finished off by gunners summoned from the Arsenale.

Back on the riva degli Schiavoni is the church of **La Pietà** (*see p87*), where Vivaldi was choir master. In calle della Pietà, alongside the church, is the **Piccolo Museo della Pietà** (*see p87*), dedicated to the Pietà (a foundling home) and the composer.

Head on eastwards past the **Ca' di Dio**, once a hostel for pilgrims setting out for the

Holy Land and now an old people's home, and the *forni pubblici* (public bakeries), where the biscuit (*bis-cotto*, literally 'twice-cooked') – that favourite, scurvy-encouraging staple of ancient mariners – was reputedly invented.

Crossing the bridge over the rio dell'Arsenale, you can see the grand Renaissance entrance to the **Arsenale** shipyard (*see right*). Once a hive of empire-building industry, it's now an expanse of empty warehouses and docks, though parts have been beautifully restored and are used for Biennale-related events (*see p31*).

Just beyond the rio dell'Arsenale, the model-packed **Museo Storico Navale** (*see p86*) lovingly charts Venice's shipbuilding history. A little further on, the wide and lively **via Garibaldi** forks off to the left. This road, like the nearby *giardini pubblici* (public gardens), is a legacy of French occupation in the early 19th century. Via Garibaldi leads eventually to the island of **San Pietro**, where the former cathedral (*see p88*) stands among modest, washing-garlanded houses.

Back on the lagoon, the riva degli Schiavoni changes its name after the rio dell'Arsenale to become the riva dei Sette Martiri, named after seven partisans executed here in 1944 (a striking statue – located by the Giardini vaporetto stop – recalls the event). Just beyond here, the shady *giardini pubblici* occupies the place where four suppressed convents once

stood. A Renaissance archway from one has been reconstructed in a corner of the gardens. In another corner lies the entrance to the **Biennale** (*see p31*); the international pavilions, ranging in style from the seedy to the pompous, used to remain locked up except for those few weeks every two years when a major contemporary art bonanza would be set up; other more recently created events such as the Biennale dell'Architettura mean the pavilions get more frequent airings.

The *riva* ends in the sedately residential district of **Sant'Elena**. This, in Venetian terms, is a 'modern' district. In 1872 work began to fill in the *barene* (marshes) that lay between the edge of the city and the ancient island of Sant'Elena, with its charming Gothic church (*see p87*). Also tucked away here is Venice's football stadium – though fans are hoping for a new mainland ground sometime in the not-too-distant future (*see p81* **Stadium Controversy**).

Sights & Museums

Arsenale

Castello, campo dell'Arsenale. (www.arsenaledi venezia.it) Vaporetto Arsenale. **Map** p77 E4 ㉕
The word *arsenale* derives from the Arabic *dar sina'a*, meaning 'house of industry': the industry, and efficiency, of Venice's Arsenale was legendary:

EXPLORE

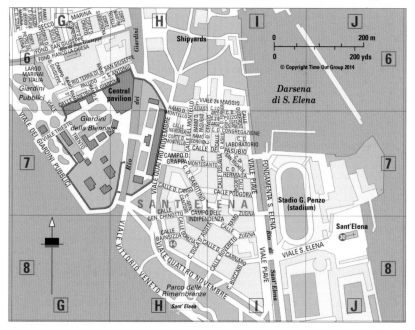

La Pietà

the *arsenalotti* could assemble a galley in just a few hours. Shipbuilding activities began here in the 12th century; at the height of the city's power, 16,000 men were employed. Production expanded until the 16th century, when Venice entered its slow but inexorable economic decline.

The imposing land gateway by Antonio Gambello (1460) in campo dell'Arsenale is the first example of Renaissance classical architecture to appear in Venice, although the capitals of the columns are 11th-century Veneto-Byzantine. The winged lion gazing down from above holds a book without the traditional words *Pax tibi Marce* (Peace to you, Mark) – unsuitable in this military context. Outside the gate, four lions keep guard. Those immediately flanking the terrace were looted from Athens in 1687; the larger one stood at the entrance to the port of Piraeus and bears runic inscriptions on its side, hacked there in the 11th century by Norse mercenary soldiers in Byzantine service. The third lion, whose head is clearly less ancient than its body, came from Delos and was placed here to commemorate the recapture of Corfu in 1716.

Shipbuilding activity ceased in 1917, after which the complex remained largely unused navy property until 2013 when much of it returned to town council hands… not that they're entirely sure what to do with it now. It is destined, authorities say, to become a 'scientific and cultural pole'. Exhibitions and performances will continue to be held in some of the cavernous spaces within its walls: the *Artiglierie* and the grandiose *Gaggiandre*, dockyards designed by Sansovino. In campo della Tana, on the other side of the rio dell'Arsenale, is the entrance to the *Corderia* (rope factory), an extraordinary building 316m (1,038 ft) long. This vast space is used to house large swathes of the Biennale (*see p31*). In May the Mare Maggio sea-, boat- and travel-themed festival (www.maremaggio.it) opens up much of the Arsenale to the curious.

Museo dell'Istituto Ellenico

Castello 3412, ponte dei Greci (041 522 6581). Vaporetto San Zaccaria. **Open** 9am-5pm daily. **Admission** €4; €2 reductions. **No credit cards.** **Map** p76 C3 ㉖

The adjacent church of San Giorgio dei Greci was a focal point for the Greek community, which was swollen by refugees after the Turkish capture of Constantinople in 1453. There have been a Greek church, college and school at this location since the end of the 15th century. The oldest piece in the museum's collection is the 14th-century altar cross behind the ticket desk. The icons on display mainly follow the dictates of the Cretan school, with no descent into naturalism, though some of the 17th- and 18th-century pieces make jarring and often kitsch compromises with Western art. The best pieces are those that are resolute in their hieratic (traditional-style Greek) flatness, such as *Christ in Glory among the Apostles* and the Great Deesis from the first half of the 14th century. St George is a popular subject: there is one splendid painting of him dating from the late 15th century. Also on display are priestly robes and other Greek-rite paraphernalia.

► *For information on the church itself, see p87.*

Museo Storico Navale

Castello 2148, campo San Biagio (041 244 1399). Vaporetto Arsenale. **Open** 8.45am-1.30pm Mon-Fri; 8.45am-1pm Sat. **Admission** €1.55. **No credit cards.** **Map** p77 E5 ㉗

This museum dedicated to ships and shipbuilding continues an old tradition: under the Republic, the models created for shipbuilders in the final design stages were kept in the Arsenale. Some of the models on display are from that collection.

The ground floor has warships, cannons, explosive speedboats and dodgy-looking manned torpedoes, plus a display of ships through the ages. On the

EXPLORE

walls are relief models in wood and papier mâché, dating from the 16th to the 18th century, of Venetian fortresses and possessions.

On the first floor are ornamental trimmings and naval instruments, plus a series of impressive models of Venetian ships. Here, too, is a richly gilded model of the Bucintoro, the doges' state barge. The second floor has uniforms, more up-to-date sextants and astrolabes, and models of modern Italian navy vessels. On the third floor there are models of Chinese, Japanese and Korean junks, cruise ships and liners, and a series of fascinating naïve votive paintings, giving thanks for shipwrecks averted or survived.

A room at the back has a display of gondolas, including a 19th-century example with a cabin, and the last privately owned covered gondola in Venice, which belonged to the larger-than-life art collector and bon vivant Peggy Guggenheim.

Piccolo Museo della Pietà 'Antonio Vivaldi'
Castello 3701, calle della Pietà (041 522 2171, www.pietavenezia.org). Vaporetto Arsenale or San Zaccaria. **Open** by appointment only. **Admission** €3. **No credit cards. Map** p76 C4

This museum chronicles the activities of the Ospedale della Pietà, the orphanage where Antonio Vivaldi was violin teacher and choir master. Numerous documents recount such details as the rules for admission of children and the rations of food allotted them; the 'Daughters of the Choir' received more generous portions of food and wine. There is also a selection of period instruments.

🆓 La Pietà (Santa Maria della Visitazione)
Castello, riva degli Schiavoni (041 523 1096). Vaporetto San Zaccaria. **Open** for services only. **Map** p76 C4 ❷

By the girls' orphanage of the same name, the church of La Pietà was famous for its music. Antonio Vivaldi, violin and choir master here from 1703 until 1740, wrote some of his finest music for his young charges. The present building, by Giorgio Massari, was begun in 1745, four years after Vivaldi's death. Music inspired its architecture: the interior, reached through a vestibule resembling a foyer, has the oval shape of a concert hall. The ceiling has a *Coronation of the Virgin* (1755) by Giambattista Tiepolo.
▶ *For concerts held in the church, see p196.*

🆓 Sant'Elena
Castello 3, Servi di Maria, campo Chiesa Sant' Elena (041 520 5144). Vaporetto Sant'Elena. **Open** 5-7pm Mon-Sat. **Map** off p85 J8 ❸

The red-brick Gothic church of Sant'Elena contains no great works of art (the church was deconsecrated in 1807, turned into an iron foundry, and not opened again until 1928) but its austere Gothic nakedness is a relief after all that Venetian ornament. In the chapel to the right of the entrance lies the body of

St Helen, the irascible mother of the Emperor Constantine and finder of the True Cross. (Curiously enough, her body is also to be found in the Aracoeli church in Rome.) To the left are the charming cloisters and rose garden tended by the three monks left in the monastery.

🆓 San Giorgio dei Greci
Castello, fondamenta dei Greci (041 523 9569). Vaporetto San Zaccaria. **Open** 9am-12.30pm, 2.30-4.30pm Mon, Wed-Sat. **Map** p76 C3 ❶

By the time the church of San Giorgio was begun in 1539, the Greeks were well established in Venice and held a major stake in the city's scholarly printing presses. Designed by Sante Lombardo, the church's interior is fully Orthodox in layout, with its women's gallery, and high altar behind the iconostasis. A heady smell of incense lends the church an Eastern mystique, enhanced by dark-bearded priests in flowing robes. The campanile is decidedly lopsided. Next to the church are the Scuola di San Nicolò (now the Museo dell'Istituto Ellenico) and the Collegio Flangini (now seat of the Istituto Ellenico di Studi Bizantini e post-Bizantini), both by Baldassare Longhena.
▶ *For information about the museum, see p86.*

🆓 San Giovanni in Bragora
Castello, campo Bandiera e Moro (041 270 2464). Vaporetto Arsenale. **Open** 9am-noon, 3.30-5pm Mon-Sat. **Map** p76 D4 ❷

San Giovanni in Bragora (the meaning of *bragora* is obscure) is an intimate Gothic structure. The church

San Giorgio dei Greci.

where composer Antonio Vivaldi was baptised (a copy of the entry in the register is on show), San Giovanni also contains some very fine paintings. Above the high altar is the recently restored *Baptism of Christ* (1492-95) by Cima da Conegliano, with a landscape recalling the countryside around the painter's home town of Conegliano. A smaller Cima, on the right of the sacristy door, shows *Constantine Holding the Cross and St Helen* (1502). On the same wall, just before the second altar, is a triptych by Bartolomeo Vivarini, *Madonna and Child and Two Saints*, dated 1478. The church also contains three paintings by his nephew Alvise Vivarini, one of them a splendidly heroic *Resurrection* (1498); the figure of Christ in this picture is based on a statue of Apollo in the Museo Archeologico (*see p56*).

San Pietro di Castello

Castello, campo San Pietro (041 275 0462, www.chorusvenezia.org). Vaporetto San Pietro. **Open** 10am-5pm Mon-Sat. **Admission** €3 (or Chorus; *see p89*). **No credit cards.** **Map** p77 H4 ⬤

Until 1807, San Pietro in Castello was the cathedral of Venice, and its remote position testifies to the determination of the Venetian government to keep the clerical authorities far from the centre of temporal power. There has probably been a church here since the seventh century, but the present building was constructed in 1557 to a design by Palladio.

The body of the first patriarch of Venice, San Lorenzo Giustiniani, is preserved in an urn elaborately supported by angels above the high altar, a magnificent piece of Baroque theatricality designed by Baldassarre Longhena (1649). In the right-hand aisle is the so-called 'St Peter's Throne', a delicately carved marble work from Antioch containing a Muslim funerary stele and verses from the Koran. The Baroque Vendramin Chapel in the left transept was again designed by Longhena, and contains a *Virgin and Child* by the prolific Neapolitan Luca Giordano. Outside the entrance to the chapel is a late work by Paolo Veronese, *Saints John the Evangelist, Peter and Paul*.

★ Scuola di San Giorgio degli Schiavoni

Castello 3259A, calle dei Furlani (041 522 8828). Vaporetto Arsenale or San Zaccaria. **Open** 2.45-6pm Mon; 9.15am-1pm, 2.45-6pm Tue-Sat; 9.15am-1pm Sun. **Admission** €3; €2 reductions. **No credit cards. Map** p76 C3 ⬤

The *schiavoni* were Venice's Slav inhabitants, who had become so numerous and influential by the end of the 15th century that they could afford to build this *scuola* (or meeting house) by the side of their church, San Giovanni di Malta. The *scuola* houses one of Vittore Carpaccio's two great Venetian picture cycles. In 1502, eight years after completing his St Ursula cycle (now in the Accademia, *see p145*), Carpaccio was commissioned to paint a series of canvases

illustrating the lives of the Dalmatian saints George, Tryphone and Jerome. In the tradition of the early Renaissance *istoria* (narrative painting cycle), there is a wealth of incidental detail, such as the decomposing virgins in *St George and the Dragon*, or the little dog in the painting of *St Augustine in his Study* (receiving the news of the death of St Jerome in a vision) – with its paraphernalia of humanism (astrolabe, shells, sheet music, archaeological fragments).

It's worth venturing upstairs to see what the meeting hall of a working *scuola* looks like. San Giorgio degli Schiavoni still provides scholarships, distributes charity and acts as a focal point for the Slav community. Opening hours are notoriously changeable.

Restaurants

Al Covo

Castello 3968, campiello della Pescaria (041 522 3812, www.ristorantealcovo.com). Vaporetto Arsenale. **Meals served** 12.45-2pm, 7.30-10pm Mon, Tue, Fri-Sun. Closed mid Dec-mid Jan & 2wks Aug. **Average** €50. **Map** p76 D4 ⬤

Though Al Covo is hidden in an alley behind the riva degli Schiavoni, it's very much on the international gourmet map. Its reputation is based on a dedication to serving the best seafood, including a sashimi of Adriatic fish and crustaceans, and *paccheri* pasta with pistacchio pesto, mussels and aubergines. The restaurant's decor should make it ideal for a romantic dinner, but in fact it's more for foodies than lovers, and service can be prickly. Chef/owner Cesare

San Pietro di Castello.

IN THE KNOW CHORUS

There are around 140 churches in Venice proper and on the lagoon islands – an immense repository of artistic and architectural wonders. Of these, 15 belong to the Chorus organisation and charge an entry fee that is ploughed back into church upkeep. A €12 pass (€8 students with ID under 29; €20 family ticket for two adults with two children; under-18s free), purchasable at the churches themselves or online through www.veneziaunica.it, gets you into all of the Chorus churches. Tickets for each church individually cost €3. For further information, see www.chorusvenezia.org.

Benelli's American wife Diane talks English speakers through the menu. Desserts are delicious.

Corte Sconta
Castello 3886, calle del Pestrin (041 522 7024, www.cortescontavenezia.it). Vaporetto Arsenale. **Meals served** 12.30-2.30pm, 7-10pm Tue-Sat. Closed Jan & mid July-mid Aug. **Average** €65. **Map** p76 D4 ㊱
This trailblazing seafood restaurant is such a firm favourite on the well-informed tourist circuit that it's a good idea to book well in advance. The main act is a procession of seafood *antipasti*. The pasta is home-made and the warm *zabaione* dessert is a delight. Decor is of the modern Bohemian trattoria variety, the ambience loud and friendly. In summer, try to secure one of the tables in the pretty, vine-covered courtyard.

Il CoVino
Castello 3829, calle del Pestrin (041 241 2705, www.covinovenezia.com). Vaporetto Arsenale. **Meals served** 12-3pm, 9.15-10pm Mon, Tue, Fri-Sun. **Average** €50. **Map** p76 D4 ㊲
Venice's newest hot gastronomic ticket in 2014, the relaunched Il CoVino, has a lot to love about it. In one corner of the tiny room, Dmitri juggles pots and pans in his open-to-view kitchen, while affable Andrea mans the very few tables. The inventive dishes (meat, fish, no pasta) on the ever-changing menu are market-fresh and very tasty. But the fact that diners are obliged to pay a set price of €36, even if they don't want all three included courses, will put some off; with wine and extras, none of which comes free, the bills is unlikely to be much less than €50 a head. There's an interesting wine list, of mainly natural unfiltered wines.

€ Dai Tosi
Castello 738, secco Marina (041 523 7102, www.trattoriadaitosi.com). Vaporetto Giardini. **Meals served** noon-2pm Mon, Tue, Thur; noon-2pm, 7-9.30pm Fri-Sun. Closed 2wks

Aug. **Average** *Pizzeria* €20. *Full meal* €35. **Map** p77/85 G6 ㊳ **Pizzeria**
In one of Venice's most working-class areas, this pizzeria is a big hit with locals. Beware of another restaurant of the same name on the street: this place (at no.738) is better. The cuisine is humble but filling, the pizzas are tasty, and you can round the meal off nicely with a killer *sgropin* (a post-prandial refresher made with lemon sorbet, vodka and prosecco). In summer, angle for one of the garden tables.

Il Ridotto
Castello 4509, campo Santi Filippo e Giacomo (041 520 8280/www.ilridotto.com). Vaporetto San Zaccaria. **Meals served** noon-2pm, 7-11pm Mon, Tue, Fri-Sun; 7-10pm Thur. **Average** €85. **Map** p76 B3 ㊴
Gianni Bonaccorsi's restaurant is a natural stop-over for upcoming chefs passing through the lagoon city. Though expertise flows in both directions, Gianni's policy of using the freshest and best of local ingredients in unfussy ways to produce something remarkably sophisticated is adhered to with memorable results. The five-course taster menu (€70) gives the best scope for experiencing Il Ridotto's range, which might include octopus on a broad bean purée with turnip tops, a superb *caciucco* fish soup or seabass served on a bed of creamed celeriac. The place – two narrow rooms – is tiny, the decor is ultra-simple and the service is warmly professional. There's a good lunch deal, at €28 for a selection of *cicheti* plus a fish or meat main. Be sure to book: gourmets whether local or visiting know that this is one of the city's best foody attractions.
► *Across the campo (no.4357), Gianni's trattoria L'Aciugheta serves decent pizzas and good cicheto snacks, and has an interesting selection of wines.*

Cafés, Bars & Gelaterie

See also p125 **Majer**.

★ Angiò
Castello 2142, ponte della Veneta Marina (041 277 8555). Vaporetto Arsenale. **Open** 7am-9pm Mon, Wed-Sun. **Map** p77 E5 ㊵
Angiò is the finest stopping point along one of Venice's most tourist-trafficked spots – the lagoon-front riva degli Schiavoni. Tables stretch towards the water's edge, with a stunning view across to San Giorgio Maggiore; ultra-friendly staff serve up pints of Guinness, freshly made sandwiches and interesting selections of cheese and wine. Closing time is pushed back to midnight or later in summer months, when music events are held on Saturday evenings.

El Refolo
Castello 1580, via Garibaldi (no phone). Vaporetto Giardini. **Open** *During Biennale* 10.30am-12.30amTue-Sun. *Rest of year* 5.30pm-12.30am Tue-Sun **No credit cards**. **Map** p77 F5 ㊶

EXPLORE

Via Garibaldi. *See p85.*

If you want to settle at one of the high stools on the pavement outside this tiny bar, be prepared to wait. Because friendly El Refolo, with its well-priced wine (from €2.50 a glass), interesting and ever-changing selection of filled rolls and excellent salami and/or cheese platters is everybody's favourite, especially when the area throngs with Biennale-goers (*see p31*). Over summer weekends, owner Massimiliano doesn't pull down the shutters until very late indeed.

Pasticceria Melita

Castello 1000-4, fondamenta Sant'Anna (no phone). Vaporetto Giardini or San Pietro. **Open** 8am-2pm, 3.30-8.30pm Tue-Sun. **No credit cards. Map** p77 G5 ㊷
The welcome in this family café-bakery is not always sunny, but the quality of the pastries behind the old-fashioned bar counter will compensate. There's no sitting down for a languorous coffee and cake session: it's a stand-up or takeaway only kind of place, but it's a favourite with locals and with zoned-in visitors to Biennale (*see p31*) events at the nearby Arsenale.

Serra dei Giardini

Castello 1254, viale Garibaldi/giardini pubblici (041 296 0360, www.serradeigiardini.org). Vaporetto Giardini. **Open** 10am-9.30pm Tue-Fri, Sun; 10am-midnight Sat. **Map** p77 F5 ㊸
This gorgeous greenhouse has stood inside the Giardini pubblici since 1894, when its purpose was to provide winter shelter for the exotic plants brought out in summer to grace the national pavilions in the neighbouring Biennale gardens. Restored and run by a local cooperative, it now houses a plant shop, spaces for children's activities, parties and exhibitions, and a café/tea shop with garden tables when the weather permits. The setting is charming, and the coffee, juices and light

meals on offer are good. The idyll can be slightly marred by less-than-charming staff.

Vincent Bar

Sant'Elena, viale IV novembre 36 (041 520 4493). Vaporetto Sant'Elena. **Open** 7am-10pm Tue-Sun. **No credit cards. Map** p85 H8 ㊹
Sant'Elena is surely the only place in Venice you'll find more residents, trees and grassy expanses than tourists and churches. Grab a seat – and a drink – outside this bar and join the locals gazing lazily across the lagoon at passing boats or keeping a watchful eye on their *bambini* as they play in the park. The big mixed salads served at lunch make a great light meal, and there are huge helpings of competently prepared pasta dishes too. Ice-cream is made on the premises.

Shops & Services

Banco Lotto N°10

Castello 3478B, salizada Sant'Antonin (041 522 1439/www.ilcerchiovenezia.it). Vaporetto Arsenale. **Open** 3.30-7.30pm Mon; 10am-1pm, 3.30-7.30pm Tue-Sat. **Map** p76 D4 ㊺ **Fashion/accessories**
The quirky dresses, bags and accessories sold in this little outlet all hail from the workshops of Venice's women's prison on the Giudecca island. Many of the designs are one-offs, and there's a strong vintage flavour, and some interesting recycling goes on too. *See also p155* **Gardens of Marvels**.

Vino e… Vini

Castello 3566, salizada Pignater (041 521 0184). Vaporetto Arsenale. **Open** 9am-1pm, 5-8pm Mon-Sat. **Map** p76 D4 ㊻ **Food & drink**
Vino e… Vini stocks a wide-ranging selection of major Italian wines, as well as French, Spanish, Californian and even Lebanese vintages.

WELL-HEADS THROUGH THE AGES

A once-practical architecture that still adds beauty to many a campo.

It's estimated that the number of well-heads in Venice is now around 2,500 – a dramatic drop from the 6,782 counted by city authorities in 1858. The ground level in squares with wells at their centre is often raised, to keep salt water out during high tide. The paving is angled towards drains, where rain water would disappear, sink through filtering systems, and then find its way into cisterns beneath the well-heads. In 1882-84, pipes were laid to bring fresh water to the lagoon city from the mainland. With no practical purpose, monumental well-heads became just one more thing that poor Venetians could flog off to wealthy foreigners.

THE MOST ANCIENT
Corte Correr (between San Zaccaria and Santa Maria Formosa, map p310 K7): a square well-head dating from the ninth or tenth century; the sculpted rosettes are 15th century.

BYZANTINE
Corte del Remer (near San Giovanni Crisostomo, map p307 H5): elegant arches in red Verona marble.

GOTHIC
Corte Veniera (off campo Santi Giovanni e Paolo, map p310 K5): a fine specimen with ogival arches.
Ca' d'Oro (*see p100*): an elaborately carved late-Gothic well in the courtyard.

RENAISSANCE
Campo Santi Giovanni e Paolo (map p310 K5): an elegant well-head with festoon-draped *putti*.
Campo San Zaccaria (map p310 K7), **Campo San Giovanni Crisostomo** (map p307 H5), **campo della Maddalena** (map p307 F3): inspired by Corinthian capitals, these have delicate carvings of foliage.
Campo Angelo Raffaele (map p308 B8): cylindrical, with charming carvings of Tobias and the guardian angel.

MANNERIST AND BAROQUE
Campo dei Frari (map p309 E6): a large cylindrical well with a swelling waist.
Campo San Marcuola (map p307 E3): a lavish well with lion heads and scrolled shields amid ornate curlicues.

19TH CENTURY
Campo San Polo (map p307 F6): this octagonal well-head is the largest in the city.

EXPLORE

Cannaregio

Already the train trip across the lagoon from Mestre on the mainland towards the northern shores of Cannaregio is a romantic idyll, but step out of Santa Lucia station and be prepared to be dazzled: you're greeted not by a dingy car park or snarling flurry of taxis but by the stunning sight of the Grand Canal itself. What comes next, if you walk to the centre, is altogether less grand: a jostling array of souvenir stalls, grotty bars and downmarket hotels on busy lista di Spagna, Cannaregio's main thoroughfare. Concealed beyond, however, is a blissfully calm area of long canalside walks and the occasional, mostly undemanding, church. The only big surprise of the area comes in the Ghetto, where a thriving Jewish community creates a sudden burst of activity amid the quiet of this second-largest *sestiere*.

EXPLORE

Santa Maria dei Miracoli.

Don't Miss

1 The Ghetto The original, and (now) the most picturesque (p102).

2 Madonna dell'Orto Where the Tintoretto clan let rip (p104).

3 Santa Maria dei Miracoli A miracle of multicoloured marble (p107).

4 Kosher Tevà The very best in Jewish pastries (p104).

5 Vittorio Costantini Venetian glass animals as they really should be. (p109).

View from **Santa Lucia Station**.

FROM THE STATION TO THE RIALTO

Vaporetto Ca' d'Oro, Ferrovia, Guglie, Rialto or San Marcuola.

Heading away from the **station** towards the Rialto, the tourist-tack-filled *lista* leads to the large campo **San Geremia**, overlooked by the church of the same name (containing the shrivelled body of St Lucy) and **Palazzo Labia**, currently occupied by the RAI (Italian state television). The palazzo contains frescoes by Tiepolo, visible by appointment (041 781 111).

Once over the **Cannaregio Canal** (*see p95*) – by way of ponte delle Guglie, a grandiose bridge with obelisks – the route assumes more character, taking in lively street markets with Venetians going about their daily business. Off to the right, in a square giving on to the Grand Canal, is the church of **San Marcuola** (*see p99*), with an unfinished façade. A bit further on, the more picturesque church of **La Maddalena**, inspired by the Pantheon in Rome, stands in the small campo della Maddalena adorned with a large assortment of fantastic chimney pots.

Beyond this, wide strada Nuova begins. Off to the left is the church of **San Marziale** (*see p99*), with whimsical ceiling paintings; on the strada Nuova itself stands the church of **Santa Fosca**, another mainly 18th-century creation. In front of the church stands a statue of Paolo Sarpi, who helped Venice resist a Papal interdict

in the 17th century and faced an assassination attempt as a result. Down a calle to the right is the entrance to the **Ca' d'Oro** (*see below*), Venice's most splendid Gothic palazzo.

The strada Nuova ends by the church of **Santi Apostoli** (*see p99*); the route to the Rialto soon becomes narrow and crooked, passing the church of **San Giovanni Crisostomo** (*see p98*) and the adjacent courtyard of the **corte Seconda del Milion**, where Marco Polo was born in 1256. Some of the Veneto-Byzantine-style houses in the courtyard date from that time. It was to this courtyard that we imagine Marco Polo returning with his father and uncle in 1295, after 24 years travelling the Far East. As the story goes, the three men turned up in the old Polo home dressed in shabby Tartar costume. Nobody recognised them until they threw back their hoods. Then, to general amazement, Marco slit open the lining of their rough clothes and out poured a glittering shower of diamonds and precious stones. The name of the courtyard derives from the title of his own account of his adventures.

There's a plaque commemorating Marco Polo on the rear of the **Teatro Malibran** (*see p197*), formerly the Teatro di San Giovanni Crisostomo, one of Venice's earliest theatres. The theatre was opened once more in 2001, its restoration fast-tracked after the city's opera house, La Fenice, burnt down.

Sights & Museums

IN THE KNOW
DEATH IN VENICE

The corte **Seconda del Milion** (*see above*) has a splendidly carved horseshoe arch. It was on the well-head in the centre of the *corte* that Dirk Bogarde collapsed in Visconti's *Death in Venice*, his hair dye and mascara trickling down his face in the rain.

Ca' d'Oro (Galleria Franchetti)
Cannaregio 3932, calle Ca' d'Oro (041 523 8790, www.cadoro.org). Vaporetto Ca' d'Oro. **Open** 8.15am-2pm Mon; 8.15am-7.15pm Tue-Sat; 10am-6pm Sun. **Admission** €6; €3 reductions; price varies during special exhibitions. **No credit cards. Map** p97 F5 **①**
In its 15th-century heyday, the façade of this pretty townhouse on the Grand Canal must have looked a psychedelic treat: the colour scheme was light blue and burgundy, with 24-carat gold highlights.

CANNAREGIO CANAL

Explore this impressive waterway.

Apart from the Grand Canal and the Giudecca, there is only one waterway in the city that is dignified by the name of 'canal', and that is the **Cannaregio Canal**. Until the 19th century, when Austrian occupiers built the rail bridge across the lagoon (the road bridge came later, in 1932), this waterway was the main route into Venice from the mainland – and it provides a suitably impressive introduction, with wide *fondamente* on each side and several imposing *palazzi*. It's spanned by two stately bridges, the **ponte delle Guglie** (Bridge of the Obelisks, 1823), and the **ponte dei Tre Archi**, the only three-arch stone bridge in Venice, designed by Andrea Tirali in 1688. Heading towards the northern lagoon from the ponte delle Guglie on the right-hand *fondamenta*, you pass the *sottoportico* leading to the Jewish Ghetto (*see pp102-104*).

Beyond this stands the **Palazzo Nani** (no.1105), a fine Renaissance building dating from the 16th century. Some 200 metres (700 feet) further on is the **Palazzo Surian-Bellotto** (no.968); in the 18th century, this was the French embassy, where Jean-Jacques Rousseau worked – reluctantly – as a secretary. Beyond, **Santa Maria delle**

Ponte dei Tre Archi.

Penitenti, with its unfinished façade, was formerly a home for the city's fallen women.

On the left bank is the **Palazzo Priuli-Manfrin** (nos.342-343), another Tirali creation dating from 1735, in a neoclassical style of such severe plainness that it could almost prefigure 20th-century purist art.

The domineering 17th-century **Palazzo Savorgnan** (no.349) – now a school – has huge coats of arms and reliefs of helmets; the owners were descended from Federigo Savornan, who, in 1385, became the first non-Venetian to be admitted to Venice's patrician ruling clique. Behind it is the **Parco Savorgnan**, a charming public garden that is one of Venice's better-kept secrets. A little further on, the ponte della Crea spans a canal that was covered over for centuries, only to be re-excavated in 1997.

After passing the ponte dei Tre Archi (with the Renaissance church of **San Giobbe**, *see p105*, off to the left), the *fondamenta* continues on to the ex-slaughterhouse, built in the 19th century by the Austrians. It has been taken over and revamped by Venice University's economics faculty.

Two fairly recent housing projects are easily reachable from the canal. From the left bank, calle delle due Corti leads to the Area Saffa, a complex built to designs by Vittorio Gregotti between 1981 and 1994; owing to the enclosed nature of the site and the use of high dividing walls, the overall effect is claustrophobic. More successful is the housing project of sacca San Gerolamo, at the end of the right bank, to designs by Franco Bortoluzzi (1987-90); the complex makes pictureque use of traditional elements, such as slabs of Istrian marble framing green-shuttered windows and large archways giving on to the lagoon.

EXPLORE

Cannaregio Canal.

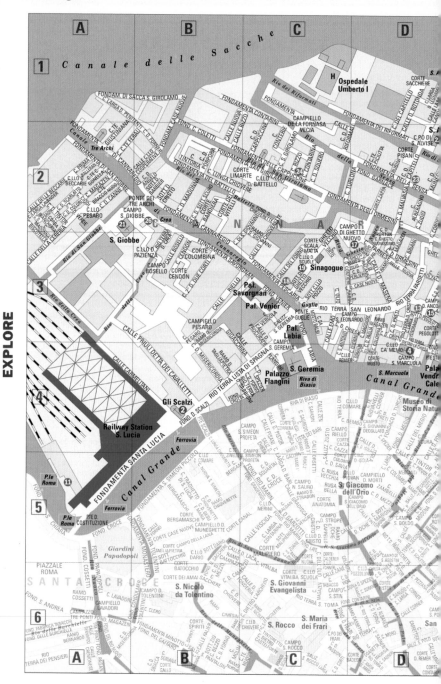

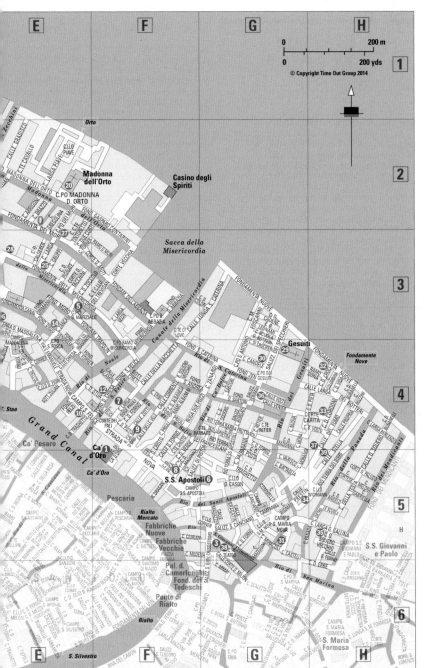

STATION SHOPPING

A different place for gifts.

If you've failed to pick up souvenirs and gifts, and you get to the station with time to kill, you have two options. With your back to the station turn left down the tourist-tack-alley lista di Spagna for blinking *gondole* and glass animals. Or stay in the station itself – perhaps with a detour off to the adjoining Palazzo Compartimentale on the right – for a shiny new development of international-brand stores, plus a restaurant and café (*see p100* **F30**) that's a great spot for filling up as you arrive or depart.

According to Trenitalia (Italian railways) figures, Venice's Santa Lucia station sees 30 million arrivals and departures each year, making it one of Italy's busiest rail hubs. So the rather quaint old-fashioned hall that had greeted visitors until 2013 was somewhat outdated. The new selection of 37 shops ranges from Muji and Mango to pizza chain Spizzico, make-up purveyors Kiko and, just in case you need an elegant notebook for your Venice jottings, Moleskine. Shops are open 8am-10pm daily.

Though the colour has worn off, the Grand Canal frontage of Ca' d'Oro – built for merchant Marin Contarini between 1421 and 1431 – is still the most elaborate example of the florid Venetian Gothic style besides the Doge's Palace.

Inside, little of the original structure and decor has survived. The pretty courtyard was reconstructed with its original 15th-century staircase and well-head a century ago by Baron Franchetti; the mosaic floor is a 19th-century imitation of the floors in San Marco. The baron also assembled the collection of paintings, sculptures and coins that is exhibited inside.

The highlight of the collection is Mantegna's *St Sebastian*, a powerful late work; the Palladian frame contrasts oddly with the saint's existential anguish. The rest is good in parts, though not necessarily the parts you would expect. A small medal of Sultan Mohammed II by Gentile Bellini (a souvenir of his years in Constantinople, being restored at the time of writing) is more impressive than the worse than faded frescoes by Titian and Giorgione removed from the Fondaco dei Tedeschi (*see p43*). There are some good Renaissance bronzes from deconsecrated churches, and small but vigorous plaster models by Bernini for the statues on the fountains in Rome's piazza Navona.

FREE Gli Scalzi
Cannaregio, fondamenta degli Scalzi (041 715 115). Vaporetto Ferrovia. **Open** 7-11.50am, 4-7pm daily. **Map** p96 B4 ❷

Officially Santa Maria di Nazareth, this church is better known as Gli Scalzi after the order of *Carmelitani scalzi* (Barefoot Carmelites) to whom it belongs. They bought the plot in 1645 and subsequently commissioned Baldassare Longhena to design the church. The fine façade (1672-80) is the work of Giuseppe Sardi; it was paid for by a newcomer to Venice's ruling patrician class, Gerolamo Cavazza, determined to make his mark on the landscape.

The interior is striking for its coloured marble and massively elaborate baldachin over the high altar. There are many fine Baroque statues, including the *St John of the Cross* by Giovanni Marchiori in the first chapel on the right and the anonymous marble crucifix and wax effigy of Christ in the chapel opposite. An Austrian shell that plummeted through the roof in 1915 destroyed the church's greatest work of art, Tiepolo's fresco, *The Transport of the House of Loreto*, but spared some of the artist's lesser frescoes, *Angels of the Passion* and *Agony in the Garden*, in the first chapel on the left, and *St Theresa in Glory*, which hovers gracefully above a ham-fisted imitation of Bernini's sculpture, *Ecstasy of St Theresa*, in the second on the right. In the second chapel on the left lie the remains of the last doge of Venice, Lodovico Manin.

FREE San Giovanni Crisostomo
Cannaregio, campo San Giovanni Crisostomo (041 522 7155). Vaporetto Rialto. **Open** 8.15am-12.15pm, 3-7pm Mon-Sat; 3-7pm Sun. **Map** p97 G5 ❸

Santi Apostoli.

This small church by Mauro Codussi is dedicated to St John Chrysostomos, archbishop of Constantinople, and shows a Byzantine influence in its Greek-cross form. It contains two great paintings. On the right-hand altar is *Saints Jerome, Christopher and Louis of Toulouse*, signed by Giovanni Bellini and dated 1513. This late work is one of his few Madonna-less altarpieces and shows the Old Master ready to experiment with the atmospheric colouring techniques of such younger artists as Giorgione. On the high altar hangs *Saints John the Baptist, Liberale, Mary Magdalene and Catherine* (c1509) by Sebastiano del Piombo, who trained under Bellini but was also influenced by Giorgione. (Novelist Henry James was deeply impressed by the figure of Mary Magdalene in Del Piombo's painting. She looked, he said, like a 'dangerous, but most valuable acquaintance'.) On the left-hand altar is *Coronation of the Virgin*, a fine relief (1500-02) by Tullio Lombardo.

FREE San Marcuola

Cannaregio, campo San Marcuola (041 713 872). Vaporetto San Marcuola. **Open** 10am-noon, 5-6pm Mon-Sat. **Map** p96 D4 ❹
There was no such person as St Marcuola; the name is a local mangling of the over-complicated *santi* Ermagora e Fortunato, two early martyrs. The church, designed by 18th-century architect Giorgio Massari, has been beautifully restored – its gleaming interior comes as a surprise after the unfinished brick façade. It contains some vigorous statues by Gianmaria Morlaiter and, in the chancel, a *Last Supper* (1547) by Tintoretto, his first treatment of the subject; the layout is uncharacteristically symmetrical but indications of the later Tintoretto can be seen in the restless movements of the disciples and the background figures. Opposite is a 17th-century copy of another Tintoretto (*Christ Washing the Feet of His Disciples*).

FREE San Marziale

Cannaregio, campo San Marziale (041 719 933). Vaporetto Ca' d'Oro or San Marcuola. **Open** 4-6.30pm Mon-Sat; 8.30-10am Sun. **Map** p97 E3 ❺
The real joy of this church is its ceiling, with its four luminous paintings (1700-05) by the vivacious colourist Sebastiano Ricci. Two of them depict *God the Father with Angels* and *St Martial in Glory*; the other two recount the miraculous story of the wooden statue of the Madonna and Child that resides on the second altar on the left – apparently, it made its own way here by boat from Rimini. The high altar has an equally fantastic Baroque extravaganza: a massive marble group of Christ, the world and some angels looms over the altar while St Jerome and companions crouch awkwardly beneath.

FREE Santi Apostoli

Cannaregio, campo Santi Apostoli (041 523 8297). Vaporetto Ca' d'Oro. **Open** 8.30am-noon, 5-7pm Mon-Sat; 4-7pm Sun. **Map** p97 G5 ❻
According to tradition, the 12 apostles appeared to the seventh-century Bishop of Oderzo, St Magnus, telling him to build a church where he saw 12 cranes together – a not uncommon sight when Venice was little more than a series of uninhabited islands poking out of marshes. Magnus followed orders, but the ancient church was rebuilt in the 17th century. Its campanile (1672), crowned by an onion dome added 50 years later, is a Venetian landmark.

The Cappella Corner, off the right side of the nave, is a century older than the rest of the structure. It was built by Mauro Codussi for the dispossessed Queen Caterina Cornaro of Cyprus; she was buried here in 1510 alongside her father and brother but subsequently removed to the church of San Salvador (*see p62*). On the altar is a splendidly theatrical *Communion of St Lucy* by Giambattista Tiepolo; the young saint, whose gouged eyes are in a dish on the floor, is bathed in a heavenly light. The chapel to the right of the high altar has remnants of 14th-century frescoes while the one to the left has a dramatically stormy painting of *The Guardian Angel* by Francesco Maffei.

Restaurants

Antica Adelaide

Cannaregio 3728, calle larga Doge Priuli (041 523 2629, www.anticaadelaide.it). Vaporetto Ca d'Oro. **Open** 7am-midnight daily. **Meals served** noon-2.30pm, 7.30-10.30pm daily. **Average** €35. **Map** p97 F4 ❼
This historic bar-*osteria* behind tack-filled Strada Nuova reopened in 2006, after painstaking restoration, with dynamic restaurateur and wine buff Alvise Ceccato at the helm. Popular around *aperitivo* time, it has also made a splash on the culinary front, with its unusual menu of revisited traditional dishes from the Veneto – like *oca in onto* (goose in its own fat) or freshwater lagoon fish done *in saor*

EXPLORE

(onions). There is a large selection of cheeses and cured meats, and a good pan-Italian wine list. Vegetarians are well catered for.

La Bottega ai Promessi Sposi

Cannaregio 4367, calle dell'Oca (041 241 2747). Vaporetto Ca' d'Oro. **Meals served** 12.30-2.30pm, 8-11pm Mon, Tue, Thur-Sun. **Average** €35. **No credit cards. Map** p97 F5 ❽

This pared-back *osteria* has a wooden counter groaning with excellent *cicheti* and a good selection of wines by the glass, to be sampled at the bar or mingling with the standing, chatting crowds that form in the narrow alley outside. In the back rooms are a few tables where diners can sample simple dishes – mainly but not exclusively seafood – with some twists on local stalwarts, such as fried *schie* (tiny grey prawns) on rocket with balsamic vinegar.

Ca' D'Oro (Alla Vedova)

Cannaregio 3912, ramo Ca' d'Oro (041 528 5324). Vaporetto Ca' d'Oro. **Meals served** 11.30am-2.30pm, 6.30-10.30pm Mon-Wed, Fri, Sat; 6.30-11pm Sun. Closed Aug. **Average** €35. **No credit cards. Map** p97 F4 ❾

Officially Ca' d'Oro, this place is known by locals as Alla Vedova – the Widow's Place. The widow has joined her *marito*, but her family still runs the show. The traditional decor remains, though the warmth of the welcome can vary. Tourists head for the tables (it's best to book), where tasty pasta dishes (like spaghetti in cuttlefish ink) and *secondi* are served; locals stay at the bar snacking on classic *cicheti*, including the best *polpette* (meatballs) in Venice.

La Cantina

Cannaregio 3689, campo San Felice (041 522 8258). Vaporetto Ca' d'Oro. **Open** 11am-10pm Mon-Sat. **Average** €35. **Map** p97 E4 ❿

The service here can verge on the plain rude. But the *aperitivo* snack offerings – including *crostini* made on the spot with whatever's in season – are so substantial that a quick drink can easily turn into a full meal, seafood platters and the occasional hot dish are delicious, and outside tables are the perfect place for watching the world bustle by. Around 30 wines are available by the glass.

F30

Cannaregio, santa Lucia railway station (041 525 6154). Vaporetto Ferrovia. **Open** 7am-11pm Mon-Thur, Sun; 7am-3am Fri, Sat. **Meals served** 11am-10.30pm daily. **Average** €15-€45. **Map** p96 A5 ⓫

Part of the recent Santa Lucia station upgrade (*see p98* **Station Shopping**), this light-filled, modern café-restaurant has a view over, and tables on the pavement by, the Grand Canal – though not as you might imagine it. *Vaporetti* bustle beneath Calatrava's bridge over to the bus terminus at piazzale Roma as you eat excellent *tramezzini* or cakes perched at the

bar, or put away a decent pizza, large mixed salad or classic pasta dish at restaurant tables inside or (weather permitting) out. Unlike the rest of the offerings in this global-label station complex, F30 is a one-off run by locals. Keen to make this a real part of the city, F30 has live music from 9pm on Saturday nights and 'Soul Fridays' with DJ set from 10pm. With food served all day, this is a great spot if you're starving as you arrive or leave by train.

Vini da Gigio

Cannaregio 3628, fondamenta San Felice (041 528 5140, www.vinidagigio.com). Vaporetto Ca' d'Oro. **Meals served** noon-2.30pm, 7-10.30pm Wed-Sun. Closed 3wks Jan-Feb. **Average** €50. **Map** p97 F4 ⓬

Vini da Gigio is strong on Venetian *antipasti*, including raw seafood; there are also a number of good meat and game options, like seared cuts of breaded lamb or tuna in a sesame seed crust. As the name suggests, wine is another forte, with good international and by-the-glass selections. The only drawback in this highly recommended restaurant is the unhurried service. Book well ahead.

Cafés, Bars & Gelaterie

See also p143 **El Sbarlefo**, *p189* **Paradiso Perduto**.

★ Boscolo

Cannaregio 1818, campiello de l'Anconeta (041 720 731). Vaporetto San Marcuola. **Open** 6.40am-8.40pm daily. **No credit cards. Map** p96 D3 ⓭

The bar at Boscolo's *pasticceria* is always packed; locals flock to enjoy an extra-strong *spritz al bitter* with one of the home-made *pizzette*. There is also an excellent assortment of Venetian sweets: *frittelle* during Carnevale, as well as *zaleti* and *pincia* (made with cornflour and raisins). Boscolo's range of chocolates in the form of interesting (and graphic) Kama Sutra positions has made this confectioner famous.

Santo Bevitore

Cannaregio 2393A, campo Santa Fosca (041 717 560, www.ilsantobevitorepub.com). Vaporetto Ca' d'Oro or San Marcuola. **Open** 9.30am-1.30am Mon-Sat. **No credit cards. Map** p97 E3 ⓮

This friendly pub-café on campo Santa Fosca, just off strada Nova, has consistently proved popular with both Venetian locals and visitors, who drop in to munch *cicheti* during the day or come to while away the evening over a beer or a glass of wine.

Shops & Services

Cibele

Cannaregio 1823, campiello dell'Anconeta (041 524 2113). Vaporetto San Marcuola. **Open** 8.30am-12.45pm, 4-7.45pm Mon-Sat. **Map** 96 D3 ⓯
Food & drink/health & beauty

DRINK, SNACK, DINE

Making sense of Venice's hostelries.

Venice's uniqueness extends into many unexpected spheres – eating and drinking included. Take, for example, the all-day bar. Unassuming places such as **Da Lele** (*see p131*) or **Alla Ciurma** (*see p116*) open their doors round about 6am. But you'll search in vain for a coffee machine: market traders or workers arriving from the mainland drop by at sunrise for their first (alcoholic) drink of the day. It keeps – they'll tell you – the damp out of your bones. This kind of central heating comes cheap: in a city where everything seems to cost over the odds, a small glass of wine (*un'ombra*) costs anything from Lele's ridiculous 60c to around €1.50. And in all but the smartest bars, the ubiquitous spritz (*see p113* **Spritz**) comes in at €2.

Or rather, it does when consumed standing. It's true anywhere in Italy that a surcharge is applied to café/bar prices when you consume sitting at a table (*see also p61* **In the Know**). But Venice takes this rule much further.

The traditional Venetian eaterie (known as a *bàcaro* – **Al Portego** (*see p82*), **Ca' d'Oro** (*see p100*), **All'Arco** (*see p116*) and **Bottega ai Promessi Sposi** (*see p100*) are fine examples) has a dark room out the back with a few tables in it. But dominating the front of the premises you'll find a high glass-fronted bar counter inside which there will be shelves piled with tapas-like snacks called *cicheti*. From creamed cod (*baccalà mantecato*) to meatballs, to sardines stewed in onion (*sarde in saor*), to tiny stuffed peppers – you'll find a huge selection, to be eaten one at a time, or piled on to a plate to make what can add up to a pretty full meal. But – except where you can perch on a bar stool or occupy any front-of-house accommodation – this is on-the-hoof food: the proper tables are for proper diners, opting for the full pasta-plus-main meals that will appear from a kitchen hidden away behind.

Cicheti are charged individually – anything between €1.50 and €3 is normal, depending on what you choose. So a well-filled plate can cost €10 or less. Sitting down for a proper meal in the same hostelry, however, may cost €30 or more (sometimes much more) a head. To complicate arrangements still further, many clients will just be

Bottega ai Promessi Sposi.

here for a drink: they're generally the ones chatting, glass in hand, in the *calle* outside.

Cichetando (dining on *cicheti*) may be a (rare) cheap option for eating out in Venice but in the more traditional places you'll have to dine early to take advantage. *Bàcari* which consider themselves old-school generally close the kitchen down by 9pm or so. A newer generation places its emphasis more on food than on drinking-with-snacks, and keeps on cooking until 10pm or 10.30pm.

At the higher end of Venice's dining scene, *trattorie* and *ristoranti* function much as in the rest of Italy, the difference being that their prices tend to be higher than elsewhere. Between the two comes the trap that many visitors fall into: the hostelry catering only to the easily-ripped-off tourist horde. You can eat exceptionally well in the lagoon city... as long as you avoid anything with a *menu turistico* in several languages and a determined enticer at the door. Pay for the best, or seek out some dark *bàcaro*: anything else will not be the real Venetian thing.

EXPLORE

A full range of natural health foods, cosmetics and medicines is on sale here. Staff will also prepare blends of herbal teas and remedies.

★ Mori & Bozzi

Cannaregio 2367, rio terà Maddalena (041 715 261). Vaporetto San Marcuola. **Open** 9.30am-7.30pm daily. Closed Sun in July & Aug. **Map** p97 E3 ⑯ **Accessories**
Women's shoes for the coolest of the cool: whatever the latest fad – pointy or square – it's here. There are enough trendy names and designer-inspired footwear to please the Carrie Bradshaw in us all. Also beautiful bags, clothes hats and accessories of all kinds.

IL GHETTO

Vaporetto Guglie or San Marcuola.

The word 'ghetto' (like 'arsenal' and 'ciao') is one that Venice has given to the world. It originally meant an iron foundry, a place where iron was *gettato* (cast). Until 1390, when the foundry was transferred to the Arsenale, casting was done on a small island in Cannaregio. In 1516, it was decided to confine the city's Jewish population to this island; here they remained until 1797.

Venetian treatment of the Jews was by no means as harsh as in many European countries, but neither was it a model of open-minded

LIVING IN THE GHETTO

Creative solutions to cramped conditions.

Today, pretty campo del Ghetto Nuovo gives little idea of the hardships suffered there through the centuries that it hosted the closed community of Jews. Note the houses on the southern and eastern sides of the campo: taller than any others in Venice, they bear witness to how the hopelessly cramped inhabitants, prevented from expanding horizontally, did so vertically. Similar upwards extensions on the other two sides of the square have since been demolished; in times past, however, the open space was hemmed in and towered over on all sides.

During the day, the *campo* would have buzzed with activity. Christians came to the Ghetto to visit not only the pawnbrokers and money-lenders but also the *strazzerie* (second-hand clothes sellers) and artisans. As successive waves of immigrants arrived, the Ghetto would have resounded with a babble of languages from around the Mediterranean, as well as the northern inflections of Polish and German.

At night, the gates were closed and guarded by armed boats that patrolled the canals circling the small island; the Jews themselves were forced to pay for this guard service.

The ground floors of the buildings around the *campo* were almost entirely devoted to commercial activities; everything else – residences, synagogues and schools – was located above. Ceilings were low and the staircases were narrow, to save space. For structural stability, the walls on the ground floor were reinforced and the interior structures made of wood. There

are reports of floors collapsing under the feet of over-enthusiastic wedding parties.

Despite hardship and chronic overcrowding, these outwardly unassuming buildings manage to contain the splendid spaces of the synagogues. The **Scola Canton** and the **Scola Tedesca**, the earliest of the synagogues, are distinguished on the exterior only by the array of five windows and by the small wooden lantern in Scola Canton; inside, however, architects created room for impressive devotional spaces, with rich carvings and decorations (again, all in wood). Clearly, religion played an enormous part in the lives of the inhabitants.

It has been calculated that when the population was at its height (and before the Jews were allowed to spill over into the adjoining areas of the Ghetto Vecchio and Ghetto Novissimo), overcrowding was such that the inhabitants had to take it in turns to sleep.

EXPLORE

benevolence. The Republic's attitude was governed by practical considerations, and business was done with Jewish merchants at least as early as the tenth century. It was not until 1385, however, that Jewish moneylenders were given permission to reside in the city itself. Twelve years later, permission was revoked amid allegations of irregularities in their banking practices. For a century after that, residence in Venice was limited to two-week stretches. In 1509, when the Venetian mainland territories were overrun by foreign troops, great numbers of Jews took refuge in the city. The clergy seized the opportunity to stir up anti-Jewish feeling and demanded their expulsion. Venice's rulers, however, had begun to see the economic advantages of letting them stay, and in 1516 a compromise was reached. In a decision that was to mark the course of Jewish history in Europe, the refugees were given residence permits but confined to the Ghetto.

Restrictions were many and tough. Gates across the bridges to the island were closed an hour after sunset in summer (two hours after in winter), reopening at dawn. During the day, Jews had to wear distinctive badges or headgear. Most trades other than money-lending were barred to them. One exception was medicine, for which they were famous: Venetian practicality allowed Jewish doctors to leave the Ghetto at night for professional calls. Another was music: Jewish singers and fiddlers were hired for private parties.

The Ghetto became a stop on the tourist trail. In 1608, traveller Thomas Coryat came to gaze at the Jews – never having seen any in England – and marvelled at the 'sweet-featured persons' and the 'apparel, jewels, chains of gold' of the women.

The original inhabitants were mostly Ashkenazim from Germany; they were joined by Sephardim escaping from persecution in Spain and Portugal and then, increasingly, by Levantine Jews from the Ottoman Empire. These latter proved key figures in trade between Venice and the East, particularly after Venice lost so many of her trading posts in the eastern Mediterranean. By the middle of the 16th century, the Levantine Jews, the richest community, were given permission to move from the Ghetto Nuovo to the confusingly named Ghetto Vecchio (the 'old Ghetto', the site of an earlier foundry); in 1633, they expanded into the Ghetto Nuovissimo. Nonetheless, the conditions here remained cramped (*see p102* **Living in the Ghetto**). Room was found for five magnificent synagogues, however. The German, Levantine and Spanish synagogues can all be visited as part of the **Museo Ebraico** tour (*see right*).

With the arrival of Napoleon in 1797, Jews gained full citizenship rights; many chose to

Il Ghetto.

EXPLORE

remain in the Ghetto. In the deportations during the Nazi occupation of Italy in 1943, 202 Venetian Jews were sent to the death camps. The Jewish population of Venice and Mestre now stands at about 500 (see www.jvenice.org for information). Only around a dozen Jewish families still live in the Ghetto, but it remains the centre of spiritual, cultural and social life for the Jewish community. Orthodox religious services are held in the Scuola Spagnola in the summer and in the Scuola Levantina in winter. Most of the city, including the Ghetto, is an eruv.

Sights & Museums

Museo Ebraico

Cannaregio 2902B, campo del Ghetto Nuovo (041 715 359, www.museoebraico.it). Vaporetto Guglie or San Marcuola. **Open** 10am-5.30pm Mon-Fri, Sun. *Guided tours* (hourly) 10.30am-4.30pm Mon-Thur, Sun; 10.30am-2.30pm Fri. **Admission** *Museum only* €4; €3 reductions. *Museum & synagogues* €10; €8 reductions. **Map** p96 D3 ⑰ This well-run museum and cultural centre – founded in 1953 – has been spruced up over recent years, with a bookshop and a new section dedicated to the history and traditions of the various 'nations' that make up Venice's Jewish community, its relationship with the city after the 1797 opening of the Ghetto, some of its famous personages and the role of usury. In the older rooms there are ritual objects in silver – Torah finials, Purim and Pesach cases, menorahs – sacred vestments and hangings, and a series of marriage contracts. The museum is best visited as part of a guided tour. This takes in three synagogues – the Scuola Canton (Ashkenazi rite), the Scuola Italiana (Italian rite) and the Scuola Levantina (Sephardic rite).Tours of the Jewish cemetery on the Lido also set out from here.

Restaurants

Gam Gam Kosher Restaurant
Cannaregio 1122, fondamenta di Cannaregio (041 275 9256, http://gamgamkosher.com). Vaporetto Guglie. **Open** noon-10pm Mon-Thur, Sun. **Average** €30. **Map** p96 C3 ⓲ **Jewish**
Gam Gam livens up evenings in the Ghetto with its tables out on the Cannaregio canal and its friendly staff coping with the hungry crowds. As the name implies, the food (and wine) is kosher, and there's a range of traditional options including latkes and malza balls, gefilte fish and falafel. But there's a definite Venetian twist to the cooking. And the non-meat, non-dairy range makes this a favourite for vegetarians and vegans. You are advised to book.

Shops & Services

Kosher Tevà
Cannaregio 1242, campo del Ghetto Vecchio (041 524 4486). Vaporetto Guglie. **Open** 10am-6.30pm Mon-Fri, Sun. **No credit cards. Map** p96 C3 ⓳ **Food & drink**
In the heart of the Ghetto, Tevà produces excellent breads, biscuits and cakes… all kosher, exactly as the shop's name implies.

NORTH & WEST

Vaporetto Orto, San Marcuola or Sant'Alvise.

If you're tired of the crowds, there's no better place for getting away from it all than the north-western areas of Cannaregio. Built around three long parallel canals, it has no large animated squares and (with the exception of the Ghetto, *see p102-104*) no sudden surprises – just occasional views over the northern lagoon. And, at night, a lively scene around a handful of restaurants and bars.

The area does, however, have its landmarks, such as the *vecchia* (old; 14th-century) and *nuova* (new; 16th-century) **Scuole della Misericordia**, the 'new' one being a huge pile designed by Sansovino, its façade never completed. It has long been awaiting conversion into a cultural institute. Behind the *scuole*, the

picturesque campo dell'Abbazia, overlooked by the Baroque façade of the **Abbazia della Misericordia** and the Gothic façade of the *scuola vecchia*, is one of the most peaceful retreats in Venice; on the façade of the latter you can still see the outlines of sculptures (now in London's Victoria & Albert Museum) by Gothic master Bartolomeo Bon. The building is used as an art restoration workshop.

Out on a limb in the far west, beyond the Cannaregio canal, renaissance **San Giobbe** (*see p105*) was the first Venetian work of master mason Pietro Lombardo.

On the northernmost canal (the rio della Madonna dell'Orto) are the churches of the **Madonna dell'Orto** (*see below*) and **Sant'Alvise** (*see p106*), as well as many fine *palazzi*. At the eastern end of the *fondamente* along this canal, **Palazzo Contarini dal Zaffo** was built for Gaspare Contarini, a 16th-century scholar, diplomat and cardinal. Behind, a large garden stretches down to the lagoon; in its far corner stands the **Casinò degli Spiriti** (best seen from fondamente Nuove). It was designed as a meeting place for the 'spirits' (wits) of the day, though the name and the lonely position of the construction have given rise to numerous ghost stories.

The Madonna dell'Orto area may have been the home of an Islamic merchant community in the 12th and 13th centuries, centring on the long-since-destroyed *Fondaco degli arabi* (a meeting place and storehouse). Opposite the church of Santa Maria dell'Orto is the 15th-century **Palazzo Mastelli**, also known as Palazzo del Camello because of its relief of a turbaned figure with a camel. The Arabic theme carries on across the bridge in **campo dei Mori** ('of the Moors'), named after the three turban-wearing stone figures set into the façade of a building here. The one with the iron nose – dubbed 'Sior Antonio Rioba' – was where disgruntled citizens or local wits would stick their rhyming complaints under cover of darkness; his name was used as a pseudonym for published satires. The three figures are believed to be the Mastelli brothers, owners of the adjacent palazzo, who came to Venice as merchants from the Greek Peloponnese (then known as Morea – which offers another possible explanation of the campo's name).

Sights & Museums

★ Madonna dell'Orto
Cannaregio, campo Madonna dell'Orto (041 719 933, www.madonnadellorto.org). Vaporetto Orto. **Open** 10am-5pm Mon-Sat; noon-6pm Sun. **Admission** €2.50. **No credit cards. Map** p97 E2 ⓴

Madonna dell'Orto.

The 'Tintoretto church' was originally dedicated to St Christopher (a magnificent statue of whom stands over the main door), the patron saint of the gondoliers (who ran the ferry service to the islands from a nearby jetty). However, a cult developed around a large, unfinished and supposedly miraculous statue of the Madonna and Child that stood in a nearby garden. In 1377, the sculpture was transferred into the church (it's now in the chapel of San Mauro), and the church's name was changed to the Madonna dell'Orto – of the Garden.

The church was rebuilt between 1399 and 1473, and a monastery was constructed alongside. The false gallery at the top of the beautiful Gothic façade is unique in Venice; the sculptures are all fine 15th-century works. But it is the numerous works by Tintoretto that have made the Madonna dell'Orto famous. Tradition has it that the artist began decorating the church as penance for insulting a doge: in fact, it took very little to persuade Tintoretto to get his palette out, and the urgent sincerity of his work here speaks for itself.

Two colossal paintings dominate the side walls of the chancel. On the left is *The Israelites at Mount Sinai*. Opposite is a gruesome *Last Judgement*. Tintoretto had no qualms about mixing religion and myth: note the classical figure of Charon ferrying the souls of the dead. His paintings in the apse include *St Peter's Vision of the Cross* and *The Beheading of St Paul* (or Christopher, according to some), in which maelstroms of swirling angelic movement. On the wall of the right aisle is the *Presentation of the Virgin in the Temple*. The Contarini Chapel, off the left aisle, contains the artist's beautiful *St Agnes Reviving the Son of a Roman Prefect*. It is the swooping angels in their dazzling blue vestments that steal the show. Tintoretto, his son Domenico and

his artistically gifted daughter Marietta are buried in a chapel off the right aisle.

When the Tintorettos get too much for you, take a look at Cima da Conegliano's masterpiece *Saints John the Baptist, Mark, Jerome and Paul* (1494-95) over the first altar on the right. The saints stand under a ruined portico against a sharp, wintry light. There used to be a small *Madonna and Child* by Giovanni Bellini in the chapel opposite, but it was stolen in 1993. The second chapel on the left contains, on the left-hand wall, a painting by Titian of *The Archangel Raphael and Tobias* (and dog) that has been moved here from the church of San Marziale (*see p99*). In a room beneath the bell tower, a small treasury contains reliquaries and other precious objects.

FREE San Giobbe

Campo San Giobbe (041 524 1889, www.chorus venezia.org). Vaporetto Crea or Ponte Tre Archi. **Open** 10am-1.30pm Mon-Sat. **Admission** €3 (or Chorus; *see p89*). **Map** p96 A2 ㉑

Job (Giobbe) has been given saint status by Venice, despite his Old Testament pedigree. The church named after him was built to celebrate the visit in 1463 of St Bernardino di Siena, a high-profile Franciscan evangelist. The first Venetian creation of Pietro Lombardo, it introduced a new classical style, immediately visible in the doorway (three statues by Pietro Lombardo that once adorned it are now in the sacristy).

The interior of what was probably the first single-naved church in Venice is unashamedly Renaissance in style. Members of the Lombardo family are responsible for the carvings in the domed sanctuary, all around the triumphal arch separating the sanctuary from the nave, and on the tombstone of San Giobbe's founder, Cristoforo Moro, in the centre of the sanctuary floor. This doge's name has given rise to associations with Othello, the Moor of Venice; some have seen the mulberry symbol in his tombstone (*moro* can mean mulberry tree as well as Moor) as the origin of Desdemona's handkerchief, 'spotted with strawberries'.

Most of the church's treasures – altarpieces by Giovanni Bellini and Vittore Carpaccio – are now in the Accademia (*see p145*). An atmospheric *Nativity*

IN THE KNOW
PAINTER PORTRAITS?

Local lore has it that Tintoretto's *Israelites at Mount Sinai*, in the church of **Madonna dell'Orto** (*see p104*), contains hidden portraits of Venice's artistic top four (Giorgione, Titian, Veronese and Tintoretto himself) in the bearers of the Golden Calf. There's no actual documentary evidence for this, though, nor for the identification of the lady in blue as Mrs Tintoretto.

EXPLORE

by Gerolamo Savoldo remains, as does an *Annunciation with Saints Michael and Anthony* triptych by Antonio Vivarini in the sacristy. The Martini Chapel, the second on the left, is a little bit of Tuscany in Venice. Built for a family of silk-weavers from Lucca, it is attributed to the Florentine Bernardo Rossellino. The terracotta medallions of Christ and the Four Evangelists are by the Della Robbia studio – the only examples of its work in Venice.

Sant'Alvise
Cannaregio, campo Sant'Alvise (041 275 0462, www.chorusvenezia.org). Vaporetto Sant'Alvise. **Open** 10am-5pm Mon-Sat. **Admission** €3 (or Chorus; *see p89*). **No credit cards**. **Map** p96 D2 ㉒

A pleasingly simple Gothic building of the 14th century, Sant'Alvise's interior was remodelled in the 1600s with extravagant, if not wholly convincing, trompe l'œil effects on the ceiling. On the inner façade is a *barco*, a hanging choir of the 15th century with elegant wrought-iron gratings. Beneath the *barco* are eight charmingly naïve biblical paintings in tempera, attributed to Lazzaro Bastiani. On the right wall of the church are two paintings by Tiepolo, *The Crowning with Thorns* and *The Flagellation*. A larger and livelier work by the same painter, *Road to Calvary*, hangs on the right wall of the chancel, with rather ill-suited circus pageantry.

Restaurants

Anice Stellato
Cannaregio 3272, fondamenta della Sensa (041 720 744). Vaporetto Guglie or Sant'Alvise. **Meals served** 12.30-2pm, 7.30-10pm Wed-Sun. **Average** €40. **Map** p96 D2 ㉓

The bar in this friendly *bàcaro* fills up with *cichetari* (snacking locals) in the hour before lunch and evening meals. Tables take up two simply decorated rooms, and spill out on to the canalside walk in summer. What emerges from the kitchen are mostly Venetian classics such as *bigoli in salsa*, some given a novel twist.

Bea Vita
Cannaregio 3082, fondamenta delle Cappuccine (041 275 9347). Vaporetto Santa Marta or Tre Archi. **Meals served** noon-2.30pm, 7.30-10.30pm Mon-Sat. **Average** €35. **Map** p96 C2 ㉔

On the long canalside promenade just north of the Ghetto, Bea Vita attracts locals with its ample portions and decent prices. After a single *antipasto* you're likely to feel full – but it's worth pushing on through the creative menu. Desserts are mouthwatering. The small wine list includes a decent by-the-glass selection. There's a good €28 taster menu.

Da Rioba
Cannaregio 2553, fondamenta della Misericordia (041 524 4379, www.darioba.com). Vaporetto Orto. **Meals served** 12.30-2.30pm, 7.30-10.30pm Tue-Sun. Closed 3wks Jan & 3wks Aug. **Average** €40. **Map** p97 E3 ㉕

Taking its name from the iron-nosed stone figure of a turbaned merchant – known as Sior Rioba – set into a wall in nearby campo dei Mori, Da Rioba is a pleasant place for lunch on warm days, when tables are laid out along the canal. This nouveau-rustic *bàcaro* attracts a predominantly Venetian clientele – always a good sign. The menu ranges from local standards like *schie con polenta* to forays like red mullet fillets on a bed of artichokes with balsamic sauce.

Dalla Marisa
Cannaregio 652B, fondamenta San Giobbe (041 720 211). Vaporetto Crea or Tre Archi. **Meals served** noon-2.30pm Mon, Wed, Sun; noon-2.30pm, 8-9.15pm Tue, Thur-Sat. Closed Aug. **Average** €35. **No credit cards**. **Map** p96 B2 ㉖

I Gesuiti.

Signora Marisa is a culinary legend in Venice, with locals calling up days in advance to ask her to prepare ancient recipes such as *risotto con le secoe* (risotto made with a cut of beef from around the spine). Pasta dishes include the excellent *tagliatelle con sugo di masaro* (in duck sauce), while *secondi* range from tripe to roast stuffed pheasant. In summer, tables spill out from the tiny interior on to the *fondamenta*. Book well ahead – and remember, serving times are rigid: turn up late and you'll go hungry. There's a €15 lunch menu.

L'Orto dei Mori

Cannaregio 3386, fondamenta dei Mori (041 524 3677, www.osteriaortodeimori.com). Vaporetto Orto or San Marcuola. **Meals served** 12.30-2.30pm, 7-10.30pm Mon, Wed-Sun. Closed 3wks Jan. **Average** €45. **Map** p97 E3 ㉗

The cook may be Sicilian but there's a definite Venetian feel to this welcoming *osteria*, especially in warmer weather when tables spill out on to this quietly picturesque *fondamenta*. On the Venetian front, there's a light *baccalà mantecato* (creamed cod) and a tasty risotto *al nero di seppia* (risotto with squid ink) but you can also snack on an untraditional *caprese* salad (with mozzarella and tomato).

Shops & Services

Nicolao Atelier

Cannaregio 2590, fondamenta della Misericordia (041 520 7051, www.nicolao.com). Vaporetto Guglie. **Open** 9am-1pm, 2-6pm Mon-Fri. **Map** p97 E3 ㉘ Carnival costumes

A very simple costume can be hire from €150 per day; the more elaborate ones can go up to as much as €300 a day. There is, however, a reduction for each additional day that you keep the costume thereafter. Costumes are also for sale and can be purchased online.

EAST

Vaporetto Fondamente Nove or Rialto.

Behind the straight edge of the Fondamenta Nuove, eastern Cannaregio is more intriguingly closed in, with many narrow alleys (including the Venetian record holder: calle Varisco, which is 52 centimetres/20 inches wide at its narrowest point), charming courtyards and well-heads, but no major sights, with the exception of the spectacularly ornate church of **I Gesuiti**, the **Oratorio dei Crociferi**, further east, the miniature marvel of **Santa Maria dei Miracoli** (for all, *see right*). Titian had a house here, with a garden extending to the lagoon; the courtyard where the house was located is raised to the dignity of a 'campo' and named after the artist.

Sights & Museums

FREE I Gesuiti

Cannaregio, salizada dei Spechieri (041 523 1610). Vaporetto Fondamente Nove. **Open** 10am-noon, 4-6pm daily. **Map** p97 G4 ㉙

The Jesuits were never very popular in Venice, and it wasn't until 1715 that they felt secure enough to build a church here. Even then they chose a comparatively remote plot on the edge of town. But once they made up their mind to go ahead, they went all out: local architect Domenico Rossi was given explicit instructions to dazzle. The result leaves no room for half measures: you love it or you hate it, and many people do the latter.

The exterior, with a façade by Gian Battista Fattoretto, is conventional enough; the interior is anything but. All that tassled, bunched, overpowering drapery is not the work of a rococo set designer gone berserk with luxurious brocades: it's plain old green and white marble. Bernini's altar in St Peter's in Rome was the model for the baldachin over the altar, by Fra Giuseppe Pozzo. The statues above the baldachin are by Giuseppe Torretti, as are the rococo archangels at the corners of the crossing. Titian's *Martyrdom of St Lawrence* (1558-59), over the first altar on the left side, cxame from an earlier church on this site, and was one of the first successful night scenes ever to be painted.

Oratorio dei Crociferi

Cannaregio 4905, campo dei Gesuiti (041 271 9012). Vaporetto Fondamente Nove. **Open** by appointment. **Admission** €6. **Map** p97 G4 ㉚

Founded in the 13th century by Doge Renier Zeno, the oratory is a sort of primitive *scuola* (*see p129* **Scuole Stories**), with the familiar square central meeting hall but without the quasi-masonic ceremonial trappings. Palma il Giovane's colourful cycle of paintings shows Pope Anacletus instituting the order of the Crociferi (cross-bearers), and dwells on the pious life of Doge Pasquale Cicogna, who was a fervent supporter of the order.

★ Santa Maria dei Miracoli

Cannaregio, campo Santa Maria dei Miracoli (041 275 0462, www.chorusvenezia.org). Vaporetto Fondamente Nove or Rialto. **Open** 10am-5pm Mon-Sat. **Admission** €3 (or Chorus; *see p89*). **No credit cards. Map** p97 G5 ㉛

Arguably one of the most exquisite churches in the world, Santa Maria dei Miracoli was built in the 1480s to house a miraculous image of the Madonna, reputed to have revived a man who had spent half an hour underwater in the Giudecca Canal, and also to have cancelled all traces of a knife attack on a woman. The building is the work of the Lombardo family, early Renaissance masons who fused architecture, surface detail and sculpture into a unique whole.

Pietro Lombardo may have been a Lombard by birth but he soon got into the Venetian way of

EXPLORE

doing things, employing Byzantine spoils left over from work on St Mark's to create a work of art displaying an entirely Venetian sensitivity to texture and colour. There is an almost painterly approach to the use of multicoloured marble in the four sides of the church, each of which is of a slightly different shade. The sides have more pilasters than necessary, making the church appear longer than it really is.

Inside, the 50 painted ceiling panels by Pier Maria Pennacchi (1528) are almost impossible to distinguish without using binoculars. Instead, turn your attention to the church's true treasures: the delicate carvings by the Lombardos on the columns, steps and balustrade, with their exquisite, lifelike details.

Restaurants

Algiubagiò

Cannaregio 5039, Fondamenta Nuove (041 523 6084, www.algiubagio.net). Vaporetto Fondamente Nove. **Open** 7am-midnight Mon, Wed-Sun. Closed Jan. **Meals served** noon-3pm, 7-10.30pm Mon, Wed-Sun. **Average** €45. **Map** p97 H4 ☺

This busy spot has morphed from bar to full-on restaurant, now with a vast waterside terrace. The menu ranges from seafood, meat, salad and cheese *antipasti*, through pasta dishes such as tagliolini with duck and autumn greens, to Angus steak (the house speciality), prepared every which way. Vegetarians are well served; and there's a small but well-chosen wine list. Right by the Fondamente Nove vaporetto

WALK LIKE A VENETIAN
Pedestrian etiquette.

EXPLORE

With their unique transport situation, Venetians have developed a particular etiquette for getting around on foot, with clear rules depending on the particular weather conditions.

In general, 'traffic' tends to flow in lanes (keep to the right) with potential for passing: a quick acceleration to the left with a polite '*permesso*' will get you past those in front. Locals take a dim view of anyone stopping in narrow alleyways or on busy bridges to gawp or – worse still – spread out their picnics. Pull off well to the side or into a quiet side-street to consult a map or admire a building. Be adventurous and explore remoter districts if you want

to avoid the high-season all-day-long traffic jam clogging the main arteries of the city, especially those near San Marco and Rialto.

Acqua alta (high water) presents other problems. Except in truly exceptional cases, all this means is that a couple of inches of water laps into the lowest parts of the city for an hour or two, then recedes. As the water rises, sirens sound five ten-second blasts two hours before the tide's high point. During the *acqua alta* season (September to April), trestles and wooden planks are stacked up along flood-prone thoroughfares, ready to be transformed into raised walkways. Venetians caught out by the rising water without wellies wait their turn patiently, then proceed slowly but surely. They expect tourists to do the same, or risk an angry telling-off.

Pedestrian etiquette extends beyond the walkways. The streets may be waterlogged, but they continue to function as a municipal road network; locals are understandably peeved if tourists doing Gene Kelly impersonations prevent them from reaching their destination dry. Remember, too, that during *acqua alta* you can't see where the pavement stops and the canal begins. Maps posted at vaporetto stops show flood-prone areas; if you don't want to get your feet wet, stick to higher ground or sit out those damp hours in your hotel room or a bar.

To see if you'll be facing this challenge, go to www.comune.venezia.it and click on '*previsione maree*' for tide forecasts. Anything over 80cm means that low-lying areas, such as piazza San Marco, will be submerged.

stop, this is the perfect place for a quick bite before heading out to the islands of the northern lagoon.

Alla Frasca
Cannaregio 5176, campiello della Carità (041 528 5433, www.osteriaviniallafrasca.com). Vaporetto Fondamente Nove. **Meals served** noon-2.30pm, 7-10.30pm Tue-Sat; noon-2.30pm Sun. **Average** €35. **Map** p97 H4 ③
Alla Frasca is a pleasant trattoria with a good seafood menu: the *zuppa di pesce* (fish soup) and spaghetti with lobster are particularly fine. With outside tables on a tiny square just south of fondamenta Nuove, it is almost ridiculously picturesque.

Boccadoro
Cannaregio 5405A, campiello Widman (041 521 1021, www.boccadorovenezia.it). Vaporetto Fondamente Nove. **Meals served** 7-11pm daily. **Average** €60. **Map** p97 G5 ③
The cuisine in this restaurant with pleasantly modern decor is very good, with a focus on fresh fish – such as tuna tartare or *cozze pepate* (peppery mussels). *Secondi* range from simple grilled fish to more adventurous seafood and vegetable pairings. In summer, there are tables outside on a small neighbourhood campo – a great playspace for bored kids.

Da Alberto
Cannaregio 5401, calle Giacinto Gallina (041 523 8153). Vaporetto Rialto. **Meals served** noon-3pm, 6.30-9.30pm Mon-Sat. **Average** €35. **Map** p97 H5 ③
This *bàcaro* with trad decor, not far from campo Santi Giovanni e Paolo, has a well-stocked bar counter, at which you can stand and snack. Served on tables in the back, the wide-ranging, sit-down menu is rigidly Venetian, offering utterly traditional *granseola* and *seppie in umido* (stewed cuttlefish), plus seafood pastas and risottos. Book ahead if you want a table.

Trattoria Storica
Cannaregio 4858, salizada Sceriman (041 528 5266). Vaporetto Fondamente Nove or Ca' D'Oro. **Meals served** 12.30-2.30pm, 6.30-10pm Mon-Sat. **Average** €35. **Map** p97 G4 ③
Located after the bridge that heads south out of campo dei Gesuiti, this family restaurant is simple, not generally overrun with tourists and good value for hearty servings of good traditional Venetian fare. This is especially true at lunchtime when there's a generous €15 set menu.

Shops & Services

Gianni Basso Stampatore
Cannaregio 5306, calle del Fumo (041 521 4681). Vaporetto Fondamenta Nove. **Open** 9am-1pm, 2.30-6pm Mon-Sat. **Map** p97 H4 ③ **Gifts & stationery**

Boccadoro.

Gianni Basso is an amiable character, who moves among his ancient printing presses, chatting about his latest jobs while pulling open drawer after drawer of superb printing blocks so that you can choose the perfect motif for your hand-printed business cards, ex libris or stationery. Around the walls are cards made for his many faithful clients: actors, writers, intellectuals – you'll recognise the names.

Libreria Marco Polo
Cannaregio 5886A, calle del Teatro Malibran (041 522 6343, www.libreriamarcopolo.com). Vaporetto Rialto or Rialto Mercato. **Open** 9.30am-7.30pm Mon-Thur, Sat; 9.30am-11.30pm Fri. **Map** p97 G5 ③ **Books & music**
Claudio Moretti's quirky bookshop is a labour of love, which carries on against all odds. Selling remainders, second-hand books (they can be exchanged too) and many more in Italian but also in English and other languages, it specialises in travel – from guides and maps to works of fiction. There are book presentations, meetings with writers and events of all kinds, plus a place to sit and peruse your acquisition over a cup of tea.

★ Vittorio Costantini
Cannaregio 5311, calle del Fumo (041 522 2265, www.vittoriocostantini.com). Vaporetto Fondamenta Nove. **Open** 9.15am-1pm, 2.15-5.30pm Mon-Fri. **Map** p97 H5 ③ **Glass**
Vittorio is internationally renowned as one of the most original Venetian glass workers. His intricate animals, insects, fish and birds are instantly recognisable for their fine workmanship.

San Polo & Santa Croce

Within the bulge created by the great bend in the Grand Canal lie the *sestieri* of San Polo and Santa Croce. Working out where one stops and the other begins is an arduous task. The area ranges from an eastern portion, tightly clustered around the Rialto market, which was the city's ancient heart and where, despite the invasion of stalls selling trashy tourist-trinkets, you can still feel its steady throb, particularly in the bustling morning market, to a quieter, residential, more down-at-heel area in the far west extending to the university zone by San Nicolò da Tolentino.

Between the two extremes come the large open space of campo San Polo, the great religious complex of the Frari and the scuole of San Rocco and San Giovanni Evangelista.

Scuola Grande di San Rocco.

Don't Miss

1 I Frari Superlative artworks in a barn of a church (p126).

2 Palazzo Mocenigo The history of Venetian fashion explained (p122).

3 Scuola Grande di San Rocco Tintoretto let rip in this temple to his genius (p129).

4 Rialto markets source of all that's good and fresh on Venetian plates (p112).

5 Da Lele A Venetian institution, your cheapest aperitivo in Venice (p131).

THE RIALTO MARKETS

Vaporetto Rialto or Rialto Mercato.

Rialto, most experts agree, derives from *Rivoaltus* (high bank). It was on this point of higher ground at the mid-point along the Grand Canal that one of the earliest settlements was founded, in the fifth century. The district has been the commercial centre of the city since the market was placed here in 1097.

The present layout of the market zone is the result of a reconstruction project by Scarpagnino, undertaken after a devasting fire in 1514. The project made use of the existing foundations, so the present street plan probably reflects quite faithfully the earliest urban arrangement, with long, narrow parallel blocks running behind the grand *palazzi* along the riva del Vin, and smaller square blocks further inland for the market workers.

At the foot of the Rialto bridge, where the tourist stalls are thick on the ground, stand (to the south) the **Palazzo dei Dieci Savi**, which housed the city's tax inspectors but is now used by the ancient but extant lagoon water authority, Il magistrato alle acque, and (to the north) the **Palazzo dei Camerlenghi**, which housed the finance department.

Beyond these, the small church of San **Giacomo di Rialto** (known affectionately as San Giacometto; *see right*) is generally agreed to be the oldest of the city's churches. All around it stretch the markets – the best place to buy your fruit, veg and seafood. In recent years, this area has taken on a new lease of life as a centre of Venetian nightlife, with a number of bars opening under the porticos of the Renaissance Fabbriche Vecchie (Scarpagnino, 1520-22), including some opening on to the Erbaria.

The name Erbaria denotes the fact that vegetables are sold here; there are other examples of such names in the streets and squares nearby (Naranzeria – oranges; Casaria – cheese; Speziali – spices), while the narrower alleys mostly bear the names of ancient inns and taverns – some still in operation – such as 'the Monkey', 'the Two Swords', 'the Two Moors', 'the Ox', and 'the Bell'. Then, as now, market traders hated to be too far from liquid refreshment.

On the other side of campo San Giacomo from the church, behind the fruit stalls, is a 16th-century statue of a kneeling figure supporting a staircase leading up to a small column of Egyptian granite, from which laws and sentences were pronounced. It was to this figure – the *Gobbo di Rialto* (the Hunchback of the Rialto, although you'll note that he is, in fact, merely crouching) – that naked malefactors

Muro Rialto.

clung in desperate and bloody relief, since the statue marked the end of the gauntlet they were condemned to run from piazza San Marco as an alternative to gaol.

The ruga degli Speziali leads to the **Pescaria** (fishmarket; open Tue-Sat mornings). The present neo-Gothic arcade (1907) replaced an iron structure of the previous century. Beyond the market extends a warren of medieval low-rent housing interspersed with proud *palazzi*. This area is traversed by two main pedestrian routes from the Rialto bridge, one running westward (*see p118*) more or less parallel to the Grand Canal, towards campo San Polo, and the other zigzagging north-westwards (*see p121*) via a series of small squares towards campo **San Giacomo dell'Orio** (*see p123*) and the station.

FREE San Giacomo di Rialto

San Polo, campo San Giacomo (041 522 4745). Vaporetto Rialto or Rialto Mercato. **Open** 9.30am-noon, 4-6pm Mon-Sat. **Map** p115 H4 ❶
The traditional foundation date for this church is that of the city itself: 25 March 421. It has undergone several radical reconstructions since then, the last in 1601. Nonetheless, the original Greek-cross plan was always preserved, as were its minuscule dimensions. The interior has columns of ancient marble with 11th-century Corinthian capitals. One 16th-century guide book to the city suggests that the domes of this church may have provided a model for those of St Mark's basilica (*see p50*).

In 1177, Pope Alexander III granted plenary indulgence to all those who visited the church on Maundy

Thursday; among the eager visitors every year was the doge. The special role of this church in Venetian history was given official recognition after 1532, when Pope Clement VII bestowed the patronage of the church on the doge, effectively annexing it to the Ducal Chapel of St Mark's. The church currently hosts an exhibition of ancient musical instruments, organised by Interpreti veneziani (*see p194*).

Restaurants

See also p116 **All'Arco**, **Alla Ciurma**, and **Naranzaria**.

Bancogiro
San Polo 122, campo San Giacomo di Rialto (041 523 2061). Vaporetto Rialto Mercato. **Meals served** noon-11pm Tue-Sun. **Average** €45. **Map** p115 H4 ❷
The location of this updated *bacaro* is splendid: the main entrance gives on to the busy Rialto square of San Giacomo, while the back door leads to a prime bit of Grand Canal frontage, with (hotly contested) tables from which to soak in the view. Bancogiro dispenses excellent wines and *cicheti* to an appreciative crowd downstairs; upstairs, the restaurant has creative seafood dishes.

Muro Rialto
San Polo 222, campo Cesare Battisti già Bella Vienna (041 241 2339, www.murovenezia.com). Vaporetto Rialto or Rialto Mercato. **Open** 9am-3pm, 4pm-2am Mon-Sat; 4pm-2am Sun. **Average** €35. **Map** p115 H3 ❸
Stylish Muro is generally packed with throngs of sophisticated but thirsty *spritz*-seekers. There's something for pretty much everyone here – from *aperitivi* and *cicheti* at the spacious downstairs bar and outside tables, to eclectic fine dining on the first floor. In the colourful area around the historic Rialto markets, Muro's sleek, modern design is complemented by the friendly staff. The €10 self-service brunch (fried fish and a glass of wine) on Saturdays in the campo outside is highly popular. Success at the mother ship has led Muro to expand into two smart new venues, both of which are restaurants serving pizza plus a range of mainly seafood fare.
Other locations Muro San Stae, Santa Croce 2048, campiello dello Spezier (041 524 1629); Muro Frari, San Polo 2604B-C, rio terà (041 524 5310).

Cafés, Bars & Gelaterie

Al Mercà
San Polo 213, campo Cesare Battisti già Bella Vienna (347 100 2583 mobile). Vaporetto Rialto or Rialto Mercato. **Open** 9am-3pm, 6-9pm Mon-Sat; 6-9pm Sun. **No credit cards. Map** p115 H3 ❹
Quite literally a hole in the wall, with standing room only in this campo in the market, Al Mercà (or Al Marcà, the spelling varies) has been serving Rialto

---

SPRITZ
Venice's favourite fizzy beverage.

It's difficult to avoid *spritz* in Venice: before lunch, early evening, after dinner – just about any time, in fact, you'll find crowds outside Venetian bars, glasses of amber-orange liquid in hand. But despite its jaunty hue and party-fun flavour, *spritz* comes in varying degrees of dangerous.

The origins of this ubiquitous drink are as obscure as its 'real' recipe. Perhaps invented by Venice's Austrian occupiers in the 19th century (they couldn't take the strength of local wines, one story goes, and so ordered it watered down), a classic version calls for one part prosecco, one part bitters and one part sparking seltz water, with a slice of orange and some ice to finish off the job.

It's quite normal these days to find common or garden mineral water being used instead of the far more carbonated seltz soda; and often still white wine replaces prosecco, making it altogether a less tingling experience.

The real threat to navigation comes from your choice of bitter. When ordering you can specify spritz all'Aperol (11% proof), with the very Venetian Select (14%) or with Campari (20+%). Whatever version you choose, a generous glass will cost somewhere between €2 and €3.50 in all but the swishest bars.

Spritz

EXPLORE

EXPLORE

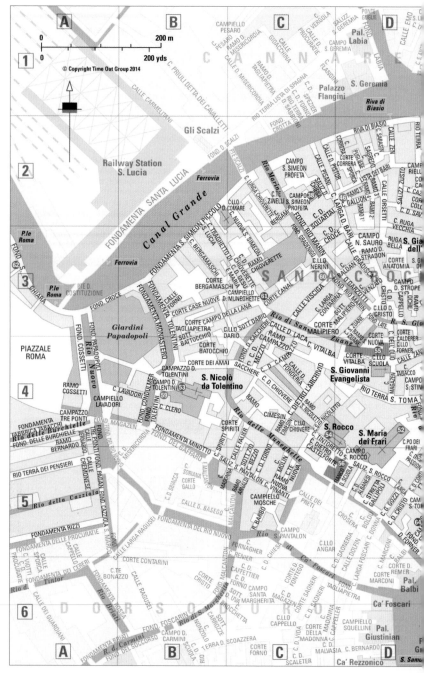

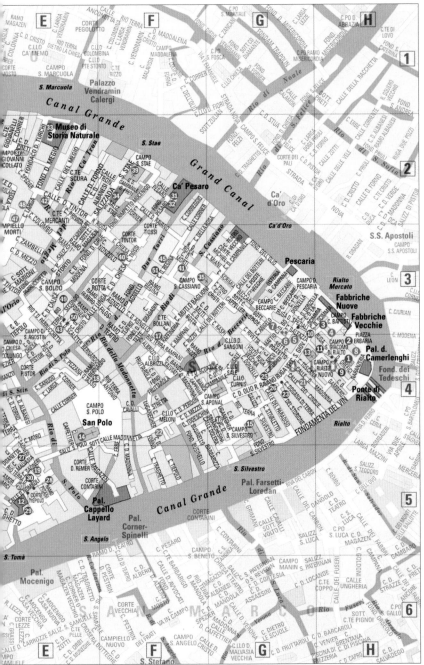

EXPLORE

Alla Ciurma.

marketgoers since 1918. Today's owners dispense the usual choice of wine, and a decent *spritz*, plus snacks – meatballs, artichoke hearts and mini-sandwiches, in addition to numerous options for panini toppings.

Alla Ciurma
San Polo 406, calle Galeazza (041 523 9514). Vaporetto Rialto or Rialto Mercato. **Open** 8am-3pm, 5.30-9pm Mon-Sat. **No credit cards.** **Map** p115 H3 ❺

Packed, loud and casually friendly, Alla Ciurma mixes market stallholders with locals and tourists in a happy confusion around a high counter packed with *cicheti* (snacks) of all kinds, including skewers of deep-fried seafood and – their speciality – king prawns wrapped in bacon. Most people drop by for a glass of wine or a *spritz* (and alcohol is consumed throughout daylight hours here by stallholders whose day begins before dawn). There are a couple of tables to consume at, beneath the boat suspended from one wall: if you can bag a seat at lunch you can enjoy good salads and an excellent *baccalà mantecato* (creamed cod).

All'Arco
San Polo 436, calle Ochialera (041 520 5666). Vaporetto Rialto or Rialto Mercato. **Open** 8am-2.30pm Mon-Sat. **No credit cards.** **Map** p115 G3 ❻

If you don't like crowds, you should steer clear of this hugely popular bacaro; throughout the day, friendly bar staff serve *ombre* (glasses of wine), stiffer stuff and wonderfully fresh *cicheti* to an enthusiastic clientele ranging from Rialto market stallholders to bewildered tourists. At €1.50 a *cicheto*, you can put together a delicious meal for very little, but it won't be a comfortable one: it's standing room only here. If you can handle that, join the crowd.

Do Mori
San Polo 429, calle dei Do Mori (041 522 5401). Vaporetto Rialto, Rialto Mercato or San Silvestro. **Open** 8am-8pm Mon-Sat. **No credit cards.** **Map** p115 G3 ❼

Do Mori claims to be the oldest *bacaro* in Venice, dating back to 1462. Batteries of copper pans hang from the ceiling, and at peak times the narrow bar is a heaving mass of bodies lunging for the excellent mini-sandwiches and the selection of fine wines. Don't point to a label at random, as prices can sometimes be in the connoisseur bracket. You won't go far wrong if you stick to a glass of the classic *spento* – prosecco minus the bubbles.

Naranzaria
San Polo 130, Erbaria (041 724 1035, www. naranzaria.it). Vaporetto Rialto or Rialto Mercato. **Open** noon-2am Tue-Sun. Closed 10 days Jan. **Map** p115 H4 ❽

From a superb location – one side gives on to campo San Giacomo, the other on to the market and the Grand Canal – this nouveau-*bacaro* offers a

EXPLORE

selection of fine wines, many of them produced by co-owner Brandino Brandolini, which can be enjoyed on foot outside with the regulars or perched at a table if you're lucky, as you absorb the view. There's also a restaurant but you're best opting for liquid refreshment and moving on: prices are high and the vibe is not always friendly.

Shops & Services

★ Attombri

San Polo 65, sottoportego degli Orafi (041 521 2524, www.attombri.com). Vaporetto Rialto or Rialto Mercato. **Open** 9am-1.30pm Mon, Fri; 9am-1.30pm, 2-6.30pm Tue-Thur; 10am-6.30pm Sat. **Map** p115 H4 **❾ Jewellery**
Underneath the arches at the north-western foot of the Rialto, Stefano and Daniele Attombri peddle

their sumptuous creations. Intricate, unique pieces combine metal wire and antique Venetian glass beads, or blown glass cameos of their own design. They also produce interior design pieces, including mirrors and lamps.
Other location San Marco 1179, Frezzeria (041 241 1442).

★ Drogheria Mascari

San Polo 381, ruga degli Spezieri (041 522 9762, www.imascari.com). Vaporetto Rialto Mercato or San Silvestro. **Open** 8am-1pm, 4-7.30pm Mon-Sat. **No credit cards. Map** p115 G3 **❿ Food & drink**
This wonderful old-fashioned grocery shop is the best place in the city to find exotic spices, nuts, dried fruit and mushrooms, as well as oils and wines from different regions in Italy. They also have a fine range of loose-leaf teas, infusions and coffee.

VENETIAN PEOPLE FR ROLFE

Fantasist, con man and score-settling novelist.

Fr(ederick) Rolfe – any ambiguity was purely intentional – was born in Cheapside in 1860 into a middle-class family. A convert to Catholicism, he was determined to become a priest, but his take on Catholicism was too extreme for his tutors and he was never ordained. Extremity was to become his hallmark.

During a stint at the Scots College in Rome, he was, he claimed, adopted by Duchess Sforza Cesarini, who bestowed the title 'Baron Corvo' on him. It was one of many of his pseudonyms, though his favourite was always Fr. Rolfe – intimating that he had, in fact, achieved that ordination that in reality had been denied to him.

A drifter and sponger, only staying in any one place long enough to antagonise the benefactors he had begun by ingratiating himself with, Rolfe churned out a series of stories and novels – laboured things, full of wish-fulfillment, personal vendetta and spite – which have left his star, never very bright, waning over the decades. His most successful opus was the extraordinary *Hadrian the Seventh*, a wild fantasy in which the protagonist, banished from his seminary, is by a series of odd coincidences elected pope. This Rolfe alter ego is, naturally, a hugely successful, reforming, brilliant pontiff until he is assassinated by a jealous rival. DH Lawrence described the novel as 'the book of a man demon, not a mere poseur'.

Rolfe spent the last seven years of his life in Venice, going from kept man in a plush apartment, to pitied guest among members of the English community, to penniless drifter, sometimes with sufficient spare cash to live out his fantasies with young boys picked up on Venice's docks. Throughout his time in the lagoon city, however, he was working away at *The Desire and Pursuit of the Whole*, a homo-erotic fantasy published posthumously in 1934. In it were poison-pen sketches of all those in Venice whom he felt had slighted him, under invented names admittedly but easily recognisable to those in the know. Little wonder, then, that when Rolfe died in 1913, he was friendless and broke, and ended up in a pauper's grave on the island of San Michele.

EXPLORE

Piedàterre

San Polo 60, sottoportego degli Orafi (041 528 5513, www.piedaterre-venice.com). Vaporetto Rialto or Rialto Mercato. **Open** 10am-12.30pm, 2.30-7.30pm Mon.Sat. **Map** p115 H4 ⓫ **Shoes** Furlane (or *friulane*) are those traditional slipper-like shoes that you'll see on the feet of many gondoliers. In this little shop at the foot of the Rialto bridge, brilliantly coloured bundles of them line the walls. The design is traditional, as is the use of recycled materials such as old tyres to make the soles. But the colours and textiles are eye-catchingly mod. There are shoes here for adults and children.

WEST FROM THE RIALTO

Vaporetto Rialto, Rialto Mercato, San Silvestro or San Tomà.

The route to campo San Polo traverses a series of busy shopping streets, passing the church of **San Giovanni Elemosinario** (*see p119*) and the deconsecrated church of **Sant'Aponal**, which has fine Gothic sculpture on its façade. To the south of this route, towards the Grand Canal, stands **San Silvestro** (*see p119*), with a good Tintoretto, while to the north is a fascinating network of quiet, little-visited alleys and courtyards.

Curiosities worth seeking out (take calle Bianca Cappello from campo Sant'Aponal) include **Palazzo Molin-Cappello**, birthplace of Bianca Cappello, who in 1563 was sentenced to death *in absentia* for eloping with a bank clerk but managed to right things between herself and the Most Serene Republic by later marrying Francesco de' Medici, Grand Duke of Tuscany. North-westwards from here is campiello Albrizzi, overlooked by **Palazzo Albrizzi**, with its sumptuous Baroque interior (unfortunately, it's closed to the public).

After the shadowy closeness of these *calli*, the open expanse of campo **San Polo** – home to the church (*see p119*) of the same name – comes as a sudden, sunlit surprise. This is the largest square on this side of the Grand Canal and, in the past, was used for popular occasions such as bull-baiting, religious ceremonies, parades and theatrical spectacles. Now the venue for an open-air film season (*see p184*) in the summer and a skating rink in the winter, its main day-to-day function for much of the year is that of a vast children's playground.

The curving line of *palazzi* on the east side of the square is explained by the fact that these buildings once gave on to a canal, which was subsequently filled in. The two *palazzi* Soranzo (nos.2169 and 2170-1) are particularly attractive Gothic buildings, with marble facing and good

capitals. In the north-west corner is a view of **Palazzo Corner** (the main façade is on rio di San Polo), a 16th-century design by Sanmicheli. Novelist Frederick Rolfe stayed here – until his hosts read the manuscript of his work, *The Desire and Pursuit of the Whole* (1909), which contained vitriolic pen-portraits of their friends. They turned him out of the house, thus earning a place for themselves too in this grudge novel.

From the south-west of the squar, salizada di San Polo leads to Palazzo Centani, the birthplace of Carlo Gondoli, the prolific Venetian playwright, which contains a small museum and library: the Casa di Carlo Goldoni (*see below*).

Sights & Museums

Casa di Carlo Goldoni

San Polo 2794, calle dei Nomboli (041 275 9325, www.visitmuve.it). Vaporetto San Tomà. **Open** 10am-5pm Mon, Tue, Thur-Sun. **Admission** €5; €3.50 reductions (*see also p53* **Museum passes**). **No credit cards. Map** p115 E5 ⓬ Officially the Casa di Goldoni e Biblioteca di Studi Teatrali (Goldoni's House and Library of Theatre Studies), this museum is really for specialists, though the attractive Gothic courtyard, with its carved well-head and staircase, is worth seeing. It is the birthplace of Venice's greatest writer, the playwright Carlo Goldoni. Over the course of his career, he transformed Italian theatre, moving it away from the clichés of the *Commedia dell'arte* tradition and introducing a comedy based on realistic observation. On the first floor, there are reproductions of prints based on Goldoni's works and a few 18th-century paintings; however, the best item is a splendid 18th-century miniature theatre

Palazzo Albrizzi.

complete with puppets of *Commedia dell'arte* figures. The library on the upper floor has theatrical texts and original manuscripts.

San Giovanni Elemosinario
San Polo, ruga vecchia San Giovanni (041 275 0462, www.chorusvenezia.org). Vaporetto Rialto, Rialto Mercato or San Silvestro. **Open** 10am-5pm Mon-Sat. **Admission** €3 (or Chorus; *see p89*). **No credit cards. Map** p115 G4 ⑬
This small Renaissance church – a Greek cross within a square – was founded in the ninth or tenth century but rebuilt after a fire in 1514, probably to a design by Scarpagnino. On the high altar is a painting by Titian of the titular saint, *St John the Alms Giver*. In the left aisle is a medieval fragment of sculptural relief (12th or 13th century) of the Nativity, which shows an ox and donkey reverently licking the face of the Christ child.

San Polo
San Polo, campo San Polo (041 275 0462, www. chorusvenezia.org). Vaporetto San Silvestro or San Tomà. **Open** 10am-5pm Mon-Sat. **Admission** €3 (or Chorus; *see p89*). **No credit cards. Map** p115 E4 ⑭
The church of San Polo (Venetian for Paolo, or Paul) faces away from the square, towards the canal, although later buildings have deprived it of its façade and water entrance. The campanile (1362) has two 12th-century lions at the base, one brooding over a snake and the other toying with a human head, which Venetians like to think of as that of Count

Carmagnola, who was beheaded for treachery in 1402. The Gothic church was extensively altered in the 19th century, when a neoclassical look was imposed on it. Some of this was removed in 1930, but the interior remains a rather awkward hybrid.
Paintings include a *Last Supper* by Tintoretto, to the left of the entrance, and a Tiepolo: *The Virgin Appearing to St John of Nepomuk*. Giambattista Tiepolo's son, Giandomenico, is the author of a brilliant cycle of Stations of the Cross in the Oratory of the Crucifix (entrance is under the organ), freshly restored. He painted these, as well as the ceiling paintings, at the age of 20.

FREE San Silvestro
San Polo, campo San Silvestro (041 523 8090). Vaporetto San Silvestro. **Open** 7.30am-noon, 4-6pm Mon-Sat. Closed some afternoons. **Map** p115 G4 ⑮
The church of San Silvestro was rebuilt in the neoclassical style between 1837 and 1843. It contains a *Baptism of Christ* (c1580) by Tintoretto, located over the first altar on the right, with the river Jordan represented as a mountain brook. Opposite this is *St Thomas à Becket Enthroned* (1520) by Girolamo da Santacroce, with the saint in startling white robes against a mountain landscape; the other two saints are 19th-century additions. Off the right aisle (ask the sacristan to let you in) is the former School of the Wine Merchants; on the upper floor there's a chapel with 18th-century frescoes by Gaspare Diziani. Opposite the church is the house (no.1022) where the artist Giorgione died in 1510.

Restaurants

All'Amarone
San Polo 1131, calle del Luganegher (041 5223 1184, www.allamarone.com). Vaporetto Rialto Mercato or San Silvestro. **Meals served** 10am-10pm Mon, Tue, Thur-Sun. **Average** €40. **Map** p115 G4 ⑯
A recent addition to the Venetian eating and drinking scene, this low-key wine bar-restaurant has a friendly feel and a very interesting wine list. Run by an Italo-French couple, Amarone offers all the usual Venetian bar snacks, plus an à la carte menu for sit-down meals of well-prepared and reasonably priced pan-Italian staples, and some good salads for a healthy light lunch. The wine list leans heavily towards the north-east but also includes vintages from elsewhere in Italy, and some kosher wines too. If anything grabs your fancy, they'll organise a vertical tasting just for you.

Antiche Carampane
San Polo 1911, rio terà delle Carampane (041 524 0165, www.antichecarampane.com). Vaporetto San Silvestro. **Meals served** 12.30-2.30pm, 7.30-11pm Tue-Sat. Closed Aug. **Average** €60. **Map** p115 F4 ⑰

EXPLORE

Fiendishly difficult to find, Antiche Carampane is a Venetian classic but be warned: there are a lot of tables packed into a very small space so don't expect privacy; and demand is so great that there are two evening sittings – at 7.30pm and 9.30pm – arrive later than you booked for and your table will be given away. What eager diners pile in here for is fine (though not cheap) seafood that goes beyond the ubiquitous standards with recherché local specialities such as *spaghetti in cassopipa* (a spicy sauce of shellfish and crustaceans). Leave room for an unbeatable *fritto misto* (mixed seafood fry-up) and their delicious desserts. Inside is cosy; outside is better.

Birraria La Corte

San Polo 2168, campo San Polo (041 275 0570, www.birrarialacorte.it). Vaporetto San Silvestro or San Tomà. **Meals served** noon-2.30pm, 6-10.30pm daily. **Average** *Pizzeria* €20. *Full meal* €35. **Map** p115 E4 ⑬ **Pizzeria**
The outside tables of this huge, no-nonsense pizzeria are a great place to observe life in the campo – and a boon for parents with small children, who can chase pigeons while mum and dad tuck into a decent pizza. The restaurant occupies a former brewery, and beer still takes pride of place over wine. There's also a regular menu with decent pasta options and some good grilled-meat *secondi*.

Da Ignazio

San Polo 2749, calle dei Saoneri (041 523 4852). Vaporetto San Tomà. **Meals served** noon-3pm, 7-10pm Mon-Fri, Sun. **Average** €50. **Map** p115 E5 ⑲
The big attraction of this tranquil, no-frills, neighbourhood restaurant is its pretty, pergola-shaded courtyard. The cooking is safe, traditional Venetian: mixed seafood *antipasti* might be followed by a good rendition of *spaghetti con caparossoli* or *risi e bisi* (risotto with peas), and grilled fish *secondi*.

Cafés, Bars & Gelaterie

Bar ai Nomboli

San Polo 2717C, rio terà dei Nomboli (041 523 0995). Vaporetto San Tomà. **Open** 7am-9pm Mon-Fri. Closed 3wks Aug. **No credit cards**. **Map** p115 E5 ⑳
This bar, much loved by Venice's students, has expanded its already impressive repertoire of sandwich combinations to more than 100 sandwiches and almost 50 *tramezzini*: try the 'Serenissima' with tuna, peppers, peas and onions or perhaps the 'Appennino' with roast beef, broccoli and pecorino – or ask them to build your own creation with their fresh ingredients.

★ Caffè del Doge

San Polo 609, calle dei Cinque (041 522 7787, www.caffedeldoge.com). Vaporetto Rialto Mercato or San Silvestro. **Open** 7am-7pm Mon-Sat; 7am-1pm Sun. **No credit cards**. **Map** p115 G4 ㉑

Italians scoff at the idea of drinking cappuccino after 11am, but rules like this go by the board at the Caffè del Doge, where any time is good for indulging in the richest, creamiest, most luscious cup of coffee in Venice. Two signature blends and a variety of single-origin coffees are available to consume or purchase. Don't overlook the pastries, and watch out for the speciality coffees.

Rizzardini

San Polo 1415, campiello dei Meloni (041 522 3835). Vaporetto San Silvestro. **Open** 7am-8.30pm Mon, Wed-Sun. Closed Aug. **No credit cards**. **Map** p115 F4 ㉒
An eye-catching *pasticceria* with pastries, cookies and snacks to go with your *caffè*, cappuccino or *aperitivo*. When owner Paolo is behind the bar, there's never a dull moment. It's especially good for traditional Venetian pastries, cookies, coffee, *frittelle* during Carnevale… anything, if you can manoeuvre up to the counter and place your order.

Shops & Services

★ Aliani Gastronomia

San Polo 654, ruga Rialto/ruga vecchia San Giovanni (041 522 4913). Vaporetto Rialto Mercato or San Silvestro. **Open** 8am-1pm, 5-7.30pm Tue-Sat. **Map** p115 G4 ㉓ **Food & drink**
This traditional family grocery stocks a selection of cold meats and cheeses from every part of Italy, plus an assortment of prepared dishes and roast meats.

Atelier Pietro Longhi

San Polo 2608, rio terà dei Frari (041 714 478, www.pietrolonghi.com). Vaporetto San Tomà. **Open** 9am-1pm, 2-6pm Mon-Fri. **Map** p115 E4 ㉔ **Costumes**
This atelier makes exquisite period costumes and accessories for rent or purchase. Prices vary greatly, but renting something simple will cost about €160 for the first day, and less for subsequent days. The atelier also organises private events and stages historical re-enactments, details of which are on their site. They'll send costumes all over the world.

Il Bottegon

San Polo 806, calle del Figher (041 522 3632). Vaporetto San Silvestro. **Open** 9am-12.45pm, 4-7.30pm Mon-Sat. **Map** p115 G4 **Homewares** ㉕
Il Bottegon is one of those everything-you-could-possibly-need/want shops that are so rare these days: crammed into this tiny space are cosmetics and toiletries, pots, pans, rugs and general hardware. If you don't see what you're looking for, ask: they'll probably pull it out from somewhere.

Francis Model

San Polo 773A, ruga Rialto/ruga del Ravano (041 521 2889). Vaporetto Rialto Mercato

Tragicomica.

or San Silvestro. **Open** 10am-7pm daily.
Map p115 G4 ㉖ **Accessories**
Beautifully coloured and crafted handbags, belts
and briefcases are produced by hand in this tiny *bottega* by a father-and-son team.

Gilberto Penzo
*San Polo 2681, calle II dei Saoneri (041 719
372, www.veniceboats.com). Vaporetto San
Tomà.* **Open** 8.30am-12.30pm, 3-6pm Mon-Sat.
Map p115 E5 ㉗ **Model boats**
Gilberto Penzo creates astonishingly detailed
models of gondolas, sandolos, topos and *vaporetti*.
Inexpensive kits are also on sale – if you would like
to practise the fine art of shipbuilding yourself.

Sabbie e Nebbie
*San Polo 2768A, calle dei Nomboli (041 719
073). Vaporetto San Tomà.* **Open** 10am-
12.30pm, 4-7.30pm Mon-Sat. Map p115 E5 ㉘
Homewares
A beautiful selection of Italian ceramic pieces are
on display here, as well as refined Japanese works.
The shop also sells handmade objects (such as
lamps and candlesticks) by Italian designers.

Tragicomica
*San Polo 2800, calle dei Nomboli (041 721 102,
www.tragicomica.it). Vaporetto San Tomà.* **Open**
10am-7pm daily. Map p115 E5 ㉙ **Masks**
A spellbinding collection of masks: mythological
subjects, Harlequins, Columbines and Pantaloons, as
well as 18th-century dandies and ladies.

ZaZú
*San Polo 2750, calle dei Saoneri (041 715 426).
Vaporetto San Tomà.* **Open** 9.30am-1.30pm,
2.30-7.30pm Mon-Sat. Map p115 E5 ㉚ **Fashion/
jewellery**
This brilliantly coloured store has clothing and jewels from the East that are very wearable in the West.
There are handbags and other accessories as well.

NORTH-WEST FROM THE RIALTO
*Vaporetto Ferrovia, Rialto Mercato, Riva
di Biasio or San Stae.*

Yellow signs pointing to 'Ferrovia' mark the
zigzagging north-western route from the Rialto,
past the fish market, and on past campo **San
Cassiano**. The uninspiring plain exterior of
the church here (*see p123*) gives no clue as to
its heavily decorated interior.

Across the bridge is campo **Santa Maria
Mater Domini** with its Renaissance church
(*see p124*). Before entering the campo, stop
on the bridge to admire the view of the curving
Grand Canal-facing marble flank of **Ca' Pesaro**
(*see 122*), the seat of the **Museo Orientale** and
Galleria d'Arte Moderna. On the far side of
the square, which contains a number of fine
Byzantine and Gothic buildings, the yellow
road sign indicates that the way to the station
is to the left *and* to the right. Take your pick.

The quieter route to the right curls parallel
to the Grand Canal. The road towards Ca'
Pesaro passes **Palazzo Agnusdio**, a small
14th-century house with an ogival five-light
window decorated with bas-reliefs of the
Annunciation and symbols of the evangelists;
the house used to belong to a family of sausage-
makers, who were given patrician status in the
17th century.

Many of the most important sights face on
to the Grand Canal, including the 18th-century
church of **San Stae** (*see p124*) and the Fondaco
dei Turchi (Warehouse of the Turks), home to
the **Museo di Storia Naturale** (*see p122*).

On the wide road leading towards San Stae
is **Palazzo Mocenigo** (*see p122*), with its
collection of perfumes, textiles and costumes.
Nearby is the quiet square of San Zan Degolà
(**San Giovanni Decollato**), with a well-
preserved 11th-century church (*see p123*).
From here, a series of narrow roads leads
past the church of **San Simeone Profeta**
(*see p124*) to the foot of the Scalzi bridge
across the Grand Canal.

Leave campo Santa Maria Mater Domini
by the route to the left, on the other hand, and
you'll make your way past the near-legendary
Da Fiore restaurant (*see p125*) to the house
(no. 2311) where Aldus Manutius set up the
Aldine Press in 1490, and where the humanist
Erasmus came to stay in 1508. To the right, by
a building with a 14th-century relief of Faith
and Justice above its doorway, the rio terà del
Parrucchetta (reportedly named after a seller
of animal fodder who used to wear a ridiculous
wig, or *parrucca*) leads to the large leafy campo
San Giacomo dell'Orio (*see p123*). The
campo (which translates as St James of the

EXPLORE

wolf, the laurel tree, the rio or the Orio family – take your pick) has a pleasantly downbeat feel, with its trees, bars and children. It's dominated by the church with its plump apses and stocky 13th-century campanile. The church has its back and sides to the square; the main entrance was directly from the water.

Sights & Museums

Ca' Pesaro – Galleria Internazionale d'Arte Moderna

Santa Croce 2076, fondamenta Ca' Pesaro (041 524 0695, www.visitmuve.it). Vaporetto San Stae. **Open** 10am-5pm Tue-Sun. **Admission** (incl Museo Orientale) €10.50; €8 reductions; *see also p53* **Museum Passes**. **Map** p115 F2 ③①
This grandiose palazzo was built in the second half of the 17th century for the Pesaro family, to a project by Baldassare Longhena. When Longhena died in 1682, the family called in Gian Antonio Gaspari, who finished it in 1710. The interior of the palazzo still contains some of the original fresco and oil-painted decorations, although the family's great collection of Renaissance paintings was auctioned off in London by the last Pesaro before he died in 1830.

The palazzo passed through many hands until its last owner, Felicita Bevilacqua La Masa, bequeathed it to the city. Into it went the city's collection of modern art, gleaned from the Biennale (*see p31*). The museum now covers a century of mainly Italian art, from the mid 19th century to the 1950s. The stately ground floor is used for temporary shows. At the foot of the staircase stands Giacomo Manzù's tapering bronze statue, *Cardinal*.

The first rooms on the *piano nobile* contain atmospheric works by 19th-century painters and some striking sculptures by Medardo Rosso. In the central hall are works from the early *Biennali* (up to the 1930s), including pieces by Gustav Klimt and Vassily Kandinsky, alongside more conventional, vast-scale 'salon' paintings. Room 4 holds works by Giorgio Morandi, Joan Mirò and Giorgio De Chirico. After rooms devoted to international art from the 1940s and '50s, the collection finishes up with works by notable post-war Venetian experimentalists such as Armando Pizzinato, Giuseppe Santomaso and Emilio Vedova.

Ca' Pesaro – Museo Orientale

Santa Croce 2070, fondamenta Ca' Pesaro (041 524 1173, www.visitmuve.it). Vaporetto San Stae. **Open** 10am-5pm Tue-Sun. **Admission** (incl Galleria d'Arte Moderna) €10.50; €8 reductions; *see also p53* **Museum Passes. Map** p115 F2 ③②
If Japanese art and weaponry of the Edo period (1600-1868) are your thing, you'll love this eclectic collection, put together by Count Enrico di Borbone – a nephew of Louis XVIII – in the course of a round-the-world voyage between 1887 and 1890. After the count's death, the collection was sold off

to an Austrian antique merchant; it bounced back to Venice after World War I as reparations.

The collection features parade armour, dolls, decorative saddles and case upon case of curved samurai swords forged by smiths who had to perform a ritual act of purification before putting their irons in the fire. There is also a dwarf-sized lady's gilded litter, and lacquered picnic cases that prove that the Japanese obsession with compactness indeed pre-dates the Sony Walkman.

Museo di Storia Naturale

Santa Croce 1730, salizada del Fondaco dei Turchi (041 275 0206, www.visitmuve.it). Vaporetto San Stae. **Open** 10am-6pm Tue-Sun. **Admission** €8; €5.50 reductions; *see also p53* **Museum Pass. Map** p115 E2 ③③
After many years of very leisurely restoration, this museum in the Fondaco dei Turchi, a Venetian-Byzantine building leased to the Turks in the 17th century as a residence and warehouse, is now back in business and looking rather fine. The Acquario delle Tegnue is devoted to the aquatic life of the northern Adriatic, and the Sala dei Dinosauri contains a state-of-the-art exhibition chronicling the Ligabue expedition to Niger (1973), which unearthed a fossil of the previously unknown *Auronosaurus nigeriensis* and a giant crocodile. With vast storerooms holding some two million items from scientific collections put together over the centuries – as well as teams of restorers making sure that time doesn't take too much of a toll on their precious artefacts – this museum is a hive of scientific activity.

Palazzo Mocenigo

Santa Croce 1992, salizada San Stae (041 721 798, www.visitmuve.it). Vaporetto San Stae. **Open** 10am-4pm Tue-Sun. **Admission** €8; €5.50 reductions (*see also p53* **Museum Passes**). **No credit cards. Map** p115 F2 ③④
Reopened late in 2013 after a major makeover, Palazzo Mocenigo is now a rather splendid showcase for life of the aristocracy in 18th-century Venice. Already extant in an earlier form by 1500, this predominantly 17th-century palazzo was the home of the Mocenigo family, which provided the Republic with seven doges; the paintings, friezes and frescoes by late 18th-century artists such as Jacopo Guarana and Gian Battista Canal glorify their achievements. A collection of period costumes – including an andrienne dress with bustles so horizontal you could rest a cup and saucer on them, antique lace and silk stockings, and a whalebone corset – are displayed among fine furniture and fittings, in rooms with walls now covered with exquisite Rubelli (*see p57* **Material Makers**) reproductions of the original fabrics.

Added to the museum during the recent restoration is a fascinating section on perfumes and perfumery, with intriguing essences in lovely glass jars to explore and sniff.

San Giacomo dell'Orio.

FREE San Cassiano

San Polo, campo San Cassiano (041 721 408).
Vaporetto Rialto Mercato or San Stae. **Open** 9am-
noon, 5-7.30pm Mon-Sat. **Map** p115 F3 ㉟
This church has a singularly dull exterior and a
heavily decorated interior, with a striking ceiling
(which has been freshly restored) by the Tiepolesque
painter Constantino Cedini.

The chancel contains three major Tintorettos:
Crucifixion, Resurrection and *Descent into Limbo.*
The *Crucifixion* is particularly interesting for its
viewpoint. As Ruskin puts it, 'The horizon is so low,
that the spectator must fancy himself lying full
length on the grass, or rather among the brambles
and luxuriant weeds, of which the foreground is
entirely composed.' In the background, the soldiers'
spears make a menacing forest against a dramatic
stormy sky. Off the left aisle is a small chapel with
coloured marbles and inlays of semi-precious stones.

On the wall opposite the altar is a painting by
Antonio Balestra, which at first glance looks like a
dying saint surrounded by *putti.* On closer inspection
it transpires that the chubby children are, in fact,
hacking the man to death: the painting represents
The Martyrdom of St Cassian, a teacher who was
murdered by his pupils with their pens. This, of
course, makes him the patron saint of schoolteachers.

★ San Giacomo dell'Orio

Santa Croce, campo San Giacomo dell'Orio
(041 275 0462, www.chorusvenezia.org).
Vaporetto Riva di Biasio. **Open** 10am-5pm
Mon-Sat. **Admission** €3 (or Chorus; *see p89*).
No credit cards. Map p114 D3 ㊱
The main entrance of San Giacomo dell'Orio faces
the canal rather than the campo. The interior is a
fascinating mix of architectural and decorative
styles. Most of the columns have 12th- or 13th-cen-
tury Veneto-Byzantine capitals; one has a sixth-
century flowered capital and one is a solid piece of
smooth verd-antique marble, perhaps from a
Roman temple sacked during the Fourth Crusade.

Note, too, the fine 14th-century ship's-keel roof. The
Sacrestia Nuova, in the right transept, was built in
1903 on the site of the Scuola del Sacramento. This
was the original home of the five gilded compartments on the ceiling with paintings by Veronese:
an *Allegory of the Faith* surrounded by four Doctors
of the Church. Among the paintings in the room
is *St John the Baptist Preaching* by Francesco
Bassano, which includes a portrait of Titian (in
the red hat).

Behind the high altar is a *Madonna and Four
Saints* by Lorenzo Lotto, one of his last Venetian
paintings. There is a good work by Giovanni
Bonconsiglio at the end of the left aisle, *St Lawrence,
St Sebastian and St Roch*; St Roch's plague sore
has an anatomical precision that is really rather
unsettling. St Lawrence also has a chapel all to
himself in the left transept, with a central altarpiece
by Veronese and two fine early works by Palma il
Giovane. As you leave, be sure to have a look at the
curious painting to the left of the main door, a naïve
18th-century work by Gaetano Zompini, showing
a propaganda miracle involving a Jewish scribe
who attempted to profane the body of the Virgin on
its way to the sepulchre.

FREE San Giovanni Decollato
(San Zan Degolà)

Santa Croce, campo San Giovanni Decollato
(041 524 0672). Vaporetto Riva di Biasio.
Open 10am-noon Mon-Sat. **Map** p115 E2 ㊲
The church of Headless Saint John – or San Zan
Degolà in Venetian dialect – is a good building to visit
if you want a relief from the usual Baroque excesses
and ecclesiastic clutter. Restored and reopened in
1994, it preserves much of its original 11th-century
appearance. The church's interior has Greek columns
with Byzantine capitals supporting ogival arches, and
an attractive ship's-keel roof. During the restoration,
a splendidly heroic 14th-century fresco of St Michael
the Archangel came to light in the right apse. The left
apse has some of the earliest frescoes in Venice,

EXPLORE

Veneto-Byzantine works of the early 13th century. The church is used for Russian Orthodox services.

FREE San Simeone Profeta

Santa Croce, campo San Simeone Profeta (041 718 921). Vaporetto Ferrovia. **Open** 9am-noon, 5-6.30pm Mon-Sat. **Map** p114 C2 ⑱
More usually known as San Simeone Grande, this small church of possibly tenth-century foundation underwent numerous alterations in the 18th century. The interior retains its ancient columns with Byzantine capitals. To the left of the entrance is Tintoretto's *Last Supper*, with the priest who commissioned the painting standing to one side, a spectral figure in glowing white robes. The other major work is the stark, powerful statue of a recumbent St Simeon, with an inscription dated 1317 attributing it to an otherwise unknown Marco Romano. The prophet has a 'face full of quietness and majesty, though very ghastly,' as Ruskin puts it. Outside, beneath the portico flanking the church, is a fine 15th-century relief of a bishop praying.

San Stae

Santa Croce, campo San Stae (041 275 0462, www.chorusvenezia.org). Vaporetto San Stae. **Open** 10am-5pm Mon-Sat. **Admission** €3 (or Chorus; *see p89*). **No credit cards. Map** p115 F2 ㊙
Stae is the Venetian version of Eustachio or Eustace, a martyred saint who was converted to Christianity by the vision of a stag with a crucifix between its antlers. This church on the Grand Canal has a dramatic late-Baroque façade (1709) by Swiss-born architect Domenico Rossi. The form is essentially Palladian but enlivened by a number of vibrant sculptures, some apparently on the point of leaping straight out of the façade. Venice's last great blaze of artistic glory came in the 18th century, and the interior is a temple to this swansong. On the side walls of the chancel, all the leading painters operating in Venice in 1722 were asked to pick an apostle. The finest of these are: Tiepolo's *Martyrdom of St Bartholomew* and Sebastiano Ricci's *Liberation of St Peter*, perhaps his best work (both left wall, lower row); Pellegrini's *Martyrdom of St Andrew* and Piazzetta's *Martyrdom of St James*, a disturbingly realistic work showing the saint as a confused old man in the hands of a loutish youth (both right wall, lower row).

FREE Santa Maria Mater Domini

Santa Croce, calle della Chiesa (041 721 408). Vaporetto San Stae. **Open** 10am-noon daily. **Map** p115 F3 ㊵
This church is set just off the campo of the same name. It was built in the first half of the 16th century to a commission by either Giovanni Buora or Maurizio Codussi. The façade is attributed to Jacopo Sansovino; the harmonious Renaissance interior alternates grey stone with white marble. The *Vision of St Christine*, on the second altar on

the right, is by Vincenzo Catena, a spice merchant who painted in his spare time. St Christine was rescued by angels after being thrown into Lake Bolsena with a millstone tied around her neck; in the painting she adores the Risen Christ, while angels hold up the millstone for her. In the left transept hangs *The Invention of the Cross*, a youthful work by Tintoretto.

Restaurants

€ Al Nono Risorto

Santa Croce 2338, sottoportico di Siora Bettina (041 524 1169). Vaporetto San Stae. **Meals served** noon-2.30pm, 7-11pm Mon, Tue, Fri-Sun; 7-11pm Thur. **Average** *Pizzeria* €18. *Full meal* €35. **No credit cards. Map** p115 F3 ㊶ **Pizzeria**
You don't come to this spit and sawdust trattoria-pizzeria for culinary excellence, but if you're looking for a pleasant courtyard in which to sit among noisy diners tucking into decent pizzas, then it might be for you. It also does traditional Venetian trattoria fare, at traditional Venetian trattoria prices.

★ € Alla Zucca

Santa Croce 1762, ponte del Megio (041 524 1570, www.lazucca.it). Vaporetto San Stae. **Meals served** 12.30-2.30pm, 7-10.30pm Mon-Sat. **Average** €30. **Map** p115 E2 ㊷
One of Venice's first 'alternative' trattorias and still one of the best – not to mention one of the best-value. By a pretty bridge, the vegetarian-friendly Pumpkin offers a break from all that seafood. The menu is equally divided between meat (ginger pork with pilau rice) and vegetables (pumpkin and seasoned ricotta quiche). Always book ahead, especially in summer for one of the few outside tables.

Vecio Fritolin.

★ Da Fiore

San Polo 2202, calle del Scaleter (041 721 308, www.dafiore.net). Vaporetto San Stae or San Tomà. **Meals served** 7.30-10.30pm Mon; 12.30-2.30pm, 7.30-10.30pm Tue-Sat. **Average** €110. *Set lunch* €50. **Map** p115 E3 ⑬

Michelin-starred Da Fiore is considered by many to be Venice's best restaurant. Host Maurizio Martin treats his guests with egalitarian courtesy, while his wife Mara concentrates on getting the food right. Raw fish and seafood is a key feature of the *antipasti*; *primi* are equally divided between pasta dishes and a series of faultless risottos. *Secondi* are all about bringing out the flavour of the fish without smothering it in sauce. It's a classic, rather than a superlative, dining experience; but that's Venice for you. There's a choice of €50 set lunch menus, and taster menus at €120 and €140 in the evening.

Il Refolo

Santa Croce 1459, campiello del Piovan (041 524 0016, www.nardini.it). Vaporetto Riva di Biasio or San Stae. **Map** p114 D2 ㉔ **Pizzeria**

Until spring 2014 this was the gourmet pizza off-shoot of the Michelin-starred Da Fiore restaurant. Then the premises passed to Nardini (*see p228*), the grappa producer from Bassano. Precisely what it will become is anybody's guess but it's pretty certain that it will be a high-profile showcase for this ancient firm... and that grappa will feature somehow. A tiny indoor space with tables out on a gorgeous lively campo, the location already makes it a hit.

Vecio Fritolin

Santa Croce 2262, calle della Regina (041 522 2881, www.veciofritolin.it). Vaporetto San Stae. **Meals served** 7-10.30pm Tue; noon-2.30pm, 7-10.30pm Wed-Sun. **Average** €55. **Map** p115 F3 ㊺

Wooden beams, sturdy tables and the long bar at the back of the main dining room set the mood in this old-style *bacaro*. But the seasonally-changing menu is more creative than the decor might lead you to expect, with dishes such as cocoa tagliatelle with squid, or a main course of turbot in a crust of black rice with sautéed baby artichokes.

Cafés, Bars & Gelaterie

★ Alaska Gelateria-Sorbetteria

Santa Croce 1159, calle larga dei Bari (041 715 211). Vaporetto Riva de Biasio. **Open** *Apr-Oct* 11am-midnight daily. *Feb-Mar & Nov* noon-9pm daily. Closed Dec-Jan. **No credit cards.** **Map** p114 D2 ㊻

The jury is out about Alaska's gelato: some find the fruit flavours insufficiently creamy, others object to the fact that novelty flavours (celery anyone?) are hardly sweet. But to those who appreciate the eccentricities, Carlo Pistacchi's ice-cream is some of

Venice's best. There are tried and true choices such as hazelnut, pistachio or yoghurt, or seasonally changing exotic flavours, such as artichoke, fennel, asparagus or ginger.

Al Prosecco

Santa Croce 1503, campo San Giacomo dell'Orio (041 524 0222, www.alprosecco.com). Vaporetto San Stae. **Open** 9am-10pm Mon-Sat. **Map** p115 E2 ㊼

Prosecco – whether sparkling or still (aka *spento*) – is second only to *spritz* in terms of daily Venetian consumption, and (as the name suggests) this bar is a good place for consuming it. But you can also drop by here for morning coffee or a light lunch. The shaded outside tables are a fantastic vantage point for observing daily life in a lively campo, but the interior is just as convivial on cool days. Exceptional wines are served by the glass, accompanied by a first-rate choice of cheeses, cold meats, marinated fish and oysters. Closes around 8pm in winter.

Majer

Santa Croce 1658, campo San Giacomo dell'Orio (041 710 677, www.majer.it). Vaporetto San Stae. **Open** 7.30am-10pm daily. **Map** p115 E2 ㊽

Everywhere you look in Venice, a sleek new branch of this hyperactive café-store seems to be luring passersby in with the perfume of freshly made cornetti and loaves: there's another on this same campo at number 1630. Most of the outlets (see below) have tables at which to consume an excellent cappuccino with one of their delicious pastries. Most also serve light lunches and snacks throughout the day. But there's also wine, bread, cakes and their own-brand coffee to take away.

Other locations Santa Croce 287A, fondamenta Pagan (041 710 836); Santa Croce 1906, salizada Carminati (041 524 6762); San Polo 2307, campiello Sant'Agostin (041 722 873); Dorsoduro 3108D, rio terà Canal (041 528 9014); Castello 1591, via Garibaldi (041 528 9014); Cannaregio 1227, calle Ghetto Vecchio (041 523 0820).

Shops & Services

See also above **Majer**.

Laberintho

San Polo 2236, calle del Scaleter (041 710 017, www.laberintho.it). Vaporetto San Stae or San Tomà. **Open** 10.30am-1pm, 3-6.30pm Mon, Sat; 9.15am-1pm, 3-7.15pm Tue-Fri. **Map** p115 E3 ㊾ **Jewellery**

The pair of goldsmiths who work in this tiny *bottega* produce startling retro and contemporary designs in gold plus some (slightly less expensive lines) in silver. In addition to the one-of-a-kind rings, earrings and necklaces on display, they will produce made-to-order pieces.

EXPLORE

Monica Daniele

*San Polo 2235, calle Scaleter (041 524 6242,
www.monicadaniele.com). Vaporetto San Silvestro
or San Stae.* **Open** *9am-1pm, 2.30-6pm Mon-Sat.*
Map p115 E3 **⑩** **Fashion**
Monica Daniele has single-handedly brought the
tabarro – that sweeping cloak seen in many an 18th-
century Venetian print – back into vogue: a heavy
woollen one will cost €500 or more. But this odd little
shop also has a range of hats, from panamas to stylish creations by the shop's owner.

Rialto Biocenter

*San Polo 2264, calle della Regina (041 523 9515,
www.rialtobiocenter.it). Vaporetto Rialto Mercato
or San Stae.* **Open** *8.30am-1pm, 4.30-8pm Mon-
Thur; 8.30am-8pm Fri, Sat.* **Map** p115 E3 **⑪** **Food
& drink**
A little bit of just about everything can be found in
this health food shop, from wholemeal pasta,
grains, honey and freshly baked breads to natural
cosmetics and incense. Now in larger premises,
they also offer a wide range of organic fruit and
veg, dairy produce, lactose-free ice-creams and sul-
phite-free wine.

FROM THE FRARI TO PIAZZALE ROMA

Vaporetto Piazzale Roma or San Tomà.

At the heart of the western side of the two
sestieri of San Polo and Santa Croce lies the
great gothic bulk of Santa Maria Gloriosa
dei Frari (aka **I Frari**; *see right*), with its
70-metre (230-foot) campanile, matched by
the Renaissance magnificence of the *scuola*
and church of San Rocco. These buildings
contain perhaps the greatest concentration
of influential works of art in the city outside
piazza San Marco and the Accademia (*see p145*).

Beyond the Frari's convent – which houses
Venice's historic archives (*see p128* **In the
Know**) – is the **Scuola di San Giovanni
Evangelista** (*see p128*), one of the six *scuole
grandi* (*see p129* **Scuole Stories**).

North of here runs rio Marin, a canal with
fondamente on both sides, lined by some fine
buildings; these include the late 16th-century
Palazzo Soranzo Capello (no.770), with a
small rear garden that figures in Henry James'
The Aspern Papers; and the 17th-century
Palazzo Gradenigo, (no.768) the garden of
which was once large enough to host bullfights.

South-west of the Frari is the quiet square
of **San Tomà**, with a church on one side and
the **Scuola dei Calegheri** ('of the cobblers')
opposite; the *scuola* (now a library) has a
protective mantle-spreading Madonna over the
door. Above it is a relief by Pietro Lombardo of
St Mark Healing the Cobbler Annanius, who

became bishop of Alexandria and subsequently
the patron saint of shoemakers.

Heading west from the Frari, the route leads
past the **church** and **scuola** of **San Rocco**
(*see p128 and p129*), both treasure troves for
Tintoretto-lovers, and ends up in a fairly bland
area of 19th-century housing. At the edge of
this stands the Baroque church of **San Nicolò
dei Tolentini** (*see p128*); the adjoining former
monastery houses part of the Venice University
Architecture Institute.

The rather forlorn **Giardino Papadopoli**,
a small park with Grand Canal views, stands
on the site of the church and convent of Santa
Croce. The name survives as that of the
sestiere, but the church is one of many
suppressed by the French at the beginning
of the 19th century. All that remains of Santa
Croce is a crenellated wall next to a hotel
on the Grand Canal. The garden was much
larger until the rio Novo was cut in 1932-33
to provide faster access from the new car park
to the St Mark's area. The canal subsequently
had to be closed to regular waterborne traffic,
in the early 1990s, owing to subsidence in the
adjacent buildings.

Beyond the garden there is little but the
carbon-monoxide kingdom of piazzale Roma
and the multi-storey car parks. One last
curiosity is the complex of bridges across the
rio Novo known as Tre Ponti (three bridges);
there are, in fact, five interlocking bridges.

Sights & Museums

★ I Frari

*San Polo, campo dei Frari (041 522 2637,
www.chorusvenezia.org). Vaporetto San Tomà.*
Open *9am-6pm Mon-Sat; 1-6pm Sun.* **Admission**
€3 (or Chorus; *see p89*). **No credit cards.**
Map p114 D4 **⑫**
A gloomy Gothic barn, the brick house of God
known officially as Santa Maria Gloriosa dei Frari
is one of the city's most significant artistic store-
houses. The Franciscans were granted the land in
about 1250 and completed a first church in 1338.
At this point they changed their minds and started
work on a larger building, which was finally completed just over a century later. The church is 98m
(320ft) long, 48m (158ft) wide at the transept and
28m (92ft) high – just slightly smaller than the
Dominicans' Santi Giovanni e Paolo (*see p79*) –
and has the second highest campanile in the city.
And while the Frari may not have as many dead
doges as its Dominican rival, it undoubtedly has
the artistic edge. This is one church where the
entrance fee is not a recent imposition: tourists
have been paying to get into the Frari for over a
century. At the entrance you are brought face to
face with the long sweep of church with Titian's
glorious *Assumption* above the high altar.

Chancel

The high altar is dominated by Titian's *Assumption*, a work that seems to open the church up to the heavens. In the golden haze encircling God the Father, there may be a reminiscence of the mosaic tradition of Venice. The upward-soaring movement of the painting may owe something to the Gothic architecture of the building, but the drama and grandeur of the work essentially herald the Baroque.

On the right wall of the chancel is the monument to Francesco Foscari, the saddest doge of all. The story of his forced resignation and death from heartbreak (1547) after the exile of his son Jacopo is recounted in Byron's *The Two Foscari*, which was turned into a particularly gloomy opera by Verdi. The left wall hosts one of the finest Renaissance tombs in Venice, the monument to Doge Niccolò Tron, by Antonio Rizzo (1473). This is the first ducal tomb in which the subject is upright; he sports a magnificent bushy beard grown as a sign of perpetual mourning after the death of his favourite son.

Monks' choir

In the centre of the nave stands the choir, with wooden stalls carved by Marco Cozzi (1468), inlaid with superb intarsia decoration. The choir screen is a mixture of Gothic work by Bartolomeo Bon and Renaissance elements by the Lombardi family.

Left transept

In the third chapel, with an altarpiece by Bartolomeo Vivarini and Marco Basaiti, a slab on the floor marks the grave of composer Claudio Monteverdi. The Corner chapel, at the end, contains a mannered statue of St John the Baptist by Sansovino; this sensitively wistful figure could hardly be more different from Donatello's work of a century earlier.

Left aisle

Another magnificent Titian hangs to the right of the side door: the *Madonna di Ca' Pesaro*. This work was commissioned by Bishop Jacopo Pesaro in 1519 and celebrates victory in a naval expedition against the Turks, led by the bellicose cleric in 1502. The bishop is kneeling and waiting for St Peter to introduce him and his family to the Madonna. Behind, an armoured warrior bearing a banner has Turkish prisoners in tow. This work revolutionised altar paintings in Venice. It wasn't just that Titian dared to move the Virgin from the centre of the composition to one side, using the splendid banner as a counterbalance; the real innovation was the rich humanity of the whole work, from the beautifully portrayed family (with the boy turning to stare straight at us) to the Christ child, so naturally active and alive, twisting away from his mother (said to be a portrait of Titian's wife) to gaze curiously at the saints clustered around him. The timeless 'sacred conversation' of Bellini's paintings here becomes animated, losing some of its sacredness but gaining in drama and realism.

Right aisle

In the second bay, on the spot where Titian is believed to be buried (the only victim of the 1575-76 plague who was allowed a city burial), is a loud monument to the artist, commissioned nearly 300 years after his death by the Emperor of Austria. On the third altar is a finer memorial, Alessandro Vittoria's statue of St Jerome, generally believed to be a portrait of his painter friend.

Right transept

To the right of the sacristy door is the tomb of the Blessed Pacifico (a companion of St Francis), attributed to Nanni di Bartolo and Michele da Firenze (1437); the sarcophagus is surrounded by a splendidly carved canopy in the florid Gothic style. The door itself is framed by Lorenzo Bregno's tomb of Benedetto Pesaro, a Venetian general who died in Corfu. To the left of the door is the first equestrian statue in Venice, the monument to Paolo Savelli (d.1405). The third chapel on the right side of this transept has an altarpiece by Bartolomeo Vivarini, in its original frame, while the Florentine Chapel, next to the chancel, contains the only work by Donatello in the city: a striking wooden statue of a stark, emaciated St John the Baptist.

Sacristy

Commissioned by the Pesaro family, this contains one of Giovanni Bellini's greatest paintings: the *Madonna and Child with Saints Nicholas, Peter, Benedict and Mark* (1488), still in its original frame. 'It seems painted with molten gems, which have been clarified by time,' wrote Henry James, his eye, as ever, firmly on the prose structure, 'and it is as solemn as it is gorgeous and as simple as it is deep.' Also in the sacristy is a fine Renaissance tabernacle, possibly by Tullio Lombardo, for a reliquary holding Christ's blood.

EXPLORE

IN THE KNOW
NOTHING THROWN AWAY

The monastery buildings of the **Frari** (*see p126*) contain the State Archives, a monument to Venetian reluctance ever to throw anything away. In 300 rooms, about 15 million volumes and files are conserved, starting from the year 883. Faced with such a daunting wealth of detailed information – from ambassadors' dispatches on foreign courts to spies' reports on noblemen's non-regulation cloaks – grown historians have been reduced to quivering wrecks.

The whole of the next bay, around the side door, is occupied by another piece of Pesaro propaganda – the mastodontic mausoleum of Doge Pesaro (d.1659), attributed to Longhena, with sculptures by Melchior Barthel of Dresden. Supporters of the Baroque have some difficulty defending this one, with its 'blackamoor' caryatids, bronze skeletons and posturing allegories.

The penultimate bay harbours a monument to Canova, carried out by his pupils in 1827, five years after his death, using a design of his own that was intended for the tomb of Titian. His body is buried in his native town of Possagno (*see p231* **Writers & Artists**), but his heart is conserved in an urn inside the monument. The despondent winged lion has a distinct resemblance to the one in *The Wizard of Oz*.

FREE San Nicolò da Tolentino
Santa Croce, campo dei Tolentini (041 710 806). Vaporetto Piazzale Roma. **Open** 8.30am-noon, 4.30-6.30pm Mon-Sat; 4.30-6.30pm Sun. **Map** p114 B4 ⑤
This church (1591-95), usually known as I Tolentini, was designed by Vincenzo Scamozzi. Its unfinished façade has a massive Corinthian portico (1706-14) added by Andrea Tirali.

The interior is a riot of Baroque decoration, with lavish use of stucco and sprawling frescoes. The most interesting paintings – as so often in the 17th century – are by out-of-towners. On the wall outside the chancel to the left is *St Jerome Succoured by an Angel* by Flemish artist Johann Liss. Outside the chapel in the left transept is *The Charity of St Lawrence* by the Genoese Bernardo Strozzi, in which the magnificently hoary old beggar in the foreground upstages the rather wimpish figure of the saint. In the chancel hangs an *Annunciation* by Neapolitan Luca Giordano; opposite is a splendidly theatrical monument to Francesco Morosini (a 17th-century patriarch of that name, not the doge) by Filippo Parodi (1678), with swirling angels drawing aside a marble curtain to reveal the patriarch lounging at ease on his tomb.

In 1780, the priests of this church handed over all their silverware to a certain 'Romano', who claimed to have a secret new method for cleaning silver and jewellery. He was never seen again.

FREE San Rocco
San Polo, campo San Rocco (041 523 4864). Vaporetto San Tomà. **Open** 9.30am-5.30pm daily. **Map** p114 C4 ⑥
If you have toured the school of San Rocco (*see p129*) and are in the mood for yet more Tintorettos (perhaps after a stiff drink or a lie down), look no further. Built in Venetian Renaissance style by Bartolomeo Bon from 1489 to 1508, but radically altered by Giovanni Scalfarotto in 1725, the church has paintings by Tintoretto, or his school, on either side of the entrance door, between the first and second altar on the right, and on either side of the chancel. Nearly all are connected with the life of St Roch; the best is probably *St Roch Cures the Plague Victims* (chancel, lower right). The altar paintings are all rather difficult to see; they're high up and not very well lit. Even if you could get a good view, you might not be much the wiser: even Ruskin, Tintoretto's greatest fan, was completely baffled as to their subject matter.

★ Scuola Grande di San Giovanni Evangelista
San Polo 2454, campiello della Scuola (041 718 234, www.scuolasangiovanni.it). Vaporetto San Tomà. **Open** 9.30am-5pm daily. Closed during conferences. **Admission** €5; €3 reductions. **No credit cards. Map** p114 D4 ⑤
Used frequently during the day for conferences and in the evening for concerts, this *scuola* is open to the public at other times: there's a list of visiting days on the website.

The Scuola Grande di San Giovanni Evangelista is one of the six *scuole grandi* (*see p129* **Scuole Stories**); founded in 1261, it is the most ancient of the still existing *scuole*. Originally attached to the church of Sant'Aponal, the *scuola* moved to its present premises in 1340. It grew in size and prestige, especially after the acquisition (1396) of a fragment of the True Cross, an event celebrated in a series of paintings now housed inside the Gallerie dell'Accademia (*see p145*). The *scuola* was closed at the Fall of the Republic then refounded in 1929 with the blessing of the Pope. Its building and its contents now carefully restored, this is one of Venice's most magnificent structures.

The *scuola* stands in a small courtyard, at the entrance of which is a screen with a superb eagle pediment carved by Pietro Lombardo. The groundfloor, with the large Sala delle Colonne, mostly maintains its medieval aspect, with fragments of medieval carvings on the walls; it was used as a space where members and pilgrims could gather.

The upper floor of the *scuola* is accessed by a magnificent double staircase, a masterpiece by the Renaissance architect Mauro Codussi.

The decoration in the Sala Capitolare is mainly 18th century. The floor is especially fine, with its geometrical patterns of multicoloured marbles that mirror the arrangement of the ceiling paintings. Giambattista Tiepolo was originally commissioned to execute the ceiling-paintings of the Apocalypse but left for Madrid without fulfilling his obligations. His son Giandomenico painted some of the smaller scenes on the ceiling (*The Woman Clothed with the Sun* and *The Four Angels and the Four Evil Winds*); despite their size they easily outshine the larger works at the centre of the sequence. The walls are hung with 17th and 18th-century paintings recounting the life of St John the Evangelist, by Domenico Tintoretto and others.

Also decorated in the 18th century was the Oratorio della Croce, where a tabernacle holding the precious piece of cross is one of the finest pieces of Venetian goldwork; it is rarely on display. This room originally contained a cycle of paintings by Gentile Bellini and Vittore Carpaccio, now in the Accademia; these days it has to make do with rather less inspired devotional works by Francesco Maggiotto, set within dainty stucco-work. Beyond this room is the Sala dell'Albergo, which contains a series of paintings by Palma il Giovane. The most spirited of these is *St John's Vision of the Four Horsemen*, recently restored.

The custodian will also open up the church of San Giovanni Evangelista across the courtyard, which has a Gothic apse but is mainly 17th- and 18th-century in its decoration.

★ Scuola Grande di San Rocco

San Polo 3054, campo San Rocco (041 523 4864, www.scuolagrandesanrocco.it). Vaporetto San Tomà. **Open** 9.30am-5.30pm daily. **Admission** €10; €8 reductions. **Map** p114 D5 🖼

The Archbrotherhood of St Roch was the richest of the six *scuole grandi* (*see below* **Scuole Stories**) in 15th-century Venice. Its members came from the top end of the mercantile and professional classes. It was dedicated to Venice's other patron saint, the French

---

SCUOLE STORIES

Venice's confraternities were part of a complicated social system.

Scuola Grande di San Rocco.

Scuola Grande di San Marco.

Scuole – a blend of art-treasure house and social institution – are uniquely Venetian establishments. Essentially, they were devotional lay brotherhoods, subject to the state rather than the church. In Venice's complicated system of social checks and balances (*see p71* **Machinery of State**), they gave citizens of wealth – but with no hope of ever entering the ruling elite – a place to feel they exerted some influence. The earliest were founded in the 13th century; by the 15th century, there were six *scuole grandi* and as many as 400 minor *scuole*.

The six *scuole grandi* had annually elected officers drawn from the 'citizen' class (sandwiched between the governing patriciate and the unenfranchised *popolani*). While members of the *scuole grandi* – such as the **Scuola Grande di San Rocco** (*see above*), the recently restored **Scuola Grande di San Marco** (*see p81*) and **Scuola Grande di San Giovanni Evangelista** (*see p128*) – were mainly drawn from the wealthier professional classes, the humbler *scuole piccole* were exclusively devotional groups, trade guilds or confraternities of foreign communities (such as the **Scuola di San Giorgio degli Schiavoni**; St George of the Slavs, *see p88*).

The wealthier confraternities devoted a great deal of time and expense to beautifying their meeting houses (the *scuole* themselves), sometimes hiring one major painter to decorate the whole building; this was the case with Tintoretto at San Rocco and Carpaccio at San Giorgio degli Schiavoni.

VENICE IMAGINED

Deals, scheming and sex: the city in the 17th-century English psyche.

The very first years of the 17th century were very good – or perhaps very bad – for Venice on the London stage. Three runaway hits set in the lagoon city received rapturous welcomes between 1604 and 1606. The city, clearly, had made its mark on the English psyche.

Venice enters English literature care of **William Shakespeare**. The Bard never actually set foot here, but nonetheless the city of *Othello* (first performed 1604) and *The Merchant of Venice* (first performed 1605) is a more fully realised place than, say, the Sicily of *Much Ado About Nothing*. Clearly, Venice was already as powerful an icon as New York is today; the Rialto

The Merchant of Venice.

and gondolas could be mentioned as casually as Wall Street and yellow cabs. Shakespeare's Venice is very much a mercantile city, a place of deals, exchanges and bonds.

But it is also a place of licentiousness and scheming, where people aren't always what they seem. Desdemona, according to Iago, is a 'super-subtle Venetian'. Ben Jonson took the subterfuge to new depths in his *Volpone* (first performed in 1606) in which the wily manipulator of that name dupes grasping would-be heirs out of their own wealth in a show of nastiness that ends in the Ospedale degli Incurabili (*see p145*).

plague protector and dog-lover St Roch (also known as St Rock or San Rocco), whose body was brought here in 1485. To celebrate the feast day of St Roch (16 August), admission to the *scuola* is free on that day.

The *scuola* operated out of rented accommodation for many years, but at the beginning of the 16th century a permanent base was commissioned. The architecture, by Bartolomeo Bon and Scarpagnino, is far less impressive than the interior decoration, which was entrusted to Tintoretto in 1564 after a competition in which he stole a march on his main rivals – Salviati, Zuccari and Veronese – by presenting a finished painting rather than the required sketch.

In three intensive sessions spread out over the following 23 years, Tintoretto went on to make San Rocco his epic masterpiece. Fans and doubters alike should start here; the former will no doubt agree with John Ruskin that paintings such as the *Crucifixion* are 'beyond all analysis and above all praise,' while the latter may well find their prejudices crumbling. True, the devotional intensity of his works can shade a touch too much into kitsch for the 21st-century soul; but his feel for narrative structure remains timeless.

To follow the development of Tintoretto's style, pick up the free explanatory leaflet and the audio guide and begin in the smaller upstairs hall – the Albergo. Here, filling up the whole of the far wall, is the *Crucifixion* (1565). More than anything it is the perfect integration of main plot and sub-plots that strikes the viewer; whereas most paintings are short stories, this is a novel. Note that some restoration

work was underway as this guide went to press.

Tintoretto began work on the larger upstairs room in 1575, with Old Testament stories on the ceiling and a Life of Christ cycle around the walls, in which the artist experimented relentlessly with form, lighting and colour. Below the canvases is a characterful series of late 17th-century wooden carvings, including a caricature of Tintoretto himself, just below and to the left of his painting of *The Agony in the Garden*.

Finally, in the ground-floor hall – which the artist decorated between 1583 and 1587, when he was in his sixties – the paintings reach a visionary pitch that has to do with Tintoretto's audacious handling of light and the impressionistic economy of his brush strokes. The *Annunciation*, with its domestic Mary surprised while sewing, and *Flight into Egypt*, with its verdant landscape, are among the painter's masterpieces.

Restaurants

€ Frary's

San Polo 2559, fondamenta dei Frari (041 720 050). Vaporetto San Tomà. **Meals served** noon-3pm, 6-11pm Mon, Wed-Sun. **Average** €30. **Map** p114 D4 ⑰ **Middle Eastern**
A friendly, reasonably-priced spot specialising in Arab cuisine, though there are some Greek and Kurdish dishes too, plus gluten-free options. Couscous comes with a variety of sauces: vegetarian, mutton, chicken or seafood. The *mansaf* (rice with chicken, almonds and yoghurt) is good.

Cafés, Bars & Gelaterie

Caffè Dersut
San Polo 3014, campo dei Frari (041 303 2159).
Vaporetto Tomà. **Open** 6am-8pm Mon-Sat; 8am-
2pm Sun. **No credit cards. Map** p114 D5 ⑱
Right by the side of the Frari (*see p126*) and no distance from the Scuola di San Rocco (*see p129*), this
coffee bar is a great place to refuel after an excess of
art. An outlet for the Treviso-based coffee roasters
of the same name, the café serves excellent breakfast
coffee and pastries, good fresh fruit juices and
smoothies, plus sandwiches for a light lunch.

Da Lele
Santa Croce 183, campo dei Tolentini (no phone).
Vaporetto Piazzale Roma. **Open** 6am-8pm Mon-Fri;
6am-2pm Sat. **No credit cards. Map** p114 B4 ⑲
Gabriele's (Lele's) place is the first authentic *osteria*
for those arriving in Venice – or the last for those
leaving; look for the two barrels outside – and the
crowds of people milling – and you've found this
Venetian institution. It's so small in here, there isn't
even room for a phone – but there are local wines
from Piave, Lison and Valdobbiadene on offer, as
well as rolls that are filled to order with meat and/or
cheese. A basic but good glass of chardonnay costs
just 60c, a mini-*panino* 90c (don't leave it too late if
you're hungry or they'll run out of bread). Don't
bother asking for coffee: no room for the machine.

Pasticceria Rio Marin
Santa Croce 784, rio Marin (041 718 523).
Vaporetto Riva di Biasio. **Open** 6.30am-8pm Mon,
Tue, Thur-Sun. Closed Aug. **Map** p114 C3 ⑳
Just a short hop across the Grand Canal from the
train station, Bianca and Dario's delicious cakeshop
is a rewarding stopover on arrival in (or departure
from) Venice – or at any other time, for that matter.
There's a world of choice here. Individual portions
can be consumed with a coffee or drink at one of the
tables along the rio Marin. Alternatively, treats such
as a wonderful creation with cream and fresh fruit
can be purchased family-size to take away.

Shops & Services

Ceramiche La Margherita
Santa Croce 659, corte Canal (393 210 0272,
www.lamargheritavenezia.com). Vaporetto San
Stae. **Open** 9.30am-1pm, 3.30-7pm Mon-Sat.
Map p114 C3 ㉛ **Homewares**
A delightful collection of handpainted terracotta
designed by the owner. Plates, bowls, teapots, ornaments and mugs are all available in a variety of
colours and patterns.

Coop
Santa Croce 506A, piazzale Roma (041 296
0621). Vaporetto Piazzale Roma. **Open** 8.30am-
8pm daily. **Map** p114 A3 ㉜ **Food & drink**

In a city where old-fashioned grocers and butchers
were increasingly thin on the ground, the appearance
of Coop and InCoop cornershops all over is a welcome
development. Most (including branches listed below)
are open Mon-Sat. If you need to restock on Sunday,
though, you'll need to make your way to piazzale
Roma. This is good supermarket food at good prices
(for Venice). This branch caters to tourists, with a
handy salad bar, snacks and Venetian specialities
conveniently lumped together.
Other locations Castello 5898, calle Larga (041
522 9214); Santa Croce 1493, campo San Giacomo
dell'Orio (041 275 0218); Giudecca 484, calle
dell'Olio (041 241 3381).

Guarinoni
San Polo 2861, calle del Mandoler (041 522
4286). Vaporetto San Tomà. **Open** 9am-noon,
3-7pm Mon-Sat. **Map** p114 D5 ㉝ **Furnishings**
An assortment of antique furnishings from as early
as the 16th century is sold here. The shop also has
a workshop that restores gilded ceilings.

VizioVirtù
San Polo 2898A, calle del Campaniel (041 275
0149, www.viziovirtu.com). Vaporetto San Tomà.
Open 10am-7.30pm daily. **Map** p114 D5 ㉞ **Food
& drink**
At the San Tomà vaporetto stop, VizioVirtù serves
up gluttonous pleasures. Here, you can witness
chocolate being made while nibbling on a spicy pra-
line or sipping an iced chocolate. This cornucopia of
cocoa has unusual delights such as blocks of chocolate Parmesan, and cocoa *tagliatelle* (the chef recom-
mends teaming it with game sauces).

IN THE KNOW THE ROMANTICS

For the Romantics, Venice's decadence
was delicious. **William Beckford, Lord
Byron** and **Percy Bysshe Shelley** thrilled.
They sought shudders by visiting the
prisons of the Palazzo Ducale (Doge's
Palace; *see p56*); they saw romance in the
mix of decay and splendour. Byron's twofold
reaction to Venice makes him the most
interesting expatriate writer of the period.
In his immensely fashionable poem *Childe
Harold's Pilgrimage*, he draws Venice as a
dream. Its past is melodramatic: dungeons,
the Council of Ten (*see p71* **Machinery
of State**), vendettas. It's a purely literary
creation, not based on observation. But
in *Beppo*, Byron draws a very different
picture, describing Venice at Carnevale
time: a menacing Turk turns out to be a
lost husband; and when this husband finds
his wife has taken a lover, all three settle
down to live together happily ever after.

EXPLORE

Dorsoduro

Cradling the southern flank of Venice proper, Dorsoduro – literally 'hard back' – stretches from its smart, artsy eastern district of elegant *palazzi* and quiet *campielli* to the little-visited docks and university area in the *sestiere*'s far western reaches. The concentration of art – from the very contemporary at the Punta della Dogana through the modern at the Peggy Guggenheim Collection to the grand masters at the Gallerie dell'Accademia – is unique. But there are fine churches here too, including the magnificent Santa Maria della Salute, a Venetian icon in its pre-eminent position at the entrance to the Grand Canal. In between the geographical and social extremes comes the wholly democratic and buzzing campo Santa Margherita, around which much of the city's nightlife action takes place.

EXPLORE

Santa Maria della Salute.

Don't Miss

1 Peggy Guggenheim Collection Great modern art in a pleasant palazzo (p147).

2 Gallerie dell'Accademia One of the world's great art collections (p145).

3 Campo Santa Margherita Venice's buzzy night-time spot (p138).

4 Zattere Wide canal-side promenade with wonderful views to the Giudecca (p145).

5 Santa Maria della Salute A Venice icon, dramatic outside, restful inside (p148).

EXPLORE

IN THE KNOW
LOGGIA OUT FRONT

Only two churches in Venice have loggias out front, and both are very old indeed. One is **San Nicolò dei Mendicoli** (*see p135*) and the other is **San Giacomo di Rialto** (*see p112*).

WEST

Vaporetto Santa Marta, San Basilio or Zattere.

This was one of the first areas in the lagoon to be settled. One seventh-century church here is called **San Nicolò dei Mendicoli** (*see p135*) – 'of the beggars' – a hint that the locals have never been in the top income bracket. In the past they were mostly fishermen or salt-pan workers. The area gave its name to one of two factions into which the proletariat was divided: the *nicolotti*. The *nicolotti* enjoyed a certain form of local autonomy under a figure known as the *gastaldo*, who, after his election, would be received with honours by the doge.

The area is still noticeably less sleek than the centre, although fishing was superseded as a source of employment by the port long ago, and subsequently by the Santa Marta cotton mill – now stunningly converted into the **Istituto Universitario di Architettura di Venezia (IUAV)**. Massive redevelopment schemes were talked about for much of this downbeat district, with plans to revitalise it in a vast 'university meets London Docklands' style project, to a design by the late Catalan architect Enric Miralles. The plans included an auditorium, a conference hall, a restaurant

and a huge centralised university library, thus providing Venice's universities with something approaching a genuine campus. After various legal disputes, these ambitious schemes fell through and the two universities of Venice fell back on a more modest development plan, converting some of the ex-warehouses into classrooms and lecture halls; these constitute the Polo didattica di San Basilio, which was inaugurated in March 2008.

Moving eastwards, the atmosphere remains unpretentious around the churches of **Angelo Raffaele** (*see below*) and **San Sebastiano** (*see p135*), with its splendid decoration by Paolo Veronese. Northwards from here, on the rio di Santa Margherita, are some grander *palazzi*, including **Palazzo Ariani**, with Gothic tracery that is almost oriental in its intricacy, and, further up, the grand **Palazzo Zenobio** (*see p135*), now an Armenian school and institute, containing Tiepolesque frescoes and giving on to an elaborate garden where plays are sometimes performed in the summer.

On the southern shore, the final and widest stretch of the **Zattere** (*see also p145*) passes several notable *palazzi*, including the 17th-century façade of the **Scuola dei Luganegheri** (sausage-makers' school), with a statue of the sausage-makers' protector, St Anthony Abbot, whose symbol was a hog.

Sights & Museums

FREE Angelo Raffaele

Dorsoduro, campo Angelo Raffaele (041 522 8548). Vaporetto San Basilio. **Open** 9am-5.30pm daily. **Map** p136 B3 ❶
Tradition has it that this church was founded by St Magnus in the eighth century, but the present free-standing building – one of only two churches in the

San Sebastiano.

city that you can walk around – dates from the 17th century. The ceiling has a lively fresco by Gaspare Diziani of *St Michael Driving out Lucifer*, with Lucifer apparently tumbling out of the heavy stucco frame into the church. There are matching *Last Suppers* on either side of the organ (by Bonifacio de' Pitati on the left, and a follower of Titian on the right).

But the real jewels of the church are on the organ loft, where five compartments, painted by Giovanni Antonio Guardi (or perhaps his brother Francesco), recount the story of *Tobias and the Angel* (1750-53). They are works of dazzling luminosity, quite unlike anything else done in Venice at the time. The paintings and the story they recount play a significant role in Sally Vickers' novel *Miss Garnet's Angel* (2000).

Palazzo Zenobio

Dorsoduro 2598, fondamenta del Soccorso (041 241 2397). Vaporetto San Basilio. **Open** during events only. **Map** p136 C3 ❷

Built towards the end of the 17th century to a design by Antonio Gaspari, Palazzo Zenobio's broad façade and two wings extending backwards are an unusual design for Venice; the central window crowned by a curved tympanum owes more to the works of the Roman architect Borromini than to local examples. In 1850, the palace was acquired by the Armenian Mechitarist monks of San Servolo and served as a college for Armenian students until 1997. Since then, it has been used as a guesthouse (very basic rooms: call 06 8530 1756 for information and bookings) and hired out for special events. But it's also the venue for exhibitions during the Biennale (*see p31*) and for other occasional shows: grab any opportunity to get inside.

The interior is sumptuously decorated with 18th-century frescoes and stucco-work. The showpiece of the palace is the Sala degli Specchi, the ballroom frescoed by the French artist Louis Dorigny. He created an elaborate ceiling with mythological figures cavorting amid trompe l'œil pillars and columns. The side rooms are frescoed in a more delicate Tiepolesque style. The large formal garden has weatherbeaten statues and peaceful avenues.

FREE San Nicolò dei Mendicoli

Dorsoduro, campo San Nicolò (041 275 0382). Vaporetto San Basilio or Santa Marta. **Open** 10am-noon, 4-7pm daily. **Map** p136 A3 ❸

San Nicolò is one of the few Venetian churches to have maintained its 13th-century Veneto-Byzantine structure, despite numerous refurbishments over the years. When the church underwent a thorough restoration in the 1970s, traces of the original foundations were uncovered, confirming the church's seventh-century origins. The 15th-century loggia at the front is one of only two extant examples of a once-common architectural feature; it originally served as a shelter for the homeless.

The interior contains a marvellous mishmash of architectural and decorative styles that creates an effect of cluttered charm. The structure is that of a 12th-century basilica, with two colonnades of stocky columns topped by 14th-century capitals. Above are gilded 16th-century statues of the Apostles. The paintings are mainly 17th century. There are also some fine wooden sculptures, including a large statue of San Nicolò made in the 15th century in the workshop of sculptor Bartolomeo Bon. In the small campo outside the church is a column with a diminutive winged lion.

★ San Sebastiano

Dorsoduro, fondamenta di San Sebastiano (041 275 0642, www.chorusvenezia.org). Vaporetto San Basilio. **Open** 10am-5pm Mon-Sat. **Admission** €3 (or Chorus; *see p89*). **No credit cards**. **Map** p136 B4 ❹

This contains perhaps the most brilliantly colourful church interior in Venice, and it's all the work of one man: Paolo Veronese. His first commission was for the sacristy (*see below*). From then on, there was no stopping him: between 1556 and 1565 he completed three large ceiling paintings for the nave of the church, frescoes along the upper parts of the walls, organ shutters, huge narrative canvases for the chancel, and the painting on the high altar.

In July 2008, restoration work began on the ceiling paintings. They depict scenes from the life of Esther (*Esther Taken to Ahasuerus, Esther Crowned Queen by Ahasuerus* and *The Triumph of Mordecai*). Esther was considered a forerunner of the Virgin, interceding for Jews in the same way that the Virgin interceded for Christians – or (more pertinently) for Venice. These works are full of sumptuous pageantry: no painter gets more splendidly shimmering effects out of clothing, which is probably why Veronese's nude St Sebastians are the least striking figures in the compositions.

The enormous canvases on the side walls of the chancel depict, on the right, *The Martyrdom of St Sebastian* and, on the left, *St Sebastian Encouraging St Mark and St Marcellan*. Other paintings in the church include *St Nicholas*, a late painting by Titian, in the first altar on the right. Paolo Veronese and his brother Benedetto are buried here.

The sacristy (10am-5pm Sat, 1-5pm Sun) contains ceiling paintings of the *Coronation of the Virgin* and the four panels of *The Evangelists*, which are among Veronese's earliest works in Venice (1555). Around the walls are works by Bonifacio de' Pitati and

EXPLORE

IN THE KNOW
DWARF IN VENICE

Film buffs should recognise the church of **San Nicolò dei Mendicoli** (*see p135*) from Nicolas Roeg's dwarf-in-Venice movie *Don't Look Now*. Other locations used include the recently opened **Palazzo Grimani** (*see p78*), where the gruesome final scene was shot.

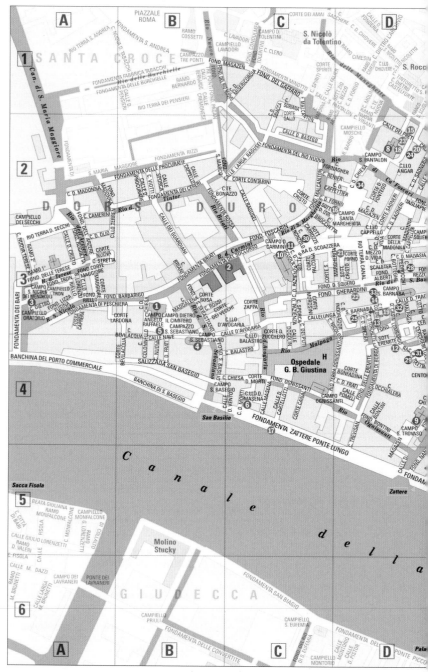

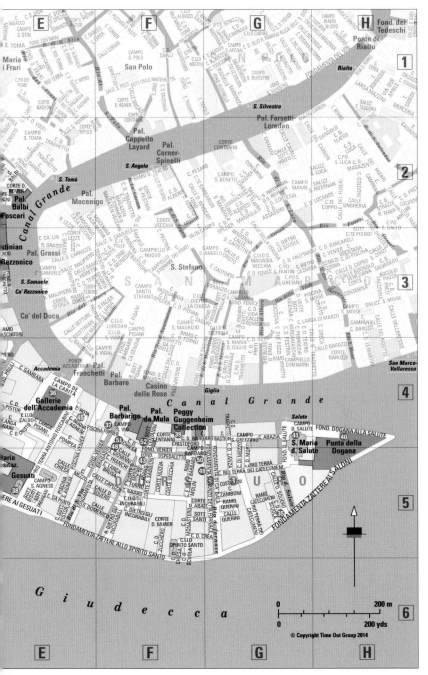

0   200 m

0   200 yds

© Copyright Time Out Group 2014

others. Restoration work on the frescoes and structure of the church will continue for some years.

Restaurants

Pane, Vino e San Daniele

Dorsoduro 1722, campo dell'Angelo Raffaele (041 523 7456). Vaporetto San Basilio. **Meals served** noon-2.30pm, 7-10.15pm daily. **Average** €35. **Map** p136 B3 ➎

This nouvelle-*osteria* belongs to a chain specialising in the wine and ham of the Friuli region, but the place has a character of its own, determined partly by its high proportion of university patrons, and partly by the fact that the Friulian imprint is varied by dishes reflecting the chef's Sardinian roots, including *coniglio al mirto* (rabbit baked with myrtle). It functions as a bar all day (9am-11pm daily) – handy if you just want a drink in the pretty square.

Riviera

Dorsoduro 1473, fondamenta Zattere Ponte Longo (041 522 7621). Vaporetto San Basilio or Zattere. **Meals served** 12.30-3pm, 7-10.30pm Tue-Sun. **Average** €90. **Map** p136 C4 ➏

Riviera is rarely less than an experience. The setting is spectacular to start with: in warm weather tables on the *fondamenta* afford views across the splendid Giudecca canal, to San Giorgio Maggiore and the Redentore. The service is warm, the ever-present owner – former musician GP Cremonini – makes your enjoyment his business. What's on the plate – mainly but not solely seafood based – is creative, excellent… and pricey: this is a place for special occasions.

NORTH & CENTRE

Vaporetto Accademia, Ca' Rezzonico, San Basilio or Zattere

A long, irregular-shaped campo with churches at both ends, **campo Santa Margherita** buzzes day and night, from shoppers at the morning market (Mon-Sat) to hurrying students and scavenging pigeons during the day, and hordes of Venice's twentysomethings thronging bars at night.

There are several ancient *palazzi* around the square, with Byzantine and Gothic features. Isolated in the middle is the **Scuola dei Varoteri**, the School of the Tanners. At the north end is the former church of **Santa Margherita**, long used as a cinema and now beautifully restored as a conference hall for the university; the interior (sneak in the back for a quick gawp if there's anything going on) is so theatrical, it's difficult to imagine how it was ever used for religious purposes. St Margaret's dragon features on the campanile, and the sculpted saint also stands triumphant on the beast between the windows of a house at the

north end of the square. A miraculous escape from the dragon's guts for some reason makes her the patron saint of pregnant women. At the other end of the square are the **scuola** and **church of the Carmini** (for both, *see p141*).

North out of Santa Margherita is campo **San Pantalon**. Its church (*see p139*) has an extraordinary Hollywood-rococo interior. If you walk out of the church towards the canal, an alley to the left will take you into little campiello d'Angaran, where there is a carved roundel of a Byzantine emperor, which possibly dates from the tenth century. Returning to the campo, you'll see a slab in the wall by the canal, which indicates the minimum lengths allowed for the sale of various types of fish.

Leaving campo Santa Margherita by the southern end, on the other hand, you reach the picturesque rio di San Barnaba. At the eastern end of the *fondamenta* is the entrance to **Ca' Rezzonico** (*see p139*), designed by Longhena and now the museum of 18th-century Venice.

The middle of the three bridges across the canal is ponte dei Pugni, with white marble footprints indicating that this was one of the bridges where punch-ups were held between the rival factions of the *nicolotti*, from the western quarters of the city, and the *castellani*, from the east. These violent brawls were tolerated by the authorities, who saw them as a chance for the working classes to let off steam in a way that was not disruptive to the state. They were banned, however, in 1705, after a particularly bloody fray.

Across the bridge is campo San Barnaba. The church of **San Barnaba** (often used for contemporary art shows) has a picturesque 14th-century campanile; the campo is a fine place for sitting outside a bar and watching the world go by. Katharine Hepburn fell into the canal flanking the campo in the film *Summertime*, causing permanent damage to her eyesight. In *Indiana Jones and the Last Crusade*, on the other hand, Harrison Ford entered the church (a library in the film)

IN THE KNOW BARNABOTTI

In the final years of the Venetian Republic, penniless patricians used to end up in **San Barnaba** (*see above*), where apartments were provided by the state for their use. The *barnabotti*, as they were known, could make a few *zecchini* by peddling their votes in the *maggior consiglio*; otherwise they hung around in their tattered silk, muttering (after 1789) subversive comments about Liberty, Fraternity and Equality.

Campo Santa Margherita.

into Venice's nobility. The Rezzonicos' bid for stardom was crowned in 1758 by two events: the election of Carlo Rezzonico as Pope Clement XIII, and the marriage of Ludovico Rezzonico into one of Venice's oldest noble families, the Savorgnan.

Giambattista Tiepolo was called upon to celebrate the marriage on the ceiling of the Sala del Trono; he replied with a composition so playful it's easy to forget that it's all about purchasing rank and power. Giovanni Battista Crosato's over-the-top ceiling frescoes in the ballroom have aged less well but, together with the Murano chandeliers and intricately carved furniture by Andrea Brustolon, they provide an accurate record of the lifestyles of the rich and famous.

There are historical canvases by Giovanni Battista Piazzetta and Antonio Diziani, plus other gems. Detached frescoes of *pulcinellas* by Giandomenico Tiepolo capture the leisured melancholy of the moneyed classes as *La Serenissima* went into terminal decline. Originally painted for the Tiepolo family villa, they were moved here in 1936 and recently restored. There are some good genre paintings by Pietro Longhi, and a series of pastel portraits by Rosalba Carriera, a female 'prodigy' who was kept busy by English travellers eager to bring back a souvenir of their Grand Tour. On the third floor is the Egidio Martini gallery, a collection of mainly Venetian works, and a reconstruction of an 18th-century pharmacy, with fine majolica vases.

A staircase at the far end of the entrance hall leads to the 'Mezzanino Browning', where the poet Robert Browning died in 1889. This contains the Mestrovich Collection of Veneto paintings, donated to the city by Ferruccio Mestrovich as a sign of gratitude for the hospitality afforded to his family after they had been expelled from Dalmatia in 1945.

FREE San Pantalon
Dorsoduro, campo San Pantalon (041 523 5893). Vaporetto San Tomà. **Open** 10am-noon, 1-3pm Mon-Sat. **Map** p136 D2 ❸

The dedicatee of this church is St Pantaleon, a court physician to Emperor Galerius, who was arrested, tortured and finally beheaded during Diocletian's persecution of the Christians in the late 3rd century. The saint's story is depicted inside the church in an extraordinary ceiling painting – a huge illusionist work, painted on 40 canvases, by the Cecil B De Mille of the 17th century, Gian Antonio Fumiani. It took him 24 years to complete the task (1680-1704), and at the end of it all he fell with choreographic grace from the scaffolding to his death. Veronese depicts the saint in less melodramatic fashion in the second chapel on the right, in what is possibly his last work, *St Pantaleon Healing a Child*.

To the left of the chancel is the Chapel of the Holy Nail. The nail in question, supposedly from the Crucifixion, is preserved in a small but richly decorated Gothic altar. On the right wall is a fine *Coronation of the Virgin* by Antonio Vivarini and Giovanni d'Alemagna.

and, after contending with most of Venice's rat population, emerged from a manhole on to the pavement outside.

From the campo, the busy route towards the Accademia (*see p145*) passes alongside the rio della Toletta (where a small plank or *tola – tavola* in Italian – once served as a bridge) towards rio San Trovaso. This handsome canal has twin *fondamente* lined by fine Gothic and Renaissance palaces housing secondary schools and university buildings. On the campo of the same name is the church of **San Trovaso** (*see p140*), with two identical façades, one on to the canal and one on to its own campo. Backing on to the campo is a picturesque *squero*, one of the few remaining yards where gondolas are made.

Sights & Museums

Ca' Rezzonico
(Museo del Settecento Veneziano)
Dorsoduro 3136, fondamenta Rezzonico (041 241 0100, www.visitmuve.it). Vaporetto Ca' Rezzonico. **Open** 10am-5pm Mon, Wed-Sun. **Admission** €8; €5.50 reductions (*see also p53* **Museum Passes**). **Map** p137 E3 ❼

The Museum of 18th-century Venice is a gleaming (if somewhat chilly) showcase for the art of the Republic's twilight years. For most visitors, the paintings on display here will appear less impressive than the palazzo itself, an imposing Grand Canal affair designed by Baldassare Longhena for the Bon family in 1667. Bon ambitions exceeded Bon means, and the unfinished palace was sold on to the Rezzonico family – rich Genoese bankers who bought their way

EXPLORE

FREE **San Trovaso**

Dorsoduro, campo San Trovaso (041 522 2133).
Vaporetto Zattere. **Open** 8-11am, 2.30-5.30pm
Mon-Sat. **Map** p136 D4 ⑨

This church overlooking a quiet campo has two almost identical façades, both modelled on the sub-Palladian church of Le Zitelle (*see p154*) on the Giudecca. The story goes that San Trovaso was built on the very border of the two areas of the city belonging to the rival factions of the *nicolotti* and *castellani*; in the event of a wedding between members of the two factions, each party was able to make its own sweeping entrance and exit. There was no actual saint called Trovaso: the name is a Venetian telescoping of martyrs San Protasio and San Gervasio.

There are five works by the Tintoretto family in the church; three are probably by the son, Domenico, including the two on either side of the high altar, which are rich in detail but poor in focus. In the left transept is a smaller-than-usual version of one of Tintoretto's favourite subjects, *The Last Supper*; the tavern setting is strikingly realistic.

In the chapel to the left of the high altar is *The Temptations of St Anthony the Abbot*, with enough vices to tempt a saint – note the harlot with 'flames playing around her loins,' as John Ruskin so coyly put

WINE OF NORTH-EAST ITALY
The best tastes of the region.

The wine-growing area that stretches from the Veneto north-east to Friuli is, after Tuscany and Piedmont, one of Italy's strongest: even in Venice's humbler establishments, the house wine is often surprisingly refined and locals are proud of it.

The grape-growing area is divided into two regions, the **Veneto** and **Friuli-Venezia Giulia**. The latter has the strongest reputation, mostly centred on the Collio and Colli Orientali appellations. This pair of appellations can be confusing. The names Collio and Colli Orientali don't tell you what you're getting in the glass: they are umbrella affairs. You might order a Colli Orientali tocai friuliano, or refosco; or a Collio merlot, or sauvignon.

The Veneto region is coming on, too. Long considered good only for full-bodied red Amarone and Valpolicella, the region is undergoing an image makeover, thanks to energetic winemakers who use local grape varieties like corvina and garganega to turn out some fine and complex reds. Even Soave has come good in the hands of producers like Pieropan or Inama. The Veneto is also home to Italy's favourite fizz, prosecco.

The following are the wines you are most likely to find in the wine bars and *bacari*.

RED
Cabernet: When Venetians ask for a glass of cabernet, they generally mean cabernet franc. A staple of the Veneto's upland wine enclaves, the grape yields an honest, moreish red with an unmistakable grassy aroma. For Veneto area cabernets, look out for Mattiello, Costozza and Cavazza. In Friuli, cabernet sauvignon and cabernet franc have a foothold. Russiz Superiore and La Boatina make some of the best.

Raboso: The classic Venetian winter-warming red, raboso is rough, acidic, tannic and lacking in pretension. The best kind is served from a huge demijohn in your local *bacaro*.

Refosco: A ruby-red with hints of grass and cherries, locals like to keep this variety to themselves. Try the meaty version produced by Dorigo.

Valpolicella, Recioto della Valpolicella & Amarone: Standard Valpolicella suffers from overstretched DOC boundaries and overgenerous yields. But the best, bottled as Valpolicella classico or Valpolicella superiore, can be very good. Amarone and Recioto, the area's two famous *passito* wines, are made from partially dried Valpolicella grapes. Recioto is the sweet version, Amarone the dry. The best producers include Allegrini (Recioto), Bussola, Cantina Sociale Valpolicella, Corte Sant'Alda, Dal Forno, Masi (Amarone), Quintarelli (Amarone), Viviani and Zenato.

WHITE & SPARKLING
Soave & Recioto di Soave: In the Soave classico area, a few winemakers are showing that this blend of garganega and trebbiano is capable of great things: look out in particular for Pieropan's La Rocca or Calvarino selections. In the 1980s, a few producers revived the tradition of Recioto di Soave, a dessert wine made from raisinised garganega grapes. The best producers include Anselmi, Ca' Rugate, Gini, Inama, Pieropan and Suavia.

EXPLORE

it. On the side wall is a painting in the international Gothic style by Michele Giambono, *St Chrisogonus on Horseback* (c1450); the saint is a boyish figure on a gold background, with a shyly hesitant expression and a gorgeously fluttering cloak and banner. In the Clary chapel (right transept) are Renaissance marble reliefs (c1470) showing angels playing musical instruments or holding instruments of the Passion, attributed only to the conveniently named 'Master of San Trovaso'.

FREE **Santa Maria dei Carmini**
Dorsoduro, campo dei Carmini (041 522 6553). Vaporetto Ca' Rezzonico or San Basilio. **Open**
7am-noon, 2.30-7pm Mon-Sat; 8.30am-noon, 2.30-7pm Sun. **Map** p136 C3 ⑩
The church officially called Santa Maria del Carmelo has a tall campanile topped by a statue of the Virgin. It is richly decorated inside, with 17th-century gilt wooden statues over the arcades of the nave and, above, a series of Baroque paintings illustrating the history of the Carmelite order. The best paintings in the church are a *Nativity* by Cima da Conegliano, on the second altar on the right, and *St Nicholas of Bari* by Lorenzo Lotto, opposite; the latter has a dreamy landscape containing tiny figures of St George and the dragon. To the right of the Lotto painting is a Veronese *Holy Family*, moved here from the church of San Barnaba. In the chapel to the right of the high altar is a graceful bronze relief of *The Lamentation over the Dead Christ*, including portraits of Federico da Montefeltro and Battista Sforza, by the Sienese sculptor, painter, inventor, military architect and all-round Renaissance man Francesco di Giorgio.

Scuola dei Carmini
Dorsoduro 2617, campo dei Carmini (041 528 9420, www.scuolagrandecarmini.it). Vaporetto Ca' Rezzonico or San Basilio. **Open** 11am-5pm daily. **Admission** €5; €2-€4 reductions. **No credit cards. Map** p136 C3 ⑪
Begun in 1670 to plans by Baldassare Longhena, the building housing this *scuola* (*see p129* **Scuole Stories**) run by the Carmelite order was spared the Napoleonic lootings that dispersed the fittings of most other *scuole*. So we have a good idea of what an early 18th-century Venetian confraternity HQ must have looked like, from the elaborate Sante Piatti altarpiece to the staircase with its excrescence of gilded cherubs.

In the main hall of the first floor is one of the most impressive of Giambattista Tiepolo's Venetian ceilings: the airy panels were painted from 1740 to 1743. Don't even try to unravel the story – a celestial donation that supposedly took place in Cambridge, when Simon Stock received the scapular (the badge of the Carmelite order) from the Virgin. What counts, as always with Tiepolo, is the audacity of his off-centre composition. If the atmosphere were not so ultra-refined, there would be something disturbing in the Virgin's sneer of cold contempt and those swirling clouds. The central painting fell from the wood-worm-ridden ceiling in August 2000 but has been beautifully restored. In the two adjoining rooms are wooden sculptures by Giacomo Piazzetta and a dramatic *Judith and Holofernes* by his more gifted son Giovanni Battista Piazzetta.

Restaurants

Ai Artisti
Dorsoduro 1169A, fondamenta della Toletta (041 523 8944, www.enotecaartisti.com). Vaporetto Accademia or Ca' Rezzonico. **Meals served** noon-4pm, 7-10pm Mon-Sat. Closed 3wks Dec-Jan. **Average** €40. **Map** p136 D4 ⑫

Friulian whites: The Collio and Colli Orientali appellations turn out some of Italy's most graceful white wines. Four varietals dominate: sauvignon (the Ronco delle Mele cru produced by Venica & Venica is to die for); pinot bianco; pinot grigio; and tocai friuliano (a dry summery white). Producers who do great things with two or more of these varietals include Ascevi, Castello di Spessa, Collavini, Dorigo, Gravner, Humar, Jermann, Kante, Keber, Le Vigne di Zamò, Livio Felluga, Marco Felluga, Miani, Pecorari, Polencic, Primosic, Princic, Puiatti, Rodaro, Ronco dei Tassi, Ronco del Gelso, Ronco del Gnemiz, Russiz Superiore, Schioppetto, Scubla, Toros, Venica & Venica, Villa Russiz and Volpe Pasini. Other white varieties grown in these areas include chardonnay and ribolla gialla, a local grape that makes for fresh and lemony wines. Finally, there is Picolit, the hugely expensive Italian take on Sauternes, made from partially dried grapes.
Prosecco di Conegliano & Valdobbiadene: The classic Veneto dry white fizz, prosecco comes from vineyards around Valdobbiadene and Conegliano, in the rolling hills north of Treviso. The most highly prized (and expensive) version of prosecco is known as Cartizze. A more rustic, unfizzy version – known as *prosecco spento* or simply *spento* – is served by the glass in *bacari*. The best producers include Bisol, Bortolomiol, Col Vetoraz, Le Colture, Nino Franco and Ruggeri & Co.

EXPLORE

El Sbarlefo.

This tiny trattoria expands out on to the pretty canal-side walk in the warmer months, which is good because the demand is overwhelming: you are advised to book. In the kitchen, Francesca prepares everything from scratch, from a menu that changes day by day depending on what's good in the market. On Monday, meat dominates because the boats don't go out on Sunday; other days, you might find delicious prawn-stuffed squid, or a fillet of john dorey lightly pan-fried with artichokes. If prices seem to be on the high-ish side, bear in mind that main courses have vegetables included (unusual in Italy).

La Bitta

Dorsoduro 2753A, calle lunga San Barnaba (041 523 0531). Vaporetto Ca' Rezzonico. **Meals served** 6.30-11pm Mon-Sat. **Average** €40. **Map** p136 D3 ⑲

La Bitta, a warm and rustic *osteria* with a small courtyard, stands out by having virtually no fish on the menu. Dishes like *straccetti di pollo ai finferli* (chicken strips with chanterelle mushrooms) or *oca in umido* (stewed goose) make a welcome change. There's also a good selection of cheeses, served with honey or chutney, and intelligent by-the-glass wine options.

Oniga

Dorsoduro 2852, campo San Barnaba (041 522 4410, www.oniga.it). Vaporetto Ca' Rezzonico. **Meals served** noon-2.30pm, 7-10.30pm Mon, Wed-Sun. Closed 3wks Jan. **Average** €40. **Map** p136 D3 ⑭

With tables outside on campo San Barnaba, Oniga has a friendly, local feel. The menu is adventurous Venetian and changes frequently but the pasta is consistently excellent. Fish and meat figure among the *secondi*: the pork chop with potatoes and figs is good. Marino is a wine expert, and will guide you through the select list.

Cafés, Bars & Gelaterie

Café Noir

Dorsoduro 3805, crosera San Pantalon (041 528 0956). Vaporetto San Tomà. **Open** 8am-2am Mon-Sat; 7pm-2am Sun. **No credit cards.** **Map** p136 D2 ⑮

Warm and intimate Café Noir is a winter favourite among the university and twentysomething crowd, who while away their days over panini and a cuop of hot chocolate. As it livens up later, it fills up inside and out with imbibers of *spritz* and a good choice of wine.

★ Café Rosso

Dorsoduro 2963, campo Santa Margherita (041 528 7998, www.cafferosso.it). Vaporetto Ca' Rezzonico. **Open** 7am-1am Mon-Sat. **No credit cards. Map** p136 D2 ⑯

Laid back and eclectic, the campo's oldest bar says 'Caffè' over the door, but it's universally known as 'Caffè Rosso' – perhaps for the decor, or for the political leanings of its boho-chic clientele. It attracts a mixed crowd of all ages who spill out from its single room to sip a *spritz* in the campo or to choose from the impressive wine list.

★ El Chioschetto

Dorsoduro 1406A, fondamenta delle Zattere (348 396 8466 mobile). Vaporetto Zattere. **Open** *Mar-Nov* 8.30am-2am daily. *Dec-Feb* weather permitting. **No credit cards.** **Map** p136 D4 ⑰

A much-loved spot not only for scrumptious panini and nibbles, but also for the tranquillity of sitting outside along the Giudecca Canal with a glass of wine and a sweeping view from industrial Marghera to Palladian San Giorgio Maggiore. There is no inside seating. From April to September there's live blues and jazz out on the *fondamenta* on Wednesday and Sunday evenings (6-9pm).

El Sbarlefo

Dorsoduro 3757, calle San Pantalon (041 524 6650). Vaporetto San Tomà. **Open** 10am-midnight daily. **No credit cards. Map** p136 D2 ⑱

Chic and sophisticated with great loungey background music, this new arrival in an ever-livelier corner of northern Dorsoduro updates the typical Venetian *bàcaro* with real class. By-the-glass wines range from the simple-but-good to some really excellent labels; the bar snacks offer a gourmet twist on Venetian traditions.

Other locations Cannaregio 4556C, salizada del Pistor.

Grom

Dorsoduro 2761, campo San Barnaba (041 099 1751). Vaporetto Ca' Rezzonico. **Open** 11am-10pm Mon-Thur, Sun; 11am-12.30am Fri, Sat. **Map** p136 D3 ⑲

Founded in Turin and now spreading as far afield as New York, the Grom *gelato* empire has also begun to colonise Venice, serving their trademark ice-cream with high-quality ingredients such as *sfusato* lemon from Amalfi, *tonda gentile* hazelnut from Lombardy, and pistachios from Bronte in Sicily. Note that prices are higher than most other *gelaterie* in town.

Other locations Cannaregio 3844, Strada Nuova; San Polo 3006, campo dei Frari.

Impronta Café

Dorsoduro 3815, crosera San Pantalon (041 275 0386). Vaporetto San Tomà. **Open** 7am-2am Mon-Fri; 9am-2am Sat. **Map** p136 D2 ⑳

Modern and minimalist, Impronta is an all-day operation, from excellent coffee and *cornetti* at breakfast time to nightcaps into the wee hours. Through its opening hours, it tends to be packed: with students in term time and everyone else all year. The restaurant food (served 11am-midnight) is good and reasonably priced, and there's a list of 150-odd wines with which to wash it down. But you might prefer just to turn up for an aperitivo and experience the vibe in this buzzing area of town.

★ Orange

Dorsoduro 3054A, campo Santa Margherita (041 523 4740, www.orangebar.it). Vaporetto Ca' Rezzonico. **Open** 9am-2am daily. **No credit cards. Map** p136 D3 ㉑

Orange calls itself a 'restaurant and champagne lounge' but it's far from being as exclusive as this may sound: on any night of the year, you'll find a horde of young locals and students, spritz in hand, spilling out from the sleek orange interior and across the campo. The young staff are efficient and friendly, the cocktails are creative and cheap, the garden inside is wildly popular and the patio heaters out on the square keep smokers warm on the coldest of nights. There's food too, at lunch and dinner: standards are good, servings are large and prices are not bad.

Osteria ai Pugni

Dorsoduro 2836, fondamenta Gherardini (346 960 7785 mobile). Vaporetto Ca' Rezzonico. **Open** 6.30am-12.30am daily. **No credit cards. Map** p136 D3 ㉒

There's always a warm welcome at this friendly bar at the foot of the Pugni bridge, where locals and students pile in from breakfast time until late at night for time-appropriate beverages and snacks. As the day wears on, a selection of good sandwiches and *cicheti* (bar snacks) appears on the counter. There's a sister establishment on neighbouring campo San Barnaba; called Ai Artisti, (Dorsoduro 2771; open 7am-9pm Mon-Fri, 8am-late Sat, 9am-late Sun), it is similarly friendly but not to be confused with the nearby restaurant of the same name.

Tonolo

Dorsoduro 3764, calle San Pantalon (041 523 7209). Vaporetto San Tomà. **Open** 7.45am-8pm Tue-Sat; 7.45am-1pm Sun. Closed Aug. **No credit cards. Map** p136 D2 ㉓

This Venice institution has been operating in the same spot since 1953. The coffee is exceptional. On Sundays, the place fills up with locals buying sweet offerings to take to lunch – don't be shy about asserting your rights or you may never get served. All the delectable pastries come in miniature sizes to make sampling a little bit easier.

Shops & Services

★ 3856 di Elvira Rubelli

Dorsoduro 3749, calle San Pantalon (041 720 595). Vaporetto San Tomà. **Open** 10am-7.30pm Mon-Sat; 11am-6pm Sun. **Map** p136 D2 ㉔ Fashion/accessories

This boutique is particularly popular with fashion-conscious students. Jewellery, scarves and bags sit alongside clothes and shoes. There's great attention to quality and colours of fabrics here.

★ Annelie

Dorsoduro 2748, calle lunga San Barnaba (041 520 3277). Vaporetto Ca' Rezzonico. **Open** 9.30am-1pm, 4-7.30pm Mon-Sat. **Map** p136 C3 ㉕ Homewares/children

A delightful shop run by a delightful lady who has a beautiful selection of sheets, tablecloths, curtains, shirts and baby clothes, either fully embroidered or with lace detailing. Stocks antique lace too.

Arras

Dorsoduro 3235, campiello Squellini (041 522 6460, http://.arrastessuti.wordpress.com). Vaporetto Ca' Rezzonico. **Open** 9am-1pm Mon, Fri; 9am-1.30pm, 2-6.30pm Mon-Thur; 10am-7pm Sat. **Map** p136 D3 ㉖ Accessories

In this venture involving disabled people, a variety of handwoven fabrics are created in a vast range of gorgeous colours and textures. These unique textiles

EXPLORE

are then worked into bags, clothing and scarves. Customised designs can be ordered. Arras also has ceramics and homeware... and it produces brilliantly coloured robes for priests too.

Cafoscarina 2

Dorsoduro 3259, campiello degli Squellini (041 240 4801, www.cafoscarina.it). Vaporetto Ca' Rezzonico or San Tomà. **Open** 9am-1pm, 2.30-7pm Mon-Fri; 10am-1pm Sat. **Map** p136 D3 ㉗ **Books & music**

This is the official bookstore of the Università Ca' Foscari, selling mostly scholarly texts on a wide variety of topics. On the other side of the campiello (Dorsoduro 3224) is Cafoscarina 3, which stocks a good selection of books in English.

★ Ca' Macana

Dorsoduro 3172, calle delle Botteghe (041 277 6142, www.camacana.com). Vaporetto Ca' Rezzonico. **Open** 10am-7.30pm daily. **Map** p136 D3 ㉘ **Carnival masks**

This workshop packed with traditional papier-mâché masks from the commedia dell'arte theatre tradition makes all its own masks, unlike so many of the carbon-copy shops that plague the city. This is where Stanley Kubrick came to stock up when making *Eyes Wide Shut*. Explanations of the mask-making process, as well as courses, are given by the artist in residence. **Other locations** Dorsoduro 1169, fondamenta della Toletta; Dorsoduro 3215, calle del Capeler (courses).

Canestrelli

Dorsoduro 1173, calle della Toletta (041 277 0617, www.venicemirrors.com). Vaporetto Accademia. **Open** 11am-1.30pm, 3.30-7.30pm Mon-Sat. **Map** p136 D4 ㉙ **Mirrors**

Designer-producer Stefano Coluccio specialises in beautifully framed convex mirrors.

Fustat

Dorsoduro 2904, campo Santa Margherita (041 523 8504). Vaporetto Ca' Rezzonico. **Open** 9.30am-12.30pm Mon-Sat. **Map** p136 C3 ㉚ **Homewares**

All the pottery in this little workshop/outlet is handmade by the owner, Cinzia Cingolani. Demonstrations of the making of raku ware and courses are also offered periodically.

Libreria Toletta & Toletta Studio

Dorsoduro 1214, calle Toletta (041 523 2034, www.latoletta.com). Vaporetto Accademia or Ca' Rezzonico. **Open** 9.30am-7.30pm Mon-Sat; 3-7pm Sun. **Map** p136 D4 ㉛ **Books & music**

Toletta offers 20%-40% off the usual retail prices. Italian classics, art, cookery, children's books and history (mostly in Italian) all feature, along with a vast assortment of dictionaries and reference books. Next door is the Toletta Studio, which specialises in architecture. Toletta Cube (address below; closed at lunch,

and Sun from June to Aug) is their newest shop, just across the calle, and it carries art and photography books as well as posters, cards and gadgets. **Other locations** Dorsoduro 1175, calle Toletta (041 241 5660).

★ Madera

Dorsoduro 2762, campo San Barnaba (041 522 4181, www.maderavenezia.it). Vaporetto Ca' Rezzonico. **Open** 10am-1pm, 3.30-7.30pm Tue-Sat. **Map** p136 D3 ㉜ **Homewares/accessories**

Fusing minimalist design with traditional techniques, the young architect and craftswoman behind Madera creates unique objects in wood. She also sells exceptional lamps, ceramics, jewellery and textiles by other crafts people, many of them Venice-based. Some of the homeware is now just down the road in calle Lunga San Barnaba (2729).

★ Signor Blum

Dorsoduro 2840, campo San Barnaba (041 522 6367, www.signorblum.com). Vaporetto Ca' Rezzonico. **Open** 10am-7pm daily. **Map** p136 D3 ㉝ **Jigsaw puzzles**

Mr Blum's colourful handmade wooden puzzles of Venetian *palazzi*, gondolas and animals make great gifts for children and adults alike.

★ Vinaria Nave de Oro

Dorsoduro 3664, campo Santa Margherita (041 522 2693). Vaporetto Ca' Rezzonico. **Open** 9am-1pm, 5-8pm Mon, Tue, Thur-Sat; 9am-1pm Wed. **No credit cards. Map** p136 D2 ㉞ **Food & drink**

Bring your own bottles here and the staff will fill them with anything from pinot grigio to merlot. For something different, try *torbolino*, a sweet and cloudy first-pressing white wine. **Other locations** Castello 5786B, calle del Mondo Nuovo (041 523 3056); Cannaregio 1370, rio terà San Leonardo (041 719 695).

EAST

Vaporetto Accademia, Salute or Zattere.

The eastern reaches of Dorsoduro, from the rio di San Trovaso, past the **Accademia** (*see p145*) and the **Salute** (*see p148*) to the punta della Dogana, is an area of elegant, artsy prosperity, home to artists, writers and wealthy foreigners. Ezra Pound spent his last years in a small house near the Zattere; Peggy Guggenheim hosted her collection of modern artists in her truncated palazzo on the Grand Canal (now the **Peggy Guggenheim Collection** *see p147*); artists use the vast spaces of the old warehouses on the Zattere as studios. On Sunday mornings, campo San Vio is some corner of a foreign land, as British expats home in on the Anglican church of **St George**.

Overlooking the campo, the **Galleria Cini** (*see p146*) houses a charming collection of Ferrarese and Tuscan art.

It is a district of quiet canals and cosy *campielli*, perhaps the most picturesque being campiello Barbaro, behind pretty, lopsided **Ca' Dario** (rumoured, due to sudden deaths of owners over the centuries, to be cursed). But all that money has certainly driven out the locals: nowhere in Venice are you further from a simple *alimentari* (grocery store).

The colossal magnificence of Longhena's church of Santa Maria della Salute brings the residential area to an end. Beyond is the old Dogana di Mare (Customs House). Debate about redeploying this empty space raged for years: in the end, the contract for redevelopment went to French magnate Francois Pinault. With the **Punta Della Dogana** gallery (*see p147*) open and building work over, it is once again possible to stroll around the *punta*, with its spectacular view across the water towards St Mark's.

South from punta della Dogana, the mile-long stretch of **Le Zattere**, Venice's finest

Madera.

promenade after the riva degli Schiavoni, leads westwards past the churches of **I Gesuati** (*see p14*) and **Santa Maria della Visitazione** (*see p150*) to the San Nicolò zone.

This long promenade bordering the Giudecca Canal is named after the *zattere* (rafts) that used to moor here, bringing wood and other materials across from the mainland. The paved quayside was created by decree in 1519. It now provides a favourite strolling ground, punctuated by some spectacularly situated (if somewhat shadeless) benches for a picnic.

The eastern end is usually quiet, with the occasional flurry of activity around the rowing clubs now occupying the 14th-century salt warehouses, one of which now hosts the **Fondazione Vedova** gallery (*see below*).

Westward from these are the new premises of the **Accademia di Belle Arti** (the school of fine arts that was recently evicted from the Accademia), the church of **Spirito Santo** and the long 16th-century façade of the grimly named **Ospedale degli Incurabili** (the main incurable disease of the time was syphilis). In Ben Jonson's play *Volpone*, the title character's property is confiscated and he himself sent to this hospital at the end of the play.

The liveliest part of the Zattere is around the church of I Gesuati. Venetians flock here at weekends and on warm evenings to savour ice-cream or sip drinks at canalside tables.

Sights & Museums

Fondazione Vedova

Dorsoduro 50, fondamenta zattere ai Saloni (041 522 6626, www.fondazionevedova.org). Vaporetto Salute or Zattere. **Open** 11.30am-6.30pm Tue-Sun. **Admission** varies. **Map** p137 G5 ❸

A selection of works by Venetian artist Emilio Vedova (1919-2006) is now housed in a stunning new gallery, designed by Renzo Piano, in the Magazzini del Sale (salt warehouses). Immense canvasses by this leading member of the European avant-garde are suspended from moving brackets in what curators describe as a 'dynamic' exhibition.

★ Gallerie dell'Accademia

Dorsoduro 1050, campo Carità (041 522 2247, www.gallerieaccademia.org). Vaporetto Accademia. **Open** 8.15am-2pm Mon; 8.15am-7.15pm Tue-Sun. **Admission** €9; €6 reductions; under-18s and EU students free (includes Palazzo Grimani, *see also p78*); price varies for special exhibitions. *Audio guide* €6. **Map** p137 E4 ❸

Early in 2014 the Accademia galleries threw open the doors of a long-awaited extension, which added to the existing exhibition halls parts of the Scuola della Carità (the oldest of the Venetian *scuole*, founded in the 13th century), the monastery of the Lateran Canons (a 12th-century structure remodelled by

EXPLORE

IN THE KNOW
BY ANY OTHER NAME...

Paolo Veronese's vast *Christ in the House of Levi* in the **Accademia** gallery (*see p145*) was painted as a *Last Supper*. In 1573, the Inquisition took offence at a *Last Supper* in which figures of 'buffoons, drunkards, Germans, dwarves' supposedly insulted church decorum, and threatened Veronese with heresy charges. The artist – with admirable chutzpah – simply changed its name.

Andrea Palladio with a superb oval staircase by the architect now on view) and the church of the Carità. At the time of writing, the new area was bare; a complete overhaul was scheduled as the artworks were rehung. The description below refers to the original body of the gallery; the arrangement of works inside may be altered considerably in time.

The Accademia is the essential one-stop shop for Venetian painting, and one of the world's greatest art treasure houses. It was Napoleon who made the collection possible: first, by suppressing hundreds of churches, convents and religious guilds, confiscating their artworks for the greater good of the state; and second, by moving the city's Accademia di Belle Arti art school here, with the mandate both to train students and to act as a gallery and storeroom for all the evicted artworks, which were originally displayed as models for pupils to aspire to. The art school moved to a new site on the nearby Zattere in 2004, leaving the freed-up space for the gallery extension.

In its old layout, the collection is arranged chronologically, with the exception of the 15th- and 16th-century works in rooms 19-24 at the end. It opens with 14th- and 15th-century devotional works by Paolo Veneziano and others – stiff figures against gold backdrops in the Byzantine tradition. This room was the main hall of the *scuola grande*: note the original ceiling of gilded cherubim. Rooms 2 and 3 have devotional paintings and altarpieces by Carpaccio, Cima da Conegliano and Giovanni Bellini (a fine *Enthroned Madonna with Six Saints*).

Rooms 4 and 5 bring us to the Renaissance heart of the collection: here are Mantegna's *St George* and Giorgione's mysterious *Tempest*, which has had art historians reaching for symbolic interpretations for centuries. In Room 6, the three greats of 16th-century Venetian painting – Titian, Tintoretto and Veronese – are first encountered. But the battle of the giants gets under way in earnest in Room 10, where Tintoretto's ghostly chiaroscuro *Transport of the Body of St Mark* vies for attention with Titian's moving *Pietà* – his last painting – and Veronese's huge *Christ in the House of Levi*.

Room 11 covers two centuries, with canvases by Tintoretto (the exquisite *Madonna dei Camerlenghi*),

Bernardo Strozzi and Tiepolo. The series of rooms beyond brings the plot up to the 18th century, with all the old favourites: Canaletto, Guardi, Longhi and soft-focus, bewigged portraits by female superstar Rosalba Carriera.

Rooms 19 and 20 take us back to the 15th century; the latter has the rich *Miracle of the Relic of the Cross* cycle, a collaborative effort by Gentile Bellini, Carpaccio and others, which is packed with telling social details; there's even a black gondolier in Carpaccio's *Miracle of the Cross at the Rialto*.

An even more satisfying cycle has Room 21 to itself. Carpaccio's *Life of St Ursula* (1490-95) tells the story of the legendary Breton princess who embarked on a pilgrimage to Rome with her betrothed so that he could be baptised into the true faith. All went swimmingly until Ursula and all the 11,000 virgins accompanying her were massacred by the Huns in Cologne (the initial 'M' – for martyr – used in one account of the affair caused the multiplication of the number of accompanying maidens from 11 to 11,000, M being the Roman numeral for 1,000). More than the ropey legend, it's the architecture, the ships and the pageantry in these meticulous paintings that grab the attention. Perhaps most striking, amid all the closely thronged, action-packed scenes, is the rapt stillness and solitude of *The Dream of St Ursula*.

Room 23 is the former church of Santa Maria della Carità: here are devotional works by Vivarini, the Bellinis and others. Room 24 – the Albergo room (or secretariat) of the former *scuola* – contains the only work in the whole gallery that is in its original site: Titian's magnificent *Presentation of the Virgin*.

Galleria Cini

Dorsoduro 864, piscina del Forner (041 271 0111, www.cini.it). Vaporetto Accademia. **Open** *Feb-June, Sept-Nov* 10am-6pm Tue-Sun. **Closed** Dec, Jan, July, Aug. **Admission** €6.50; €5.50 reductions. **No credit cards. Map** p137 F4 ⑳
This lovely collection of Ferrarese and Tuscan art was put together by industrialist Vittorio Cini, who created the Fondazione Cini on the island of San Giorgio Maggiore (*see p159*). It's small but there are a few gems, like the unfinished Pontormo double *Portrait of Two Friends* (on the first floor), and Dosso Dossi's *Allegorical Scene* (on the second), a vivacious character study from the D'Este Palace in Ferrara. There are also some delicate, late-medieval ivories and a rare, 14th-century wedding chest decorated with chivalric scenes.

I Gesuati

Dorsoduro, fondamenta Zattere ai Gesuati (041 275 0642, www.chorusvenezia.org). Vaporetto Zattere. **Open** 10am-5pm Mon-Sat. **Admission** €3 (or Chorus; *see p89*). **No credit cards. Map** p137 E5 ㉝
This church is officially Santa Maria del Rosario, but it is always known as the Gesuati, after the minor religious order that owned the previous church here.

Peggy Guggenheim Collection.

The order merged with the Dominicans – the present owners – in 1668. I Gesuati is a great piece of teamwork by a trio of remarkable rococo artists: architect Giorgio Massari, painter Giambattista Tiepolo and sculptor Giovanni Morlaiter.

The façade deliberately reflects the Palladian church of the Redentore opposite, but the splendidly posturing statues give it that typically 18th-century touch of histrionic flamboyance. Plenty more theatrical sculpture is to be found inside the church, all by Morlaiter. Above is a magnificent ceiling by Tiepolo, with three frescoes on Dominican themes. These works reintroduced frescoes to Venetian art after two centuries of canvas ceiling paintings. The central panel shows St Dominic passing on to a crowd of supplicants the rosary he has just received from the cloud-enthroned Madonna. Tiepolo also painted the surrounding grisailles, which, at first sight, look like stucco reliefs.

There is another brightly coloured Tiepolo on the first altar on the right, *The Virgin and Child with Saints Rosa, Catherine and Agnes*. Tiepolo here plays with optical effects, allowing St Rosa's habit to tumble out of the frame. In his painting of three Dominican saints on the third altar on the left, Giovanni Battista Piazzetta makes use of a narrower and more sober range of colours, going for a more sculptural effect.

★ Peggy Guggenheim Collection
Dorsoduro 701, fondamenta Venier dei Leoni (041 520 6288, www.guggenheim-venice.it). Vaporetto Accademia or Salute. **Open** 10am-6pm Mon, Wed-Sun. **Admission** €14; €8-€12 reductions. **Map** p137 F4 ③
This remarkable establishment, tucked behind a high wall off a quiet street (but with a Grand Canal frontage), is the third most visited museum in the city. It was founded by one of Venice's most colourful expat residents, Peggy Guggenheim.

She turned up in the lagoon city in 1949 looking for a home for her already sizeable art collection. A short-sighted curator at the Tate Gallery in London had described her growing pile of surrealist and modernist works as 'non-art'. Venice, still struggling to win back the tourists after World War II, was less finicky, and Peggy found a perfect, eccentric base in Palazzo Venier dei Leoni, a truncated 18th-century Grand Canal palazzo.

There are big European names in her art collection, including Picasso, Duchamp, Brancusi, Giacometti and Max Ernst, plus a few Americans such as Calder and Jackson Pollock. Highlights include the beautifully enigmatic *Empire of Light* by Magritte and Giacometti's disturbing *Woman with Her Throat Cut*. The flamboyant *Attirement of the Bride*, by Peggy's husband, Max Ernst, often turns up as a Carnevale costume. But perhaps the most startling exhibit of all is the rider of Marino Marini's *Angel of the City* out on the Grand Canal terrace, who thrusts his manhood towards passing *vaporetti*. (Never the shrinking wallflower, Peggy took delight in unscrewing the member and pressing it on young men she fancied.)

Another wing has been given over to Futurist works on long-term loan from the collection of Gianni Mattioli. The gallery has a pleasant garden and café.

★ Punta della Dogana
Dorsoduro 2, campo della Salute (041 523 1680, www.palazzograssi.it). Vaporetto Salute. **Open** 10am-7pm Mon, Wed-Sun. **Admission** €15

EXPLORE

(€20 Punta & Palazzo Grassi; *see p65*; €10 (€14 both) reductions. **Map** p137 H4 ⓵
Inaugurated in June 2009 after a remarkable makeover by Japanese archistar Tadao Ando, the Punta della Dogana gallery confirms Venice's key place on Europe's contemporary art circuit. French tycoon Francois Pinault beat the Peggy Guggenheim Collection (*see p147*) with his bid for the lease on this 17th-century bonded warehouse – much to the annoyance of many Venetians who felt that Pinault's outpost at Palazzo Grassi (*see p65*) was more than enough. On show here are revolving exhibitions based around Pinault's own immense contemporary art collection.

★ FREE Santa Maria della Salute

Dorsoduro, campo della Salute (041 241 1081, www.seminariovenezia.it). Vaporetto Salute.
Open 9am-noon, 3-5.30pm daily. **Admission**
Church free. *Sacristy* €2. **No credit cards**.
Map p137 G4 ⓵
This magnificent Baroque church, queening it over the entrance of the Grand Canal, is almost as recognisable an image of Venice as St Mark's or the Rialto bridge. It was built between 1631 and 1681 in thanksgiving for the end of Venice's last bout of plague, which had wiped out at least a third of the population in 1630. The church is dedicated to the Madonna, as protector of the city.

The terms of the competition won by 26-year-old architect Baldassare Longhena presented a serious challenge, which beat some of the best architects of the day. The church was to be colossal but inexpensive; the whole structure was to be visually clear on entrance, with an unimpeded view of the high altar, the ambulatory and side altars coming into sight only as one approached the chancel; the light was to be evenly distributed; and the whole building should *creare una bella figura* – show itself off to good effect.

Longhena succeeded brilliantly in satisfying all of these requisites – particularly the last and most Venetian of them. The church takes superb advantage of its dominant position and pays homage to both the Byzantine form of San Marco across the Grand Canal and the classical form of Palladio's Redentore, across the Giudecca Canal.

The architect said he chose the circular shape with the reverent aim of offering a crown to the Madonna. She stands on the lantern above the cupola as described in the Book of Revelations: 'Clothed in the sun, and the moon under her feet, and upon her head a crown of twelve stars.' Beneath her, on the great scroll-brackets around the cupola, stand statues of the apostles – the 12 stars in her crown. This Marian symbolism continues inside the church, where in the centre of the mosaic floor, amid a circle of roses, is an inscription, *Unde origo inde salus* (from the origin comes salvation) – a reference to the legendary birth of Venice under the Virgin's protection.

Longhena's intention was for the visitor to approach the high altar ceremoniously through the main door, with the six side altars only coming into view upon reaching the very centre of the church, where they appear framed theatrically in their separate archways. However, the main door is rarely open and often the central area of the church is roped off, so you have no choice but to walk round the ambulatory and visit the chapels separately.

The three on the right have paintings by Luca Giordano, a prolific Neapolitan painter who brought a little southern brio into the art of the city at a time (the mid 17th century) when most painting had become limply derivative.

On the opposite side is a clumsily restored *Pentecost*, by Titian, transferred here from the island monastery of Santo Spirito (demolished in 1656). The high altar has a splendidly dynamic sculptural group by Giusto Le Corte, the artist responsible (with assistants) for most of the statues inside and outside the church. This group represents *Venice Kneeling before the Virgin and Child*, while the plague, in the shape of a hideous old hag, scurries off to the right, prodded by a tough-looking *putto*. In the midst of all this marble hubbub is a serene Byzantine icon of the *Madonna and Child*, brought from Crete in 1669 by Francesco Morosini, the Venetian commander later responsible for blowing up the Parthenon.

Sacristy

The best paintings are in the sacristy (opens at 10am). Tintoretto's *Marriage at Cana* (1551) was described by Ruskin as 'perhaps the most perfect example which human art has produced of the utmost possible force and sharpness of shadow united with richness of local colour'. He also points out how difficult it is to spot the bride and groom in the painting.

On the altar is a very early Titian of *Saints Mark, Sebastian, Roch, Cosmas and Damian*, saints who were all invoked for protection against the plague; the painting was done during the outbreak of 1509-14.

VENETIAN PEOPLE TADAO ANDO

The Japanese architect who's made his mark on the city.

Self-taught and without the shadow of an academic qualification, Japanese architect Tadao Ando has put his stamp on Venice thanks to his close collaboration with French magnate and collector of contemporary art Francois Pinault.

When Pinault bought the Grand Canal-side **Palazzo Grassi** (*see p65*) from Fiat in 2005, he called on Ando to rationalise the exhibition spaces inside the immense 18th-century pile. The result was clean but cold.

Two years later, Pinault was handed the lease on the **Punta della Dogana**, a 17th-century bonded warehouse at a strategic and hugely scenic spot facing across St Mark's basin to the Doge's Palace. Once again, Ando was given charge of the makeover of the immense, unstructured spaces inside the triangular customs building. He set to work with his usual gusto, sweeping aside the bureaucratic complications that can make renovations

in Italy a decades-long calvary. The result is a stunning series of halls with a subtle play of wood and brick, concrete (Ando's signature material) and dazzling light off the water that laps all around.

At Palazzo Grassi, where work took seven months, as at Punta della Dogana (14 months), the rapidity with which Ando got things done left Italians bewildered, but not bowed. In his notes for the catalogue of the inaugural show at the Punta, *Mapping the Studio*, Ando expressed his 'great respect for this emblematic building' but also let slip some pique that furious protests from residents had stymied his plans to erect two towering concrete columns symbolising 'dialogue between the history and the future' by the campo della Salute entrance.

Ando's latest Venetian outing was a bagatelle in comparison: the **Teatrino Grassi** (*see p65*) is a sheer space of curves and diagonals in shiny white.

EXPLORE

Teatrino Grassi.

Three later works by Titian (c1540-49) hang on the ceiling, violent Old Testament scenes also brought here from the church of Santo Spirito: *The Sacrifice of Abraham, David Killing Goliath* and *Cain and Abel*. These works established the conventions for all subsequent ceiling paintings in Venice: Titian decided not to go for the worm's-eye view adopted by Mantegna and Correggio, which sacrificed clarity for surprise, and instead chose an oblique viewpoint, as if observing the action from the bottom of a hill. More Old Testament turbulence can be seen in Salviati's *Saul Hurling a Spear at David* and Palma il Giovane's *Samson and Jonah*, in which the whale is represented mainly by a vast lolling rubbery tongue.

FREE Santa Maria della Visitazione
Dorsoduro, fondamenta Zattere ai Gesuati (041 522 4077). Vaporetto Zattere. **Open** 8am-noon, 3-6pm daily. **Map** p137 E5 ⓸
Confusingly, this has the same name as the Vivaldi church on the riva degli Schiavoni – though the latter is usually known as La Pietà (*see p87*). Santa Maria della Visitazione is now the chapel of the Istituto Don Orione, which has taken over the vast complex of the monastery of the Gesuati next door.

Designed by Tullio Lombardo or Mauro Codussi and built in 1423, the church has an attractive early Renaissance façade. It was suppressed (that rascal Napoleon again) at the beginning of the 19th century and stripped of all its works of art with the exception of the original coffered ceiling, an unexpected delight containing 58 compartments with portraits of saints and prophets by an Umbrian painter of Luca Signorelli's school, one of the few examples of central Italian art in Venice. To the right of the façade is a lion's mouth for secret denunciations: the ones posted here went to the *Magistrati della sanità*, who dealt with matters of public health.

Restaurants

See also p151 **Osteria Al Squero**.

Ai Gondolieri
Dorsoduro 366, fondamenta Ospedaletto (041 528 6396, www.aigondolieri.com). Vaporetto Accademia or Salute. **Meals served** noon-3pm, 7-11.15pm Mon, Wed-Sun. **Average** €85. **Map** p137 F5 ⓸
If you're looking to splash out, Ai Gondolieri offers a creative menu that belies its ultra-traditional decor and service. It's also, unusually for Venice, fish-free. Rooted in the culinary traditions of northeast Italy, dishes include a warm salad of venison with blueberries, *panzerotti* (pasta parcels) filled with Jerusalem artichokes in Montasio cheese sauce, and pork fillet in pear sauce with wild fennel. Enquire about the price before tasting truffle delights in autumn.

Cafés, Bars & Gelaterie

Cantinone (già Schiavi)
Dorsoduro 992, fondamenta Nani (041 523 0034). Vaporetto Accademia or Zattere. **Open** 8am-8pm Mon-Sat. **Map** p137 E4 ⓸
Two generations of the Gastaldi family work in the Cantinone (also, confusingly, known as Il Bottegon) filling glasses, carting cases of wine, and preparing huge panini with mortadella or more delicate *crostini* with, for example, creamed pistachio or cream cheese with fish roe. Give yourself ample opportunity to select from the day's offerings by coming before the crowds pour in at 1pm. When the bar itself is full, you'll be in good company on the bridge outside – a good setting for the Venetian ritual of *spritz* and prosecco consumption.

Santa Maria della Salute. *See p148.*

IN THE KNOW ANOTHER VENETIAN ECCENTRIC

Peggy Guggenheim wasn't the first eccentric female to occupy **Palazzo Venier dei Leoni**, which now houses the Peggy Guggenheim Collection (*see p147*); from 1910-1924 the building was the home of the Marchesa Luisa Casati, who liked to parade through piazza San Marco with a pair of cheetahs on diamond-studded leashes.

★ Da Gino

Dorsoduro 853A, calle Nuova Sant'Agnese (041 528 5276). Vaporetto Accademia. **Open** 6am-7.30pm Mon-Sat. **No credit cards. Map** p137 E4 ㊺

You will always be greeted with a smile by the Scarpa family; they take customer service seriously in a city where so many tourists make for some cranky hosts. Gino's serves some of the best *tramezzini* and made-to-order panini around. At the time of writing, the rumour that the bar was about to change hands wouldn't die, despite (somewhat hasty) denials from the Scarpas themselves…

Gelateria Lo Squero

Dorsoduro 989-990, fondamenta Nani (347 269 7921 mobile). Vaporetto Accademia or Zattere. **Open** 11am-9pm daily. **No credit cards. Map** p137 E4 ㊻

Simone Sambo makes some of the finest ice-cream in Venice. He's hard-pressed to pinpoint a favourite flavour, but can happily rattle off those in his current repertoire – which always depends on the freshest ingredients available. His mousse series (blueberry, strawberry, chocolate and hazelnut, among others) is so light and creamy, it's served in a waffle cone so it doesn't fly away.

Osteria al Squero

Dorsoduro 944, fondamenta Nani (335 600 7513 mobile). Vaporetto Zattere or Accademia. **Open** 9am-9.30pm Tue-Sun. **No credit cards. Map** p136 D4 ㊼

This simple, friendly *bàcaro*, located opposite one of Venice's very few remaining gondola building/repairing yards (*squero*), looks like it has been here since time immemorial, but that's an illusion. The former teachers who run the place, however, have perfectly captured the spirit of the traditional Venetian drinking den, adding only some truly gourmet *cicheti* at very reasonable prices: many customers turn up for a single glass of wine, and end up making a full meal out of a plate of these delicious tidbits. There are no tables, just benches and perching places; on fine days, much of the clientele will be standing out on the *fondamenta*, gazing across at the *squero*.

Shops & Services

Cornici Trevisanello

Dorsoduro 662, fondamenta Bragadin (041 520 7779). Vaporetto Accademia. **Open** 9am-1pm, 3-7pm Mon-Fri; 9am-1pm Sat. **Map** p137 F4 ㊽ **Frames**

This workshop is home to a father, son and daughter team that makes beautiful gilded frames, many with pearl, mirror and glass inlay. Custom orders and shipping are not a problem.

Le Forcole di Saverio Pastor

Dorsoduro 341, fondamenta Soranzo de la Fornace (041 522 5699, www.forcole.com). Vaporetto Salute. **Open** 8am-6pm Mon-Fri. **Map** p137 F5 ㊾ **Oar-makers/gifts**

The place to come when you need a new *forcola* or pair of oars for your favourite gondola. Saverio Pastor is one of only three recognised *marangon* (oar-makers) in Venice; he specialises in making the elaborate walnut-wood rests (*forcole*) that are the symbols of the gondolier's trade. There are also bookmarks, postcards and some books (in English) on Venetian boatworks.

Genninger Studio

Dorsoduro 364, campiello Barbaro (041 522 5565, www.genningerstudio.com). Vaporetto Accademia or Salute. **Open** 9.30am-6.30pm Mon-Sat; 11am-6pm Sun. **Map** p137 F5 ㊿ **Accessories/homewares**

After years in a studio with a Grand Canal frontage, designer Leslie Ann Genninger has moved her brilliantly coloured creations to pretty campiello Barbaro: her flame-worked and blown beads, custom jewellery, knick-knacks, lighting and mirrors offer a contemporary take on Venetian luxury and decadence.

Marina & Susanna Sent

Dorsoduro 669 & 681, campo san Vio (041 520 8136, www.marinaesusannasent.com). Vaporetto Accademia. **Open** 10am-6pm daily. **Map** p137 F4 (51) **Accessories**

Some of Venice's finest contemporary glass jewellery is created by the Sent sisters. There's also a good selection of the work of the contemporary design house Arcade.

Other locations: San Marco 2090, ponte San Mosie (041 520 4014); Murano, fondamenta Serenella 20 (041 527 4665).

Il Pavone

Dorsoduro 721, fondamenta Venier dei Leoni (041 523 4517). Vaporetto Accademia. **Open** 9.30am-1.30pm, 2.30-6.30pm daily. **Map** p137 F4 (52) **Gifts & stationery**

This is a place to seek out for handmade paper with floral motifs in a variety of colours. Il Pavone also stocks boxes, picture frames and other objects, all decorated in the same style.

EXPLORE

La Giudecca & San Giorgio

Once a place of flourishing monasteries and lush gardens, the gondola-shaped island of La Giudecca, just across the water to the south of Venice proper, might appear run-down today. Its nature changed in the 19th century when city authorities began converting abandoned religious houses into factories and prisons. The factories have almost all closed down, but the prisons remain in use. Giudecca now has a reputation as one of the poorer areas in the city, but it manages to attract more than its fair share of celebrities, and locals in the know come here for its community spirit and alternative arty scene.

With its splendid Palladian church facing the Doge's palace across the lagoon, the island of San Giorgio is an immediately recognisable Venetian icon.

San Giorgio campanile.

Don't Miss

1 San Giorgio campanile The view from the belltower is unique (p159).

2 Fortuny Tessuti Artistici An Aladdin's cave of fabulous fabrics (p157).

3 Alla Palanca Great fare, great waterside view (p156).

4 Le Stanze del Vetro Exquisite Venetian glass on display (p158).

5 The Borges maze An amazing labyrinth inside Fondazione Cini (p159).

EXPLORE

EXPLORE

Molino Stucky.

LA GIUDECCA

Vaporetto Palanca, Redentore or Zitelle.

The Giudecca was once known as 'Spinalonga', from an imagined resemblance to a fish-skeleton (*spina* means fish bone). Some claim that the present name derives from an early community of Jews, and others to the fact that the island was a place of exile for troublesome nobles, who had been *giudicati*, 'judged'. The exile was sometimes self-chosen, however, as people used the islands as a place of rural retreat. Michelangelo, when exiled from Florence in 1529, chose to mope here; three centuries later, during his steamy and highly public love affair with George Sand, Alfred de Musset wrote in praise of the flowery meadows of 'la Zuecca'.

The Giudecca's industrial heritage is in the process of being shaken up: some of the factories remain abandoned, contributing to the run-down appearance of the south side of the Giudecca, but a few have been converted into new residential complexes. The greatest transformation has been that of the **Molino Stucky**, the vast turreted and crenellated Teutonic mass at the western end of the Giudecca. The largest building in the lagoon, it was built as a flour mill in 1896 and continued to function until 1955. After decades of rat-ridden abandonment, it now hosts the Hilton Hotel with its conference centre, rooftop **Skyline Bar** (*see p157*) and swimming pool, and private flats.

The *palazzi* along the northern *fondamenta* enjoy a splendid view of Venice and attract well-heeled outsiders (Elton John and Giorgio Armani, for example) in search of picturesque holiday homes. Apart from the Hilton, there are a number of other major hotels, including the swanky **Cipriani** (*see p278*), at the eastern end. The island's disused warehouses are popular as studios for artists.

The main sights of the Giudecca are all on this northern *fondamenta*: **Santa Eufemia** (*see p156*), the Palladian churches of **Le Zitelle** ('the spinsters': the convent ran a hospice for poor girls who were trained as lace-makers), which is nearly always closed, and **Il Redentore** (*see p156*), as well as several fine *palazzi*.

Near Le Zitelle is the neo-Gothic **Casa De Maria**, with its three large inverted-shield windows. The Bolognese painter Mario De Maria built it for himself from 1910 to 1913. It's now home to **Tre Oci** (www.treoci.org), a space hosting regular photography exhibitions. It is the only private palazzo to have the same patterned brickwork as the Doge's Palace.

On the fondamenta Rio della Croce (no.149, close to the Redentore) stands the **Palazzo Munster**, a former infirmary for English sailors. The vitriolic Anglo-Catholic writer Frederick Rolfe (*see p117* **Venetian People**) received the last sacraments here in 1911, after slagging the hospital off in his novel *The Desire and Pursuit of the Whole*. (He then lived for two more vituperative years.)

Opposite is another expat landmark, the so-called **Garden of Eden**, pleasure ground of Frederic Eden, a disabled Englishman who, like Byron, discovered that Venice was

GARDEN OF MARVELS

Behind prison walls, female inmates grow organic vegetables.

Before it became an industrial hub in the late 19th century, the Giudecca was Venice's garden island, home to secluded *palazzi* and monasteries, each with its extensive *orto* (vegetable garden) producing fruit and vegetables. In one (very) out-of-the-way corner of this little-visited island, a group of women continues this tradition.

Behind the high walls of a 13th-century former convent on the fondamenta delle Convertite, the inmates of the **Casa di Reclusione Femminile** (women's prison) grow organic vegetables in a 6,400-square-metre (1.6-acre) plot. To sample the produce of the *Orto delle Meraviglie* – the 'Garden of Marvels', as the vegetable garden is known – turn up outside the prison walls on a Wednesday morning. Throughout the year, whatever this lovingly tended, chemical-free oasis yields goes on sale to the public.

Produce from the garden also makes its way into the prison's cosmetics lab, where gloriously perfumed toiletries with the label *Veneziana Coloniali e Spezie* are made for some of the city's swishest hotels.

But the activities of the 80-odd inmates don't stop there. The prison's leather workshop produces a contemporary line of bags, wallets and other accessories in leather and recycled PVC, on sale at a tiny green kiosk in campo Santo Stefano (open 10am-8pm Mon-Sat), which also sells hand-printed T-shirts, hoodies and bags made in the silk-screen workshop.

When not producing costumes for La Fenice (*see p69*) the tailors' shop turns out reproduction historical clothing (for sale and hire), as well as a very smart contemporary line of women's clothes, bags and accessories, available at **Banco Lotto No.10** (Castello 3478, salizada Sant'Antonin), near the church of San Giovanni in Bragora.

For further information, check the websites www.rioteradeipensieri.org and www.ilcerchiovenezia.it.

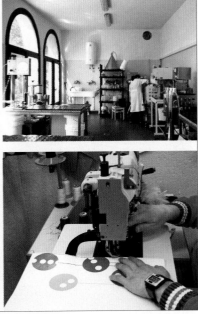

EXPLORE

the perfect city for those with disabilities – particularly if they could afford their own gondola and steam launch. After a period in which it belonged to the ex-Queen of Yugoslavia, the garden passed into the hands of the Austrian artist Fritz Hundertwasser. Since his death in 2000, it has belonged to a foundation in his name, which has, reportedly, allowed the garden to remain verdant but totally unkempt.

Sights & Museums

Il Redentore
Giudecca, campo del Redentore (041 275 0462, www.chorusvenezia.org). Vaporetto Redentore. **Open** 10am-5pm Mon-Sat. **Admission** €3 (or Chorus; *see p89*). **No credit cards.** **Map** p156 D2 ❶
Venice's first great plague church was commissioned to celebrate deliverance from the bout of 1575-77. An especially conspicuous site was chosen, one that could be approached in ceremonial fashion. The ceremony continues today, on the third Sunday of July, when a bridge of boats is built across the canal. Palladio designed an eye-catching building whose prominent dome appears to rise directly behind the Greek-temple façade, giving the illusion that the church is centrally planned, as was traditional with sanctuaries and votive temples outside Venice. A broad flight of steps leads to the entrance.

The solemn, harmonious interior, with a single nave lit by large 'thermal' windows, testifies to Palladio's study of Roman baths. But the Capuchin monks, the austere order to whom the building was entrusted, were not pleased by its grandeur; Palladio attempted to mollify them by designing their choir stalls in a plain style. The best paintings are in the sacristy, which is rarely open; they include a *Virgin and Child* by Alvise Vivarini and a *Baptism* by Veronese.

Santa Eufemia
Giudecca, fondamenta Santa Eufemia (041 522 5848). Vaporetto Palanca. **Open** usually closed to the public. **Map** p156 B2 ❷
This church has a 16th-century Doric portico along its flank. The interior owes its charm to its mix of styles. The nave and aisles are mostly 11th century, with Veneto-Byzantine columns and capitals, while the decoration consists mainly of 18th-century stucco and paintings. Over the first altar on the right is *St Roch and an Angel* by Bartolomeo Vivarini (1480).

Restaurants

★ € Alla Palanca
Giudecca 448, fondamenta del Ponte Piccolo (041 528 7719). Vaporetto Palanca. **Meals served** noon-2.30pm Mon-Sat. **Average** €30. **No credit cards.** **Map** p156 C2 ❸

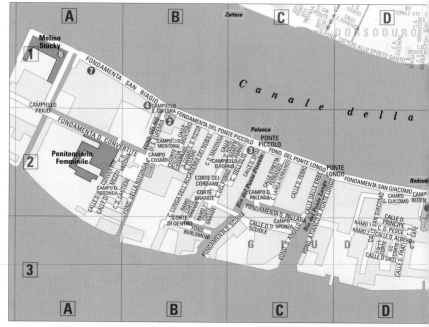

One of the cheapest meals-with-a-view in Venice is on offer at this hugely friendly bar-trattoria on the Giudecca quay. It's a lunch-only place: the rest of the day (7.30am-8.30pm) it operates as a bar. Sit at a quayside table and order from a good-value menu that includes some surprisingly gourmet options: tagliatelle with prawns and *funghi porcini*, or tuna steaks in balsamic and sesame. Finish up with a delicious chocolate mousse with candied fruit.

Harry's Dolci
Giudecca 773, fondamenta San Biagio (041 522 4844, www.cipriani.com). Vaporetto Sant'Eufemia. **Open** 10.30am-11pm Mon, Wed-Sun. Closed Nov-Mar. **Meals served** noon-3pm, 7-10.30pm Mon, Wed-Sun. **Average** €80. **Map** p156 B1 ➍
Arrigo Cipriani's second Venetian stronghold (after Harry's Bar; *see p69*), this open-air restaurant is a fair-weather-only venue. The cuisine is supposedly more summery than *chez* Harry, but in practice many dishes are identical. Outside of mealtimes, you can order just a coffee and one of the delectable pastries made on the premises. Come prepared for mosquitoes.

Mistrà
Giudecca 53C, calle Michelangelo (041 522 0743). Vaporetto Zitelle. **Meals served** noon-3pm, 6.30-10.30pm Tue-Sun. **Average** €30. **Map** p157 F2 ➎
At lunchtime, Mistrà is not a bad spot, with its open-to-view kitchen and friendly mix of workers from local galleries and boatyards. There's pizza as well as fish-based Venetian classics at reasonable prices. The place aims to go upmarket in the evenings but the result doesn't merit the higher price tag.

Cafés, Bars & Gelaterie

See also p156 **Alla Palanca**.

Skyline Bar
Molino Stucky Hilton Hotel, Giudecca 810, campo San Biagio (041 272 3310). Vaporetto Palanca. **Open** 5.30pm-1am Tue-Sun. **Map** p156 A1 ➏
It's a hike across to the Hilton Hotel in the former Molino Stucky flour mill (*see p154*) – and the bar is an expensive extravaganza – but sit out on the rooftop terrace and survey Venice beneath you, beyond the grand sweep of the Giudecca Canal, and you'll probably feel that it's all worth it. Meals and light snacks are served but forget the expensive food and just savour the view, with a drink in hand.

Shops & Services

★ Fortuny Tessuti Artistici
Giudecca 805, fondamenta San Biagio (041 528 7697, www.fortuny.com). Vaporetto Palanca. **Open** *Apr-Sept* 10am-1pm, 2-6pm Mon-Sat. *Oct-Mar* 10am-1pm, 2-6pm Mon-Fri. **Map** p156 A1 ➐ **Fabric**

EXPLORE

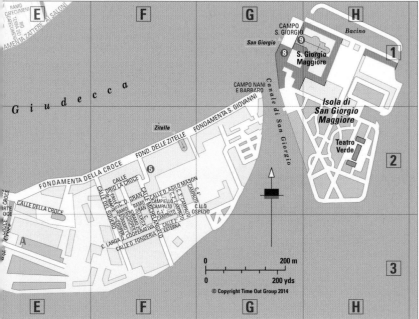

This wonderful factory showroom space glows with the exquisite colours and patterns of original Fortuny prints. At €427 a metre, you may not be tempted to buy, but it's worth the trip just to see it. The marvellous garden inside the factory can be visited by appointment. Check the Fortuny blog (through the website) for occasional clearance sales and cut-price discontinued lines. *See also p57* **Material Makers**.

ISOLA DI SAN GIORGIO

Vaporetto San Giorgio.

Sights & Museums

The island of **San Giorgio**, facing St Mark's across the lagoon, realised its true potential under set designer extraordinaire Andrea Palladio, whose church of **San Giorgio Maggiore** (*see p159*) is one of Venice's most recognisable landmarks. Known originally as the Isola dei Cipressi (Cypress Island), it soon became an important Benedictine monastery and centre of learning – a tradition that is carried on today by the **Fondazione Giorgio Cini** (*see below*), which operates a research centre and craft school on the island.

Fondazione Giorgio Cini, Benedictine Monastery & Le Stanze del Vetro

(041 524 0119, www.cini.it). Vaporetto San Giorgio. **Open** *Monastery* (guided tours every hour) 10am-4pm Sat, Sun. Mon-Fri by appointment only. *Le Stanze del Vetro* 10am-7pm Mon, Tue, Thur-Sun during

exhibitions. **Admission** *Monastery* €10; €8 reductions. *Le Stanze del Vetro* free. **No credit cards. Map** p157 G1 ❽

There has been a Benedictine monastery here since 982, when Doge Tribuno Memmo donated the island to the order. The monastery continued to benefit from ducal donations, acquiring large tracts of land both in and around Venice and abroad. After the church acquired the remains of St Stephen (1109), it was visited yearly by the doge on 26 December, the feast day of the saint. The city authorities often used the island as a luxury hotel for particularly prestigious visitors, such as Cosimo de' Medici in 1433. Cosimo had a magnificent library built here; it was destroyed in 1614, to make way for a more elaborate affair by Longhena.

In 1800, the island hosted the conclave of cardinals that elected Pope Pius VII, after they had been expelled from Rome by Napoleon. In 1806, the French got their own back, supressing the monastery and sending its chief artistic treasure – Veronese's *Marriage Feast at Cana* – off to the Louvre, where it still hangs. For the rest of the century, the monastery did ignominious service as a barracks and ammunition store. In 1951, industrialist Vittorio Cini bought the island to set up a foundation in memory of his son, Giorgio, killed in a plane crash in 1949.

The Fondazione Giorgio Cini uses the monastery buildings for its activities, including artistic and musical research (it holds a collection of Vivaldi manuscripts, plus illuminated manuscripts), and a naval college. A portion of the complex was given back to the Benedictines; there are currently a handful of monks in the monastery. The foundation is now open to the public at weekends for guided tours (in Italian, English, French and German). There are two beautiful cloisters – one by Giovanni Buora (1516-40), the other

San Giorgio.

ISLAND GREENERY

Some Giudecca gardens are secret. Others are open to all.

Once famous for its gardens, the Giudecca island keeps its greenery well hidden these days. The Garden of Marvels (*see p155*) inside the women's prison is off-limits, as is what remains of the Garden of Eden (*see p154*) – an Englishman's verdant retreat made for Frederick Eden in the 1880s.

But the magnificent courtyards – one with a maze – inside the **Fondazione Cini** (*see p158*) are visitable, as is the garden inside the **Fortuny Tessuti Artistici** (*see 157*) which is open by appointment and beautiful to see despite being in the middle of a painstaking restoration as this guide went to press. Also worth a peek if you're craving greenery is the gem that lies behind the Bauer group's Palladio and Villa F hotels (for both, *see p278*); four separate gardens have been restored and brought back to life, adding contemporary verve to historically documented elegance.

Maze, Fondazione Cini.

by Palladio (1579) – an elegant library and staircase by Longhena (1641-53), and a magnificent refectory (where Veronese's painting hung) by Palladio (1561). The tour also includes the splendid garden, including a JL Borges-inspired maze by the late British designer Randoll Coate, behind the monastery.

Inside the monastery complex, Le Stanze del Vetro (www.lestanzedelvetro.it) is an exhibition space which hosts excellent shows on Venetian glass.

★ FREE San Giorgio Maggiore

(041 522 7827). Vaporetto San Giorgio.
Open 8.30am-8pm daily. **Admission**
Church free. *Campanile* €6; €4 reductions.
No credit cards. Map p157 G1 ❾

This unique spot cried out for a masterpiece. Palladio provided it. This was his first complete solo church; it demonstrates how confident he was in his techniques and objectives. With no hint of influence from the city's Byzantine tradition, Palladio here develops the system of superimposed temple fronts with which he had experimented in the façade of San Francesco della Vigna (*see p78*). The interior maintains the same relations between the orders as the outside, with composite half-columns supporting the gallery and lower Corinthian pilasters supporting the arches. The effect is of luminosity and harmony, decoration being confined to the altars. Palladio believed that white was the colour most pleasing to God, a credo that happily matched the demand from the Council of Trent for greater lucidity in church services.

There are several good works of art. Over the first altar is an *Adoration of the Shepherds* by Jacopo Bassano, with startling lighting effects. The altar to the right of the high altar has a *Madonna and Child with Nine Saints* by Sebastiano Ricci.

On the side walls of the chancel hang two vast compositions by Tintoretto, a *Last Supper* and the *Gathering of Manna*, painted in the last years of his life. The perspective of each work makes it clear that they were intended to be viewed from the altar rails. Tintoretto combines almost surreal visionary effects (angels swirling out from a lamp's eddying smoke) with touches of superb domestic realism (a cat prying into a basket, a woman stooping over her laundry). Tintoretto's last painting, a moving *Entombment*, hangs in the Cappella dei Morti (open for 11am Mass on Sundays in winter only). It's possible that Tintoretto included himself among the mourners: he has been identified as the bearded man gazing intensely at Christ's face.

In the left transept is a painting by Jacopo and Domenico Tintoretto of the *Martyrdom of St Stephen*, placed above the altar containing the saint's remains (brought from Constantinople in 1109).

From the left transept, follow the signs to the campanile. Just in front of the ticket office stands the huge statue of an angel that crowned the bell tower until it was struck by lightning in 1993. To the left of the statue, a corridor gives access to the lift that takes you up to the bell tower. The view from the top of the tower is extraordinary: the best possible panorama across Venice itself and the lagoon.

Lido & Lagoon

Venice lies more or less in the middle of a saltwater lagoon, separated from the open sea by two slender sand barriers – the Lido and Pellestrina. It is, on the whole, another world out here, inhabited by fishermen and rowers and flocks of lazy water birds. In high season, much- visited islands such as Murano and Burano can seem only marginally less crowded than St Mark's or the Rialto. But even at the busiest times, the views from the vaporetto of the lagoon's empty reaches are enough to soothe the most frayed of nerves. Other islands, such as Sant'Erasmo, are always bucolically tranquil and almost entirely tourist-free.

San Michele cemetery.

Don't Miss

1 **Santa Maria Assunta** The Last Judgement mosaic is breathtaking (p174).

2 **San Michele cemetery** Seek out the final resting place of some famous names (p164).

3 **Lido seafront** The rows of pastel bathing huts are gorgeously *Death In Venice* (p162).

4 **Museo dell'Arte Vetrario** Everything you need to know about Venetian glass (p166).

5 **Burano's** painted houses The whole island looks like a colour chart (p170).

EXPLORE

San Nicolò.

The Lido

Vaporetto Lido–Santa Maria Elisabetta.

The **Lido** is the northernmost of the two strips of land that separate the lagoon from the open sea. It is no longer the 'bare strand/Of hillocks heaped from ever-shifting sand' that Shelley described in *Julian and Maddalo*, nor is it the playground for wealthy aesthetes that fans of *Death in Venice* might come in fruitless search of. These days, Venice-by-the-sea is a placidly residential suburb, where pale young boys in sailor-suits are in very short supply – an escape from the strangeness of Venice to a normality of supermarkets and cars.

Things perk up in summer when buses are full of city sunbathers and tourists staying in the Lido's overspill hotels. However, the days of all-night partying and gambling are long gone. In 2001, the Lido Casinò closed. Now the only moment when the place stirs to anything like its former vivacity is at the beginning of September when the film festival (*see p184*) rolls into town for two weeks, with its bandwagon of stars, directors, PR people and sleep-deprived, caffeine-driven journalists.

The Lido has few tourist sights as such. Only the church of **San Nicolò** on the riviera San Nicolò – founded in 1044 – can claim any great antiquity. It was here that the doge would come on Ascension Day after marrying Venice to the sea in the ceremony known as *lo sposalizio del mare* (*see p29* **Festa e Regata della Sensa**). Inside is the tomb of Nicola Giustiniani, a Benedictine monk who was forced to leave holy orders in 1172 to assure the future of his illustrious family, of which he was the sole heir. He married the doge's daughter, had lots of kids, then went back to being a monk. After his death he was beatified for his spirit of self-sacrifice.

Fans of art nouveau and deco have plenty to look at on the Lido. On the Gran Viale there are two gems: the tiled façade of the **Hungaria Hotel** (no.28), formerly the Ausonia Palace, with its Beardsley-esque nymphs; and **Villa Monplaisir** at no.14, an art deco design from 1906. There are other smaller-scale examples in and around via Lepanto. For full-blown turn-of-the-century exotica, though, it's hard to beat the **Hotel Excelsior** (*see p278*) on lungomare Marconi, a neo-Moorish party-piece, complete with minaret.

The bus ride south along the lagoon-side promenade of the Lido is uneventful but passes some submerged history. The old town of **Malamocco**, near the south end of the island, was engulfed by a tidal wave in 1107; it had been a flourishing port controlled by Padua. The new town, built further inland, never really amounted to much; today, its sights consist of a few picturesque streets and a pretty bridge.

Offshore from Malamocco is the tiny island of **Poveglia**, once inhabited by 200 families, descendants of the servants of Pietro Tradonico, a ninth-century doge murdered by his rivals. His servants barricaded themselves inside the Palazzo Ducale and only agreed to leave when safe conduct to this new home was promised.

GETTING THERE & AROUND

The main Lido–Santa Maria Elisabetta **vaporetto** stop (often just called 'Lido') is served by frequent boats from Venice and the mainland. The San Nicolò stop, to the north, is served by the no.17 car ferry from Tronchetto.

Bus routes: the A heads south from the main vaporetto stop through Malamocco and Alberoni to the very tip of the Lido. The B covers some of the same route, going south from the main vaporetto stop as far as Malamocco; in the other direction, the B cuts across the centre of the island and does the sea coast route northwards as far as the beach at San Niccolò. The V does a shorter route, cutting across the island from Santa Maria Elisabetta then trundling south past the seafront hotels and beaches. Buses 11 and N, with small variations, provide an epic ride, southwards from the vaporetto stop to the tip of the Lido, right on to the Pellestrina ferry, then along that sandbank-island to the ferry stop for Chioggia (*see p203*).

Cycling is a good way of getting around the pancake-flat Lido; for bike hire, *see p282*.

TOURIST INFORMATION

From June to September, there's a tourist information office at Gran Viale 6A, Lido (041 526 5721, www.turismovenezia.it, open 9.30am-1pm, 3-6.30pm daily).

Restaurants

Al Mercà

Via Enrico Dandolo 17A (041 243 1663). Vaporetto Lido. **Meals served** *June-Oct* 10.30am-3pm, 6.30pm-midnight Tue-Sun. Closed Nov-May. **Average** €40. **Map** p163 A3 ❶

A success from the word go, Al Mercà is the Lido's coolest dining hang-out with a lively aperitivo scene in the evening before eating begins. Charming hosts serve excellent mixed seafood *antipasti*, fishy pasta dishes and grilled fish to contented diners out on the portico of the former produce market. Best to book. Note that Al Mercà only operates in the warmer months.

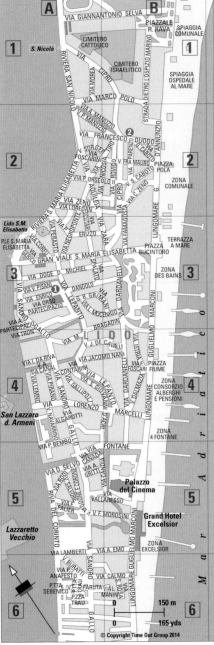

The Lido's Adriatic shore.

San Michele in Isola. ❷

La Favorita

Via Francesco Duodo 33 (041 526 1626).
Vaporetto Lido. **Meals served** 7.30-10.30pm Tue;
12.30-2.30pm, 7.30-10.30pm Wed-Sun. Closed Jan.
Average €55. **Map** p163 B2 ❷

With a lovely vine-shaded pergola for summer dining, this is an old-fashioned and reassuring sort of
place that does textbook Venetian seafood classics
like *spaghetti ai caparossoli* or *scampi in saor*
(sweet-and-sour sauce), plus a few more audacious
dishes such as pumpkin gnocchi with scorpion fish
and radicchio. Service is professional, and the wine
list has a fine selection of bottles from the north-east.

The Northern Lagoon

SAN MICHELE

Vaporetto Cimitero (4.1 or 4.2).

Halfway between Venice and Murano, this is
the island where tourists begin their lagoon
visit. For many Venetians, it's the last stop:
San Michele is the city's cemetery (open
Apr-Sept 7.30am-6pm daily, Oct-Mar 7.30am-
4.30pm daily). Early in the morning, *vaporetti*
are packed with locals coming over to lay
flowers. This is not a morbid spot, though:
it is an elegant city of the dead, with more
than one famous resident.

These days San Michele is more a temporary
parking lot than a final resting place: the island
reached saturation point long ago, and even
after paying through the nose for a plot,
families know that after a suitable period –
generally around ten years – the bones of their
loved ones will be dug up and transferred to an
ossuary elsewhere.

An orderly red-brick wall runs around the
whole of the island, with a line of tall cypress
trees rising high behind it – the inspiration
for Böcklin's famously lugubrious painting
Island of the Dead. The island was originally
a Franciscan monastery, but during the
Napoleonic period the grounds that used
to extend behind the church were seconded
for burials in an effort to stop unhygienic
Venetians from digging graves in the *campi*
around parish churches.

Before visiting the cemetery, take a look
at the recently restored church of **San
Michele in Isola** (open 7.30am-12.15pm,
3-4pm daily); turn left after entering the
cemetery and pass through the fine cloisters.
The view of the façade is particularly striking.
Designed by Mauro Codussi in the 1460s, this
white building of Istrian stone was Venice's
first Renaissance church.

In a booth to the left of the entrance by
the vaporetto stop, staff hand out maps,
which are indispensable for celebrity hunts.
In the Greek and Russian Orthodox section
of the cemetery are the elaborate tomb of
Sergei Pavlovich Diaghilev, who introduced
the Ballets Russes to Europe, and a simpler
monument to the composer Igor Stravinsky
and his wife. The Protestant (*Evangelico*)
section has a selection of ships' captains
and passengers who ended their days in
La Serenissima, plus the simple graves
of Ezra Pound and Joseph Brodsky.

There's a rather sad children's section and
a corner dedicated to the city's gondoliers, their
tombs decorated with carvings and statues of
gondolas. Visit the cemetery on the *Festa dei
morti* – All Souls' Day, 2 November – and
the vaporetto is free, but seriously packed.

MURANO

Vaporetto Colonna, Da Mula, Faro, Museo, Navagero or Venier (multiple lines).

After San Michele, the vaporetto continues to **Murano**, one of the larger and more populous islands. In the 16th and 17th centuries, when it was a world centre of glass production and a decadent resort for pleasure-seeking Venetians, Murano had a population of more than 30,000. These days only around 5,000 people live here, many workers commuting from the mainland.

Murano owes its fame to the decision taken in 1291 to transfer all of Venice's glass furnaces to the island because of a fear of fire in the main city. Their products were soon sold all over Europe. The secrets of glass were jealously guarded within the island: any glass-maker leaving Murano was proclaimed a traitor. Even today, there is no official glass school: the delicate skills of blowing and flamework are only learned by apprenticeship to one of the glass masters. At first sight, Murano looks close to being ruined by glass tourism. Dozens of 'guides' swoop on visitors as they pile off the ferry, to whisk them off on tours of furnaces. Even if you head off on your own, you'll find yourself on fondamenta dei Vetrai, a snipers' alley of shops selling glass knick-knacks, most

of which are made far from Murano. But there *are* some serious glass-makers on the island and even the tackiest showroom usually has one or two gems.

There's more to Murano, however, than glass. At the far end of fondamenta dei Vetrai is the nondescript façade of the 14th-century parish church of **San Pietro Martire** (*see p167*), which holds important works of art including Bellini's impressive altarpiece triptych.

Beyond the church, Murano's Canal Grande is spanned by Ponte Vivarini, an unattractive, 19th-century iron bridge. Before crossing, it is worth looking at the Gothic **Palazzo Da Mula**, just to the left of the bridge; this splendid 15th-century building has been recently restored and transformed into council offices. In the morning you can stroll through its courtyard, which contains a monumental carved Byzantine arch from an earlier (12th- or 13th-century) building.

On the other side of the bridge, a right turn takes you along fondamenta Cavour; 200 metres further along, it veers sharply to the left, becoming fondamenta Giustinian. The 17th-century Palazzo Giustinian, situated far from the tacky chandeliers and fluorescent clowns, is the **Museo dell'Arte Vetraria** (*see p166*), the best place to learn about the history of glass. Just beyond this is Murano's

EXPLORE

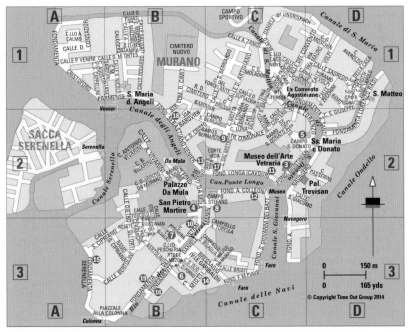

greatest architectural treasure: the 12th-century basilica of **Santi Maria e Donato** (*see p167*), with its apse towards the canal.

Return to Ponte Vivarini and walk to the end of fondamenta Sebastiano Venier. The church of **Santa Maria degli Angeli** backs on to the convent where Casanova conducted one of his most torrid affairs, with a libertine nun named Maria Morosoni.

Sights & Museums

Museo dell'Arte Vetrario
Fondamenta Giustinian 8 (041 739 586). Vaporetto Museo. **Open** 10am-5pm daily. **Admission** €5.50; €3 reductions (*see also p289* **Tourist information**). Map p165 C2 ❸

The museum was undergoing restoration as this guide went to press, with only five rooms open to the public; reopening was scheduled for late 2014. Housed in beautiful Palazzo Giustinian, built in the late 17th century for the bishop of Torcello, the museum has a huge collection of Murano glass. As well as the famed chandeliers, which were first produced in the 18th century, there are ruby-red beakers, opaque lamps and delicate Venetian *perle* – glass beads that were used in trade and commerce all over the world from the time of Marco Polo. One of the earliest pieces is the 15th-century Barovier marriage cup, decorated with portraits of the bride and groom. In one room is a collection of 17th-century oil lamps in the shapes of animals, some of which are uncannily Disney-like. On the ground floor is a good collection of Roman glassware from near Zara on the Istrian peninsula.

GONE FISHING
Relaxation Venetian-style.

Fishing is a time-honoured Venetian pastime, the Giardini embankment (*see p85*) and the Zattere (*see p145*) being two popular haunts. Angling supplies can be purchased at **Nautica & Pesca** (Cannaregio 4792, calle del Spezier, 041 241 3899, www.nauticaepesca.com), which sells everything from lugworms to wellies.

Armed with your rod and worms, you may have a yen for a boat. **Cristiano Brussa**'s hire shop in Cannaregio (fondamenta di Cannaregio 1030, 041 275 0196, www.cristianobrussa.com) has boats available by the hour or the day. No licence is needed. A valid ID document must be left at the hire shop while you've got the boat, and credit cards aren't accepted.

If you envisage yourself battling it out with the big boys on the high seas, contact **Big Game Fishing** (campo Stringari 13, Sant'Elena, 041 528 5123, www.biggamesportfishing.it). Staff will rig you out and escort you to the Adriatic. Smaller fish like mackerel make up the normal catch but tuna, shark and other monsters of the deep are possible.

If, on the other hand, you fancy messing about on the water without expending energy, contact Alfredo Zambon (335 623 3328, www.ilnuovotrionfo.org) to experience life on board the **Nuovo Trionfo**, a traditional *trabaccolo* built in 1926. The boat – a two-masted, 17-metre (65-foot) vessel once common on the Adriatic but now the only one of its kind left – has been beautifully restored by an association that aims to

Nuovo Trionfo.

preserve and promote the traditional wooden boats of Venice. Year-round, and from April to October in particular, an extensive range of activities is offered on the lagoon for up to 30 people: from a cruise or sailing excursion to special events, dinners or tours of the main islands of the lagoon. A half-day tour on the *trabaccolo* will set you back around €800, while the full-day experience costs €1,300. The **Guide to Venice** tour company (*see p290*) can arrange to have an English-speaking guide for your sailing trip.

EXPLORE

★ FREE San Pietro Martire

Fondamenta dei Vetrai (041 739 704). Vaporetto Colonna or Faro. **Open** 9am-6pm Mon-Fri; 1-6pm Sat; 8am-5pm Sun. **Map** p165 B2 ❹

Behind its unspectacular façade, the church of San Pietro Martire conceals an important work by Giovanni Bellini, backed by a marvellous landscape: *The Virgin and Child Enthroned with St Mark, St Augustine and Doge Agostino Barbarigo*. There is also a Tintoretto *Baptism*, two works by Veronese and his assistants (mainly the latter) and an ornate altarpiece (*Deposition*) by Salviati, which is lit up by the early morning sun. The sacristy (offering of €1.50) contains remarkable woodcarvings from the 17th century and a small museum of reliquaries and other ornaments.

FREE Santi Maria e Donato

Campo San Donato (041 739 056). Vaporetto Museo. **Open** 8am-7pm daily. **Map** p165 C2 ❺

Although altered by over-enthusiastic 19th-century restorers, the exterior of this church is a classic of the Veneto-Byzantine style, with an ornate blind portico on the rear of the apse. Inside is a richly coloured mosaic floor, laid down in 1140 (at the same time as the floor of the basilica di San Marco), with floral and animal motifs. Above, a Byzantine apse mosaic of the Virgin looms out of the darkness surrounded by a field of gold.

Restaurants

Acquastanca

Fondamenta Manin 48 (041 319 5125, www. acquastanca.it). Vaporetto Faro. **Meals served** noon-3.30pm, 7-10.30pm Mon, Fri; noon-3.30pm Tue-Thur, Sat. **Bar open** 9am-4pm, 6-11pm Mon, Fri; 9am-4pm, 6-8.30pm Tue-Thur, Sat. **Average** €35. **Map** p165 B3 ❻

In a former bakery, this new arrival on the Murano eating scene is helmed by two local ladies and frequented, to date, more by their fellow islanders than by visitors. It's an all-day kind of place, where you can drop by for a cappuccino, a bar snack or a whole meal. In the kitchen, Caterina updates fishy Venetian classics, while out front Giovanna uses skills picked up over many years as events manager at Harry's Bar (*see p69*) to create an atmosphere far more understated than at that brash watering hole.

B-Restaurant alla Vecchia Pescheria

Murano, campiello Pescheria 4 (041 527 957). Vaporetto Faro. **Meals served** noon-3.30pm Mon, Tue; noon-3.30pm, 6-10pm Thur-Sun. Closed 3 wks Dec. **Average** €35. **Map** p165 B3 ❼

A sideline for the glass-making Berengo dynasty, this trattoria in Murano's old fish market is chic and stylish inside, with tables beneath big green umbrellas outside on a pretty square in fine weather. The

Santi Maria e Donato.

welcome is friendly, and some very good, rather creative seafood cooking is served up at reasonable prices (for Venice). The crew that runs the place is young and lively; large groups can be catered for; and children are very welcome in this family-run eaterie where the campo outside sometimes resembles a kiddies' playground. The hours given above refer to meal times: but B-Restaurant opens early in the morning for breakfast, and is a fine place for a pre-dinner aperitivo too.

Busa alla Torre

Murano, campo Santo Stefano 3 (041 739 662). Vaporetto Faro. **Meals served** noon-3.30pm daily. **Average** €45. **Map** p165 C2 ❽

In summer, tables spill out into a pretty square opposite the church of San Pietro Martire. The service is deft and professional. The cuisine is reliable, no-frills seafood cooking, with good *primi* that might include ravioli filled with *branzino* (bream) in a spider-crab sauce, or tagliatelle with *canoce* (mantis shrimps). Note the lunch-only opening. *Photo p168.*

La Perla ai Bisatei

Murano, campo San Bernardo 1 (041 739 528). Vaporetto Museo or Venier. **Meals served** noon-3pm daily. **Average** €25. **No credit cards. Map** p165 C2 ❾

La Perla is a rare gem in Venice: spit-and-sawdust, local, family-run, unreconstructed, with great mainly fishy dishes at sub-Venetian prices and

Busa alla Torre. *See p167.*

an atmosphere that makes anyone who wanders this far into the heart of Murano feel like they've stumbled across a roomful of old friends. The traditional Venetian fare – both seafood and meat – is well prepared, served in generous helpings and very fresh.

Cafés, Bars & Gelaterie

See p167 **Acquastanca** and
B-Restaurant alla Vecchia Pescheria

Shops & Services

Berengo Fine Arts
Fondamenta dei Vetrai 109A (041 739 453, www.berengo.com). Vaporetto Colonna or Faro. **Open** 9am-5.30pm daily. **Map** p165 B3 ⑩ **Glass**
Adriano Berengo commissions various international artists to design brilliantly coloured sculptures – in glass, of course.

Davide Penso
Shop & workshop: riva Longa 48. (041 527 4634, www.davidepenso.com). Vaporetto Museo. **Open** 9.30am-6.30pm daily. **Map** p165 C2 ⑪ **Glass jewellery**
Davide Penso makes and shows exquisite glass jewellery. His own creations are all one-off or limited edition pieces with designs drawn from nature: zebra-striped, mother-of-pearl or crocodile-skinned. The shop sometimes closes 1.30-2.30pm.

Galliano Ferro
Fondamenta Colleoni 6 (041 739 477, www.gallianoferro.it). Vaporetto Faro. **Open** by appointment. **No credit cards. Map** p165 C2 ⑫ **Glass**

Inspired by 18th-century classics of design, Ferro's rich, vibrant and intricate works in glass are some of Murano's most sought-after pieces. There are early 20th-century and Islamic art-inspired designs available too.

Luigi Camozzo
Fondamenta Venier 3 (041 736 875, www.luigi camozzo.com). Vaporetto Venier. **Open** 10am-6pm Mon-Fri; by appointment Sat, Sun. **Map** p165 B2 ⑬ **Glass**
It would be over-simplifying things to describe Luigi Camozzo as a glass-engraver. Using a variety of different tools, he carves, sculpts and inscribes wonderfully soft, natural bas-reliefs into glass. Drop by and you may even catch him in action.

Manin 56
Fondamenta Manin 56 (041 527 5392). Vaporetto Faro. **Open** 10am-6pm daily. Closed Jan. **Map** p165 B3 ⑭ **Glass**
Sells modern (though slightly staid) lines in glassware and vases from prestigious houses such as Salviati and Vivarini.

Marina e Susanna Sent
Fondamenta Serenella 20 (041 527 4665, www.marinaesusannasent.com). Vaporetto Colonna. **Open** 10am-5pm Mon-Fri. **Map** p165 A3 ⑮ **Jewellery**
In the Sent sisters' recently expanded Murano workshop, you'll find clean, modern jewellery in glass, in interesting counterpoise to innovative jewellery in other materials, including wood, coral, paper and rubber.
Other locations San Marco 2090, ponte San Moise (041 520 4014); Dorsoduro 669 & 681, campo San Vio (041 520 8136).

Rossana e Rossana. *See p170.*

EXPLORE

MURANO GLASS

How it's made – and where to buy it.

Murano has been the capital of glass since 1291. In that year, Venice's rulers banished all glass furnaces to this island to avert the kind of conflagrations that would regularly devastate swathes of what was then a largely wooden city. Over the following centuries, the island refined its particular craft. Its vases, chandeliers, mirrors and drinking vessels were shipped all over the world by Venice's great merchant fleet.

Nowadays, the assault of glass-blowing hustlers coupled with shop windows packed with glass *objets* of dubious taste and even more dubious origin make it hard to see the island's speciality as a noble art. But behind the tack, Murano remains a special place where centuries of glass-making techniques are still jealously preserved.

Murano glass is divided into medium to large furnace-made pieces (blown glass, sculpture and lamps) and smaller pieces (beads and animals) fashioned from sticks of coloured glass in the heat of a gas jet. Once made, these objects may be engraved or patterned with silver, and multi-piece objects need assembling – all of which keeps much of Murano's population employed.

But unless you have your wits about you, you may never get beyond shops and warehouses packed with glass shipped from the Far East. Most hotel porters and concierges in Venice have agreements of some kind with these emporia: don't expect disinterested advice on where to go.

Tourist-trade Murano outlets with 'authentic' furnaces being used by 'authentic' glass-blowers rarely sell the articles you'll see produced, whatever the salesmen tell you. Glass shops range from the excellent to the downright rip-off: labels proclaiming '*vetro di Murano*' mean very little ('*vetro artistico di Murano*' is meant to offer a firmer guarantee, though some top producers refuse to bow to this, believing that their reputation is all the guarantee needed).

So, how do you go about making sure you get the real thing? Real Murano glass is fiendishly expensive. There's no such thing as a real €30 vase, or a genuine €5 wine glass… at those prices you can be sure you're taking home something 'authentically' Chinese. If you want genuine without paying much for it, you'll have to resort to the odd glass bead. Moreover, the best workshops don't allow tourists in to gawp, though sometimes you can peer through an open front gate. And, occasionally, they'll invite you in if you really intend to purchase. If you're after a true Murano glass experience, just be brave: ring that doorbell and see if they'll humour you and allow you a peek.

In the outlets listed in our Murano: Shopping section (*see left*) you'll find fine examples of the real thing. More great glass can be found at L'Isola – Carlo Moretti (*see p67*), Galleria Marina Barovier (*see p67*), Caterina Tognon (*see p70*) and Vittorio Costantini (*see p109*).

EXPLORE

Burano.

Murano Collezioni

Fondamenta Manin 1C (041 736 272, www.
muranocollezioni.com). Vaporetto Colonna.
Open 10.30am-5.30pm Mon-Sat. Closed 2wks
Jan. **Map** p165 B3 ⑯ **Glass**
This shop sells pieces by some of the lagoon's most
respected producers, including Carlo Moretti,
Barovier e Toso, and Venini. Room to move about
and good lighting will help you make your choice.

Rossana e Rossana

Riva Longa 11 (041 527 4076, www.ro-e-ro.com).
Vaporetto Museo. **Open** 10am-6pm daily. **Map**
p165 C2 ⑰ **Glass**
The place to come for traditional Venetian glass,
from filigree pieces to Veronese vases and elegant
goblets that are based on models that were popular
in the early years of the last century – all produced
by master glass-maker Davide Fuin. *Photo p168.*

Seguso Viro

Fondamenta Venier 29 (041 527 4255, www.
segusoviro.com). Vaporetto Museo or Venier.
Open 11am-4pm Mon-Sat. **Map** p165 B2 ⑱
Glass
Giampaolo Seguso comes from a long line of
Venetian glass-makers. His modern blown glass
pieces are enhanced by experiments working around
Murano traditions.

Venini

Fondamenta Vetrai 47 (041 273 7204, www.
venini.com). Vaporetto Colonna. **Open** 9.30am-
5.30pm Mon-Sat. **Map** p165 B3 ⑲ **Glass**
Venini was the biggest name in Murano glass for
much of the 20th century, and remains in the fore-
front. Classic designs are joined by more innovative
pieces, including a selection designed by major international glass artists.
Other location San Marco 314, piazzetta dei
Leoncini (041 522 4045).

BURANO & MAZZORBO

Vaporetto Burano or Mazzorbo (12, N).

Mazzorbo, the long island next to Burano,
is a haven of peace, rarely visited by tourists.
It is worth getting off here just for the sake of
the quiet walk along the canal and then across
the long wooden bridge that connects Mazzorbo
to Burano. The view from the bridge across
the lagoon to Venice is stunning, and there's
always a chance you'll have it to yourself.

Mazzorbo was settled around the tenth
century. When it became clear that Venice itself
had got the upper hand, most of the population
simply dismantled their houses brick by brick,
transported them by boat to Venice, and rebuilt
them there. Today Mazzorbo is a lazy place of
small farms with a pleasant walk to the 14th-
century Gothic church of **Santa Caterina**
(opening times vary), whose wonky tower still
has its original bell dating from 1318 – one of
the oldest in Europe. Winston Churchill, a keen
amateur painter, set up his easel here more than
once after World War II. Facing Burano is an
area of attractive, modern, low-cost housing,
in shades of lilac, grey and green, designed
by the architect Giancarlo De Carlo.

You could almost believe that they invented
the adjective 'picturesque' to describe **Burano**.
Together with its lace, its multicoloured houses
make it a magnet for tourists armed with
cameras. The locals are traditionally either
fishermen or lace-makers, though there are
fewer and fewer of the latter, despite the best
efforts of the island's Scuola di Merletti (Lace
School, now also home to the **Museo del**
Merletti; *see p172*).

The street leading from the main quay
throbs with souvenir shops selling lace, lace
and more lace – much of it machine-made in

the far east. But Burano is big enough for the visitor to meander through its quiet backstreets and avoid a lace overload. It was in Burano that Carnevale (*see p28*) was revived in the 1970s; the modest celebrations here are still far more authentically joyful than the antics of masked tourists cramming piazza San Marco.

Fishermen have lived on Burano since the seventh century. According to local lore they painted their houses different colours so that they could recognise them when fishing out on the lagoon – though in fact only a tiny proportion of the island's houses can actually be seen from the lagoon. Whatever the reason, the *buranelli* still go to great efforts to decorate their houses, and social life centres on the *fondamente* where the men repair nets or tend to their boats moored in the canal below, while their wives – at least in theory – make lace.

Lace was first produced in Burano in the 15th century, originally by nuns, but the trade was quickly picked up by fishermen's wives and daughters. So skilful were the local lace-makers that in the 17th century many were paid handsomely to work in the Alengon lace ateliers in Normandy. Today, most work is done on commission, though interested parties will have to get to know one of the lace-makers in person, as the co-operative that used to represent the old ladies closed down in 1995.

Burano lace.

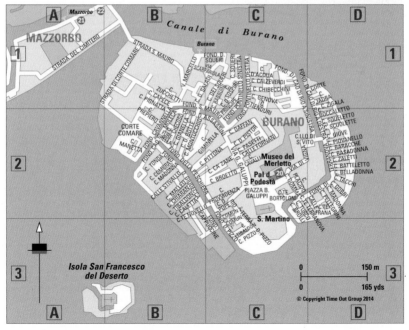

EXPLORE

Baldassare Galuppi.

The busy main square of Burano is named after the island's most famous son, Baldassare Galuppi, a 17th-century composer who collaborated with Carlo Goldoni on a number of operas and who was the subject of a poem by Robert Browning. The square is a good place for sipping a glass of prosecco. Across from the lace museum is the church of **San Martino** (open 8am-noon, 3-7pm daily), containing an early Tiepolo *Crucifixion* and, in the chapel to the right of the chancel, three small paintings by the 15th-century painter Giovanni Mansueti; the *Flight into Egypt* presents the Holy Family amid an imaginative menagerie of beasts and birds. There's a lively morning fish market (Tue-Sat) on the fondamenta della Pescheria.

Sights & Museums

Museo del Merletti
Piazza B Galuppi 187, Burano (041 730 034, http://museomerletto.visitmuve.it). Vaporetto 9, 12, N. **Open** 10am-5pm Tue-Sun. **Admission** €5; €3.50 reductions; *see also p289* **Tourist information. No credit cards. Map** p171 C2 ⑳

Following a major revamp, the Lace School's rooms with painted wooden beams are looking resplendent. In a chronological layout, the display covers elaborate examples of lace-work from the 17th century onwards. There are fans, collars and parasols, and some of the paper pattern-sheets that lace-makers use. Some of Burano's remaining lace-makers can regularly be found at work here, displaying their handicraft to visitors.

Restaurants

Alla Maddalena
Mazzorbo 7B (041 730 151). Vaporetto Mazzorbo. **Meals served** noon-3pm Mon-Wed, Fri-Sun. **Average** €40. **Map** p171 A1 ㉑
Opposite the jetty on the island of Mazzorbo is this lunch-only trattoria, which serves good lagoon cuisine. During the hunting season, wild duck is sourced directly from local hunters; the rest of the year, seafood dominates. Book ahead for Sunday lunch in summer, when the waterside tables and those in the quiet garden behind fill up. Service, though professional, is not always cheerful.

Venissa
Mazzorbo, fondamenta Santa Caterina 3 (041 527 2281, www.venissa.it). Vaporetto Mazzorbo. **Meals served** noon-2.30pm, 7-9.30pm Mon, Tue-Sun. **Average** €95. **Map** p171 A1 ㉒
Inside a high-walled vineyard, with a hotel attached (*see p279*), Venissa serves exquisite fare inspired by super-fresh local produce, conjured up by Michelin-starred chef Antonia Klugmann. Many of the raw ingredients come from the on-site vegetable garden, but fish caught by Venetian fishermen also feature heavily. There are taster menus at €75 and €95. With the main restaurant open only six months a year, a less formal eating alternative/winebar is planned for 2014, to supplement Venissa's offer year-round. The initiative is the brainchild of prosecco producers Bisol, who have brought back to life the well-nigh-forgotten Dorona grape here. Book to arrive an hour before lunch and enjoy (€25) a tour of the walled estate, plus a tasting of Venissa's own wine.

SAN FRANCESCO DEL DESERTO

From behind the church of San Martino on Burano there is a view across the lagoon to the idyllic monastery island of **San Franceso del Deserto**. The island, with its 4,000 cypress trees, is inhabited by a small community of Franciscan monks. Getting there can be quite a challenge. If you take the water taxi from Burano, expect to pay at least €60 for the return ride. Individuals or smaller groups should call the Laguna Fla boat hire service (339 778 1132) which chargees €10 per person return (no credit cards).

The other-worldly monk who shepherds visitors around will tell the story (only in Italian) of how the island was St Francis's first stop in Europe on his journey back from the Holy Land in 1220. He planted his stick, it grew into a pine and birds flew in to sing for him; there are certainly plenty of them in evidence in the cypress-packed gardens today. The medieval monastery – all warm stone and cloistered calm – is about as far as you can get from the worldly bustle of the Rialto.

Sights & Museums

★ Convento di San Francesco del Deserto
041 528 6863, www.sanfrancescodeldeserto.it. **Open** 9-11am, 3-5pm Tue-Sun. **Admission** by donation.

TORCELLO

Vaporetto Torcello (9, N).

This sprawling, marshy island is where the history of Venice began. **Torcello** today is a picturesquely unkempt place with a resident population of about 15 (plus infinitely more mosquitoes). It's difficult to believe that in the 14th century more than 20,000 people lived here. It was the first settlement in the lagoon, founded in the fifth century by the citizens of the Roman town of Altino on the mainland. Successive waves of emigration from Altino were sparked off by barbarian invasions, first by Attila and his Huns, and, in the seventh century, by the Lombards. But Torcello's dominance of the lagoon did not last: Venice itself was found to be more salubrious (malaria was rife on Torcello) and more easily defendable. Even the bishop of Torcello chose to live on Murano, in the palace that now houses the glass museum (*see p166*). But past decline is present charm, and rural Torcello is a great antidote to the pedestrian traffic jams around San Marco.

From the ferry jetty, the cathedral **campanile** (*see right*) can already be made out; to get there, simply follow the path along the main canal through the island. Halfway along the canal is the ponte del Diavolo (one of only two bridges in the lagoon without a parapet), where there is an *osteria* called **Al Ponte del Diavolo** (041 730 401, closed dinner, all Mon and Dec-Jan, average €40) that caters mainly to tourists and local wedding/baptism/communion parties. For the classic Torcello restaurant **Locanda Cipriani**, *see p174*.

Torcello's main square has some desultory souvenir stalls, the small but interesting **Museo di Torcello** (*see p174*) with archaeological finds from around the lagoon, a battered stone seat known arbitrarily as Attila's throne, and two extraordinary churches.

The 11th-century church of **Santa Fosca** (open 10am-5pm daily, free) looks somewhat like a miniature version of Istanbul's Santa Sophia, more Byzantine than European with its Greek-cross plan and external colonnade; its bare interior allows the perfect geometry of the space to come to the fore. Next door is the imposing cathedral of **Santa Maria Assunta** (*see p174*) with its campanile (bell tower). The view of the lagoon from the top was memorably described by Ruskin: 'Far as the eye can reach, a waste of wild sea moor, of a lurid ashen grey.' And he concluded with the elegiac words: 'Mother and daughter, you behold them both in their widowhood, Torcello and Venice.' Long open to the public, the campanile – hit by lightning and declared unstable some years

EXPLORE

Santa Maria Assunta. *See p174.*

ago – was still shrouded in scaffolding as this guide went to press, with an end to work tentatively forecast for Easter 2014.

Note that there is an €8 cumulative ticket for the museum and the cathedral, which also includes the cathedral audioguide (usually €2).

Sights & Museums

Museo di Torcello
Palazzo del Consiglio (041 730 761). Vaporetto Torcello. **Open** 10am-5pm Tue-Sun. **Admission** €3. **No credit cards.**
The Museum of Torcello has a small but worthwhile collection of sculptures and archaeological finds from the cathedral and elsewhere in Torcello. Among the exhibits on the ground floor are late 12th-century fragments of mosaic from the apse of Santa Maria dell'Assunta, and two of the *bocche di leone* (lions' mouths) where citizens with grudges could post their denunciations. Upstairs are Greco-Byzantine icons, painted panels, bronze seals and pottery fragments, and an exquisite carved ivory statuette of an embracing couple dating from the beginning of the 15th century.

★ Santa Maria Assunta
041 270 2464. Vaporetto Torcello. **Open** 10.30am-5pm daily. **Admission** €5. **No credit cards.**
Dating from 639, the basilica of Santa Maria Assunta is the oldest building on the lagoon. The interior has an elaborate 11th-century mosaic floor, but the main draws are the vivid mosaics on the ceiling vault and walls, which range in date from the ninth century to the end of the 12th. The apse has a simple but stunning mosaic of a *Madonna and Child* on a plain gold background, while the other end of the cathedral is dominated by a huge mosaic of the *Last Judgement*. The theological rigour and narrative complexity of this huge composition suggest comparisons with the *Divine Comedy*, which Dante was writing at about the same time, however the anonymous mosaicists of Torcello were even more concerned than him with striking fear into the hearts of their audience. It's worth picking up an audioguide (€2) for a very good explanation of the church's history and artistic treasures. *Photo p173.*

Restaurants

Locanda Cipriani
Torcello, piazza Santa Fosca 29 (041 730 150/ http://locandacipriani.com). Vaporetto Torcello. **Meals served** noon-3pm Mon, Wed-Sun. Closed Jan. **Average** €80.
There is a lot to like about the high-class Locanda Cipriani, which was one of Hemingway's haunts. The setting, just off Torcello's pretty square, is idyllic; tables are spread over a large vine-shaded

terrace during the summer. And although there is nothing remotely adventurous about the cuisine, it's good in an old-fashioned way. Specialities such as *risotto alla torcellana* (with seasonal vegetables) are done to perfection, and the desserts are tasty treats for rich kids. Dinner is served (7-9pm) on Friday and Saturday, by prior arrangement only.
▶ *If you want to stay at the locanda, see p278.*

LA CERTOSA
Vaporetto Certosa (4.1 or 4.2, request stop).

Situated between Sant'Elena and Le Vignole, **La Certosa** was the seat of a monastery, which from 1422 was run by the Certosini monks of Florence. Napoleon suppressed the monastery and the army moved in, staying until 1968, when the island fell into decay; it was later earmarked to become a park. In 2004, the remaining warehouses and huts became the home of a sailing club (www.ventodivenezia.it), that runs a sailing school and a hotel (*see p279*). The rest of the island is open to the public, and makes for a pleasant walk, though views are limited by perimeter walls. If you are lucky, you'll meet the island's goats scrabbling through the thick vegetation.

SANT'ERASMO
Vaporetto Capannone, Chiesa, or Punta Vela (13, N); Forte Massimiliano (18).

The largest island in the northern lagoon, Sant'Erasmo is a well-kept secret, with a tiny population that contents itself with growing most of the vegetables eaten in *La Serenissima* (on Rialto market stalls, the sign 'San Rasmo' is a mark of quality). Venetians refer to the islanders of Sant'Erasmo as *i matti* ('the crazies') because of their shallow gene pool – everybody seems to be called Vignotto or Zanella. There are cars on this island, but as they are only used to drive the few miles from house to boat and back, few are in top-notch condition, a state of affairs favoured by the

---

IN THE KNOW
HARRY'S OFFSHOOTS

The three big Cipriani concerns in Venice – the **Hotel Cipriani** (*see p278*), **Harry's Bar** (run by Arrigo Cipriani, son of the founder; *see p69*) and the **Locanda Cipriani** (run by Arrigo's sister Carla; *see p174*) on Torcello have no business links; in fact, all have been involved in a long-running legal battle for the right to use the name 'Cipriani'.

La Certosa.

fact that the island does not have a single policeman. It also lacks a doctor, pharmacy and high school, but there is a supermarket and a tiny primary school. There are also some restaurants: **Ca' Vignotto** (via Forti 71, 041 528 5329, www.vignotto.com, average €30-€50, closed dinner Tue, Wed, Sun and all Mon), where bookings are essential, and a fishermen's bar-trattoria – **Ai Tedeschi** (041 521 0738, open 9am-11pm daily) – hidden away on a small sandy beach by the **Forte Massimiliano**. This latter is a moat-surrounded 19th-century Austrian fort that has been restored. Before restoration, it was used by a local farmer to store his tools. Nowadays it opens to the public on summer afternoons (3-7pm Wed-Sun) and some weekend mornings too. Occasionally it hosts exhibitions.

The main attraction of the island lies in the beautiful country landscapes and lovely walks past traditional Veneto farmhouses, through vineyards and fields of artichokes and asparagus – a breath of fresh air after all the urban crowding of Venice. For those wanting to get around more swiftly, bicycles can be hired from the guesthouse **Lato Azzurro** (041 523 0642; €5 for the first two hours, then €1 per hour after; no credit cards). It's a ten-minute walk southwards from the vaporetto stop Capannone.

By the main vaporetto stop (**Chiesa**) is the 20th-century church (on the site of an earlier one founded before 1000; opening hours vary); it's technically named Santi Erme and Erasmo, but it's widely known as simply 'Chiesa'. Over the entrance door is a gruesome painting, attributed to Domenico Tintoretto, of the martyrdom of St Erasmus, who had his intestines wound out of his body on a windlass. The resemblance of a windlass to a capstan resulted in St Erasmus becoming the patron saint of sailors.

If you're around on the first Sunday in October, don't miss the *Festa del mosto*, held to inaugurate the first pressing of new wine. This is perhaps the only chance you'll ever get to witness – or even participate in – a *gara del bisato*: a game in which an eel is dropped into a tub of water blackened by squid ink. Contestants have to plunge their heads into the tub and attempt to catch the eel with their teeth.

LAZZARETTO NUOVO & VIGNOLE

Vaporetto 13 (request stop).

Opposite Sant'Erasmo's Capannone vaporetto stop is the tiny island of **Lazzaretto Nuovo**. In the 15th century, the island was fortified as a customs depot and military prison; during the 1576 plague outbreak it became a quarantine centre. The island is now home to a research centre for the archaeologists of the Archeo Club di Venezia, who are excavating its ancient remains, including a church that may date back to the sixth century. Guided tours (041 244 4011, www.lazzarettonuovo.com) are available from April to October. A donation is expected.

On the smaller island of **Vignole** (also served by the 13 vaporetto, on request), there is a medieval chapel dedicated to St Erosia.

San Lazzaro Degli Armeni.

EXPLORE

The Southern Lagoon

The southern part of the lagoon – between
Venice, the Lido and the mainland – has 14
small islands, a few of which are still inhabited,
though most are out of bounds to tourists.
La Grazia was for years a quarantine hospital
but the structure has now been closed. The
huge **San Clemente**, originally a lunatic
asylum and later a home for abandoned cats,
was more recently a plush hotel that had
»closed down at the time of writing.

The islands of **San Servolo** and **San
Lazzaro** (for both, *see below*) are served by
vaporetto 20, and both are well worth visiting.

SAN SERVOLO

From the 18th century until 1978, San Servolo
was Venice's mental hospital (in his poem *Julian
and Maddalo*, Shelley describes a visit that he
paid there with Byron); it is now home to Venice
International University (*see p288*). In 2006,
the **Museo del Manicomio di San Servolo**
(San Servolo Asylum Museum; 041 524 0119)
was inaugurated. The museum is open for
guided visits only (€3; minimum 5 people);
booking is essential. It reveals the different
ways in which mental illnesses have been
treated over the years; there are not only
examples of the more or less brutal methods
of restraint (chains, straitjackets, handcuffs)
but also early examples of such treatments
as hydro-massage and electrotherapy. The
tour ends in the reconstructed 18th-century
pharmacy, which relied partly on medicines
obtained from some of the exotic plants grown
on the island. After the tour, it is possible to visit
the island's extensive and charming gardens.

SAN LAZZARO DEGLI ARMENI

A further five minutes on the no.20 will take you
to the island of **San Lazzaro degli Armeni**.
There are tours (041 526 0104) of the island every
afternoon for visitors from the mid-afternoon boat
(times vary seasonally) from San Zaccaria. The
cost is €6 (€3 reductions; no credit cards).

A black-cloaked Armenian priest meets the
boat and takes visitors on a detailed tour of the
Monastero Mechitarista. The tiny island is a
global point of reference for Armenia's Catholic
minority, visited and supported by Armenians
from Italy and abroad. Near the entrance stand
the printing presses that helped to distribute
Armenian literature all over the world for 200
years. They are now silent, with the monastery's
retro line in dictionaries and liturgical texts
farmed out to a modern press.

Originally a leper colony, in 1717 the island
was presented by the doge to an Armenian

abbot called Mekhitar, who was on the run from the Turkish invasion of the Peloponnese. There had been an Armenian community in Venice since the 11th century, centring on the tiny Santa Croce degli Armeni church, just around the corner from piazza San Marco, but the construction of this church and monastery made Venice a world centre of Armenian culture. The monastery was the only one in Venice to be spared the Napoleonic axe: the emperor had a soft spot for Armenians and claimed this was an academic rather than a religious institute.

The tour takes in both the cloisters and the church, rebuilt after a fire in 1883. The museum and the modern library contain 40,000 priceless books and manuscripts, and a bizarre collection of gifts donated over the years by visiting Armenians that range from Burmese prayer books to an Egyptian mummy.

The island's most famous student was Lord Byron, who used to take a break from his more earthly pleasures in Venice and row over three times a week to learn Armenian (as he found that his 'mind wanted something craggy to break upon') with the monks. He helped the monks to publish an Armenian-English grammar, although by his own confession he never got beyond the basics of the language. You can buy a completed version of this, plus a number of period maps and an illustrated children's Armenian grammar, in the shop just inside the monastery gate.

BATTLING THE SEA

Protecting a much-loved natural environment.

For Venetians, the greatest threat has always been the open sea, and efforts have been devoted over the centuries to strengthening the natural defences offered by Pellestrina and the Lido. In the 18th century, the *murazzi* were created: an impressive barrier of stone and marble blocks all the way down both islands.

Nowadays, the threat is seen as coming from the three *bocche di porto* (the lagoon's openings to the sea) between the Lido and Cavallino, between the Lido and Pellestrina and between Pellestrina and Chioggia. Works to create the highly controversial mobile dyke system known as Mose – which when fully operational should protect the lagoon from tides of up to three metres – are scheduled for completion in 2016.

There are 34 islands on the saltwater lagoon, most of them uninhabited, containing only crumbling masonry, and home to seagulls and lazy lizards. The lagoon itself covers some 520 square kilometres (200 square miles) – the world's biggest wetland. This wild, fragile environment is where Venetians take refuge from the tourist hordes, escaping by boat for picnics on deserted islands, or fishing for bass and bream. Others set off to dig up clams at low tide (most without the requisite licence), or organise hunting expeditions for duck, using the makeshift hides known as *botte* ('barrels', which is what they were originally, sunk into the floor of the lagoon). Many just head out after work, at sunset, to row.

EXPLORE

Arts & Entertainment

Children

There's nothing quite so special as experiencing Venice with a small child: this is truly a wonderland, with water where the streets should be, and a city-wide playground of hidey-holes and creepy corners. Of course, a solid diet of dim churches and interminable art galleries may quell their curiosity. But Venice has so much more than that to offer children.

Older offspring might baulk at so much culture, but there's plenty for them here too. The www.venicebackstage.org website has diagrams and cut-away drawings of the unique mechanics of this extraordinary place. With an idea of the complexity of what they're walking through and over, they should find much to keep their interest alive.

SIGHTSEEING

Plan your day's activities with imaginative foresight, allow for a good deal of walking and make sure you factor in plenty of ice-cream stops. You'll be surprised, too, how much you'll learn by letting your kids take the lead: bedazzled by the wonder of it all, they may well end up drawing your attention to fascinating aspects of the city that might otherwise have passed you by.

Little ones are amazed by the sheer oddness of the place: exploit it, and remember that hours hanging over bridges spotting fish-finger delivery boats is part of the Venetian experience too. Older kids may be inveigled into the right frame of mind with a pre-emptive gift of Cornelia Funke's novel *The Thief Lord*; if

IN THE KNOW
ALMOST A GONDOLA

Most children will demand a gondola trip. Remember that this expensive experience (*see p282*) can be substituted by – or supplemented with – rides on the humbler but more useful *traghetti* (*see p281*) that ply across the Grand Canal at points distant from bridges. Let your kids stand up in the boat like real Venetians.

that intrigues them, a visit to **campo Santa Margherita** (*see p138*) will be indispensable.

When you're done watching boats slipping under the city's 400-plus bridges, offer your kids a glimpse of illustrious craft of the past at the **Museo Storico Navale** (*see p86*), where Venice's maritime history is charted in scale models of ships built in the Arsenale over the centuries.

Venetians have always devoted much time to games and sport; visit the **Museo Querini Stampalia** (*see p75*), where a collection of 18th-century scenes includes some very unlikely amusements: one painting, *La Guerra dei Pugni* by Antonio Strom, shows one of the mass boxing matches that occurred frequently on bridges. The initial four competitors started out with one foot on the white inlaid footprints on the corners of the top step: these markers are still there today on **ponte dei Pugni** (*see p138*), ponte della Guerra near campo San Zulian or ponte di Santa Fosca near the campo of the same name.

Don't forget to introduce your kids to the most famous Venetian game of all. With the lagoon behind you, and the lagoon-facing façade of the Doge's Palace in front of you, make your way to the third column from the left. Place your back firmly against it, then walk round it, all the way. Can you circumnavigate it without holding on to the pillar and without slipping off the shoe-worn marble pavement?

Most of Venice's museums are singularly hands-off, but some may still appeal to kids. If the vast Tintorettos and echoing halls of the **Palazzo Ducale** (*see p56*) inspire only yawns, combine your visit with a tour of the palace's secret corridors, the *Itinerari Segreti* (not advisable for toddlers), which will take you into dungeons and torture rooms. The **Museo di Storia Naturale** (*see p122*) is home to an aquarium and some very impressive fossils.

Break your children into art with visits to less demanding exhibits, such as the **Scuola di San Giorgio degli Schiavoni** (*see p88*), where Vittorio Carpaccio's *St George* cycle is packed with fascinating detail. The grand Tintorettos in the **Madonna dell'Orto** (*see p104*), particularly *The Last Judgement*, are full of the kind of gruesome details – such as bodies with skulls for heads scrabbling their way out of the earth – likely to appeal to kids.

Don't be scared off from big galleries such as the **Accademia** (*see p145*); you may link up with one of the gallery's more child-friendly guides, who will bend over backwards to interest your offspring in the collection. And the **Musei Civici** (*see p55*) organises family events, usually on Sunday afternoons (in Italian only at present).

To win a little picture-viewing time in churches, try pointing out to your children that the red marble used in so many church floors contains amazing fossils. While they embark on mini-palaeontological excursions, you can concentrate on the artworks.

When the culture all gets too much, take Junior up a **campanile** for a bird's-eye view of the city. The one in piazza San Marco (*see p55*) is the highest; **San Giorgio Maggiore**'s (*see p159*) affords a more detached vantage point. Time your ascent to coincide with the striking of an hour – noon is particularly deafening. Give the kids the satisfaction of making their own panting way up to the top of the campanile at the basilica on **Torcello** (*see p173*), via steep sloping ramps rather than stairs; a fine view over the lagoon is the reward.

TIPS FOR TINIES
Keeping little visitors happy.

Entertaining your very small children while you catch some culture in Venice can be an arduous task, but a few organisations are making it just that bit easier for you.

The wonderful **Fondazione Querini Stampalia** (*see p75*) welcomes three- to six-year-olds in its Casa Macchietta space, which is manned by Italian, English and French speakers. There are drawing materials and music, books to read and drama workshops to keep youngsters entertained while you peruse the art, visit the library or just have a quiet cappuccino in the Fondazione's café. The facility is open 1-6pm Tue-Fri, and costs €5 per child for a two-hour session.

There's no charge at all for using the facilities for one- to four-year-olds in **Ca' Giustinian**, the headquarters of the Biennale arts umbrella organisation (San Marco 1364A, calle del Ridotto,

open Apr-Oct 9am-8.30pm daily, Nov-Mar 9am-8.30pm Mon-Sat). The large ground-floor room in a 15th-century palazzo with Grand Canal frontage is a brightly coloured haven for infants and weary parents, equipped with books, drawing materials, bottle warmers and changing tables. When you've had enough of keeping your tinies happy, the Ombra del Leone (*see p70*) bar across the hall does great light lunches and cocktails, to be enjoyed on the splendid waterfront terrace when the weather permits.

The municipal library at campo San Provolo, just east of piazza San Marco, is another place to reward your youngsters. Officially called **Biblioteca Pedagogica Lorenzo Bettini** (Castello 4704, 041 522 0557), it has books in Italian, English and other languages, for children from infancy to adolescence.

Fondazione Querini Stampalia.

PARKS, BEACHES & ENTERTAINMENT

Most Venetian kids spend their free time in their local *campi* (squares). Ball games are officially forbidden there, but you will find them going on in most of them anyway, particularly in the larger ones like campo Santa Maria Formosa and campo San Polo. Venetian kids are used to letting foreign visitors join in. In campo Santa Maria Formosa and campo Santo Stefano, small play areas for toddlers have been set up next to the churches.

Although well hidden, there are public parks in the city too, and most of them – including the **giardini pubblici** (*see p85*) and the **Parco Savorgnan** (*see p95*) – have been fitted up with swings and slides. Out in **Sant'Elena** (*see p87*), things improve with a grassy play area along the lagoon, and a roller skating/cycling rink.

On the mainland, the brand new **Parco San Giuliano** (bus 12 from piazzale Roma) is one of Italy's largest urban parks. The still-small trees don't offer much shade on a blazing summer day, but there are play areas, football pitches, a lake and a roller skating rink.

In summer, break up the culture with a trip to the **Lido** and its beaches (*see p162*). Most of the main ones are sewn up by the big hotels, which will charge you for a small stretch of sand, sometimes with deckchair and umbrella, and certainly with huge numbers of near neighbours. Pleasant **Sant'Erasmo** – a large, rural island – can be cycled around in an hour or so (for bike hire *see p175* **Lato Azzurro**). There's a small beach straight across the island from the ferry landing stage. Alternatively, head for the beaches of **Lido di Jesolo** (*see p175*).

Local feast days also provide entertainment, usually in the shape of puppet theatres. Watch walls for posters announcing *feste*. Particularly picturesque is the feast of Saints Peter and Paul in the parish of **San Pietro in Castello** (*see p88*), celebrated on 29 June.

GETTING AROUND

The frequent absence of barriers between pavement and canal presents a problem for mobile toddlers: safety reins might be a good idea. Pre-walkers present another dilemma. After heaving a pushchair over the umpteenth bridge in a day, a baby backpack may seem like a gift from heaven.

Vaporetto travel is not cheap. Children under five travel free; after that they pay full fare, though discounted passes are available (*see p281*). But if you look on it as a Venetian experience in itself, the cost will not seem so outrageous. It is perfectly acceptable to take your pram or pushchair on to the vaporetto – although it's probably better to avoid the smaller boats in rush hour. A complete circle on line 2 from the San Marco-San Zaccaria stop on the riva degli Schiavoni will you across to the Giudecca, then up to the station and port areas, giving them a glimpse of Venice's industrial underbelly as well as a triumphal march down the Grand Canal.

BOOKS

The excellent children's guide (in English) *VivaVenice* by Paolo Zoffoli and Paola Scibilia (Elzeviro, 2002) has games, informative illustrations and interesting facts. *Venice for Kids* by Elisabetta Pasqualin (Fratelli Palombi, 2004) is one of a series of books on Italian cities. On the fiction front, Terry Jones's fantasy story *Nicobobinus* and Anthony Horowitz's *Scorpia* both begin with exciting scenes set in Venice. And the city's alleys, *campi* and canals provide an important backdrop for the scamps of Cornelia Funke's *The Thief Lord*.

ROWING RACES

Oars to the fore.

If there's rowing going on – and there very often is – then the sight of a flotilla of boats being rowed full tilt across the lagoon or down the Grand Canal may keep both you and your children happy.

The regata delle Befane – in which rowers dressed as the old witch who brings children presents at Epiphany (6 January) whip down the Grand Canal from San Tomà to the Rialto at 10am – is a light-hearted affair. But others are hard-fought battles between the city's famously excellent rowers displaying their own particular style of forward-facing rowing.

There are 120 'serious' fixtures on the lagoon during the rowing season from April to September, plus more to accompany every big Venetian feast day. **Carnevale** (*see p28*), **Festa della Sensa** (*see p29*) and **Il Redentore** (*see p30*) all have their accompanying rowing events. The most sumptuous of all the Venetian regattas, however, is the **Regata Storica** (*see p30*) on the first Sunday in September.

More riotously jolly is the **Vogalonga** (*see p29*), which follows a 30-kilometre (18-mile) route around Venice and the northern lagoon. The race is held in spring or early summer and is open to anyone with a boat and an oar. Rowers descend from all over the country and much further afield.

Film

If you pitch up in town during the world's longest-running film festival in late summer, you might mistake Venice for cinema heaven. But outside the once-a-year jamboree, the scene is less exciting. The renaissance in 2012 of the Multisala Rossini cinema has certainly livened things up and provided a little more choice for ardent cinemagoers. Many former picture palaces, however, now house supermarkets: a pretty accurate reflection of local demand, with a diminishing population translating into decreasing numbers of moviegoers.

WHERE TO GO, WHAT TO SEE

Besides the festival at the beginning of September, when the Lido's bikini-clad hordes rub shoulders with journalists, photographers and a constellation of international stars, the only other ray of hope is **Circuito Cinema**, a city hall-backed film promotion initiative that runs and programmes a group of local arthouse cinemas.

The Circuito's cinemas include the **Giorgione Movie d'Essai**, **Multisala Astra** on the Lido and – restored and reopened in 2012 – the **Multisala Rossini** not far from campo Santo Stefano. See www.comune.venezia.it/cinema or www.venicemoviebook.it for details of others.

In Italy, the dubber is king, and the dearth of original-language films infuriates cinema lovers. The Giorgione, Rossini and Astra offer a limited selection of films in the *versione originale*.

ASSOCIATIONS

Circuito Cinema

Information: Palazzo Mocenigo, Santa Croce 1991, salizada San Stae (041 524 1320, www.comune.venezia.it/cinema). Vaporetto San Stae. **Map** p307 F4.
The Circuito Cinema operates as a publisher and as a cine-club organising a series of themed seasons and workshops. It also airs original-language films, mostly classics or arthouse movies. Its annual (July-June) CinemaPiù card (€30; €20 for students)

gives discounts to all of Venice's cinemas. It can be bought from the Giorgione, Rossini and Astra cinemas (for all, *see below*), and in the summer at the San Polo open-air cinema (*see p184*).

CINEMAS

Giorgione Movie D'Essai

Cannaregio 4612, rio terà dei Franceschi (041 522 6298). Vaporetto Ca' d'Oro. **No credit cards. Map** p310 H4.
This two-screener run by Circuito Cinema (*see left*) combines the usual fare with themed seasons and kids' films (on Saturday and Sunday at 3pm).

Multisala Astra

Via Corfù 9, Lido (041 526 5736). Vaporetto Lido. **No credit cards.**
The council-run Astra is a two-screener usually offering the same fodder as the Giorgione (*see above*) a week before or after. During the Film Festival, the Astra is home to the Venice Film Meeting, which promotes locally made films.

Multisala Rossini

San Marco 3997A, salizada de la Chiesa o del Teatro (041 241 7274). Vaporetto Rialto or Sant'Angelo. **No credit cards. Map** p309 G7.
The three-screen Rossini reopened in 2012 to the delight of Venice's film-lovers. Besides a mix of big hits, smaller productions and retrospectives (and occasional screenings in *linga originale*), the very centrally located Rossini has a bar run by the Marchini dynasty (*see p64*), a restaurant and even an in-house supermarket.

OPEN-AIR CINEMA

★ Arena di Campo San Polo
Campo San Polo. Vaporetto San Silvestro or San Tomà. **Date** late July-early Sept. **No credit cards. Map** p307 F6.
This large square is home to Venice's second most important cinematic event. Around 1,000 cinema-goers a night brave the mosquitoes to fill this open-air arena. Films are generally reruns of the previous season's blockbusters, plus the odd pre-view. During the Film Festival, you can catch some original-language films a day or two after their Lido screening. For programme details, see the city council website: www.comune.venezia.it.

VIDEOTHEQUES

Casa del Cinema – Videoteca Pasinetti
Palazzo Mocenigo, Santa Croce 1990, salizada San Stae (041 524 1320). Vaporetto San Stae. **Open** *Video archive* 8.30am-1.30pm Mon-Fri. **Shows** *Video-projected cinema classics* 6pm, 9pm Tue, Fri. **Admission** by CinemaPiù card (€30), valid July-June. **No credit cards. Map** p307 F4.
This council-run video archive was founded in 1991 to collect and conserve an incredible volume of audiovisual material concerning Venice, in all formats: feature film, TV documentary, newsreel, amateur video, and so on. More than 3,000 videos are kept here, and there's a screening room where brief film seasons are held.

FESTIVALS

Circuito off – Venice International Short Film Festival
Associazione Artecolica, Cannaregio 3831, calle Fontana (041 241 1265, www.circuitooff.com). Vaporetto Ca' d'Oro. **Date** 1st wk Sept. **Map** p307 G4.
This short-film festival, run by the Associazione Artecolica, includes competitions, retrospectives and videos. In 2014, it was held in the Teatrino Grassi (*see p65*).

★ Mostra Internazionale d'Arte Cinematografica (Venice International Film Festival)
Palazzo del Cinema, lungomare Marconi 90, Lido (041 521 8711, www.labiennale.org). Vaporetto Lido. **Date** 11 days, starting late Aug/early Sept. **Map** p163 B5.
The 11-day Venice Film Festival takes place along the main, sea-facing Lido esplanade, between the old Hotel des Bains and the Excelsior (*see p278*). Here stands the marble-and-glass Palazzo del Cinema, where official competition screenings take place. Other screens can be found in the 1,700-seater PalaLido marquee, inside the Casinò and at the Palabiennale marquee.

Press accreditation guarantees virtually unlimited access to the festival and permits priority entry to a number of special screenings, mostly in the morning and early evening. Arrange this at least two months in advance by contacting the Biennale press office (041 521 8859, www.labiennale.org). 'Cultural' accreditation is another option; it allows access to a more restricted range of screenings. This should be arranged before the end of June. A special deal for people under 26 or over 60 offers a six-day or 11-day festival pass.

Individual tickets are available on the day before screenings from the ticket office at piazzale Casinò (lungomare Marconi, Lido, open 8am-midnight daily); Palabiennale (via Sandro Gallo, open 8am-midnight); and at the offices of La Biennale (Ca' Giustinian, San Marco 1365A, calle del Ridotto, open 8am-1.30pm, 3.30-6pm). Same-day tickets are occasionally available..

▶ *For other elements of the Biennale, see p31.*

Further afield

In these days of funding cuts, smaller film festivals struggle to survive. The itinerant **Veneto Film Festival** (www.venetofilm festival.it) swam against the tide, launching in 2012 and looking comparatively healthy as this guide went to press. Also flourishing is the **Vittorio Veneto Festival** (www.vittoriofilm festival.com) of films for children and teenagers. Both of these are spring events.

The longest running and best attended local cinema event is just over the border into the Friuli region, the Silent Film Festival (*see below*).

Le Giornate del Cinema Muto
Information: Cineteca del Friuli, Palazzo Gurisatti, via Bini 50, Gemona (0432 980 458, www.giornatedelcinemamuto.it). **Date** early Oct.
At Europe's most prestigious silent movie festival, highlights include an international forum of musicians for silent movies, retrospectives and films such as the British documentary *The Battle of the Somme* (1916). Accreditation costs €65 (students under 26 €40) and allows unlimited viewings (except opening and closing nights). Non-accredited viewers pay €8 per screening during the day and €10 in the evening.

Venice International Film Festival.

Gay & Lesbian

Venice has everything and (next to) nothing: enchanting, romantic, tolerant and indulgent, the city offers gay travellers the perfect holiday venue... with hardly an LGBT-specific venue in sight, in the *centro storico* at least.

It's ideal, in fact, for culturally inclined romantics – just don't come looking for a fast-paced scene.The atmosphere heats up (a little) in summer, when the city is crowded, though even then, you'll need some imagination to make out any real action – either that or transport to *terra ferma* where Mestre, Marghera and Padua offer something lacking, alas, in Venice proper: real nightlife.

GENERAL INFORMATION

The national gay rights group **ArciGay** (www.arcigay.it) sponsors activities, festivals, counselling and AIDS awareness. ArciGay membership (annual ArciUNO card €15) is needed to enter several venues listed below; it can be purchased at the door of venues requiring it, though many will waive the requirement for tourists.

In Venice, the city council's Osservatorio LGBT keeps a weather eye out for acts of discrimination or intolerance around the lagoon and posts news of any LGBT-related events and initiatives on its blog http://queervenice.blogspot.it (Italian only).

VENICE & AROUND
City to sand

In the old city centre, with its quiet gay scene tucked away in the private sphere, dinner parties or quiet drinks at the local *bacaro* define the way the city's gay community go about their business. Out in the lagoon, gay-friendly B&Bs are seductively hidden away on islands such as Sant'Erasmo (**Lato Azzurro**, *see p175*).

The summer provides more scope for fun, when gay visitors in large numbers descend on the rather secluded **Alberoni Beach** and surrounding dunes, which indulge nude

sunbathing and cruising. **Il Muro**, one of the city's oldest cruising institutions, is no longer as popular as it once was, but still attracts a number of discreet post-midnight visitors.

Alberoni Beach, Lido
Vaporetto Lido then bus.
Alberoni is *the* place to cruise in summer. The dunes and pine forest are where the action is. If the weather's good, cruising starts as early as April; but if you enjoy being spoilt for choice, go for Saturdays and Sundays in July and August. Take the B/ bus (Alberoni Spiaggia) from Santa Maria Elisabetta to the last stop, then turn right and walk about ten minutes.
▶ *For more about Lido bus routes, see p281.*

Il Muro (The Wall)
Vaporetto San Marco Vallaresso. **Map** p310 H8.
Behind the Procuratie Nuove, by the Giardinetti Reali (at the lagoon end of the piazzetta di San Marco; turn right and keep on walking), Il Muro has seen better days as the city's after-dark cruising area. Now rarely frequented from October to May, it can still pull a crowd during summer. But even with no one about, the place has a romantic charm all its own. *Photo p186.*

Where to stay

In a city so used to, and tolerant of, an immense diversity of travellers, you'll be hard pressed to find a hotel that *isn't* gay-friendly. That said, there are some clear favourites, including

Al Ponte Mocenigo (*see p274*), **Ca' del Nobile** (*see p267*), **Locanda Sturion** (*see p275*), **San Samuele** (*see p268*), **Casa Verardo** (*see p270*) and **Il Lato Azzurro** (*see p175*) on the rural lagoon island of Sant'Erasmo.

Others, not listed in the Hotels chapter of this guide, include **B&B Fujiyama** (Dorsoduro 2727A, calle lunga San Barnaba, 041 724 1042, www.bedandbreakfast-fujiyama.it), **Alle Guglie B&B** (Cannaregio 1308, calle del Magazen, 320 360 7829, www.alleguglie.com) and the **Molino Stucky Hilton** (Giudecca 810, fondamenta San Giacomo, 041 272 3311, www.molino stuckyhilton.com).

Where to eat & drink

Buzzy Campo Santa Margherita (*see p138*) and the area around San Pantalon is the focal point for the trendier young Venetians. Its bars and *pizzerie* are all extremely busy during summer. Not the cruisiest of places, but certainly friendly.

There's plenty of evening life in the bars around the north-western foot of the Rialto bridge. **Alla Zucca** (*see p124*), ten minutes or so walk to the north-west, is one of Venice's most gay-friendly restaurants.

PDM Bar Porto de Mar

Via delle Macchine 41-3, Marghera (041 921 24, www.portodemar.com). Bus 2 or 7 from piazzale Roma/train to Mestre station, then 10mins walk. **Open** 10.30pm-4am Fri, Sat; 10.30pm-2am Sun. **Admission** with ArciGay membership, *see p185*; extra charge for special events.

The Venetian expression '*porto de mar*' loosely translates as hubbub, but literally means sea port. This venue, with darkroom, bar and outside area used for cruising in summer, is worth the trip just for a glimpse of the old port before it is fully regenerated. The bar's popular with a younger crowd, but is also very welcoming if you're the wrong side of 40. Glitter (www.glitterdisco.com) makes Friday and Saturday nights sparkle.

Il Muro. *See p185*.

Saunas

Metrò Venezia Club

Via Cappuccina 82B, Mestre (041 538 4299, www.clubmetrovenezia.it). Bus 2 or 7 from piazzale Roma/train to Mestre, then 5mins walk. **Open** 2pm-2am daily. **Admission** (with ArciGay membership; *see p185*) €12; under-30s €10, after 8pm €12; €12 all-day session with sauna Tue, Thur.

The Venice area's longest-running gay venue, Metro has a bar, a dry sauna, steam sauna, private rooms, darkroom and solarium. Massage and hydromassage are also available. Trade here is very brisk.

Tours

Venice à la Carte

041 296 0425, 349 144 7818 mobile, www. tourvenice.org. **Rates** varies according to tour. **No credit cards**.

Tailor-made tours of Venice and the Veneto villas, catering to a wide variety of cultural interests and credit limits, organised by Alvise Zanchi, a native Venetian and expert tour guide.

▶ *For other guided tours of Venice, see p290.*

PADUA

We have listed only those gay places that are most easily accessible by public transport or taxi (*see p281* and *p282*) from Venice or Mestre. Cruising can be very risky, especially around Padua station, and should be avoided, even during the day.

For general tourist information about Padua, and where to stay and eat, *see pp204-207*.

Nightlife

Flexo Club

Via D Turazza 19, int. 3 (049 807 4707, www.flexo padova.it). **Open** 10pm-2am Wed-Sun. **Admission** (with ArciGay membership; *see p185*) varies.

Flexo has a cocktail bar, disco, solarium, cruising area, darkrooms, gym, beauty centre, hydro-massage and a large cruising garden – pretty much everything you could ever want. It has also softened its no-women policy. Check the website for bear and fetish events too.

Saunas

Metrò Padova Sauna

Via D Turazza 19, int. 1 (049 807 5828, www. metropadovasauna.it). **Open** 2pm-2am daily. **Admission** (with ArciGay membership; *see p185*) €12 Mon, Wed; €16.50 (€12 after 8pm) Tue, Thur; €18 (€12 after 8pm) Fri-Sun. Under-30s €10 flat fee. Sauna with two whirlpool tubs, one of which is outside, steam rooms, dry rooms, private rooms and a bar serving snacks.

Nightlife

Endless partying was what Venice was once famous for. These days, you'll be hard-pressed to find much of a scene. There's hardly a dancefloor in the city – but then again, that's not what Venice is about. If you're happy to settle for drinks, chat and the occasional bout of live music in one of the city's late-night bars, fine; if you're after serious clubbing, you'll have to go further afield. A typical Venetian night out starts with a post-work and pre-prandial *spritz* (or three) in one of the bars around the Rialto market area, which might develop into a *giro de ombre*, a bar-crawl Venetian-style. And for those still standing when the traditional *bacari* close, there's a network of late-opening bars hidden away all over town – on Cannaregio's 'party' fondamenta della Misericordia, or Dorsoduro's 'alternative' drawing room of campo Santa Margherita.

THE SCENE

Live music

Stringent noise pollution regulations and lack of adequate venues have effectively pulled the plug on large music events; recent years have seen waivers for **Carnevale** (*see p28*) and other summer events being introduced, then rescinded, as authorities bow to pressure from residents. Rock 'n' roll royals who do dates in Venice are usually confined to the very formal setting of one of the local theatres. There's better news for jazz heads as regular series of high-quality jazz and experimental music are organised by local cultural organisations such as **Caligola** (www.caligola.it).

Thanks to the tenacity of the handful of bar owners still willing to wrestle with red tape and persist in the face of party-pooper petitioning neighbours, it's still possible to play and hear live music in various *locali* around town. Venetian vibes tend to be laid-back, and these small, free gigs are almost always reggae, jazz or blues – with the occasional rock, Latino or world session. Clubs and venues on the nearby mainland draw bigger acts.

Club culture

For serious club culture, make for the mainland. In winter, a short bus or train ride to Mestre or Marghera (just across the bridge and well served by night buses) is all it takes to dance until dawn. In summer, most of the dance action moves out to the seaside resort of **Lido di Jesolo** (*see p189*), the place to be for house and techno, with a smattering of Latino.

Information & tickets

Day-to-day listings are carried by the two local papers, *Il Gazzettino* and *La Nuova Venezia*. For a fuller overview of concerts and festivals, with English translations, monthly listings magazine *Venews* (www.venezianews.it) is indispensable. Also keep your eyes peeled for posters advertising upcoming events. Tickets are usually available at the venue, but in some cases can be bought in advance at Hellovenezia outlets (*see p289*), or online via www.ticketone.it.

Unless specified, the bars listed below have no extra charge for music. Smoking is strictly forbidden in indoor public spaces, except in designated rooms with extraction systems.

LATE BARS & MUSIC BARS

Many of the drinking establishments listed in the various Explore chapters are also open well into the evening.

San Marco

Bacaro Jazz

San Marco 5546, salizada del Fontego dei Tedeschi (041 528 5249, www.bacarojazz.com). Vaporetto Rialto. **Open** 11am-2am daily. **Map** p310 H5.
Venice's most central late-night watering hole, Bacaro Jazz is a place to mingle with fellow tourists or foreign students rather than meet the locals. It hots up during happy hour (4-7pm), and the background jazz and wide range of killer cocktails keep the party going into the early hours.

Caffè Centrale

San Marco 1659B, piscina Frezzeria (041 296 0664, www.caffecentralevenezia.com). Vaporetto San Marco Vallaresso. **Open** 7pm-1am Mon-Sat. **Map** p309 H7.
Only the exposed bricks of the original 16th-century palazzo's walls will remind you you're in Venice: this chic, contemporary restaurant and lounge bar is more New York or London. There's a studied air of coolness here, and the crowd that gathers for pre- and post-dinner aperitivi and cocktails is a sophisticated one. The cool spills into a dinner menu that would best be described as fussy, but the food is fresh (though not cheap) and vegetarians are catered for. Be prepared for fashion TV and music videos coming at you from screens all around the room.

Torino@Notte

San Marco 4591, campo San Luca (041 522 3914). Vaporetto Rialto. **Open** 9pm-1am Tue-Sat. **Map** p309 G7.
This dreary daytime snack bar (don't whatever you do, be tempted to eat a meal here…) switches management after dark and transforms into a happening hotspot. DJ sets and live music (some Wednesdays, and sometimes at weekends) keep the mix of students and older musos grooving to acid jazz, fusion and funky tunes, while Carnevale brings a week of live gigs in the campo outside.

Castello

Inishark

Castello 5787, calle del Mondo Novo (041 523 5300, www.inisharkpub.com). Vaporetto Rialto. **Open** 6pm-1.30am Tue-Sun. **No credit cards.** **Map** p311 J6.
Tucked away in a small calle near Santa Maria Formosa, this Irish-style pub has the best Guinness on tap in town and great snacky food to soak up the black stuff. Though the friendly owners are Venetian through and through, the crowd that packs in here most nights is very international, with many coming for the four TV screens showing UK premier league, Italian Serie A, and major international football fixtures, plus key rugby matches.

Cannaregio

See also p100 **Santo Bevitore.**

Irish Pub

Cannaregio 3847, corte dei Pali già Testori (041 099 0916, www.theirishpubvenezia.com). Vaporetto Ca' d'Oro. **Open** 10am-2am daily. **Map** p307 G4.

FESTIVALS

What's on, where.

Hard economic times have taken their toll on the festival scene in Venice and the Veneto, with funding being pulled on one event after the other. It pays to keep an eye on posters around town, though: happenings can pop up as often as they die off.

Estate Village

Parco San Giuliano, Mestre (www.villagestate.it). **Date** June-mid July. **Open** 7pm-2am Mon-Fri; 3pm-2am Sat, Sun. *Concerts* 9pm. **Admission** donation appreciated.
Mainly local bands – including cover bands and Venetian rastas – keep crowds of locals amused in this six-week *festa*, which in 2013 made the move from Marghera to the Parco San Giuliano, though there's no guarantee this will become its permanent home. Free nightly live music is followed by dancing and DJ sets, as well as a host of bars and food stalls to keep the party going.

Venezia Jazz Festival

Information: Via Corriva 10, Cavasagra di Vedelago (0423 452 069, www.veneto jazz.com). Concerts: various venues in Venice. **Date** late July. **Admission** varies.
Jazz legends descend on Venice for a week in late August to play gigs in fantastic settings around the city. But jazz heads should check the Veneto Jazz website at any time of the year: this organisation keeps standards high with an extraordinary programme of music all around the Veneto region, in every month of the year.

ARTS & ENTERTAINMENT

Expats, locals and tourists of all ages prop up the bar in Venice's oldest Irish pub (previously known as the Fiddler's Elbow). Party-pooping neighbours have put a stop to the regular live music nights, but this is no deterrent to regulars, who pack the place out for the sports events shown on four plasma screens.

Paradiso Perduto
Cannaregio 2540, fondamenta della Misericordia (041 720 581, http://ilparadisoperduto.wordpress. com). Vaporetto San Marcuola. **Open** 6pm-midnight Mon-Thur; noon-1am Fri, Sat; noon-midnight Sun. **No credit cards. Map** p307 G3.
Probably the most famous Venetian haunt after Harry's Bar (*see p69*), this 'Paradise Lost' is well worth finding. Arty types of all ages take their places at the long *osteria* tables for the mix of seafood and succulent sounds (mainly jazz and salsa), which go live every Monday, and a surprising number of other nights, despite the city's stringent noise regulations.

San Polo & Santa Croce

See p113 **Muro Rialto**, *p116* **Naranzaria**.

Dorsoduro

See p142 **Café Noir**, *p142* **Café Rosso**, *p143* **El Sbarlefo**, *p143* **Impronta Café**, *p143* **Orange**.

La Giudecca & San Giorgio

See p157 **Skyline Bar**.

CLUBS

Piccolo Mondo
Dorsoduro 1056A, calle Contarini-Corfù (041 520 0371, www.piccolomondo.biz). Vaporetto Accademia. **Open** 10.30pm-4am daily. **Admission** €12 incl first drink. **Map** p309 E8.
Called 'El Souk' in better days, this 'small world' remains one of the few places to dance in Venice proper. You may, therefore, find yourself on its dancefloor. If you do, you'll be mixing with ageing medallion men, lost tourists and foreign students so desperate to dance, they'll go anywhere.

★ Venice Jazz Club
Dorsoduro 3102, fondamenta dei Pugni (041 523 2056, www.venicejazzclub.com). Vaporetto Ca' Rezzonico. **Open** 7pm-2am Mon-Wed, Fri, Sat. **Admission** €20 incl first drink. **Map** p308 C8.
The intimate setting and nightly live music make this club, just behind campo Santa Margherita, a perfect place for a night out for fans of high-quality jazz. Concerts start at 9pm, and some food is served.

FURTHER AFIELD
Lido di Jesolo

Most of Jesolo's clubs open at 11pm, but nobody who's anybody shows up until 1am. Save money (rather than face) by picking up flyers offering reduced entrance before 1am. The clubs listed below are perennial favourites.

GETTING TO LIDO DI JESOLO
The Lido di Jesolo bus (information www.atvo.it) leaves from piazzale Roma, but it's more fun to get the double-decker *motonave* from San Zaccaria-Pietà, on the riva degli Schiavoni, to Punta Sabbioni and bus it from there. There are regular boats making the return journey, with a change at Lido between 1am and 6am. Note that if you drop before dawn, you'll need a lift or taxi (approximately €50) back to the boat stop at Punta Sabbioni as no buses link up with the boats during the night.

Area Club/Beast. *See p190.*

ARTS & ENTERTAINMENT

Il Muretto

Via Roma Destra 120, Lido di Jesolo (0421 371 310, www.ilmuretto.net). **Open** *Mar-Sept* 11pm-5am Wed, Fri, Sat, Sun. **Admission** €20-€50.

The home of Italian house – and a Jesolo legend – Il Muretto has been going for over 40 years yet remains super-trendy. A mass of ecstatic youth floods the dancefloor for serious house music expertly spun by highly respected resident DJs and guests who are living legends in clubland: Rampling, Oakenfold, Kevorkian, Tenaglia and the Chemical Brothers, to name just a few.

★ Terrazza Mare Teatro Bar

Via A da Giussano 1, Lido di Jesolo (0421 370 012, www.terrazzamare.com). **Open** *Apr-Sept* 6pm-4am daily. **Admission** free-€10.

This once-humble beach bar by the lighthouse is more of a cultural space than a club, organising music, exhibitions, and theatre and dance productions, in addition to club nights. With free entry (except special events), no heavy-handed bouncers or label-led dress code, the informal atmosphere attracts a mixed group of groovers, who flock here in their thousands.

Vanilla Club

Via Buonarroti 15, Lido di Jesolo (0421 372 446, www.vanilla.it). **Open** 11.30pm-5am Mon-Sat. **Admission** €10-€30.

New Age Club.

House, hip hop and R&B are the resident sounds in the Vanilla Club, located in the Acqualandia complex. There might also be a dash of disco sounds to boogie to under the palm trees.

Mestre & Marghera

Area Club/Beast

Via Don Tosatto 9, Mestre (329 948 1959 mobile, www.beastclub.it). Train to Mestre, then bus 3. **Open** 11.30pm-4am Fri-Sat. **Admission** €15-€30.

The first venue in the Venice region to specialise in hardcore techno; it plays host to big-name DJs and attracts well-heeled clubbers. *Photo p189.*

TAG Club

Via Giustizia 19, Mestre (334 824 5710 mobile). Train to Mestre. **Open** *Sept-May* 10pm-8am Fri, Sat. **Admission** (incl 1st drink) €10. **No credit cards.**

A small but lively club just behind the train station in Mestre that puts on an eclectic range of concerts and exhibitions and pop/rock nights. 'Afterhours' parties follow, starting after 3am and featuring house music mixed by well-known DJs.

★ Al Vapore

Via Fratelli Bandiera 8, Marghera (041 930 796, www.alvapore.it). Train to Mestre, or bus 6 or 6/ from piazzale Roma. **Open** 7.30am-3pm, 6pm-2am Tue-Fri; 6pm-2am Sat, Sun. **Admission** free-€15 (incl 1st drink) .

This music bar has been putting on jazz, blues, soul and rock gigs for years and is very active on the local scene. Popular Jazz Buffet nights take place in the week, with funky DJ sets and a free buffet. At weekends, well-known Italian and international musicians perform on the tiny stage. There's no charge on Fridays, but drinks cost more. Over the summer months, Al Vapore moves to Estate Village (*see p188* **Festivals**).

The Veneto

New Age Club

Via Tintoretto 14, Roncade, Treviso (0422 841 052, www.newageclub.it). Venice–Trieste motorway, exit Quarto d'Altino; follow signs for Roncade. **Open** *Oct-May* 9.30pm-5am Fri; 11.30pm-5am Sat. **Admission** *Disco* free after 12.30am for ARCI members Fri (annual membership €9 at the door); €9 (incl 1st drink) Sat. *Concerts* €8-€25. **No credit cards.**

You'll need a car to get to this spot, but if you're a pop, rock or metal fan it can be well worth it for some of the big acts that pass through to play on its small stage. Interpol, the Veils, Supergrass and Black Rebel Motorcycle Club have been among recent guests. A rock disco follows the gigs.

Performing Arts

Looking back to the days – in the 18th and 19th centuries – when Venice boasted no fewer than 18 hugely active theatres with in-house playwrights churning out any number of works for an entertainment-hungry audience, you might think that contemporary Venice has become a backwater in the performing arts sector. But this town of fewer than 60,000 souls still boasts one of Europe's great opera houses, La Fenice, high-profile international festivals of the very latest in dance, theatre and music with the Biennale di Venezia, and a number of very serious musical research bodies staging some equally serious public events. At the other end of the scale, numerous commercial organisations cater to a less rigorous public happy to crown their rose-tinted Venetian idyll with costumed renditions of Vivaldi's greatest hits.

THE SCENE

Limited in quantity it may be, but – Vivaldi renditions aside – Venice's serious performance scene today is high on quality, thanks largely to the efforts of the Biennale arts umbrella organisation (*see p197*). Stages here tend to be multi-purpose, with **La Fenice** (*see p195*), for instance, hosting opera, dance and other performances, and the **Teatro Malibran** (*see p195*) offering classical music and ballet.

THEATRICAL TRADITIONS

The popular *Commedia dell'arte* offerings of playwrights Pietro Chiari and Carlo Gozzi – who went on to produce fairy-tale works including the original *Turandot* – were ousted from centre stage when the city's most enduringly popular playwright, Carlo Goldoni, came on the scene in the mid 18th century. A law student who ran away from school to join a band of travelling players, Goldoni reformed the genre by bringing to the stage his satirical observations, usually in dialect, of Venetians and their foibles.

So popular was opera in *La Serenissima* that, it's been calculated, almost 1,300 operas were produced in Venice in just over a generation. After the fall of the Republic, composers such as Donizetti, Bellini and Rossini regularly provided new works for the La Fenice opera house. Besides Verdi's *Rigoletto* and *La Traviata*, La Fenice hosted premières of Benjamin Britten's *The Turn of the Screw* and Igor Stravinsky's *The Rake's Progress*. In the 20th century, Luciano Berio and Venice's greatest modern composer, Luigi Nono, were commissioned to write for the opera house.

The **Teatro Carlo Goldoni** (*see p195*) in Venice and the **Teatro Toniolo** (*see p195*) in Mestre tend to serve up standard theatrical fare. You can find more cutting-edge work in Venice's smaller theatres: the **Teatro Fondamenta Nuove** (*see p195*), which initially opened for contemporary dance productions but has now branched out into all forms of experimental expression; the **Teatrino Groggia** (*see p193*); and the **Teatro Junghans** (www.accademiateatraleveneta.it), on the Giudecca, a theatre school that sometimes hosts productions by its own students, plus the occasional festival production; as well as at Mestre's **Teatrino della Murata** (*see p195*). The **Teatro a**

Teatrino Grassi.

l'Avogaria (*see p193*) explores the outer reaches of Venetian and Italian theatre, often using theatre for didactic purposes, while the **Centro Culturale Candiani** (*see p195*), in Mestre, puts on contemporary pieces. The inauguration in 2013 of the **Teatrino Grassi** (*see p65*) gives the city another space, though how much theatrical performance will be staged here is still unclear.

The summer provides welcome relief in terms of contemporary theatre, dance and music, when performances abound during the **Biennale di Venezia, Danza-Musica-Teatro** (*see p197*), which brings high-quality international productions and artists. Many of these productions take place in theatre spaces created inside the Arsenale: the **Teatro alle Tese** and the **Teatro Piccolo Arsenale** (for both, *see p195*).

DANCE

The Teatro Fondamenta Nuove hosts an annual dance festival in the autumn, but most dance events are limited to the summer months, when the Biennale provides contemporary performances. The Teatro Toniolo and Centro Culturale Candiani also have fairly mainstream contemporary dance offerings. The seasons at La Fenice and Teatro Malibran always include classical ballet features. In the summer, tango aficionados can watch or even join performances in campo San Giacomo dell'Orio, on the steps of the station or in front of the Salute basilica (www.tangoaction.com).

CLASSICAL MUSIC & OPERA

Venice has become a victim of its own musical tradition, with Vivaldi pouring out of its *scuole* and churches, usually performed by bewigged

and costumed players. For many, experiencing Vivaldi in Venice is an absolute must. But more discerning music-lovers might feel somewhat Baroqued out by the predictable programmes performed by local groups, whose technical ability rarely goes beyond the so-so to fairly good range. Exceptions are the **Venice Baroque Orchestra**, **Interpreti Veneziani** (*see p194* **Choosing your Vivaldi**), and the orchestra of La Fenice, one of the best in the country. As well as its opera and ballet seasons, La Fenice has at least two concert seasons a year. The Teatro Malibran shares the Fenice's programmes and also has its own chamber music season, with performances by the **Società Veneziana dei Concerti**. Mestre's Teatro Toniolo also has a symphony and chamber music season. Most other musical events take place in Venice's churches or *scuole* (*see p195*).

St Mark's basilica holds a smattering of ceremonial concerts throughout the year, with the patriarch deciding who is to attend. But lovers of sacred music should catch one of two regular Sunday appointments: the sung Mass at St Mark's (9am) and the Gregorian chant on the island of **San Giorgio** (11am).

Visiting music groups often come to town to give one-off, free performances in Venice's churches; look out for posters around town.

THE SEASON

Venice's theatre and dance season stretches from November to June – though La Fenice keeps on going most of the year, closing only for August. Tourist-oriented classical music concerts are held all year. Smaller theatre groups take advantage of the summer temperatures from June onwards and move into Venice's open spaces (*see p195*).

But the colder months are not without their serious attractions: look out for concerts held throughout the city during late December to provide some Christmas sparkle.

INFORMATION & TICKETS

Tickets for concerts and performances can usually be purchased at theatre box offices immediately prior to shows; the tourist information office near piazza San Marco (*see p289*) and Hellovenezia offices (*see p289*) sell tickets for 'serious' events; most travel agents and hotel receptions will obtain tickets for classical music concerts.

For high-profile or first-night productions at prestigious venues such as La Fenice, Teatro Carlo Goldoni, Teatro Malibran or Teatro Toniolo, the limited number of seats not taken by season-ticket holders will sell out days or even weeks in advance: tickets should be reserved at the theatres themselves or on their websites at least two weeks before performances.

Local newspapers *Il Gazzettino* and *La Nuova Venezia* carry listings of theatrical events, as does the bilingual monthly *Venews*.

THEATRES

Teatrino Groggia

Cannaregio 3150, Parco di Villa Groggia (041 524 4665, www.comune.venezia.it/teatrino groggia). Vaporetto Sant'Alvise. **No credit cards.** **Map** p307 E1.

> ## IN THE KNOW
> ## PHOENIX FROM THE FLAMES
>
> The curtain first went up in 1792 at **La Fenice** (*see p195*), built to replace the Teatro San Benedetto, which had burnt down in 1774. Living up to its name (*fenice* means 'phoenix'), the theatre has burned to the ground twice since opening and has twice risen from the ashes – most recently in 2003 after a devastating fire in 1996. The latest rebuilding restored it to its former glory, with the bonus of updated stage machinery and surtitles for the audience.

Tucked away in the trees, this excellent little space in the northern part of Cannaregio has earned a firm following for its variety of multimedia performances, experimental music and drama, and shows for children in the beautiful garden.

Teatro a l'Avogaria

Dorsoduro 1607, corte Zappa (041 099 1967, www.teatro-avogaria.it). Vaporetto Ca' Rezzonico or San Basilio. **No credit cards.** **Map** p308 C8. This experimental theatre (entry to which is by voluntary donation) was founded in 1969 by renowned director Giovanni Poli. It was at the Teatro a l'Avogaria that he continued the experimental approach he developed in the 1950s. Since his death in 1979, Poli's disciples have pressed on

ARTS & ENTERTAINMENT

Teatro La Fenice. *See p195.*

CHOOSING YOUR VIVALDI

How to improve your listening pleasure.

Chances are you won't be in Venice long before you're accosted by a costumed, bewigged (and often rather bedraggled) youth pushing a flyer for 'the' Vivaldi concert into your hand.

With its superb venues and unique atmosphere, Venice lends itself magnificently to early music – though in Venice this is all too often reduced to a quick romp through Vivaldi's *Four Seasons*. If you're going to indulge in a concert – and this *is* an indulgence, with few outfits offering tickets at less than €25, whatever the technical standard – you'll need to examine your priorities.

If you really want the whole costumed shebang, try **I Musici Veneziani**, who perform in the **Scuola Grande di San Teodoro** (*see p196*); if you're a true music buff, however, you may feel you're paying for the 'experience' rather than any musical finesse.

Performing beneath Carpaccio's dramatic painting of St Vitalis on his charger in the church of **San Vidal** (*see p196*), the **Interpreti Veneziani** are a serious musical ensemble, playing to a high standard. There's quite a bit of showmanship here too, with lots of cameraderie and high-fiving among performers at the end of movements. But they pack in the punters nightly, and most go away very happy.

To be absolutely sure to avoid disappointment, serious music aficionados should check out the programme at **La Fenice** (*see p195*) and the **Teatro Malibran** (*see p195*): besides the opera season at the former, there are numerous symphony and chamber music concerts throughout the year, and though getting tickets for these still requires forethought, it is easier than acquiring opera places.

Teatro Malibran

If, on the other hand, you're happier to experience your early music while exploring Venice's *calli* in your own headphoned world, opt for a recording by the **Venice Baroque Orchestra** (www.venicebaroque orchestra.it). Once upon a time, lucky music-lovers could catch this award-winning, globetrotting ensemble at the Scuola Grande di San Rocco. Nowadays you're more likely to catch them in the US or the Far East.

Formed in 1997 by conductor, harpsichordist, organist and Baroque scholar Andrea Marcon, the ensemble rediscovers neglected works of the Venetian Baroque, and performs them on period instruments. The group has won widespread acclaim for its performances of previously unpublished works by Claudio Monteverdi and Antonio Vivaldi, and for its revival of lost operas including Handel's *Siroe* (in 2000), *L'Olimpiade* by Baldassare Galuppi (in 2006) and the Venetian *serenata Andromeda liberata* (2004), which was composed at least in part by Vivaldi.

The orchestra's revolutionary playing technique does away with the mechanical, tinkly, so-called 'sewing machine' style that is usually the norm for Baroque music: it will make you feel as if you're hearing *The Four Seasons* for the very first time.

Interpreti Veneziani.

with his experiments, staging works by lesser-known playwrights from the 15th to 19th centuries. Places must be booked at the number above between 2.30 and 4.30pm. The theatre opens its doors 15 minutes before performances.

Teatro alle Tese & Teatro Piccolo Arsenale
Castello 2169, campo della Tana (041 521 8898, www.labiennale.org). Vaporetto Arsenale. **Tickets** varies. **Map** p311 N8.
Two spectacular spaces inside the Arsenale (*see p85*) used for Biennale productions.

Teatro Carlo Goldoni
San Marco 4650B, calle Carbonera (041 240 2011, www.teatrostabileveneto.it). Vaporetto Rialto. **Map** p309 G6.
The Goldoni regularly serves up Venetian classics by its namesake and 20th-century classics regularly feature on the programme, as do, more recently, more contemporary Italian pieces.

Teatro Fondamenta Nuove
Cannaregio 5013, fondamenta Nuove (041 522 4498, www.teatrofondamentanuove.it). Vaporetto Fondamente Nove. **No credit cards.** **Map** p308 C3.
Opened in 1993 in an old joiner's shop, this theatre stages contemporary dance and avant-garde drama, as well as high-quality experimental music performances. It also organises film festivals, symposiums, exhibitions and workshops.

★ Teatro La Fenice
San Marco 1965, campo San Fantin (041 2424, 041 786 654, www.teatrolafenice.it). Vaporetto Giglio. **Map** p309 G8.
Restored and positively gleaming, La Fenice is back in business offering opera, ballet and concert seasons. Rehearsals allowing, 40-minute tours (€9; €6.50 reductions) can be booked at the box office. *Photo p193.*
▶ *For more information about tours, see p69.*

★ Teatro Malibran
Cannaregio 5873, calle dei Milion (041 786 603, www.teatrolafenice.it). Vaporetto Rialto. **Map** p310 H5.
Inaugurated in 1678 as Teatro San Giovanni Crisostomo, this 900-seater was built on the site where Marco Polo's family palazzo once stood. The theatre now shares the classical music, ballet and opera season with La Fenice; in addition, it has its own chamber music season.

Further afield

For details of opera performances in Verona's Roman **Arena**, *see p212* **Opera in the Arena**. And for that city's **Teatro Romano**, *see p215.*

★ Centro Culturale Candiani
Piazzale Candiani 7, Mestre (041 238 6111, www.centroculturalecandiani.it). Bus 2 from piazzale Roma.
This 1970s arts centre contains an auditorium, video library, exhibition space and outdoor arena. Alfresco performances are held from June to September. Entertainment ranges from Bach to contemporary classics, plus regular film screenings.

Teatrino della Murata
Via Giordano Bruno 19, Mestre (041 989 879, www.teatromurata.it). Bus 2 from piazzale Roma.
The tiny Teatrino della Murata (which contains a mere 70 seats) is situated in a former warehouse under the remains of the ancient city walls. Funded by the city and regional councils, it specialises in showcasing multicultural theatre.

Teatro Toniolo
Piazzetta Battisti 1, Mestre (041 396 9222, box office 041 971 666, www.culturaspettacolo venezia.it). Bus 2 or 7 from piazzale Roma.
Founded in 1913, the Teatro Toniolo serves up an assortment of performances, from vernacular favourites to contemporary plays. With its new stagings of Italian and foreign classics, musicals, cabaret, classical and pop music concerts, and contemporary dance and ballet, there is definitely something to suit all tastes. *Photo p196.*

CHURCHES, SCUOLE & PALAZZI

For information on musical events in Venice's churches, check the local press (*see p286*).

Ateneo San Basso
San Marco 315A, piazzetta dei Leoncini (041 528 2825, www.virtuosidivenezia.com). Vaporetto San Marco Vallaresso. **Shows** 8.30pm Mon-Sat. **Tickets** €25; €20 reductions. **No credit cards.** **Map** p310 J7.
Just off St Mark's square, the Ateneo San Basso puts on the *Four Seasons* and other Vivaldi works – though not many.

★ Basilica dei Frari
San Polo, campo dei Frari (041 719 308, www.basilicadeifrari.it). Vaporetto San Tomà. **Map** p307 E6.
The lofty Gothic Frari is one of the best venues in Venice for catching high-standard performances of sacred music. It has regular seasons in the autumn and spring; organ recitals and a number of free or low-cost afternoon concerts are held especially over Christmas and the New Year. If you go to one of the winter concerts, wrap up warm.
▶ *For further information on this magnificent basilica, see p126.*

Palazzo Barbarigo Minotto
*San Marco 2504, fondamenta Duodo o
Barbarigo (340 971 7272, www.musica
palazzo.com). Vaporetto Giglio.* **Shows** 8.30pm
daily. **Tickets** €70. **Map** p309 F8.
In the beautiful surroundings of a 17th-century
palazzo, performances include a variety of classic
opera arias, Neapolitan songs and complete operas
with few instruments and a piano to accompany
the singers. During the evening, the small audience
follows the performers around the salons of the
palazzo, from the frescoed Sala Tiepolo on to the
bedroom for the more intimate 'love duets'.

Palazzo Bru Zane
*San Polo 2368, campiello Forner (041 521
1005, www.br-zane.com). Vaporetto San Tomà
or San Stae.* **Shows** vary. **Tickets** €15; €5
reductions. **Map** p306 D5.
Stuccoed and frescoed Palazzo Bru Zane is home
to the Centre for French Romantic Music, a busy
research and performance institute which hosts
concerts, operas, seminars and special musical
events for children where under-12s go free and
their parents pay €10. There are free tours of the
palazzo every Thurday, at 2.30pm (Italian), 3pm
(French) and 3.30pm (English). Check the website
for programme details.

Palazzo delle Prigioni
*Castello 4209, ponte della Paglia (041 984 252,
www.collegiumducale.com). Vaporetto San
Zaccaria.* **Shows** 9pm daily. **Tickets** €25;
€20 reductions. **Map** p310 J8.
Just over the Bridge of Sighs from the Doge's
Palace, the prisons host concerts by the Collegium
Ducale Orchestra – which performs its Venetian
Baroque and German Romantic repertoires several
times a week – and also jazz evenings courtesy of
the Venice Jazz Quartet.

La Pietà
*Castello, riva degli Schiavoni (041 522 1120,
www.chiesavivaldi.it). Vaporetto San Zaccaria.*
Shows 8.30pm daily in season. **Tickets** €25;
€20 reductions. **Map** p310 K8.
I Virtuosi Italiani perform early music concerts in
what must surely be the easiest sell in Venice:
Vivaldi in the Vivaldi church. *See also p87.*

San Vidal
*San Marco 2862B, campo San Vidal (041 277
0561, www.interpretiveneziani.com). Vaporetto
Accademia.* **Shows** 9pm Mon-Sat (8.30pm in
winter). **Tickets** €27; €22 reductions.
Map p309 E8.
For highly professional renditions of Vivaldi and
other mainly baroque favourites, visit the church of
San Vidal (*see p66*), where the no-frills Interpreti
Veneziani play to a backdrop of Carpaccio's San
Vitale on a white horse over the high altar. Tickets

Teatro Toniolo.
See p195.

can be purchased on the door, or at the Museo della
Musica (*see p68*). *See also p194* **Choosing Your
Vivaldi**.

Santa Maria della Salute
*Dorsoduro, campo della Salute (041 274 3928).
Vaporetto Salute.* **Shows** 3.30pm Mon-Fri.
Map p309 G9.
The basilica's magnificent 18th-century organ is
played during vespers every week day.

Scuola Grande di
San Giovanni Evangelista
*San Polo 2454, campiello della Scuola (041 718
234, www.scuolasangiovanni.it). Vaporetto San
Tomà.* **Shows** 9pm, days vary. **Tickets** *Opera*
€30-€35; €25-€30 reductions. *Concerts* €20;
€5-€10 reductions. **Map** p306 D5.
This 14th-century *scuola*, with an imposing marble
staircase and paintings by Tintoretto and Tiepolo,
hosts concerts of ancient music played by the
Venetia Antique Ensemble, and shrink-wrapped
opera by an outfit called Opera House. Check the
websites for occasional free concerts by visiting
choirs and orchestras.

Scuola Grande di San Teodoro
*San Marco 4810, salizzada San Teodoro
(041 521 0294, www.imusiciveneziani.com).
Vaporetto Rialto.* **Shows** 8.30pm daily. **Tickets**
€25-€35; €20-€30 reductions. **Map** p310 H6.
If your heart is set on performers in wigs, head for
the Scuola Grande di San Teodoro, where the local
I Musici Veneziani orchestra dishes up Vivaldi and
a medley of opera arias.

ARTS & ENTERTAINMENT

OTHER MUSIC VENUES

Fondazione Cini
Isola di San Giorgio (041 528 9900, www.cini.it).
Vaporetto San Giorgio. **Map** p157 G1.
The foundation draws on its impressive archives to organise music seminars, workshops, masterclasses and concerts of rare or neglected music. Concerts are held at the Fondazione HQ on San Giorgio or at Palazzo Cini (Dorsoduro 864, piscina del Forner, 041 521 0755). Just turn up at the venues in time for the concerts, which are free.
▶ *For more about the Cini Foundation, see p158.*

FESTIVALS

Biennale di Venezia, Danza-Musica-Teatro
041 521 8711, www.labiennale.org. **Date** *Dance* mid-late June. *Theatre* July-Aug. *Music* Oct.
Venice's Biennale festival umbrella has expanded its dance, music and theatre department. The rich, international programme is staged in newly restored venues inside the Arsenale –the Teatro Tese and the smaller Teatro Piccolo Arsenale (for both, *see p195*), and in squares and venues around the city. There are also workshops and a host of side events.

Festival dei Matti
338 896 2711, www.festivaldeimatti.org. **Venues** various. **Tickets** €10; €8 reductions. **Date** Nov.
Organised by the Teatro Goldoni (*see p195*), the Festival dei Matti ('of the Crazies') explores madness in a themed programme – 'Exiles' in 2013, 'Policy/ Poetry' in 2014 – which aims to explore the creative and communicative potential of mental illness of all kinds and degrees. Plays, debates and workshops are held in venues including the Teatro Goldoni, the

Santa Maria della Salute.

Teatrino Groggia (*see p193*), the Telecom Italia Future Centre (*see p63*) and others. Buy tickets at the Teatro Goldoni or via its website.

Festival Galuppi
041 271 9090, www.festivalgaluppi.it. **Venues** various. **Tickets** €24; €18 reductions. **Date** late Aug-mid Oct.
This festival is dedicated to the Venetian composer Baldassarre Galuppi. Listen to 18th-century classical music in otherwise inaccessible venues, such as the islands of San Francesco del Deserto and Lazzaretto Nuovo. Tickets can be bought at venues, or through Hellovenezia (*see p189*).

Le Giornate Wagneriane
Associazione R Wagner, Ca' Vendramin Calergi, Cannaregio 2040, campiello Vendramin (041 276 0407, 338 416 4174). **Venues** various.
Date Nov-Dec.
Wagner is the star of a series of world-class concerts organised by the Associazione R Wagner; the Giornate Wagneriane also includes conferences on the great man, and visits to the house he occupied while in Venice. Concerts are free, but get tickets in advance: call or email arwv@libero.it. Venues used in the past have included Palazzo Bru Zane (*see p196*) and La Fenice (*see p195*).

Venice Open Stage
Dorsoduro, campazzo San Sebastiano (http:// veniceopenstage.jimdo.com). *Vaporetto San Basilio or Zattere.* **Tickets** free. **Date** June-July.
Map p308 B8.
Run by Venice's IUAV university, this outdoor festival brings together productions from drama schools for ten days of spectacle and experimentation.

Further afield

OperaEstate
Via Vendramin 35, Bassano del Grappa (0424 524 214, www.operaestate.it). **Date** July-Sept.
The Bassano town council organises this summer feast of dance, theatre, opera, music and cinema in Bassano and more than 30 other towns around the Veneto, including breathtakingly beautiful Asolo (*see p227*), the chessboard town of Marostica, and Montecchio Maggiore. Jazz and classical music are on offer through the summer. You can also catch dance performances featuring major international stars and a bag of treats in the theatre.

Settimane Musicali al Teatro Olimpico
Contrà San Pietro 67, Vicenza (0444 302 425, 347 492 5005, www.olimpico.vicenza.it). **Date** May-June.
In the sumptuous setting of Palladio's masterpiece, the Teatro Olimpico (*see p223*), Vicenza's annual music festival focuses on a theme or composer each year, with conferences and concerts as well as films.

ARTS & ENTERTAINMENT

Escapes & Excursions

Escapes & Excursions

Venice offers so much but it's not, of course, the whole story. Across the lagoon, on terra ferma, the Veneto region provides those things that Venice cannot or does not: Roman remains, gorgeous landscapes, masterpieces by Giotto, ski slopes, beach resorts, beetling mountains and vineyards stretching as far as the eye can see.

There's art out here aplenty as well, and though Venice boasts some superb churches by Palladio, you'll have to visit his Basilica Palladiana in Vicenza to experience the great architect's take on urban restyling, and the villas in the countryside around Vicenza for his stately rural retreats.

ACROSS THE WATER

The environmental ravages of the economic miracle have spared some lovely untouched and under-visited corners of the Veneto, particularly in the hills and mountains: the Colli Euganei beyond **Padua** (*see p204*) and the Colli Berici south of **Vicenza** (*see p216*) roll pleasantly above the industrial sprawl. But the Veneto is largely defined by its towns.

Treviso (*see p225*) has frescoed *palazzi* and an economic vitality – of which the Benetton empire is the most famous flag-bearer – that gives it a lively, dynamic feel. Beyond, in the gentle foothills of the Dolomites, are the wine-producing centres of **Conegliano** (*see p228*) and **Valdobbiadene** (*see p227*); **Asolo** and **Possagno** (for both, *see p227*), given up respectively to the leisured laziness of *il dolce far niente* (literally, 'sweet doing nothing') and the cold neoclassical visions of **Antonio Canova**; and **Bassano del Grappa** (see *p227*), home of the fiery spirit of that name. (For more on the region's wines, see *p140* **Wines of north-east Italy**).

Beyond **Belluno** (*see p228*), the mountains begin in earnest, bringing hordes of beau monde skiers to the elegant resort of **Cortina d'Ampezzo** (*see p229*) and queues of summer hikers to attempt one of the numerous *alte vie* (high-altitude footpaths) that traverse the pink-granite Dolomites.

Heading north-east from Venice, a straggle of seaside resorts with high-density beach umbrellas, campsites and discos stretches all the way from **Lido di Jesoloto** (*see p189*) to the border of the Veneto.

But for many visitors – especially those who don't read the small print on their travel itinerary – the first experience of the Veneto is **Mestre** or **Chioggia** (for both, *see p202*). At the southern end of the lagoon, Chioggia is half fishing port and half high-rise tourist resort. Industrial Mestre – with its plethora of modern overspill hotels – is not as bleak a prospect as it first appears: it has nightlife, cinemas, theatre… and there's plenty of transport across the lagoon back to Venice.

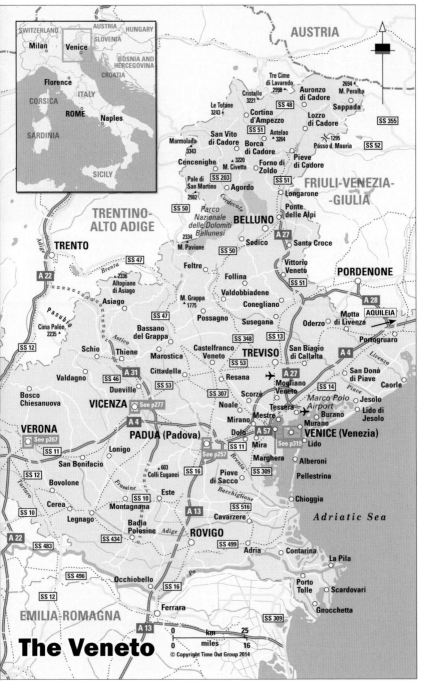

The Veneto

© Copyright Time Out Group 2014

ESCAPES & EXCURSIONS

Choggia

In the Shadow of Venice

MESTRE

Facing Venice from the mainland, Mestre was an insignificant walled town from the tenth century (the only notable remnant of these medieval fortifications is the tower in the main piazza). It began to grow exponentially only in the last century, with the creation of the industrial port of Marghera, when the lure of jobs attracted workers from all over Italy. From the 1950s, lagoon-dwelling Venetians began to move here too, fleeing high house prices in Venice itself, or simply seeking 'luxurious' trappings such as cars and supermarkets.

Though it's only a ten-minute bus or train ride from Venice proper, Mestre is a world away. The town and its environs now host the hotels where the overspill of the Venice tourist trade ends up. If your hotel seems too cheap to be true, you may find that you're being sold a room on terra ferma.

This is not entirely bad. As Mestre's population expanded, the town galloped outwards and upwards in grim concrete. Defined by what it is not (that is, Venice), Mestre has only recently begun to strive for its own identity. An evening visit to piazza Ferretto – the attractive square at Mestre's heart – will give you a sense of the extent to which Mestre is youth-oriented. Mestre has more cinemas than Venice; and both the centre and the environs are home to some great clubs, gay and straight (see p184 and p189).

It is also fair to say that the ugliness of Mestre has been somewhat exaggerated. Pedestrianised piazza Ferretto is as fine a central square as you will find in many small Italian towns, and there are attractive arcaded streets to the north (via Palazzo) and a pleasant market area to the east of the square. The churches of **San Rocco** (via Manin 39, 041 983 702, www.duomodimestre.com), with its 18th-century decorations, and **San Girolamo** (via San Girolamo 28, 041 534 9348), with its restored Gothic interior, are worth a look. There are also some fine classical villas, particularly in the greener areas north of town.

In recent years, Mestre has established some cultural independence from Venice: its theatres (see p195) provide musical and dramatic seasons that rival almost anything the lagoon city has to offer (opera excluded). The **Centro Culturale Candiani** (see p195) has spaces for exhibitions, workshops and multimedia events.

In 2004, Mestre's need for green space was answered by the opening of **Parco San Giuliano**, a 70-hectare (175-acre) area of former wasteland between the town and the lagoon, with bicycle tracks, woods, canals, play areas, a roller-skating rink and a lake. A pedestrian footbridge crosses the busy ring road to connect the park to the centre. The walk across the park is worth it for the view over the lagoon to Venice – and that, of course, sums up Mestre's problem.

CHIOGGIA

A small town of Roman origin at the southern end of the lagoon, the fishing port of Chioggia spreads over a rectangular island split down the middle by the Canal Vena; to the east is the long arm of the beach resort of Sottomarina. From piazzetta Vigo, the long, wide corso del Popolo extends the whole length of the island, parallel to the canal. On either side, narrow lanes lead off to the lagoon.

San Domenico.

The only sight not on the corso is the church of **San Domenico** (via Canali 4, 041 400 513), on its very own island at the end of the street that begins across a balustraded bridge from piazzetta Vigo, where the ferry ties up. A barn-like, 18th-century reconstruction, it houses Vittore Carpaccio's last recorded work, a gracefully poised St Paul (after the second altar on the right; 1520). Other works of note are a huge wooden crucifix – possibly a German work of the 14th century – and a Rubens-like Tintoretto. More charming is the collection of naïve ex-voto paintings placed by grateful fishermen in a side chapel.

Halfway down the corso is the **Granaio**, the former municipal granary, built in 1322 but heavily restored in the 19th century; it now hosts the fish market (open 8am-noon Tue-Sun). Nearby, the church of **San Giacomo** (corso del Popolo 1202, 041 400 584, www.sgiacomo apostolo.altervista.org), has a high altar in elaborate faux-Baroque (1907), which contains the Madonna della Navicella, an image of the Virgin as she appeared to a Sottomarina peasant in 1508.

Just beyond the Granaio is the small piazza XX Settembre. Here stands the church of the **Santissima Trinità** (041 405 968), a small, elegant 18th-century building by Andrea Tirali, which has been restored and converted into a museum. Some interesting paintings have been moved here since the restoration, including two large 17th-century works on the life of St Nicholas: *The Consecration of St Nicholas* by Pietro Damini is especially splendid, offering a fine display of colourful clerical robes.

More interesting than the church itself is the grandiose *Oratorio dei Battuti*, which begins just behind the high altar. This large space, built for a philanthropic confraternity of laymen devoted to the Madonna (and originally to flagellation), was decorated with a cycle of ceiling paintings by a number of the major names of 17th-century Mannerist painting in Venice. Particularly fine is the *Resurrection* by Alvise del Friso.

Leaving the church, cross the bridge to your right, to the church of the **Filippini** (rione San Giacomo 1154, 041 400 196), an 18th-century building with an extraordinary Chapel of Reliquaries (third on the right).

Near the end of the corso, two churches stand side by side on the right. The smaller one is **San Martino** (via Sottomarina 1468, 041 400 054), a Venetian Gothic jewel built in 1393. Next door, the huge 17th-century **Duomo** (rione Duomo 77, www.cattedralechioggia.it) was built to a design by Baldassare Longhena after a fire destroyed the original tenth-century church. Only the 64-metre (210-foot) campanile across the road remains from the earlier structure (though it was completed in the 14th century). Inside the Duomo, the chapel to the left of the chancel contains a series of grisly 18th-century paintings depicting the torturously prolonged martyrdom of the two patron saints of Chioggia, Felix and Fortunatus (Happy and Lucky).

The road to the left of the Duomo leads to the **Museo Diocesano** (piazzale Poliuto Penzo 1, 041 550 7477). It contains a collection of religious art, including two fine polyptychs by Paolo Veneziano.

The **Torre di Santa Maria** marks the end of the old town; just beyond, in campo Marconi, is the deconsecrated church of San Francesco, which has been turned into the **Museo Civico della Laguna Sud** (041 550 0911). The museum provides a good introduction to aspects of lagoon life. There's a small gallery with an attractive triptych by Ercole del Fiore (1436), *Justice between Saints Felix and Fortunatus*.

ESCAPES & EXCURSIONS

Cappella degli Scrovegni.

Cities of the Veneto

PADUA

Agricultural communities lived in the Padua area from around 1200 BC, but it was the Romans who transformed this fertile spot into the thriving town of Patavium; the ruins of their Arena lie just outside the Musei Civici complex. Little else survived the attacks of Attila and his Huns in 452. After becoming an independent republic in 1164, the city's political and cultural influence peaked under the Carrara family (1338-1405). Venice (1405-1797), Austria, Napoleon and again Austria had their turns ruling; however, Paduans played an active role in freeing northern Italy from foreign dominion. In 1866 the Austrians were banished, and Padua and the Veneto were annexed to the united Kingdom of Italy.

If you only see one sight, make it the dazzling **Cappella degli Scrovegni** (Scrovegni Chapel, piazza Eremitani 8, 049 820 4551, www.cappelladegliscrovegni.it), Giotto's masterpiece. Booking is obligatory.

Externally unassuming, this building was commissioned by Enrico Scrovegni in 1303. Enrico is pictured, dressed in violet – the colour of penitence – offering the chapel to Mary in the *Last Judgement* fresco at the far end. The two sculptures on the altar, *Two Angels* and *The Virgin and Child*, are by Giovanni Pisano. But it's Giotto's magnificent fresco cycle that utterly dominates the interior. Painted c1304-13, it tells the story of mankind's salvation through the

lives of the Virgin and of Christ, and depictions of stories of Mary's parents, Joachim and Anne. The story of Christ unfolds in the middle and lower rows, with the middle of the right-hand wall dominated by the scene of Judas's kiss.

The high dado at the base of the walls is decorated with fine grisaille paintings of the seven Virtues and Vices. Particularly striking are the figures of Envy blinded by her own serpentine tongue and Prudence equipped with pen and mirror. In the huge *Last Judgement*, covering the west wall of the Chapel, suffering souls are tortured by demonic beasts.

The chapel is part of the **Complesso Eremitani**, also encompassing the **Pinacoteca** (picture gallery), **Museo Archeologico** and a museum of applied arts. The archeological wing contains remains from

---

IN THE KNOW PACKAGE DEALS

The **Padovacard** (€16 for 48 hours, €21 for 72 hours) allows free access for one adult and one child (under 14) to ten of Padua's major attractions, and discounted entrance to 20 more, plus free travel on local buses and trams, and free parking at the car park in central piazza Y Rabin. It is easiest to buy your card online before you arrive; this will also allow you to book a slot for the **Cappella degli Scrovegni** (*see left*). For further information, see www.padovacard.it or call 049 876 7911.

Roman Padua. Upstairs, the **Pinacoteca-Museo d'Arte Medioevale e Moderna** starts with Giovanni Bellini's intriguing *Portrait of a Young Senator*. Works by Titian, Palma il Vecchio, Domenico Tintoretto, Veronese and the collection's only female artist, Chiara Varotari (1584-1663) follow. Next up is a Giotto *Crucifixion* that originally hung in the Scrovegni Chapel. There are also fine works by the Bassano family, Pozzoserrato and Luca Giordano, altarpieces by Romanino and Tintoretto, and several sculptures by Canova. The final painting, by Giorgio Fossati (1706-85), is a bird's-eye view of the Prato della Valle (*see p207*), showing how the city looked in the 18th century when the area was used as a fair.

Nearby, the 13th-century church of **Gli Eremitani** (piazza Eremitani 9, 049 875 6410) has frescoes by Mantegna, begun in 1448 when he was just 17 years old. Some were almost totally destroyed in World War II bombing raids, but fortunately, the *Martyrdom of St Christopher*, the *Carrying of the Body of St Christopher* and *Our Lady of the Assumption* survived; the *Martyrdom of St James* and *St*

Christopher Converts the Knights were restored. Bizarrely, the church housed the original tomb of the very Protestant Prince Frederick William of Orange, who died here in 1799. It was removed to Delft, Holland in 1896, but a bronze copy of the marble *Pietà* (1806-08) by Antonio Canova that adorns the tomb can still be seen in the vestibule opposite the chapel.

Towards the city centre, corso Garibaldi becomes pedestrianised and more pleasant, arriving at **Gran Caffè Pedrocchi** (via VIII Febbraio 15, entrance from piazzetta Pedrocchi, 049 878 1231, www.caffepedrocchi.it). Opened to the public in 1831, this café (and it still functions as such) was designed by Venetian architect Giuseppe Jappelli. The upper floor contains a condensed tour of Western culture: the Etruscan, Greek, Roman, Herculaneum, Renaissance, Moorish and Egyptian rooms, all lavishly decorated, surround the ballroom, or Sala Grande. The first-floor rooms also house the **Museo del Risorgimento e dell'Età Contemporanea**, with military memorabilia.

To the west of here lie Padua's three main *piazze*, ringed and linked by attractive cobbled

THE BRENTA CANAL

Cruise from Venice to Padua, passing a couple of Palladio's villas en route.

Stretching for 36 kilometres (22 miles) between Venice and Padua, the Brenta waterway was canalised in the 16th century. Goethe fondly remembered cruising down the canal in 1786, enjoying 'the banks studded with gardens and summer houses.' Nowadays, though, many of the gardens and summer houses have long since been replaced by housing estates and industrial sites.

A number of Palladian villas still grace the canal, part of which can be navigated in a boat, *Il Burchiello*, which chugs up the Brenta from Venice as far as Strà. The boat journey includes the *ville* Widmann, Pisani and Foscari.

Villa Foscari, aka 'La Malcontenta' (via dei Turisti 9, Malcontenta, 041 520 3966, www.lamalcontenta.com), is one of the most acclaimed creations of Andrea Palladio. The origin of the villa's nickname is hotly disputed, but is said to refer to an unhappy (*malcontenta*) woman who was housed there in isolation. Some say she was a disgraced Foscari wife; others that, when the family abandoned the villa shortly after the fall of the Venetian Republic in 1797, rumours of a mysterious female outcast arose to keep undesirables away. With its double staircase and elegant Greek temple façade, the Villa Foscari has been the inspiration for thousands of buildings throughout Europe and America.

The boat trip ends at the (non-Palladian) **Villa Pisani** (via Doge Pisani 7, Strà,

Villa Foscari.

049 502 074, www.villapisani.beniculturali.it), a remarkable early 18th-century house.

The budget traveller can enjoy a similar route at a fraction of the price by taking ACTV's 53 bus (bound for Padua) from piazzale Roma, leaving at 09 and 41 minutes past the hour.

SITA – Divisione Navigazione 'Il Burchiello'
Via Orlandini 3, Padua (049 820 6910, www.ilburchiello.it). **Services** (Mar-Nov) *Venice–Padua* Departure from Pietà boat stop (near San Zaccaria, Venice) 9am Tue, Thur, Sat. *Padua–Venice* Departure from piazzale Boschetti 8.15am Wed, Fri, Sun. **Rates** (incl entrance to Villa Foscari, to Barchessa Valmarana or Widmann, to Villa Pisani and return bus journey) €94; €55-€84 reductions. Online booking advisable.

Brenta Canal.

Palazzo del Capitanio.

streets, boutiques and shady loggias. Between piazza della Frutta and piazza delle Erbe is the **Palazzo della Ragione** (via VIII Febbraio, 049 820 5006), which houses the huge public chamber known to locals as **Il Salone**, built in 1218-19 to provide the city with a prison and public offices. Between 1306 and 1309 it was converted to accommodate the law courts, and the external loggia of the piano nobile was added. Inside, the Salone is frescoed with representations of the zodiac, months and seasons, but is mostly empty apart from a huge wooden horse, created for a tournament in 1466. In the north-east corner of the hall sits the *Pietra del vituperio* (stone of shame) where, according to 1261 statutes, insolvent debtors had to sit in their underwear, repeating the words *cedo bonis* (I renounce my worldly goods) before being banished. Those who tried to return risked a repeat of the punishment – plus having three buckets of water poured over their heads.

Piazza dei Signori is dominated by the **Palazzo del Capitanio**. To the south lies the underwhelming **Duomo** (piazza Duomo, church 049 662 814, baptistry 049 656 914), Padua's cathedral, and its fabulously frescoed 12th-century baptistry. The first church on this site was destroyed in 899 by rampaging Huns; in 1551, Michelangelo won a competition with his design for a new church, but it's clear from the uninspiring final form that his plans were not adhered to. Construction wasn't completed until 1754. Inside are paintings by Stefano dell'Arzere, Tiepolo, Paris Bordone and a panel painting of a Byzantine-style *Virgin and Child*, a copy of an original by Giotto. The real jewel is the 12th-century baptistry next door, frescoed from floor to ceiling by the 14th-century Florentine Giusto de Menabuoi.

Between piazza del Duomo and via VIII Febbraio is the tranquil old **Ghetto**, now a beautifully renovated pedestrian zone with shops and bars lining the cobbled streets. The area was closed off in 1603 by four gates restricting its Jewish inhabitants' movements, and remained that way until 1797. One synagogue remains on via Solferino; beneath the 16th-century loggia in Nanto stone is a plaque commemorating the deaths of 46 Paduan and 8,000 Italian Jews during the Holocaust. All that is left of the Sinagoga Tedesca (German Synagogue) – the city's oldest synagogue, destroyed in 1943 by anti-Semitic *padovani* – is a plaque on via delle Piazze.

Back on via VIII Febbraio, as you continue south the street becomes via Roma, passing **Santa Maria dei Servi** (1393). The church is open only for Mass, but look out for the beautifully carved wooden door (1511) by Bartolomeo Campologno.

Via Roma becomes via Umberto I before reaching the **Prato della Valle**. The extensive Prato claims to be the largest public square in Italy, its elliptical shape reflecting that of the Roman theatre which once stood on the site. Immediately left on entering the Prato is the delightful **Museo del Precinema** (049 876 3838, www.minicizotti.it), a minute museum housing a delightful display of magic lanterns (precursors to photo and film), with hand-painted glass slides, optical instruments and a Japanese puppet theatre. Further south towards the river is the beautiful medieval complex housing **La Specola** (vicolo dell'Osservatorio 5, 049 829 3469, www.pd.astro.it/museo-laspecola), the observatory, with a collection of antique telescopes, quadrants, sextants and other heavenly paraphernalia.

Facing the Prato to the south is the church of **Santa Giustina** (049 822 0411, www.abbazia santagiustina.org). A stone's throw away is **Il Santo** (piazza del Santo, 049 878 9722, www.basilicadelsanto.org). Don't let the economical local name for what is officially the Basilica di Sant'Antonio deceive you. Work on the church began soon after St Anthony's death (1231) and canonisation (1232), although the main structure remained unfinished until around 1350, when his body was moved to its present tomb in the Cappella dell'Arca. This chapel also contains some of the basilica's great artistic treasures: a series of marble bas-reliefs of scenes from the life of the saint by Jacopo Sansovino, Tullio Lombardo and Giovanni Minello. The chapel's ceiling dates from 1533. On the high altar are Donatello's bronze panels and crucifix (1444-45); behind the altar is his stone bas-relief of the Deposition and other bronzes, including a bull and a lion representing the evangelists St Mark and St Luke.

Other works of interest include Altichiero's late 14th-century frescoes in the Cappella di San Felice (on the south wall), Giusto de Menabuoi's frescoes in the Cappella del Beato Luca Belludi, and two fine funeral monuments by Michele Sanmicheli. At the back of the apse is the florid Cappella del Tesoro, to which Anthony's 'miraculous' relics were transferred in 1745 for safe-keeping. Here you can inspect the reliquary containing the saint's tongue, his original coffin and fragments of his robes, all housed in their specially built, garish Baroque setting.

In the piazza in front of the church stands the great Renaissance masterpiece, Donatello's monument to the famous *condottiere* (mercenary soldier) Erasmo da Narni (d.1443), aka Gattamelata, who is buried inside the basilica. Commissioned by the *condottiere*'s family in 1453 and cast the same year, it was the first full-size equestrian bronze to be made since antiquity. (Donatello is known to have inhabited the house at piazza del Santo 19, between 1444 and 1454.)

Nearby are the **Orto Botanico** (Botanical Garden, via Orto Botanico 15, 049 827 2119, www.ortobotanico.unipd.it); and the **Loggia e Odeo Cornaro** (via Cesarotti 37, 335 142 8861),

a theatre space and salon designed by Giovanni Maria Falconetto in the early 16th century.

Padovani flock to the cafés that line via Roma for their morning cappuccini – in fact, for any drinks any time. **Bar Fuji** (via Roma 53, 049 875 9485) goes one step further, supplementing drinks and light meals with good sushi. At **Caffè Cavour** (piazza Cavour 10, 049 875 1224, www.caffecavour.com), pastry magician Emanuele Saracino makes unmissable cakes, while the **Caffè Pedrocchi** (*see p205*) is an all-day food and beverage outlet as well as a stunning museum.

If you're on a budget, the morning market in piazza delle Erbe and piazza della Frutta will supply all you need for a picnic. But if money is no object, take a cab just out of town to **Le Calandre** (via Liguria 1, Sarmeola di Rubano, 049 630 303, www.calandre.com) where Massimiliano Alajmo – the youngest chef ever to achieve three Michelin stars – will amaze your taste buds. (You can also experience his gastronomic fireworks in Venice at **Gran Caffè Quadri**, *see p60*.)

VERONA

Verona is perhaps best known as the home town of star-crossed lovers Romeo and Juliet, but the attraction today known as Juliet's House pales in comparison with the other glories that Verona has to offer. If, across the lagoon, Venice lacks any ancient remains, Verona more than makes up for it. There's a Roman amphitheatre – the Arena – and theatre, both of which host cultural extravaganzas in the warmer months, the Arena opera season being world-famous.

After being colonised by the Romans in 89 BC, Verona became a frequent prize of conquest. By the 12th century, however, it had become an independent city-state, reaching its zenith in the 13th and 14th centuries, when the home-grown Della Scala (or Scaligero) dynasty (hence the ladder in local coats-of-arms – *scala* in Italian means 'ladder') brought a period of peace to a city that had long been racked by Montague and Capulet-style family feuding. The dynasty fell in 1387 and was replaced by Milan's Viscontis, superseded in turn by the Venetian Republic. Renaissance Verona lent its Venetian overlords its refined architect Sanmicheli and his painter-protégé, Paolo Veronese. Only in 1866 did Verona rid itself of foreign rulers, when it joined the newly united Kingdom of Italy.

Dominating the entrance to the old town in piazza Brà is the magnificent Roman **Arena** (045 800 3204, www.arena.it). The largest Roman amphitheatre in northern Italy, the Arena was capacious enough to seat the city's whole population of 20,000 when it

---

IN THE KNOW EARLY HOURS

The façade of the **Palazzo del Capitanio**, on Piazza dei Signori, may date from 1532 but it supports an elaborate mechanical clock built a century earlier. Installed in 1437, to a design by Maestro Novello, it's a reproduction of the first clock made in Italy (1344).

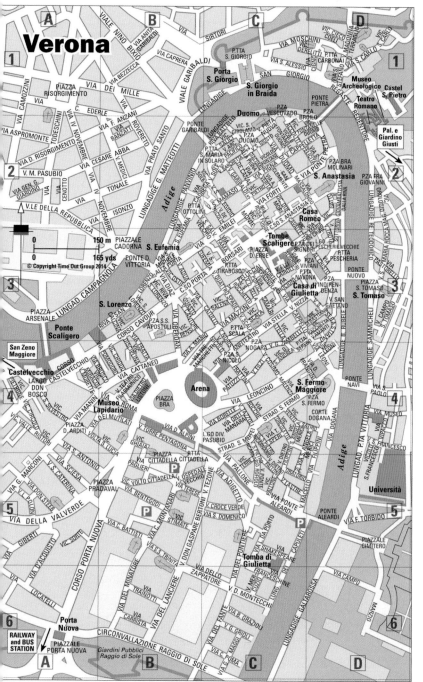

ESCAPES & EXCURSIONS

IN THE KNOW GET CARDED

An admission fee is charged by some churches and all museums in Verona. Cut costs by buying a **Verona Card** (www.veronacard.it, €15 for one day, €20 for three days), valid for all the sights that charge. It can be bought at the exchange office in the station or the ticket offices of any of the churches or museums participating in the scheme, and includes bus fares around the city. If you're limiting your sightseeing to churches, you can pick up a €6 (€5 reductions) combined entrance ticket for the ones that charge (San Zeno, San Lorenzo, Sant'Anastasia, San Fermo and the Duomo) in the churches themselves. Individually, it costs €2.50 admission to each of these; note, though, that they are covered by the Verona Card. For further information, consult www.turismoverona.eu and www.chiese verona.it.

was constructed in about AD 30. The 44 tiers of stone seats inside the 139-metre by 110-metre (456-foot by 361-foot) amphitheatre are virtually intact, as is the columned foyer. After the earthquake of 1117 destroyed most of the Arena's outer ring (the remaining four arches are known as the 'ala'), the city repaired the damage almost immediately. Originally the site of gladiatorial games and – when filled with water – naval battles, it was used by post-Roman inhabitants as a shelter during fifth- and sixth-century Barbarian invasions.

Medieval *veronesi* treated it as a red-light district and it was home to the city's cut-throats. Later, city masters used the Arena as a law court and site of the occasional execution. It functioned as a theatre in the 17th and 18th centuries, hosted circuses and hot-air balloon launches in the 19th, and became a football stadium in the early 20th century. It now provides a spectacular setting for summer operas (*see p212* **Opera in the Arena**).

The old town, nestling in the loops of the meandering Adige river, stretches out from piazza Brà. Overshadowed by the magnificent Arena, this large square is home to a number of cafés on the Liston, the Veronese promenade, and to the **Museo Lapidario Maffeiano** (045 590 087), a small collection of Greek and Roman fragments and inscriptions. A short walk north-east from the piazza along via Mazzini takes you to the heart of the city – the adjoining squares of piazza delle Erbe and piazza dei Signori.

Once the site of the Roman forum, piazza delle Erbe today is home to a somewhat tacky market (Mon-Sat), which nevertheless can't detract from the stunning surrounding buildings (all closed to the public). At the northern end is the huge 14th-century **Casa Mazzanti** with its splendid late Renaissance frescoes on the outer façade, the highly ornamented **Palazzo Maffei** and the **Torre Gardello** clock tower, built in 1370. Dotted among the stalls are the gleaming 16th-century Berlina, under which public officials were invested with their office, and a fountain (1368), whose basin is of Roman origin, as is the body of the statue known as the 'Madonna Verona', which stands above it. The tall houses

Verona.

at the square's southern end once marked the edge of the Jewish ghetto.

A detour south-east out of piazza delle Erbe along via Cappello leads to **Casa di Giulietta** (Juliet's House, via Cappello 23, 045 803 4303; *see also below* **Star-crossed Lovers**). Further down via Cappello is the **Porta Leoni**, a fragment of a Roman city gate and now part of a medieval house; excavations have exposed the full extent of the towered and arched structure.

Before the gate, at **San Fermo Maggiore** (stradone San Fermo, 045 592 813, www.chiese verona.it), you get two churches for the price of one: the intimate and solemn lower church is Romanesque; the upper church, towering and full of light, is Gothic. Its wooden ceiling resembles an upturned Venetian galleon. Among the important frescoes is an *Annunciation* by Antonio Pisanello, to the left of the main entrance. Just over the bridge from here is the district from which artist Paolo Veronese came; the modern church of **San Paolo** (via XX Settembre 2, 045 800 7790) has one of his early works, the *Madonna and Saints*.

Piazza dei Signori, the heart of medieval Verona's governance and finance, contains the 15th-century **Loggia del Consiglio** (closed to the public) topped by statues of illustrious *veronesi*, including Catullus. Linking *piazze* delle Erbe and dei Signori is the 12th-century **Palazzo della Ragione**, recently restored and now home to the **Achille Forti Gallery of Modern Art** on the first floor (cortile Mercato Vecchio, 045 800 1903, www.palazzo dellaragioneverona.it). From one of the eight elegant arches in piazza dei Signori – Arco della Costa – hangs a whale bone. According to local legend, it will fall if an adult virgin passes beneath it.

A gateway on the piazza dei Signori side of the palazzo leads into the **Mercato Vecchio** courtyard, with its huge Romanesque arches and magnificent outdoor Renaissance staircase. The palazzo is dominated by the 83-metre

STAR-CROSSED LOVERS
The (modern-day) balcony scene.

Disentangling myth and history is difficult in Verona, where locals have been milking their Romeo and Juliet connections for centuries. The Montagues and Capulets may have been real enough, but young Juliet Capulet was not laid to rest in the Roman sarcophagus in the former **convent of San Francesco al Corso** (via del Pontiere 35), where Mme de Stael and Lord Byron went into Romantic raptures (and which Charles Dickens, more prosaically, described as 'a sort of drinking trough'). And the Capulets certainly never lived in what's now known as the **Casa di Giulietta** (Juliet's house, *see above*). This doesn't stop starry-eyed visitors in droves paying for a ticket that allows them into a rather stark interior, where they can pen and post their letters to Juliet before taking a quick bow on the famous balcony.

Generations of visitors have crowded the courtyard of this pretty 13th-century palazzo, gazing enraptured at a balcony cunningly tacked on to the first floor in the 1920s,

leaving their entwined signatures on graffiti-covered walls and having a furtive rub of the shiny right breast of a 20th-century bronze of Shakespeare's best-loved heroine. But it wasn't until 2009 that Verona's town council had the bright idea of turning the place into the world's most sought-after wedding location… at a price.

Now, for a fee ranging from €600 (for local residents) to €800 (for EU citizens) or even €1,000 (for those from outside the EU), lovers can tie the knot in the courtyard beneath the balcony. The various tariffs, the city council insists, reflect the different costs of the paperwork involved in getting people wed. And they're a bargain compared to civil services in Venice, where EU citizens can pay anything up to €1,800 and those from outside the EU up to €4,200.

For the record, **Romeo's house** – which at least may have actually belonged to the Montague family – is not open to the public. It's just across from the **Della Scala tombs** (*see p213*), at Arche Scaligere 4.

OPERA IN THE ARENA

A night to remember in Verona's magnificent Roman Arena.

With its ancient history of bloodshed and torment, Verona's **Arena** (*see p208*) seems particularly suited to grand productions of tragic magnitude – but any of the operas that are performed at this 2,000-year-old amphitheatre every night from June to September will certainly be pure magic. For classics by Puccini, Bizet, Verdi and co, the atmosphere is charged with excitement as music lovers start squeezing on to the (unnumbered) stone terraces a good two hours before the performance begins.

Some might have already eaten at the self-service restaurant **Brek** (piazza Brà 20, 045 800 4561, www.brek.com) directly opposite. Others stock up at the local supermarket (PAM, at via dei Mutilati 3) and settle down with their picnics. All bring or rent a cushion, as a night perched on a piece of ancient marble can seem long and painful, whatever is happening on stage. Occupants of the *poltronissime*, the red-cushioned stalls seats, can saunter in just before the show commences, perhaps after having tucked into one of the

pre-opera menus (served from 6.30pm) in the courtyard of the baroque **Ristorante Maffei** (piazza delle Erbe 38, 045 801 0015, www.ristorantemaffei.it). Armani-clad industrialists show off their expensive seats and their even more expensive consorts. Differences dissipate as darkness descends; a hush falls over the 15,000-strong audience as the overture is played to the flickering of *mocoleti*, the candles traditionally lit all around the amphitheatre for the prelude. In the Arena's 80-plus years of operatic history, divas such as Renata Tebaldi, Angela Gheorghio and Maria Callas – who made her international debut here as *La Gioconda* in 1947 – have all trod the boards, together with tenors from Beniamino Gigli to José Carreras. Scenic extravaganzas have been staged, with designers such as Franco Zeffirelli called upon to recreate the River Nile or Sevillian mountains. Casts of hundreds have included horses, elephants and even camels, one of which managed to escape one year and lope off around town.

Centre-stage drama once turned into a backstage fracas when director Roberto Rossellini conjured up over-realistic smoke effects during a performance of *Othello*, nearly choking the leading man, tenor Mario del Monaco. The fuming *divo* threw a hissy fit and Rossellini was sent packing before the show could go on. Fully front-stage tragedy turned to comedy more recently when a voluptuous 'calamity' Carmen fell out of her costume, taking the puff out of her dying gasp.

(272-foot) **Torre dei Lamberti** (1462). From the next courtyard on the right you can descend into the archaeological site of the **Scavi Scaligeri** (Corte del Tribunale, piazza Viviani (045 800 7490, www.comune. verona.it/scaviscaligeri). The excavations give a feel for the city's historical layering, as you move between Roman mosaics and roads, interspersed at random with medieval and Lombard remains.

At the eastern exit from piazza dei Signori are the **Della Scala family tombs** (*tombe* or *arche scaligere*, via Santa Maria in Chiavica, www.turismoverona.eu). Though the site can only be visited from June to September, the Gothic tombs of medieval Verona's 'top dogs', the Della Scala family, can always be seen from the outside. Dating from 1277 to the end of the 14th century, the lavish tombs (carved by the most sought-after stonemasons of the era) give a good idea of the family's sense of its own importance. Note the family's odd taste in first names. The monument to Cangrande (Big Dog, d.1329), above the doorway to the church of Santa Maria Antica, shows the valiant duke smiling in the face of death, guarded by crowned dogs (this is a copy; the original is in the Castelvecchio, *see p215*). Poking out from above the fence are the spire-topped final resting places of Cansignorio (Lord Dog, d.1375) and Mastino II (Mastiff the Second, d.1351). Among the less flamboyant tombs is that of Mastino I (d.1277), founder of the doggy dynasty. (Verona is quietly boastful about the fact that the poet Dante lived in exile at the court of the Della Scala family from 1304. He dedicated his *Paradiso* to Cangrande I.)

Next door, the intimate church of **Santa Maria Antica** (via Arche Scaligere 3,

But even the rare glitches can't detract from the show; hours of magical music with natural acoustics and the stunning setting make a night in the world's largest open-air opera house a matchless experience.

After the final curtain, the crowd go their separate ways with the final notes still ringing in their ears; some go off to star-spot at the **Liston** (via Dietro Liston 19, 045 800 4515, www.listonristorantepizzeria.it), where cast and conductors are known to eat after the show. Others dive into the narrow street behind the Arena for dinner at **Trattoria Tre Marchetti** (vicolo Tre Marchetti 19B, 045 803 0463, www.tremarchetti.it), which has served meals since 1291; or to the simpler **Bacaro dell'Arena** (vicolo Tre Marchetti 1B, 045 590 503, www.bacarodellarena.it), which stays open until 2am on opera nights. Those who've already booked at the **Bottega del Vino** (via Scudo di Francia 3, 045 800 4535, www.bottegavini.it), will have Veronese dishes awaiting them and a choice of over 3,000 wines to uncork as they discuss the show.

Fondazione Arena di Verona
Via Dietro l'Anfiteatro 6B (045 800 5151, www.arena.it). **Performances** *June-Aug* 9pm Tue-Sun. **Tickets** €21-€198. **Map** p253 B3.
Seats are sometimes available on the day of the show, especially midweek.

IN THE KNOW
ROMAN & MEDIEVAL REMAINS

The **Arena** (*see p208*), **Teatro Romano** (*see p214*) and **ponte Pietra** (*see p214*) are Verona's major Roman remains. Many modern buildings stand on Roman foundations; some have fragments of Roman marble-work in their fabric. Verona's medieval architecture dates mostly from after the great earthquake of 1117. In the building boom that followed, the city was adorned with some of its finest buildings: the basilica of **San Zeno** (*see p215*), the **Duomo** (*see p217* and the Gothic churches of **Sant'Anastasia** (*see p214*) and **San Fermo** (*see p211*). Ancient, medieval and modern are knitted together with the ever-present pink-tinged stone and marble.

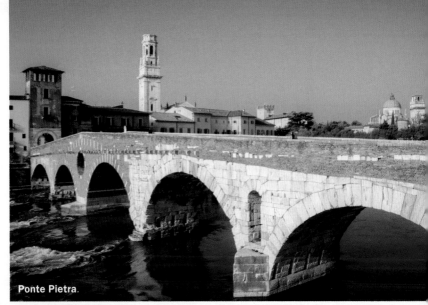
Ponte Pietra.

045 595 508) was the Della Scala family chapel. Indirectly, the church has loaned its name to Milan's famous opera house, **La Scala**. When Beatrice Regina della Scala married and moved to Milan, she had her own prayer chapel built on the site of the future opera house in 1381; it was modelled on and named after this chapel.

Moving northwards, the peaceful, narrow streets are a captivating labyrinth dotted with medieval and Renaissance *palazzi*. In via Pigna, take a look at the carved marble Roman pine cone (*pigna*) before heading north down via San Giacomo alla Pigna towards the **Duomo**, or south towards the imposing church of **Sant'Anastasia** (piazza Sant'Anastasia, 045 592 813, www.chieseverona.it).

This imposing brick Gothic church is best visited early in the morning, when sunlight streams in to illuminate Antonio Pisanello's glorious fresco (1433-38; above the terracotta-clad Pelligrini chapel) of St George girding himself to set off in pursuit of the dragon that has been pestering the lovely princess of Trebizond. Carved scenes from the life of St Peter Martyr adorn the unfinished façade, while inside, two delightful *gobbi* (hunchbacks) crouch down to support the holy water font; the one on the left was carved by Paolo Veronese's father in 1495. On the left of the church stands the tiny, deconsecrated **San Pietro in Martire** (aka San Giorgetto dei Domenicani), with three Gothic funerary monuments on its exterior.

Close by, **ponte Pietra** is Verona's oldest bridge and, for centuries, was the only link between the city centre and the suburbs beyond. The two stone arches on the left bank of the river are Roman and date from before 50 BC. The other three brick arches date from between 1200 and 1500. The bridge was reconstructed using original stones in 1957 after being destroyed by retreating Germans.

Across the bridge are some of Verona's most beautiful churches, including **San Giorgio in Braida** (piazzetta San Giorgio 1, 045 834 0232), a great domed Renaissance church, probably designed by the Veronese military architect Michele Sanmicheli between 1536 and 1543, containing a *Baptism of Christ* by Tintoretto above the entrance door, a moving *Martyrdom of St George* by Paolo Veronese and a beautiful, serene *Madonna and Child with Saints Zeno and Lawrence* by local dark horse Girolamo dai Libri. There's also **Santa Maria in Organo** (piazzetta Santa Maria in Organo, 045 591 440), a Renaissance church with what Giorgio Vasari described as the most beautiful choir stalls in Italy. A humble monk, Fra Giovanni da Verona (d.1520), worked for 25 years cutting and assembling these infinitely complex, coloured, wooden images of animals, birds, landscapes, cityscapes, religious scenes and musical and scientific instruments in dozens of intricate intarsia panels.

Also beyond the bridge is the **Museo Archeologico** (regaste Redentore 2, 045 800 0360, www.turismoverona.eu) with a collection of local remains and a spectacular view; the remains of the first-century BC **Teatro Romano** are in the same complex,

and theatre performances are staged here
in summer. The area around **Castel San
Pietro** (closed to the public) – part of the
city's medieval and Renaissance fortifications,
heavily redesigned by Austrian occupiers in
the mid 19th century – offers a bird's-eye view.
Head south-east from the bridge along regaste
Redentore and its continuations for the pretty
Giardino Giusti (via Giardino Giusti 2, 045
803 4029), a statue-packed garden with tall
cypresses laid out in 1580. The wild upper level
climbs the steep slopes of the hill behind, which
offers superb viewing and picnic opportunities.
Back towards the river is the church of **San
Tomaso Cantuariense** (piazza San Tomaso
1, 045 803 356, www.parrocchiasantomaso.it),
where Mozart, aged 13, played the organ on
his visit to the city, birthplace of his future
arch-rival, Salieri.

Corso Porta Borsari, Roman Verona's busy
main street, leads out of the north end of piazza
delle Erbe towards the **Porta Borsari**, the
best-preserved of the city's Roman gates;
it probably dates from the reign of Emperor
Claudius (AD 41-54). In a small garden
along corso Cavour is the **Arco dei Gavi**, a
triumphal arch attributed to Vitruvius, dating
from about 50 BC. Here also is the medieval
fortress of **Castelvecchio** (Corso Castelvecchio
2, 045 806 2611, www.www.turismoverona.eu),
adorned with swallow-tail battlements. By the
time Duke Cangrande II della Scala began
building this castle in 1355, the family needed
a fortress for waging war and as a refuge from
overtaxed Veronese citizens: **ponte Scaligero**,
the magnificent fortified medieval bridge, was
intended as an emergency escape route. The
castle is now a museum and exhibition venue,
with interiors beautifully redesigned in the
1960s by Venetian architect Carlo Scarpa.
The museum contains important works by
Mantegna, Crivelli, Pisanello, Giovanni Bellini,
Veronese, Tintoretto, Giambattista Tiepolo,
Canaletto and Guardi, plus a magnificent
collection of 13th- and 14th-century Veronese
religious statuary. An armoury and local
jewellery complete the collection.

Outside the centre, to the west of piazza
Brà, is the stunning basilica of **San Zeno
Maggiore** (piazza San Zeno 2, 045 592 813,
www.chieseverona.it). One of the most
spectacularly ornate Romanesque churches in
northern Italy, it was built between 1123 and
1138 to house the tomb and shrine of San Zeno,
an African who became Verona's first bishop
in 362 and is now the city's much-loved patron
saint. The façade, with its great rose window
and graceful porch, is covered with some
magnificent Romanesque marble sculpture.
Scenes from the Old Testament and the life of
Christ mingle with hunting and jousting scenes,

San Zeno Maggiore.

attributed to the 12th-century sculptors Nicolò and Guglielmo. The porch is supported by columns resting on two carved marble lions; they serve as a frame for the great bronze doors. Nicknamed 'the poor man's bible', the doors' 48 panels have scenes from the Bible and from the life of San Zeno, and a few that experts have been hard-pressed to pin down, including a woman suckling two crocodiles. The panels on the left-hand door date from about 1030 and came from an earlier church.

Inside the lofty church (note the magnificent ceiling built in 1386), a staircase descends into the crypt, which contains the tomb of San Zeno. The magnificent triptych – known as the *Pala di Mantegna* after its author, Andrea Mantegna – painted in 1457-59 for this very spot, has dominated the altar ever since (save three years in Florence for restoration recently). The enduring love affair between San Zeno and the city that adopted him may have something to do with the huge, early 12th-century marble statue of the African bishop having a grand old chuckle, which is found in a niche to the left of the apse. His black face, with its distinctly African features, is unique in Italian religious statuary. When he wasn't converting Veronese souls to Christianity, he is said to have spent his time fishing in the river Adige, seated on a rock. Covering the inside walls of the basilica are frescoes dating from the 12th to the 14th centuries, but perhaps more interesting than the paintings

themselves is the 15th- to 17th-century graffiti scratched into them.

To the right of the church is a massive bell tower, 72 metres (236 feet) high, begun in 1045. To the left is a lower tower, which is all that remains of the Benedictine monastery that stood on the site before the basilica was built, and which, according to local lore, stands over the grave of Pepin, Charlemagne's disinherited hunchback son. Behind is a Romanesque cloister.

If the Liston, by piazza Brà, is the area where locals head for a great concentration of cafés and bars, the area inside the great bend in the river Adige is also home to some good places to eat and drink.

Cappa Café (piazzetta Brà Molinari 1A, corner of via Ponte Pietra, 045 800 4516, www.cappacafe.it), with its fine view over the ponte di Pietra, is a good place to start the evening with an aperitivo on the terrace. Visitors daunted by the local yen for donkey and horse flesh (*see below* **In the Know**) will appreciate **Hostaria la Vecchia Fontanina** (piazzetta Chiavica 5, 045 591 159, www.ristorantevecchiafontanina.com), which has plenty of non-meat options among its more typical dishes. Under the porticos in a picturesque street, **Sottoriva** (via Sottoriva 9A, 045 801 4323) is a traditional Veronese *osteria*, proud of its venerable status and good, simple cooking. Not far from the Arena, **Al Bersagliere** (via Dietro Pallone 1, 045 800 4824, www.trattoriaalbersagliere.it) is an old curiosity shop, packed with the owner's strange collection. The menu covers all the local traditions, and the wine list sticks mainly to good labels from the north-east.

VICENZA

Vicenza was a Roman settlement, and the city's ancient layout is still virtually intact. It became an important Lombard and Frankish centre, but was destroyed by Magyar ravagers in 899, only to flourish again later in the Middle Ages. In 1404, Vicenza came under the rule of Venice, and a veritable building boom began. Bridling under the Venetian yoke, Vicenza's leading families proclaimed their superiority by commissioning sumptuous townhouses and country villas. But Venetian nobles were also encouraged to develop country estates in order to strengthen the Republic's grip on the surrounding territory. It was into this cauldron of Renaissance one-upmanship that **Andrea Palladio** (*see p220* **Villa Visits: Andrea Palladio**) fell in the 1540s. The mark he left here would influence architecture the world over for centuries to come.

Now a major hub of the north-eastern economic miracle, Vicenza oozes wealth.

IN THE KNOW EAT & DRINK

Verona's cuisine is a mix of Middle European heft and Italian sensibility. Boiled and roasted meats are popular, served with *cren*, the local take on horseradish sauce, and *pearà*, made of bone marrow, bread and pepper. Braised horsemeat (*pastissada de caval*) is another local speciality, as is donkey ragù. Vegetarians take heart: *bigoli*, a sort of thick spaghetti, is often served with meat-free sauces. Pumpkin-stuffed ravioli is a speciality.

The vineyards around Verona produce some of Italy's most recognisable wine exports: Soave, Bardolino and Valpolicella (*see p200* **Wines of North-East Italy**). The ultra-serious wine competition Vinitaly (www.vinitaly.com) takes place here every spring (see www.veronafiere.it for information), keeping the lightweight export names for everyday use and the better-kept secrets like Amarone and Valpolicella Classico for special occasions.

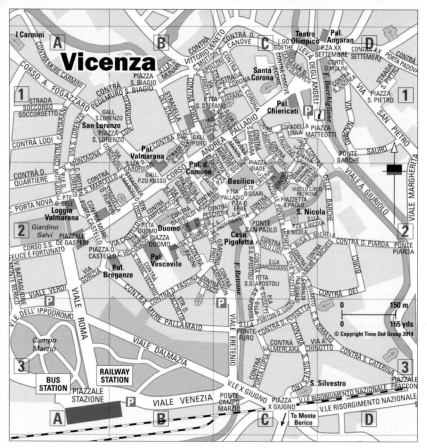

The city is home to Italy's precious-metalworking industry, and the VicenzaOro trade fair (www.vicenzaoro.com) takes place here several times a year. The city's two main claims to fame – Palladio and gold – come together along the streets of the *centro*, where shop windows in ground floors of glorious Palladian *palazzi* glisten with world-class jewels, exorbitant geegaws and designer togs.

Despite its Roman origins, Vicenza's character is very much medieval and Renaissance. Just outside the town walls, to the west of the centre, is the statue-dotted **Giardino Salvi**. This pleasant public park houses Palladio's **Loggia Valmarana**, a Doric-style temple spanning the waters of a canal. Nearby is a Baroque loggia by Baldassare Longhena.

Inside the walls, piazza del Castello takes its name from a castle built in 1337-38 by the Della Scala family, who ruled here from 1311 to 1404. The tower in the corner of the piazza

is all that remains of the castle. The adjoining gate, **Porta Castello**, was constructed in 1343 on the site of the city's Roman gate. The piazza is home to the odd-looking **Palazzo Porto Breganze**, a tall awkward fragment in the southern corner, designed by Palladio but never finished.

Palladio had a hand in five of the grandiose *palazzi* lining corso Palladio (all are closed to the public). The first palazzo of note, on the left-hand side as you exit piazza del Castello, is the magnificent **Palazzo Thiene Bonin Longare**, begun in 1562. At no.45 is **Palazzo Capra**, almost certainly designed by the young Palladio between 1540 and 1545.

A quick turn right into contrà Battisti (streets in Vicenza's centre are called '*contrà*' instead of '*via*') leads to the **Duomo** (piazza Duomo 8, 0444 320 996, www.vicenza.chiesacattolica.it), a mainly 12th-century structure that was badly bombed in World War II and has since been restored. The site is believed to have been occupied from around the fifth century by a Christian basilica, modified in the ninth, tenth and 11th centuries. The Palladian dome has been restored, as has the Gothic pink marble façade, attributed to Domenico da Venezia (1467). The banal brick interior contains an important polyptych by Lorenzo Veneziano, dated 1366.

Opposite the Duomo is the entrance to the incredibly preserved **Criptoportico Romano** (piazza Duomo, 0444 226 626), the only surviving remnant of Roman Vicetia and all that remains of a large, first-century *domus* (Roman townhouse). The 90 metres (295 feet) of vaulted tunnels formed part of the foundations supporting a walled internal garden. Well ventilated in summer, and possibly heated in winter, the space was most likely used for the storage of food and wine.

Back on corso Palladio, a detour to the left leads to **San Lorenzo** (piazza San Lorenzo, 0444 321 960), a sparse Gothic brick church with a magnificent marble portal encasing an exquisite 14th-century lunette depicting the Madonna and Child. Inside, the Poiana altar in the right transept is a late Gothic assemblage of paintings and frescoes by various artists, including a 1500 frescoed lunette of the crucifixion by Bartolomeo Montagna. The peaceful 16th-century cloister contains a medieval well-head.

Still on the corso, no.92 is **Palazzo Pojana** (1564-66), which consists of two separate buildings that were cunningly joined together by Palladio. **Palazzo Trissino Baston**, at no.98, was designed in 1592 by Palladio's student Vincenzo Scamozzi but not completed until 1667; the interior can be visited (by appointment only, 0444 221 111).

In the vast and elegant piazza dei Signori, south of the corso, is the 82-metre (269-foot) **Torre di Piazza** clocktower, which dates from the 12th century. The Gothic Palazzo della Ragione (piazza dei Signori, 0444 323 681,

Vicenza.

Piazza dei Signori & Torre di Piazza.

www.museicivicivicenza.it), seat of city government, is known to all as the **Basilica Palladiana**, thanks to the loggia tacked on the side by Palladio. (*Basilica* is used in the Roman sense of the word: a public place where justice is dispensed.) 'It is not possible to describe the impression made by Palladio's Basilica…' gushed Goethe about Palladio's most famous piece of urban restyling. When the palazzo's original loggia collapsed in 1496, city fathers canvassed the leading architects of the day; luckily for Palladio, who was only 17 at the time, they dithered for 20 years before accepting the audacious solution he proposed in 1546. Palladio's double-tiered loggia, comprising Serlian windows, encases the original Gothic palazzo in a unifying Renaissance shell. The basilica is now used as an exhibition space and opens only for shows, many of which are free.

Opposite is Palladio's **Loggia del Capitanato**, a fragment of a building, built to celebrate Venice's victory over the Turks in the Battle of Lepanto in 1571.On the same side is the complex of the **Monte di Pietà**, the city's 16th-century pawn shop.

Piazza delle Erbe is dominated by a medieval tower where wrongdoers were taken to be tortured. In the labyrinth of streets to the south of the piazza is the **Casa Pigafetta** (contrà Pigafetta 9). Dating from 1444 and built in late Spanish Gothic style, this strange, highly decorated townhouse was the birthplace

of Antonio Pigafetta, who was one of only 21 survivors of Magellan's epoch-making circumnavigation of the globe (1519-22).

Coming off corso Palladio to the north of piazza Signori is contrà Porti, a real palazzo feast. The clannish Porto family all built their houses in one street. At no.11 is the **Palazzo Barbaran Da Porto**, designed and built by Palladio (1569-71), with an interior by Lorenzo Rubini. After a 20-year restoration, it is now home to the **Museo Palladiano** (0444 323 014, www.palladiomuseum.org), which offers an intelligently curated look at Palladio's works, techniques and times, and hosts temporary exhibitions on architectural themes.

Casa Porto (no.15) is an undistinguished 15th-century building that was badly restored in the 18th century, but is of interest as the home of Luigi Da Porto (d.1529), writer of the first known account of the Romeo and Juliet story. At no.19 the exquisite, late Gothic **Palazzo Porto Colleoni** is a typical 15th-century attempt to beat the Venetians at their own game. **Palazzo Iseppo Da Porto**, at no.21, is one of Palladio's earliest creations; its interior is decorated with frescoes by Tiepolo, but, again, it's not open to the public.

At the end of the street, over the Bacchiglione river, contrà San Marco is a wide street lined with fine 16th- and 17th-century *palazzi*, including **Palazzo Da Schio**, an elegant townhouse designed by Palladio in the 1560s. Back on corso Palladio, **Palazzo Caldogno**

Casa Pigafetta.

VILLA VISITS
ANDREA PALLADIO

Pay homage to Italy's most influential architect.

Andrea di Pietro della Gondola was born in Padua in 1508, but it was in Vicenza (where he was apprenticed to a stonecarver at the age of 13) that he really made his mark. Here, a chance meeting in the 1530s with Count Giangiorgio Trissino, the wealthy leader of a group of Humanist intellectuals dedicated to reviving classical culture, led to his new life as an architect, and a new name, 'Palladio', given to him by Trissino.

The countryside around Vicenza where Palladio built his masterpieces – his domestic villas – once compared favourably with the Tuscan hills. Ugly light industry and sprawling retail have put paid to that. But many of the visitable *ville* are saved by the fact that they have their own parks and gardens to act as a buffer. You'll need transport (it is possible to reach most by public transport – using rural FTV buses that depart from near Vicenza station, www.ftv.vi.it – but it will be a hassle) and some rose-tinted spectacles so as not to notice the blighted landscape. Persevere: it's worth it.

What follows is a selection of Palladio's most important villas.

Villa Cornaro
Via Roma 92, Piombino Dese (049 936 5017). **Open** *May-Sept* 3.30-6pm Sat. *Oct-Apr* by appointment; groups only. **Admission** €7. **No credit cards**.
Constructed in 1552-53, this villa introduced to Western architecture the two-storey projecting portico-loggia motif and the aesthetically pleasing golden ratio.

Villa Godi Valmarana ora Malinverni
Via Palladio 44, Lugo di Vicenza (0445 860 561, www.villagodi.com). **Open** *Apr-Sept* 3-7pm Tue; 9am-2pm Sat; 10am-7pm Sun. *Mar, Oct, Nov* 2-6pm Fri-Sun. **Admission** €7. **No credit cards**.
Commissioned by Pietro Godi, this was Palladio's first independent job and remains one of his most radically pared-back designs.

Villa Pisani
Via Risaie 1, Bagnolo frazione di Lonigo (0444 831 104, www.villapisani.net). **Open** by appointment. **Admission** €7; €6 reductions. **No credit cards**.
Dating from 1540, this is one of Palladio's starkest, simplest villas.

Villa Poiana
Via Castello 43, Poiana Maggiore (0444 898 554, 041 220 1297, www.villapoiana.it). Bus for Noventa Vicentina. **Open** *Apr-Oct* 10am-1pm, 2-6pm Wed-Fri; 10am-6pm Sat, Sun. *Nov-Mar* by appointment. **Admission** €5; €3 reductions. **No credit cards**.
This villa demonstrates Palladio's skill as an architect of smaller dwellings. Completed around 1550, its façade is dominated by a Serlian arch (a central arched opening flanked by two rectangular ones) topped by telephone-dial openings. The interior has frescoes by Bernardino India and Anselmo Canera.

Villa Emo.

Villa Cornaro.

Villa Saraceno

Via Finale 8, Finale di Agugliaro (0444 891 371, www.landmarktrust.org.uk). **Open** *Apr-Oct* 2-4pm Wed. *Oct-Mar* by appointment. **Admission** by donation.

In 1988, the lovely Villa Saraceno (1550) was bought by Britain's Landmark Trust and restored. It was built for a gentleman farmer, and has an attic-granary lit by large grilled windows to keep the wheat ventilated. The villa is available as self-catering accommodation; see the website for details.

Villa Thiene

Piazza IV Novembre 2, Quinto Vicentino (0444 584 211). **Open** 9am-1pm, 3-8.30pm Tue-Thur; 9am-1pm, 3-9.30pm Fri; 10am-9.30pm Sat, Sun. **Admission** free.

Now the town hall of the unremarkable town of Quinto Vicentino, imposing Villa Thiene is only a fraction of what was to be an even more immense villa, designed by Palladio in 1546. The interior was frescoed in the mid 16th century by Giovanni De Mio and Bernardino India. Visitors can visit only a couple of rooms and the gardens, subject to permission.

OUTSIDE VICENZA

Palladio also designed villas outside the Vicenza area, including these two west of Treviso. For his **Villa Foscari 'La Malcontenta'**, *see p206* **The Brenta Canal**.

Villa Barbaro a Maser

Via Cornuda 7, Maser (0423 923 004, www.villadimaser.it). **Open** *Apr-June, Sept, Oct* 10am-6pm Tue-Sat; 11am-6pm Sun. *Mar, July, Aug* 10.30am-6pm Tue, Thur, Sat. *Nov-Feb* 11am-5pm Sat, Sun. **Admission** €6; reductions €3-€5. **No credit cards**.

Built for the Barbaro brothers between 1550 and 1557, this is an out-and-out exercise in rural utopianism. Two traditional parts of the Veneto farmhouse have been dressed up in a new classical disguise: those two arcaded wings flanking the main porticoed building are actually *barchesse*, or farmhouse wings; while the mirror-image, sundial-adorned chapel fronts on either end are, in fact, dovecotes. Behind these is a nymphaeum – a semicircular pool surrounded by statues. Inside, the light, airy rooms house sumptuous trompe l'œil frescoes by Paolo Veronese.

Villa Emo

Via Stazione 5, Fanzolo di Vedelago (0423 476 334, www.villaemo.org). **Open** *May-Oct* 3-7pm Mon-Sat; 9.30am-12.30pm, 3-7pm Sun. *Nov-Apr* 10am-12.30pm, 2.30-5.30pm Mon-Sat; 9am-12.30pm, 2-6pm Sun. **Admission** €6; €4-€5 reductions. Gardens only €1.50. **No credit cards**.

A tad more rustic, Villa Emo contains joyous frescoes by Giambattista Zelotti, one of the major fresco artists of the late Italian Renaissance.

Courtyard of **Teatro Olimpico**

Da Schio (no.147) is a flamboyant 14th-century jewel, which once had gilded capitals – hence its other name, Ca' d'Oro. Under the portico is a lapidarium of stone fragments collected by Giovanni da Schio (1798-1868).

The **Gallerie di Palazzo Leoni Montanari** (contrà Santa Corona 25, 0444 991 291, www.palazzomontanari.com) hosts a curious collection of two very different fields of art. On permanent display are 14 masterpieces by the 18th-century Venetian genre painter Pietro Longhi, plus several other paintings of Venice, including an interesting Canaletto. There's also an extraordinary collection of ancient Russian icons. It's worth a visit for the magnificent interiors alone, especially in the Galleria della Verità. Temporary exhibitions change every few months. Also in contrà Santa Corona is the **Museo Naturalistico Archeologico** (0444 320 440, www.museicivicivicenza.it).

On the corner of this street and the corso, the magnificent Gothic brick church of **Santa Corona** (0444 321 924) was completed in 1270 to house a thorn from Christ's crown and is Palladio's final resting place. It recently underwent a major restoration. The interior, consisting of three unequally sized naves, contains an *Adoration of the Magi* (1573) by Paolo Veronese in the third chapel on the right. In the crypt is the Valmarana Chapel, designed by Palladio. The beautifully elaborate high altar (1670) by Francesco Antonio Corberelli is a masterpiece of intricate marble inlay. The church's highlight, however, in the fifth chapel

on the left of the nave, is a beautiful 1502 *Baptism of Christ* by Giovanni Bellini.

The main street ends in piazza Matteotti, where two of Vicenza's real artistic treats await. Palazzo Chiericati (1550), one of Palladio's finest townhouses, is now the city's art gallery, the **Museo Civico** (0444 321 348, www.musei civicivicenza.it). It holds a fascinating collection of works by local painters, and Bartolomeo Montagna (1450-1523) in particular. The highlight is a 1489 Cima da Conegliano alterpiece, *Madonna Enthroned with Child between Saints Giacomo and Girolamo* (James and Jerome). There are also works by Van Dyck, Tintoretto, Veronese and Tiepolo, and a *Crucifixion* by the Flemish master Hans

---

IN THE KNOW EAT & DRINK

The *vicentini* have been eating *baccalà alla vicentina* – dried cod stewed in milk and oil – since at least 1269. Another firm favourite in the Veneto is *bollito misto* (mixed boiled meat, far more appetising than it sounds). Expect to see some combination of sausage (*cotechino*), whole hen (*gallina*) or chicken (*pollo*), veal's tongue (*lingua*), calf's head (*testina*) and a cut of beef (*manzo*). This is served with various sauces: *salsa verde* (parsley and capers), *mostarda* (spicy preserved fruit), *cren* (horseradish) and *peàra* (a combination of breadcrumbs and bone marrow).

Memling, the central part of a triptych whose side panels are in New York.

Also on piazza Matteotti is Palladio's final masterpiece, the remarkable **Teatro Olimpico** (0444 222 800, www.museicivicivicenza.it). Designed in 1579-80, just a few months before the architect's death, it was the first permanent indoor theatre to be built in Europe since the fall of the Roman Empire. His son, Silla, and his star pupil, Vincenzo Scamozzi, took over, and the two took considerable liberties with the original blueprint. The decorative flamboyance of the wood and stucco interior contrasts notably with the modest entrance and severe external walls.

Based on Roman theatres described by Vitruvius, it has 13 semicircular wooden steps, crowned by Corinthian columns holding up an elaborate balustrade topped with elegant 'antique' sculpted figures. The permanent stage set, designed by Scamozzi, with its seven trompe l'œil street scenes, represents the city of Thebes in Sophocles' *Oedipus Rex*, which was the theatre's first performance, on 3 March 1585. The elaborately frescoed antechambers to the theatre were also designed by Scamozzi and were used for meetings and smaller concerts of the Accademia Olimpica, the learned society of Humanists that commissioned the place. Don't miss the chiaroscuro fresco in the entrance hall depicting a delegation of Japanese noblemen who visited Vicenza in 1585.

Performances were brought to a halt by Counter-Reformation censorship. It wasn't until after World War II that the theatre once again realised its potential as a venue. A season of classical dramas in September and October usually includes a staging of *Oedipus Rex* (in Italian), while concerts take place in May and June – see www.olimpicovicenza.it for performance details.

Perched on one of the hilltops that surround Vicenza to the south is the **Santuario di Monte Berico** (viale X Giugno 87, 0444 559 411, www.monteberico.it, *photo p225*), a breathtakingly beautiful spot with fantastic views. The church itself was largely rebuilt in the 18th century; its interior contains Veronese's *Supper of St Gregory the Great* (1572) in the refectory, as well as a moving *Pietà* by Bartolomeo Montagna and a fine collection of fossils. The Virgin is said to have appeared twice here – in 1426 and 1428, making it a popular destination with pilgrims. An attractive loggia built by Francesco Muttoni leads up viale X Giugno to the church. It's a 20-minute walk beneath a shady 18th-century loggia from the centre, but there's also a dedicated bus service (Mon-Sat, no number – ask at the stop) from the station, though it is irregular.

VILLA VISITS BEYOND PALLADIO

More Vicenza villas.

Andrea Palladio was not the only gainfully employed architect in Vicenza in, and after, his day. His shadow, however, was long and his influence very clear. Below is a selection of the other most important country villas in Vicenza province.

Villa Cordellina Lombardi
Via Lovara 36, Montecchio Maggiore (0444 908 112, www.provincia. vicenza.it/villa-cordellina-lombardi).
Open *Apr-Oct* 9am-1pm Tue, Fri; 9am-1pm, 3-6pm Wed, Thur, Sat, Sun.
Admission €3; €2 reductions.
No credit cards.
This beautifully restored villa, built between 1735 and 1760 in the grand Palladian style, contains some flamboyant frescoes by Giambattista Tiepolo. There is also a charming French-style park, and a garden.

Villa Pisani Ferri 'Rocca Pisana'
Via Rocca 1, Lonigo (0444 831 625, www.comune.lonigo.vi.it).
Open by appointment. **Admission** €5. **No credit cards**.
Built in 1576 on the ruins of a medieval castle, this villa was designed by Palladio's pupil Vincenzo Scamozzi. Like La Rotonda (*see p225*), La Rocca has four main windows facing the four compass points, and a dome with a hole. But whereas the Rotonda hole is covered with glass, the hole here is open, allowing air to circulate.

Villa Trissino Marzotto
Piazza GG Trissino 2, Trissino (0445 962 029, www.villatrissinomarzotto.it).
Open *Mar-July, Sept, Oct* 9am-noon Wed, Sat. *Aug, Nov-Feb* by appointment.
Admission Villa €5. Garden €5.
No credit cards.
This elaborate complex is set in one of the most charming of Italy's private parks. The upper villa and the park were designed by Francesco Muttoni between 1718 and 1722. The garden is a typically 18th-century mixture of art and nature; the lower villa acts as a theatrical focal point.

ESCAPES & EXCURSIONS

VILLA ITINERARY
DAY TRIPS FROM VICENZA

Explore the villas around Vicenza on these driving itineraries.

Villa Cordellina Lombardi.

The majority of villas are private homes, so opening hours are subject to change at short notice – phone ahead.

NORTH-EAST OF VICENZA

It's quite a hike up to Lugo di Vicenza, home to some magnificent Palladian villas, so allow a generous half-day. Head north-east out of Vicenza on the SS53. About four kilometres out of town, beyond a motorway flyover, the SP29 branches right towards Quinto Vicento, where Palladio's **Villa Thiene** (*see* p220 **Villa Visits**) is now the town hall.

Backtrack on the SS53 towards Vicenza for about 500 metres, then join the A31 heading north towards Thiene. Where the motorway ends, veer right and follow the SP68 to Caltrano, then Lugo di Vicenza. In the centre of the village, via Giacomo Matteotti becomes via Palladio, which has two fine villas by the architect: **Villa Godi Valmarana ora Malinverni** (*see* p220 **Villa Visits**) and **Villa Piovene Porto Godi** (not open to the public). For a luxury lunch break or indulgent dinner, get back on the SP68, head for Zugliano, then Sarcedo, and continue on the SP63 to Montecchio Precalcino, home to the excellent **Locanda di Piero** (via Roma 32, 0445 864 827,

www.lalocandadipiero.it). Vicenza is about ten kilometres south of here on the SP248.

NORTH-WEST OF VICENZA

If you're making this an afternoon drive, you could set out after a lunch at the **Antica Trattoria Monterosso** (via Roma 40, 0444 371 362, www.trattoriamonterosso.com) in Alta Villa Vicentina. Take the SR11 south-west out of Vicenza, following the railway line towards Verona. The restaurant is in the village centre, by the motorway.

Back on the SR11, continue west to Montecchio Maggiore, home to the charming **Villa Cordellina Lombardi** (*see* p23 **Villa Visits**) and its gardens. From here, the SP246 goes north to Valdagno; about seven kilometres outside Montecchio is Trissino, where you can visit the gardens and interiors of **Villa Trissino Marzotto** (*see* p223 **Villa Visits**).

SOUTH OF VICENZA

This whole-day circuit takes in four villas and a wonderful rural restaurant. From Vicenza, head due south on the SP247 towards Noventa Vicentina for about 15 kilometres. Palladio's **Villa Saraceno** (*see* p221 **Villa Visits**) is located on via Finale, off the SP247 to the left, two kilometres before Noventa. Pioana Maggiore, home to Palladio's beguilingly modern-looking **Villa Poiana** (*see* p220 **Villa Visits**), lies three kilometres beyond Noventa Vicentina.

Next, take the SP4 north out of Poiana Maggiore, taking a right on to the SP14 towards Lonigo after about two kilometres. Just outside Lonigo, perched on a hill overlooking the town, is **Villa Pisani Ferri 'Rocca Pisana'** (*see* p223 **Villa Visits**). Those with rumbling tummies and a generous credit facility should try luxurious **La Peca** (via A Giovannelli 2, 0444 830 214, www.lapeca.it) in Lonigo.

Continue by following the SP500 directly south out of town in the direction of Cologna Veneta for about a kilometre. Take the first right at the tiny hamlet of Bagnolo-Frazione di Lonigo. The next left leads to the classic Palladian **Villa Pisani** (*see* p220 **Villa Visits**).

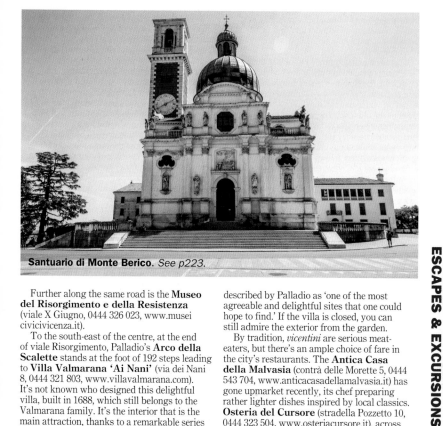

Santuario di Monte Berico. *See p223.*

Further along the same road is the **Museo del Risorgimento e della Resistenza** (viale X Giugno, 0444 326 023, www.musei civicivicenza.it).

To the south-east of the centre, at the end of viale Risorgimento, Palladio's **Arco della Scalette** stands at the foot of 192 steps leading to **Villa Valmarana 'Ai Nani'** (via dei Nani 8, 0444 321 803, www.villavalmarana.com). It's not known who designed this delightful villa, built in 1688, which still belongs to the Valmarana family. It's the interior that is the main attraction, thanks to a remarkable series of frescoes painted by Giambattista Tiepolo and his son Giandomenico in 1757. The statues of dwarves (*nani*) lining the wall to the right of the main villa were added in 1785 by Elena Garzadori, who redesigned the garden. Legend has it that the family built the statues in order to give their own dwarf daughter friendly familiars to gaze upon. The walk from the centre to the villa takes about 30 minutes.

Further along the same path is the Villa Capra Valmarana, better known as **Villa Rotonda** (via della Rotonda 45, 0444 321 793, www.villalarotonda.it). One of the most famous buildings in Western architecture, La Rotonda – designed by Palladio between 1567 and 1570, but not completed until 1606 – is not strictly speaking a villa at all, but a pleasure pavilion for retired cleric Paolo Almerico. The Rotonda was the first to be given a dome, a form previously associated with churches. Opening hours for the interior are short, but it's worth seeing the grandiose exterior and the garden,

described by Palladio as 'one of the most agreeable and delightful sites that one could hope to find.' If the villa is closed, you can still admire the exterior from the garden.

By tradition, *vicentini* are serious meat-eaters, but there's an ample choice of fare in the city's restaurants. The **Antica Casa della Malvasia** (contrà delle Morette 5, 0444 543 704, www.anticacasadellamalvasia.it) has gone upmarket recently, its chef preparing rather lighter dishes inspired by local classics. **Osteria del Cursore** (stradella Pozzetto 10, 0444 323 504, www.osteriacursore.it), across the arched ponte San Michele, offers bar nibbles and, for larger appetites, excellent versions of local specialities. Near piazza delle Erbe, lively **Osteria I Monelli** (contrà Ponte San Paolo 13, 0444 540 400, www.osteriaimonelli.it) serves a variety of mainly meat dishes. In an old farmhouse in the outskirts of Vicenza, **Trattoria da Remo** (contrà Caimpenta 14, 0444 911 007, www.daremoristorante.it) offers some of the best cooking you'll find anywhere in the Vicenza area. The boiled and roasted meats trolley is a fixture, and Remo's *baccalà alla vicentina* is spectacular.

TREVISO

Some 25 kilometres (16 miles) north of its ostentatious neighbour, Treviso likes to fashion itself as 'little Venice'. This pretty town, with its painstakingly restored *palazzi* (damaged during intensive World War II bombing) and stunning frescoed churches, is an underrated beauty. It offers Venice-style romantic canalside walks, Renaissance architecture and great art, but all on a much smaller scale and without the tourist crowds.

Treviso was important long before the Venetians muscled in during the 14th century. Originally the Roman town of Tarvisium, the city was also the seat of a Lombard duchy. The Venetian walls, dating from 1509, protect three sides of the old town; the fourth is guarded by the Sile river. Once, Treviso's stream-fed canals were used by the city's dyers, tanners and paper mills; today, their mossy walls and small bridges offer a bucolic touch to the *osterie* ranged alongside. Now, the city is famous for its millionaires, the product of its family-run businesses. The most renowned – Benetton – has progressed from its origins in the home-knitted jumpers of Giuliana Benetton, through a prominent place in the world's malls and high streets with its renowned retail outlets, to less fashionable assets, such as a sizeable chunk of Italy's motorway system.

Around the corner from the oversized Benetton store in piazza Indipendenza are piazza dei Signori and the **Palazzo dei Trecento**, the town hall dating from 1217. Across from the palazzo, in piazza Duomo, the **Duomo** (0422 545 720) contains an *Annunciation* (1570) by Titian and a beautiful *Adoration of the Magi* (1520) by Pordenone. Two other nearby churches – **San Vito** and **Santa Lucia** (piazza San Vito, 0422 545 720, www.santaluciatreviso.it) – offer splendid frescoes by Tommaso da Modena (1325-79), considered by some to be the greatest 14th-century artist after Giotto.

More works by Da Modena, including his masterpiece, *The Life of St Ursula*, are tucked away in Santa Caterina, now part of the **Musei Civici di Treviso** (piazzetta Mario Botter 1, 0422 544 864, www.museicivicitreviso.it) gallery and exhibition complex. The privately run **Casa dei Carraresi** (piazza San Leonardo 2, 0422 513 161, www.fondazionecassmarco.it) is an exhibition space with world-class pretensions.

For a fresco fest, head to the church of **San Francesco** (viale Sant'Antonio di Padova 2, 0422 582 182, http://frati-treviso.blogspot.it). Work on the ceiling of the main chapel includes the wonderful *St Francis with Stigmata*, by an anonymous 14th-century painter, though some argue it should be attributed to Da Modena. Da Modena pops up yet again with a series of frescoes in the chapter house of the Dominican monastery adjoining the Romanesque-Gothic church of **San Nicolò** (via San Nicolò 50, 0422 548 626).

The welcome in **Muscoli's** *osteria* (via Pescheria 23, 0422 583 390) isn't always the warmest, but the nibbles are outstanding, particularly with a reviving *ombra* (glass of wine). A young crowd can be found at **Osteria ai Filodrammatici** (via Filodrammatici 5, 0422 580 011), a traditional eatery where the prices can be higher than you'd expect. Just outside town, the excellent **Il Basilisco** (via Bison 34, 0422 541 822, www.ristorante basilisco.com) sources much of its super-fresh fare from the owner's native Trentino region. In the centre of town, **Trattoria Due Mori** (via Bailo 9, 0422 540 383, www.trattoria2mori.com) offers no-frills fare – including some excellent fish dishes – and alfresco seating.

Treviso.

San Nicolò, Treviso.

BEYOND TREVISO

Between Treviso and Castelfranco to the west are two fine villas by Andrea Palladio, the magnificent **Villa Barbaro a Maser** and **Villa Emo** (*see p220* **Villa Visits: Andrea Palladio**).

In **Castelfranco Veneto**, the **Duomo** (vicolo del Cristo 14, 0423 495 202, www. duomocastelfranco.it) is home to *Madonna and Child with Saints Liberal and Francis* (1504), one of the few surviving masterpieces of local artist Giorgio Barbarella, better known as Giorgione.

Another local boy is featured in the tiny village of **Possagno**, the birthplace of icy neoclassical sculptor Antonio Canova (1757-1822). Inside his family home is the **Gipsoteca Canoviana** (piazza Canova 74, Possagno, 0423 544 323, www.museocanova.it). The museum has many works, including the striking black-tack-studded plaster models for the finished statues. Modernist architect Carlo Scarpa designed the museum's extension (1955-57).

For more Scarpa, head to the cemetery in nearby **San Vito d'Altivole**. Among the more mundane remembrances is the massive Tomba Brion – 2,200 square metres (23,656 square feet) of pure Scarpa, who spent the nine years before his death in 1978 constructing the monster. He is also buried here.

The picture-postcard landscape around **Asolo** exerted so strong an attraction on writer Robert Browning (1812-1889) that he named his last collection of verse after the town (*Asolando*, 1889). Set among rolling hills covered with cypress trees, olive groves and vineyards, the town is not so much a place for sightseeing as for window-shopping, a long lunch and a leisurely walk with the town's illustrious ghosts: Caterina Cornaro, the exiled Venetian-born Queen of Cyprus, who set up court in Asolo in 1489, and the 19th-century actress Eleonora Duse.

To the west of Asolo, **Bassano del Grappa** sits astride the Brenta river. Monte Grappa, a few kilometres outside of town, gives its name

IN THE KNOW PROSECCO

The town of **Valdobbiadene** is the headquarters for the production of prosecco, a native grape that fills 33 million bottles a year. The town's tourist office (via Piva 53, 0423 976 975, www.valdobbiadene.com) provides a complete list of producers on request. The *Strada del Prosecco* (www.conegliano valdobbiadene.it) is an itinerary leading through prime wine-producing country. **Nino Franco** (www.ninofranco.it), produces one of the best *prosecchi*; they also offer great accommodation in the heart of their vineyards at **Villa Barberina** (www.villabarberina.it).

Bassano del Grappa

to both the town and Italy's fiery after-dinner drink. Technically a pomace brandy, grappa is a way of getting the most out of the vines. After the grapes are pressed for wine, the skins, seeds and stems are distilled into grappa.

The oldest and most famous name in grappa is **Nardini** (Ponte Vecchio 2, 0424 227 741, www.nardini.it). Another famous name, **Poli**, has a grappa museum (via Gamba 6, 0424 524 426, www.poligrappa.com) at the foot of Bassano's showpiece, the **Ponte degli Alpini**. The original bridge was probably built in the 1150s: what we see now is a copy of Palladio's magnificent covered wooden bridge built in 1586 (Palladio's was blown up by retreating German troops at the end of World War II).

The **Museo Civico** (piazza Garibaldi, 0424 519 450, www.museobassano.it), located inside the beautiful convent and cloistered gardens of the 14th-century church of San Francesco, has a fine collection of ceramics – Bassano's other speciality – and an archaeological section devoted to the city's Roman origins. Piazza Libertà is dominated by the medieval **Palazzo Municipale**, which is covered with faded frescoes. The **Museo degli Alpini** (via Angarano 2, 0424 503 662, www.bassano.eu), with its collection of World War I memorabilia, stands at the far end of the ponte degli Alpini.

Heading north from Treviso, the town of **Conegliano** is pleasant if unchallenging. The 14th-century **Duomo** (via XX Settembre 8, 0438 4131, www.comune.conegliano.tv.it) is home to a painting of the *Virgin and Child*

with Saints and Angels (1493) by the town's most famous son, Giambattista Cima, known as Cima da Conegliano.

Into the mountains

The hills change to mountains as you continue north towards **Vittorio Veneto**. Originally two smaller towns called Ceneda and Serravalle, Vittorio Veneto was formed and named in 1866, to commemorate the unification of Italy under King Vittorio Emanuele II. Serravalle has a well-preserved medieval *borgo* (quarter), which is unfortunately situated right on the busy *strada statale*. It's worth braving the exhaust fumes for a brief walk through the *borgo* and a glance at the frescoed **Loggia Serravallese**, which dates from 1462.

The SS51 out of Vittorio Veneto leads towards **Follina**. Here, nestled among the hills of the *prealpi* and the sleepy town centre is one of the jewels of the Veneto, the **Abbazia Santa Maria** (via Convento 3, 0438 970 231). This Romanesque abbey dates from the 12th century and features one of the most peaceful cloisters you'll ever see.

Take the *Strada d'Alemagna* – the main road (SS51) from Vittorio Veneto to Belluno – and it's hard not to rhapsodise about the area. There's no shortage of awe-inspiring views, or trails (maps available from the tourist office in Belluno) to view them from.

The medieval town of **Belluno** – known as 'the Venice of the Alps' – occupies a rocky terrace overlooking the Piave and Ardo rivers.

DEATH ON THE MOUNTAIN

The tragic history of a World War I frontline.

Behind the town of **Cortina d'Ampezzo**'s glam sophistication and breathtaking natural surroundings lies a bleak heritage of wartime suffering. The town had been part of the Habsburg empire from 1511, but when Italy entered World War I in 1915, the Austro-Hungarians swiftly abandoned it. They beat a hasty retreat into the nearby mountains, where their defences stopped the advance of the Italian forces. As winter approached, both sides began digging into a platform high up stark, rugged Monte Lagazuoi (2,752 metres/9,029 feet). Temperatures that fell to –30°C (–22°F) and snow nine metres (30 feet) deep meant that thousands of men died not in combat but from hypothermia, disease and starvation.

The tunnels, open emplacements and trenches that witnessed those chilling events are now being restored and opened to the public in an EU-financed project run by Cortina in partnership with the Austrian town of Innsbrück. Spread over a swathe of bitterly contested mountainside to the west of Cortina, the open-air **Museo della Grande Guerra** (Great War Museum; www.grande guerra.dolomiti.org) is open all year, and is free to visit.

It comprises three sites (Monte Lagazuoi, Monte Cinque Torri and the Tre Sassi Fort) within an eight-kilometre (five-mile) radius. Each is furnished with well signposted walking tracks and information panels. You can hire audio-guides for the mountain excursions at the Monte Cinque Torre chairlift or Lagazuoi cable-car ticket offices. Take torches if you're planning to explore the tunnels on Monte Lagazuoi.

An escalator carries visitors from the car park to the main piazza, emerging on to a scene that is pure enchantment. Against a beautiful backdrop of mountains and tranquillity, the 15th-century **Palazzo dei Rettori** (once home to the town's Venetian rulers; not open to the public) and 16th-century **Duomo** recall the architecture along the Grand Canal. The **Baptistry**, across from the Duomo, contains an early 18th-century carving of John the Baptist by Andrea Brustolon.

In the mountains beyond Belluno is the jet-set capital of the Dolomites, **Cortina d'Ampezzo** – beautiful, but expensive. Summer sport pursuits range from the obvious climbing and hiking to riding and fishing. For those with thighs of thunder and butts of steel, mountain bikes can be hired from **2UE & 2UE** (via Roma 70, 0436 4121, www.dueduecortina.com). For would-be Reinhold Messners, check out the *scuola roccia* (rock-climbing school; corso Italia 69B, 0436 868 505, www.guidecortina.com), which offers individual lessons, group excursions and guided solo climbs.

To the west of Belluno, **Feltre** was once a Roman fortress on the banks of the river Piave. Today, it is a perfectly preserved 16th-century town. Among the cobbled streets and frescoed *palazzi*, the sharp-eyed visitor will notice that many of the lapidaries are chipped clean. *La Serenissima* financed a well-endowed rebuilding programme after the town was destroyed in 1510 by the troops of the Holy Roman Emperor Maximilian I. Many of the stone markers praised Venice for its aforementioned munificence. When Napoleon rolled in he took umbrage at all the praise lavished on his enemies, and ordered the words destroyed. Despite Napoleon's enmity, paintings and statues of the lion of St Mark are everywhere.

Feltre.

In Context

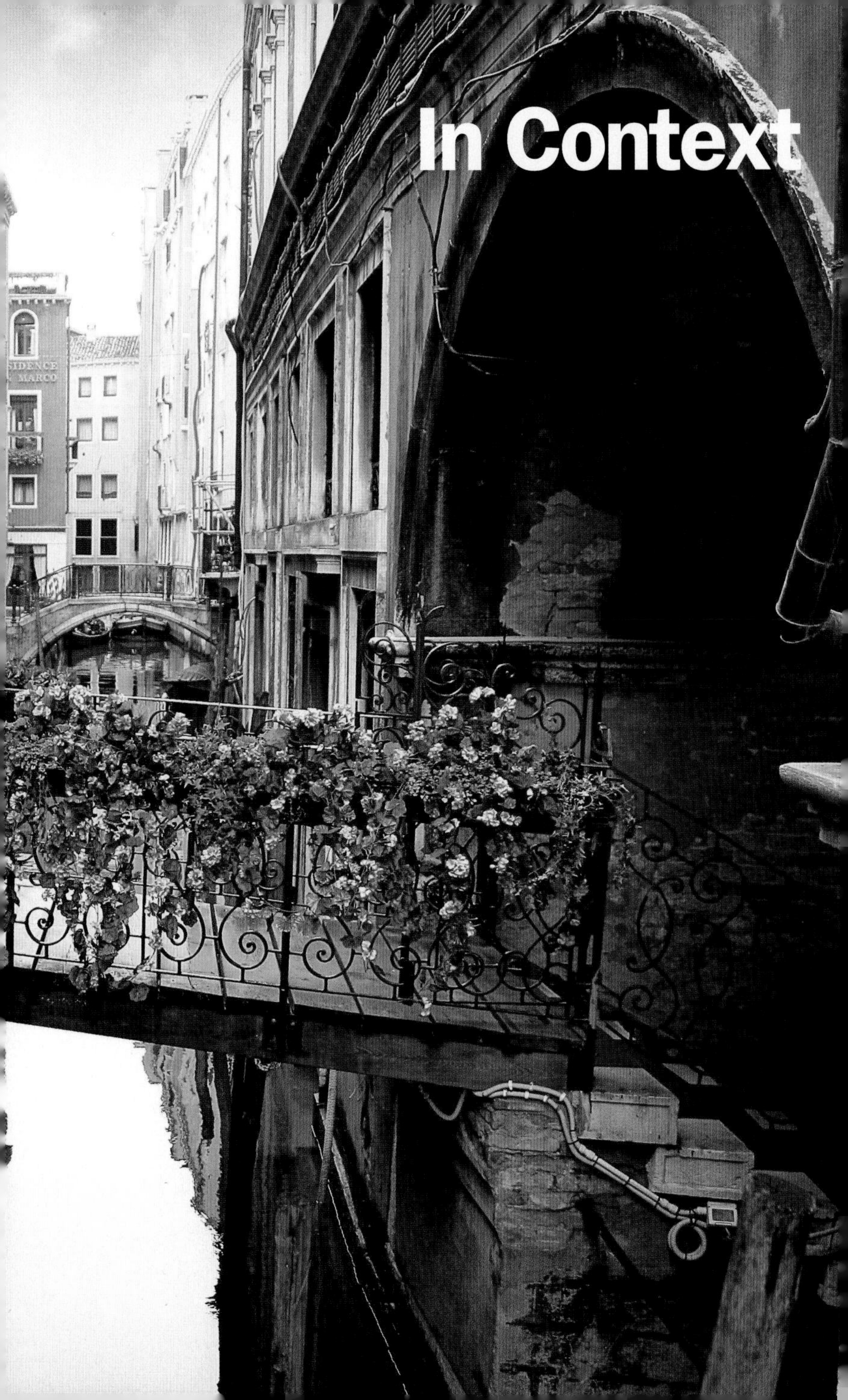

History

Desolate lagoon to city state.

TEXT: ANNE HANLEY

Venice's origins were nothing if not ignominious: in the fifth century AD, rampaging barbarians forced inhabitants of the towns in the far north east of the Italian peninsula to flee for their lives on to the sandy banks of a desolate lagoon. In the city's earliest days, that scared and scattered community eked out a living by trading in salt and fish. It's all the more wondrous, therefore, that this would develop into the Most Serene Republic of Venice, one of Europe's most powerful city-states: a republic with a rock-solid system of government that flourished for over a millennium, and a maritime power that wielded almost total control over the shipping routes of the eastern Mediterranean for six centuries. Envied for its luxurious extravagance, hated for its insolent self-assurance, Venice was the exotic odd-piece-out in the patchwork of Europe.

IN CONTEXT

LIFE ON THE LAGOON

Until the collapse of the Roman Empire in the fifth century AD, the islands of the Venetian lagoon hosted only transient fishing hamlets. The nearby cities on the mainland, on the other hand, were among the most prosperous in Roman Italy. With the final disintegration of any semblance of security in the late sixth century, there was a larger influx of population to the marshes.

These population movements were meant to be temporary, but as economic life on the mainland collapsed, the lagoon islands came to be thought of as permanent homes. They offered enormous potential in the form of fish and salt – basic necessities. Once settled in the lagoon, the fugitives could also enjoy the relative peace and tranquillity that would be denied to the peoples of mainland Europe for centuries to come.

Enormous public works were necessary almost from the start to shore up and consolidate the islands of the lagoon (*see p41* **Mud Houses**). Huge amounts of timber had to be cut down and transported here. The trunks were sunk deep into the mud as foundations for the mainly wooden buildings of the island villages. And above all, the mainland rivers, which threatened to silt up the lagoon, had to be tamed and diverted.

And yet this battle against nature helped to unite the early lagoon dwellers into a close-knit community and eventually into a republic that was to become one of the strongest and most stable states in European history. The fight against the sea never ended. Even in the 18th century, when the French army was advancing on the lagoon and the Venetian Republic was living its decline and fall, the government invested its last resources in the construction of the *murazzi*, the massive sea walls that run between the Lido, Pellestrina and Chioggia.

EASTERN PROMISE

In 552, Byzantine Emperor Justinian I was determined to reconquer Italy from the barbarians. His first object was the city of Ravenna. But his troops were confronted with an almost insuperable problem: they had made their way overland, via the Dalmatian coast on the eastern side of the Adriatic, but were blocked by the barbarian Goths who controlled the mainland to the north of

Venice. The only way they could attack and take Ravenna was to bypass the Goths, crossing the lagoon.

Already by this time, the lagoon communities had adopted a practice that was to be the keynote of Venetian diplomacy for 1,250 years: staying as far as possible from, and (where possible) profiting by, other people's quarrels. Justinian's request presented a dilemma: helping him would be seen as a declaration of war against the Ostrogoths in Ravenna, with whom the lagoon communities had reached a comfortable *modus vivendi*, assuring safety on the mainland for their traders. Yet the Eastern emperor was offering vast monetary and political rewards for transporting his troops.

The communities eventually threw in their lot with Byzantium. Justinian conquered Ravenna and marched on to Rome. From this time on the communities of the lagoon became vassals of the Eastern Empire; Venice would remain technically subject to the Byzantine emperors until considerably later than the Sack of Constantinople – an attack led by Venetians – during the Fourth Crusade in 1204.

It was not until 697, under the growing threat of the barbarian Lombards who then controlled the mainland, that the communities scattered around the lagoon – now officially recognised by Byzantium as a duchy – decided to convert their fragile confederation into a stronger, more centralised state. In this year (or maybe not: some have dismissed the story as a Venetian myth), they elected one Paoluccio Anafesto to be their first doge, as the dukes of Venice became known. Yet right from the beginning *il doge* was very different from the other feudal strongmen of Europe.

In the first application of a system that would be honed into shape over centuries (*see p71* **Machinery of State**), the doge was elected for life by a council chosen by an assembly that represented all the social groups and trades of the island communities. Technically, therefore, he was elected democratically, although the strongest groups soon formed themselves into a dominant oligarchy. Yet democracy of a kind survived in the system of checks and balances employed to ensure that no single section of the ruling elite got its hands on absolute power.

The first ducal power struggle took place in 729. The doge in question, Ipato Orso,

VENETIAN PEOPLE ST MARK

Evangelist in sausage wrapping.

'History records no more shameless example of body snatching, nor any of greater long-term significance,' remarked John Julius Norwich in describing how the relics of St Mark found their way to Venice.

As Italy's settlements began to grope their way out of the Dark Ages, a city's status was linked significantly, if not exclusively, to its religious associations: possession of significant relics conferred kudos. Rome was top of the pile, with the body of Jesus's right-hand-man St Peter. But an evangelist's remains represented an enviable windfall too: for a young republic keen to raise itself from the sludgy marshlands on which it lay, getting hold of such sought-after spoils would mean being able to compete with long-established European political and economic centres.

Venice already had a patron saint – Theodore. And the Byzantine emperor had graciously donated the remains of John the Baptist's father, St Zacharias, which were hosted in one of the city's earliest churches (San Zaccaria, *see p80*; the remains lie in the second chapel on the right). Their importance was immediately overshadowed in the year 828, however, when two of the city's merchants, Rustico di Torcello and Buono di Malamocco, convinced (or bribed) the custodians of St Mark's body in Alexandria to entrust it to them, lining the case in which it was secreted with pork to avoid closer scrutiny by the city's Muslim authorities – an episode depicted in a mosaic in St Mark's cathedral (*see p50*).

However much Venetians like to claim Mark as their own, the saint's link to the city is tenuous at best. There is very little reliable historical information surrounding the evangelist's life; much of what we 'know' is no more than foundation myth and folklore. Lagoon dwellers gave (and still give) much credence to the story that an angel appeared to St Mark as he sailed past the island of Rialto, revealing to him

that he would eventually be laid to rest on those shores. (The angel's opening gambit – *pax tibi Marce, evangelista meus;* peace to you Mark, my evangelist – is inscribed on countless carvings of the open book held by St Mark's symbol, the winged lion, around the city. His reported follow-up – *hic requiescet corpus tuum;* here your body will rest – is omitted.)

A far better claim to ownership is made by Coptic tradition. Mark, born in modern-day Libya, is believed to have founded the Christian church in Egypt when he settled in Alexandria in the second half of the first century AD. It was there that he met his sorry end: not yet willing to relinquish their pagan gods, the city's inhabitants tied him to a horse and dragged his body through the city's streets for two days.

Looted Greek horses at St Marks Basilica.

achieved the duchy's first outstanding military victory when he dislodged Lombard forces from Ravenna. Success, though, went to Orso's head, and he attempted to transform the doge's office into a hereditary monarchy. Civil war racked the lagoon for two years, ending when a furious mob forced its way into Orso's house and cut his throat. Troubles continued with the two succeeding doges: both were accused of tyranny, and were not only deposed and exiled but also ceremonially blinded.

CIVIL STRIFE, COMMERCIAL STRENGTH

The lagoon dwellers were becoming a commercial power to be reckoned with in the upper Adriatic, the eastern Mediterranean, the Black Sea and North Africa. Craftsmen were sent abroad to Dalmatia and Istria to study the art of shipbuilding; they learnt so swiftly that by the seventh century the construction and fitting out of seagoing vessels had become a thriving industry. Mercantile expansion and technical advances went hand in hand, as tradesmen brought back materials and techniques from afar – especially the Middle and Far East, where technical and scientific culture was far in advance of the West.

In 781, Pepin, son of the Frankish king Charlemagne, invaded Italy and attacked the Lombards. Wariness of mainland struggles still dominated the duchy's policy and it played for time, unsure whether to sacrifice the alliance with Byzantium to this new and powerful player on the European scene. In the end, however,

Pepin's designs on Istria and Dalmatia – part of the Venetian sphere of influence – caused relations to turn frosty. Exasperated by the duchy's fence-sitting, Pepin attacked its ally Grado on the mainland, taking all the mainland positions around Venice, and besieging the lagoon communities from the sea.

In the mid eighth century the confederation had moved its capital from Heraclea in the northern lagoon to Malamocco on the Adriatic coast, where it was at the mercy of Frankish naval forces. In 810, a strong leader emerged in the form of an admiral, Angelo Partecipazio. He abandoned the besieged capital of Malamocco, moving it almost overnight to the island archipelago of Rialto.

Next he ordered his fleet to head out of the lagoon to attack Pepin's ships, then feign terror and retreat. In hot pursuit, the deep-keeled Frankish ships ran aground on lagoon sandbanks; the locals, with their knowledge of deep-water channels, picked the crews off with ease: thousands were massacred.

After his great victory against the Franks, Partecipazio was elected doge. During his reign, work began on a ducal palace on the site of the current one, and the confederation of islands that made up the lagoon duchy was given the name 'Venetia'. Around the same time, the flourishing city of Torcello began to decline, as the surrounding lagoon waters silted up and malarial mosquitoes took over.

THE MAKING OF MYTHS

It was also around this time that Venice set about embroidering a mythology worthy of its ambitions. After Venetian merchants stole the body of St Mark (*see p237* **Venetian People**) from Alexandria and brought it back with them to their city – traditionally said to be in the year 829 – the city's previous patron, the Byzantine St Theodore, was unceremoniously deposed and the Evangelist – symbolised by a winged lion – set up in his place. A shrine to the saint was erected in the place where St Mark's basilica (*see p50*) would later rise.

Angelo Partecipazio's overwhelming success in both military and civic government led to another tussle for power. Before he died in 827, he made certain that his son Giustiniano would succeed him. When Giustiniano died two years later, his younger brother Giovanni was elected doge, despite dissent and jealousy from rival families. It was a measure of Partecipazio's importance that his surname was to feature repeatedly in the ducal roll of honour over the next century.

BLIND CUNNING

The development of the vast Venetian empire grew out of the mercantile pragmatism that dominated Venetian political thinking. They embarked upon territorial expansion for two main reasons: to secure safe shipping routes and to create permanent trading stations. Harassed by Slav pirates in the upper Adriatic, the Venetians established bases around the area from which to attack the pirate ships: gradually they took over the ports of Grado and Trieste, then expanded along the coastlines of Istria and Dalmatia. In some cases, Venetian protection against pirates was requested; in others, 'help' arrived unbidden.

With the coast well defended, the Venetians rarely bothered to expand their territories into the hinterland. There was, for many centuries, a certain mistrust of *terra ferma*; Venetian citizens were not even allowed to own land outside the lagoon until 1345.

The crusades presented Venice with its greatest opportunity yet for expanding trade routes while reaping a profit. Transporting crusaders to the Holy Land became big business for the city. More importantly, the naïve crusaders were easy prey for the professional generals – the *condottieri* – who commanded Venice's army of highly trained mercenaries: the eager defenders of the faith were, as often as not, exploited to extend and consolidate the Venetian empire.

Never was this more true than in the case of the Fourth Crusade, which set off from Venice in 1202 to reconquer Jerusalem. The Venetian war fleet was under the command of Doge Enrico Dandolo (*see p240* **Venetian People**), who, though 80 and completely blind, was a supremely cunning leader, outstanding tactician and accomplished diplomat. Other European crusader leaders were persuaded to take time out to conquer the strategic Adriatic port of Zara, thus assuring Venice's control of much of the Dalmatian coast. Even more surprisingly, they let themselves be talked into attacking Constantinople.

Venice's special relationship with the Eastern Empire had always had its ups and downs. In 1081 and 1082, Venice had done the Byzantine emperor a favour when it trounced menacing Normans in the southern Adriatic. But, in 1149, Venice's trading privileges were withdrawn in disgust at Venetian arrogance during a siege of Corfu.

'There was nothing noble about the brutal, bloody, Venetian-led sacking of Constantinople.'

IN CONTEXT

As the Fourth Crusade set out, Dandolo saw that this was an ideal opportunity to remove the Byzantine challenge to Venetian trade hegemony once and for all. He pulled the wool over his fellow crusaders' eyes, with the apparently noble argument that the Eastern emperor must be ousted and replaced by someone willing to reunite the eastern Orthodox and western Roman churches.

They acquiesced, but there was nothing noble about the brutal, bloody, Venetian-led sacking of Constantinople on 13 April 1204, nor about pillaging that followed. The Venetians looted the city's greatest treasures, including the celebrated quartet of antique Greek horses (*pictured p237*) that was transported back to Venice and placed above the entrance of St Mark's basilica. Innumerable other artefacts – jewellery, enamels, golden chalices, statuary, columns, precious marbles and much more – were plundered: they are now part of the fabric of Venice's *palazzi* and churches.

VENETIAN PEOPLE ENRICO DANDOLO

The scourge of Byzantium.

A brilliant, charismatic tactician and leader of men to some, a wily, ruthless, cynical manipulator to others, Venice's Doge Enrico Dandolo remains a resonant figure in Venetian history, perfectly reflecting that mix of heroism and pragmatism that made *La Serenissima* a political and mercantile power to be reckoned with.

Born in or around 1107, Dandolo came from a long-lived line of Venetian patricians, with a jurist father and a prelate uncle who overshadowed him until he was well into his 60s. But this gave Enrico time to hone his diplomatic acumen, and to sharpen his intense – some say pathological – dislike for the eastern Christian empire of Byzantium. By the time he was elected doge in 1192 – at around 85 – he was spoiling for a fight.

His first recorded contacts with the powerful empire came in 1171-72, when he accompanied Doge Vitale Michiel II on what was meant to be a punitive raid after Emperor Manuel Comnenus had – as part of his juggling alliances with Italian powers – confiscated the goods of the 20,000-odd Venetians living in his realm. The campaign was a disaster: plague struck the 120 Venetian ships, which not only were routed by the Byzantines but also brought the disease back to Venice with them. The doge was killed by an angry mob; Dandolo was sent back to Constantinople the following year to try to negotiate a settlement.

It was around this time that the Venetian lost his sight. There's no evidence to support the popular tale that it was the Emperor Manuel who had his eyes put out. And cataracts seem unlikely as portraits of him in very old age show him clear-eyed. Whatever the cause of his blindness, he didn't let the disability stop him.

Dandolo was handed a chance for a vendetta on a plate when the fourth crusade requested help with transport for a seaborne attack on the Muslim city of Cairo. Venice acquiesced, but levied a huge charge that placed the mainly French crusaders heavily in her debt. This, in turn, gave Dandolo immense bargaining power once the force set out in 1202. The stated aim of the crusaders may have been to defeat the Muslim infidel who had defiled the Holy Places, but Dandolo soon turned the force into an avenging host, persuading it first to descend on the (Christian) town of Zara in Dalmatia, which had dared to ally itself with Hungary against Venice, and then on Constantinople itself. Pope Innocent III had given his blessing to the Crusade but expressly forbade any attack on the eastern Christian capital of Constantinople, a magnificent city of half a million people, which he dreamed of reuniting with western Christendom in one all-conquering Christian empire.

Dandolo hid the pope's fulminations from most of the crusaders and personally led the attack on and siege of the city. In April 1204 the crusaders finally broke through Constantinople's massive walls and subjected the city to three days of carnage, burning and looting, extracting such punishment that the rift between the Roman and Orthodox church remained unbridgeable ever after. The pope excommunicated the crusaders, but Dandolo returned triumphant to Venice with far more than the 150,000 silver marks demanded in ransom, plus unimaginable artistic booty, including the four bronze horses that now grace the facade of St Mark's basilica.

The following year the indefatigable nonagenarian set off on another military campaign in Bulgaria, but this proved too much for him. In an ironic twist, he died peacefully in Constantinople, the city he had trashed, and was buried in the great church, then mosque, of Hagia Sophia, where a plaque still commemorates him.

But the booty was only a minor consideration for the Venetians and their pragmatic doge: the real prize was the one handed out when the routed Byzantine empire was carved up. The Venetians were not interested in grabbing huge swathes of territory that they knew they couldn't defend. This was left to the French and German knights, who, indeed, lost it within a few decades. Putting their intimate knowledge of eastern trade routes to excellent use, the Venetians hand-picked those islands and ports that could guarantee their merchant ships a safe passage from Venice to the Black Sea and back. These included almost all the main ports on the Dalmatian coast, certain strategic Greek islands, the Sea of Marmara and a number of strategic Black Sea ports.

For many years after the conquest of Constantinople, Venetian ships could sail from Venice to Byzantium without leaving waters controlled by their city. Venice marked the turn of events by conferring a new title on its doge: *Quartae Partis et Dimidiae Totius Imperii Romaniae Dominator* – Lord of a Quarter and Half a Quarter of the Roman Empire.

AGE OF UPRISINGS

In 1297, in what came to be known as the *Serrata del Maggior Consiglio*, the leaders of the Venetian merchant aristocracy decided to limit entry to the Grand Council to those families which had held a seat in the *maggior consiglio* in the previous four years, or to descendants of those who had belonged at any point since 1172. Under these rules, only around 150 extended families were eligible for a place, but the number of council members leapt to some 1,200.

Up-and-coming clans were understandably indignant at the thought of being forever excluded from power and from a coveted place in the *Libro d'oro* – the Golden Book – of the Venetian aristocracy. In 1310, a prosperous merchant, Baiamonte Tiepolo, harnessed the discontent in a rebellion against the aristocratic oligarchy. Had Tiepolo's standard-bearer not been felled by a loose brick knocked out of place by an old lady watching the shenanigans from her window, the uprising may have succeeded. However, as it was, his troops fled in panic, the uprising was savagely crushed, and the much-feared Council of Ten was granted draconian powers. An extensive network of spies and informers was set up to suppress any future plots.

In 1354, Doge Marino Faliero made a bid to undermine the powers of the Venetian oligarchy while increasing and consolidating his own powers as a permanent hereditary leader. This plot, too, was mercilessly suppressed and Faliero was beheaded.

The Council of Ten – along with the Venetian Inquisition that was also established after the Tiepolo plot of 1310 – wielded its special powers most effectively after the Faliero incident, ensuring that this was the last serious attempt to attack the principle of rule by elite. It was at this time that lion's-head postboxes first appeared at strategic points around the city: Venetians were encouraged to drop written reports of any questionable activity that they noticed through their marble mouths.

LAVISH LOVE AND LUXURY

While Venice's mercantile power was at its zenith from the 13th to the 15th centuries, vast fortunes were amassed and lavished on building and decorating great *palazzi* and churches. It was at this time that the city took on the architectural form still visible today. For sheer luxury, Venice's lifestyle was unequalled anywhere else in Europe.

In the 14th and 15th centuries Venice was one of the largest cities in Europe, with an estimated population of between 150,000 and 200,000. International visitors were generally astounded by *La Serenissima*'s legendary opulence and phenomenal economic dynamism.

When ships set sail from Venice for the Middle East, their holds were crammed with Istrian pine wood, iron ore, cereals, wool, and salted and preserved meats. These were traded for textiles, exotic carpets, perfumes, gold and silverware, spices, precious stones of all kinds, ivory, wax and slaves; with a virtual monopoly on all these much sought-after commodities, Venice was able to sell them on to the rest of Europe's moneyed classes at enormous profit.

The Venetian aristocracy liked to live in comfort. 'The luxury of any ordinary Venetian house,' wrote one traveller in 1492, 'is so extraordinary that in any other city or country it would be sufficient to decorate a royal palace.' The Venetians were also investing

IN CONTEXT

huge amounts of money in their summer villas on the mainland, designed and decorated by the leading Veneto architects and painters.

Venetians lavished the same kind of attention on their appearance. Fortunes were spent on the richest textiles and jewellery. Venetian women were famous for the luxury of their clothing, of their furs and of their fabrics woven with gold and silver thread. Their perfumes and cosmetics were the envy of all Europe, as were the beauty and charm of the courtesans who dominated the social and cultural life of the city.

So dedicated were Venetians to the cult of love and earthly pleasures, that the Patriarch, Venice's cardinal, was compelled to issue orders forbidding the city's nuns from going out on the town at night. Sumptuous festivals of music, theatre and dance were almost daily occurrences during these wild times. The visit of a foreign ruler, a wedding or funeral of a member of the aristocracy, a religious festival, a naval or military victory, or delivery from an epidemic – all these were excuses for public celebrations. The city's foreign communities – Jews, Armenians, Turks, Germans, French and Mongols, many of them permanent residents in this truly cosmopolitan city – would also celebrate their national or religious feast days with enormous pomp.

Despite the wealth of the city and the full employment created by its many trades and industries (at full stretch, the shipyard was capable of launching one fully equipped ship every day), life was not easy for the city's poorest residents, who lived in damp, filthy conditions. Epidemics of disease were also frequent; indeed, it is estimated that more than half the city's population died in the Black Death of 1348-49. Social tension and discontent were rife.

GENOESE JEALOUSY

Meanwhile, the enormous wealth of the Venetian Republic and its rapidly expanding empire inevitably provoked jealousy among the other trading nations of the Mediterranean – above all in the powerful city state of Genoa, Venice's main rival for trade with the East.

In 1261, the Genoese had clashed with the Venetians when the former obliged the Byzantine emperor by helping to evict Venice's high-handed merchants from Constantinople. Skirmishes between the two Italian powers continued throughout most of the 14th century, regularly flaring up into periods of open warfare, and often resulting in disastrous defeats for Venice.

By 1379, the situation had become desperate for *La Serenissima*. The Genoese fleet and army had moved into the upper Adriatic and, after a long siege, had taken Chioggia, at the southern end of the lagoon. From here the Genoese attacked and occupied much of the lagoon, including the passage to the open sea. Venice was under siege and began to starve.

Then, in 1380, the city worked another of its miracles of level-headed cunning. Almost the whole of the Genoese fleet was anchored inside the fortified harbour of Chioggia. Vittor Pisani, the admiral of the Venetian fleet, ordered hundreds of small boats to be filled with rocks. Panicked by a surprise Venetian attack on the mouth of the port, the Genoese failed to notice that the small boats were being sunk in the shallow port entrance, preventing any escape. The tables had been well and truly turned, and Venice besieged the trapped Genoese fleet until it was forced to surrender unconditionally. Genoa's days as a great naval power were over, and Venice exulted.

Ironically, however, this victory was to spell the beginning of the end for *La Serenissima*. For although the Republic had reached the climax of its prosperity and had re-acquired its supremacy in the East, concentrating its energies on fighting Genoa was to prove a costly mistake. Venice's leaders badly underestimated the threat posed by the emergence of the Turks as a military power in Asia Minor and the Black Sea area. Convinced – wrongly and ultimately fatally – that diplomacy was the way to deal with the Ottoman threat, Venice turned its attention to conquering other powers on the Italian mainland.

MAINLAND EXPANSION

For centuries, Venice had followed a conscious policy of steady neutrality towards the various powers that had carved up the Italian mainland. Europe's political upheavals from the end of the 12th century to the end of the 14th century put paid to that neutrality. The bitter rivalry between Venice and the other Italian maritime states, especially Pisa and Genoa, inevitably brought it into conflict with their mainland allies: the

Pope, the Scaligera dukes of Verona and a succession of Holy Roman emperors.

The defeat of the vast Scaligera empire (which included much of the Venetian hinterland) by Count Gian Galeazzo Visconti of Milan in 1387 brought the Milanese much too close to the lagoon for comfort. All-important trade routes through north-eastern Italy, across the Alps and into northern Europe beyond were threatened. Venice began a series of wars that led to the conquest of Verona (*see p208*) and its enormous territories in 1405, and also of near neighbours Padua (*see p204*) and Vicenza (*see p216*).

By 1420, Venice had annexed Friuli and Udine; by 1441, *La Serenissima* controlled Brescia, Bergamo, Cremona and Ravenna. The land campaign continued until 1454, when Venice signed a peace treaty with Milan. Though Ravenna soon slipped from Venice's grasp, the rest of the Republic's immense mainland territories were to remain more or less intact for almost 300 years.

PORTUGUESE SPICE THINGS UP

Even as Venice expanded into the mainland, events were conspiring to bring its reign as a political power and trading giant to a close.

SESTIERI
Dividing Venice up.

Most of the towns and cities of the Italian mainland were happy to follow the example of the ancient Romans, slicing themselves into *quartieri* (quarters) which would have been delineated by the main axis roads – the *cardo* and *decumanus* – that intersected each other at the city centre. Ever original, Venice opted to set itself apart with *sestieri* (sixths) – topological divisions that still characterise the city today.

Historians squabble about who was responsible for the breakdown. Some say that the *sestieri* date from the very earliest settlements in these marshy lagoon islands – unlikely, given that the inhabitants were few and that power, when it stabilised, lay in Torcello (*see p173*) and Malamocco (*see p162*), only shifting to what we now call Venice in the ninth century.

Some argue that ninth-century Doge Orso Partecipazio created the *sestieri* as soon as he had moved his base to Rivoalto – now known as Rialto. Still others say it was the need to raise taxes for waging war on the Byzantine Emperor Manuel Komnenus that led Doge Vitale Michiel II to carve the city into more manageable, dunnable administrative divisions in 1171.

Unwieldy and difficult to pin down, the *sestieri* nonetheless reflect Venice's largely impenetrable topography. To make orientation even more difficult, street names are considered decorative or descriptive – many, for example, are called *calle drio la chiesa* (street behind the church) or *calle forner* (bakery street) – and house numbers relate to the *sestiere* and not to the street. In Castello, the largest *sestiere*, numbers begin at one and go up almost to 7,000, often with inexplicable leaps from one front door to the next. If this seems complicated, you have to wonder how they managed before 1798, when the Austrians arrived to instill 'order' into the vanquished city-state: until then, there had been no numbers at all.

Locals and guidebooks will tell you that the *sestieri* are symbolised in each gondola's *ferro* (prow decoration), where six prongs – the six *sestieri* – point forward and a seventh – Giudecca (part of the *sestiere* of Dorsoduro) – points back. There's no historic documentation for this... but why doubt a good story?

In 1453, the Ottoman Turks swept into Constantinople, and Venice's crucial trading privileges in the former Byzantine Empire were almost totally lost. In 1487, Vasco da Gama rounded the Cape of Good Hope; in 1489, he became the first European to reach Calcutta by sea, shattering Venice's monopoly on the riches of the East. The arrival of Portuguese ships laden with spices and textiles in Portuguese ports caused a sensation in Europe and despair in Venice. The Venetians hastily drew up plans to open a canal at Suez to beat the Portuguese at their own game, but the project came to nothing. Instead, cushioned by the spoils and profits of centuries and exhausted by 100 years of almost constant military campaigning, the city sank slowly over the next two centuries into dissipation and decline.

That decline, naturally, was glorious. For most of the 16th century few Venetians behaved as if the writing were on the wall. Such was the enormous wealth of the city that the economic fall-out from the Turks' inexorable progress through the Middle East went almost unnoticed at first. Profits were not as massive as before, but the rich remained very rich and the setbacks in the East were partly counter-balanced by exploitation of the newly acquired *terra ferma* territories.

As revenue gradually declined through the 16th century, spending on life's little pleasures increased, producing an explosion of art, architecture and music. Titian, Tintoretto, Veronese and Giorgione were at work in the city. Palladio, Sanmicheli and Scamozzi were changing the face of architecture and *litterati* dazzled with their wit and learning. *La Serenissima* rang with music.

On the mainland, however, Venice's arrogant annexation of territory had not been forgotten by the powers that had suffered at her hands. When Venice took advantage of the French invasion of Italy in the final years of the 15th century to extend its territories still further, the Habsburgs, France, Spain and the papacy were so incensed that they clubbed together to form the League of Cambrai, with the sole aim of annihilating Venice.

They came very close to doing so. One Venetian military rout followed another, a number of Venetian-controlled cities defected, and others that did not were laid waste by the hostile forces. Only squabbling within the League of Cambrai stopped Venice itself from being besieged. By 1516, the alliance had fallen to pieces and Venice had regained almost all its territories.

TURKISH DELIGHT

Its coffers almost empty and its mainland dominions left in tatters, Venice was now forced to take stock of the damage that was being done by the Turks.

In 1497, as the Ottomans stormed through the Balkans, *La Serenissima* had been obliged to give up several Aegean islands and the port of Negroponte; two years later, it lost its forts in the Peloponnese, giving the Turks virtually total control of the southern end of the Adriatic. And though Venice was jubilant about securing Cyprus in 1489 – won by pressuring the king's Venetian widow Caterina Cornaro into bequeathing control of the island – the acquisition involved the Republic in almost constant warfare to keep the Turks away from this strategically vital strip of land.

In 1517, Syria and Egypt fell to the Turks; by 1529 the Ottoman Empire had spread across the southern Mediterranean as far as Morocco. The frightened European powers turned to Venice for help repulsing the common foe. But mistrust of the lagoon republic by its new allies was deep and, in their determination to keep Venice from deriving too much financial profit from the war against the Turks, the campaign itself was botched.

In 1538, a Christian fleet was trounced at Preveza in western Greece; in 1571, Venice led a huge European fleet to victory against Turkish warships in the Battle of Lepanto, in what is now the Gulf of Corinth. But despite the self-glorifying propaganda campaign that followed, it became apparent that the Turks were as strong as ever. In a treaty signed in 1573, Venice was forced ignominiously to hand over Cyprus, its second-last major possession in the eastern Mediterranean. (Crete, the final one, held out until 1669.)

TRADE DEFICIT

By the 17th century, Venice was no longer under any illusion about the gravity of its crisis. The Savi alla Mercanzia (state trading commission) noted on 5 July 1610 that 'our commerce and shipping in the West are completely destroyed. In the East only a few businesses are still functioning and

Francesco Morosini.

they are riddled with debt, without ships and getting weaker by the day. Moreover, and this must be emphasised, only a small quantity of goods is arriving in our city, and it is becoming increasingly difficult to find buyers for them. The nations which used to buy from us now have established their businesses elsewhere. We are facing the almost total annihilation of our commerce.'

Venice was down but not quite out. Between 1681 and 1687, Francesco Morosini, the brilliant strategist then in command of the Venetian fleet, reconquered much of the territory taken by the Turks, including Crete and the Peloponnese. But these moments of glory, celebrated with colossal pomp in Venice itself, were invariably short-lived.

Exhausted by debts and the sheer effort of its naval campaigns, the Venetian Republic lacked the resources needed to consolidate its victories. By 1718, it was struggling to keep its head above water as the Austrians and Turks forced it to cede most of its gains in the humiliating Treaty of Passarowitz.

By the time the Venezia Trionfante café (now Caffè Florian; see p61) opened for business in piazza San Marco in 1720, the Republic was virtually bankrupt; its governing nobility had grown decadent and politically inert. But decadence was good for the city's growing status as the party capital of Europe. Aristocratic women of all ages and marital states were accompanied in their gadding by handsome young cisibei (male escorts), whose professions of chastity fooled nobody.

Masked nuns were a common sight at the city's gambling houses and theatres; church officials who tried to confine nuns to the convent by the church of San Zaccaria would be met with a barrage of bricks.

Priests too were not slow to join in the fun: composer-prelate Antonio Vivaldi's supposed affairs with members of his famous female choir were well publicised. And though Giacomo Casanova, the embodiment of sexual excess, never actually donned a cassock, he had been a promising student of theology before he realised where his true vocation lay.

THROWING IN THE CAP

Bankrupt, politically and ideologically stagnant and no longer a threat to its former enemies, Venice directed its final heroic efforts against the forces of nature. As Napoleon prepared to invade Venice in 1797, the city was spending the meagre funds left in its coffers on building the *murazzi*, the vast stone and marble dyke designed to protect the city from the worst ravages of unpredictable Adriatic tides. On 12 May 1797, the last doge, Lodovico Manin, was deposed by the French, who, even before the Republic bowed to the inevitable and voted itself out of existence, had handed control over to Austria. Manin gave his doge's cap to the victors, saying, 'Take this, I don't think I'll be needing it any more.'

In 1805, Napoleon absorbed Venice back into his Kingdom of Italy. Until 1815, when the French emperor's star waned and Venice once again found itself under Austrian control, Napoleon's Venetian plenipotentiaries were given free rein to dismantle churches, dissolve monasteries and redesign bits of the city, including the wide thoroughfare now known as via Garibaldi and its adjoining public gardens.

The last spark of Venice's independent spirit flared up in 1848, when lawyer Daniele Manin (no relation of the last doge) led a popular revolt against the Austrians. An independent republican government was set up, holding out against siege for five heroic months. It was doomed to failure from the outset, however, and the Austrians were soon firmly back in the saddle, keeping their grip on this insignificant backwater until 1866, when a weakened Austria, badly beaten on other fronts by the Prussians, handed the city over to the newly united kingdom of Italy.

IN CONTEXT

Venetian Painting

A treasure house of art.

The lagoon city's unique atmosphere figures largely in its art. From the late Middle Ages until the mid 18th century, artists of the highest calibre, inspired by the unique colours and light of this unlikely smattering of overcrowded islands in a desolate lagoon, left their mark around the city. The result today is an anomaly: an extraordinary concentration of artistic treasures, of which the city's dwindling population is still inordinately, possessively proud.

Though little art is made in Venice these days, the city's very particular relationship with the art world continues. The 2009 inauguration of the new contemporary gallery at the Punta della Dogana means that Venice's concentration of 20th- and 21st-century art is almost as important as its Renaissance glories. For a damp town buffeted by threatening tides, Venice is truly a unique and precious repository of art.

IN CONTEXT

ART IN SITU

A key element in the effectiveness of Venetian painting is that many great pictures remain in the buildings for which they were painted. Leave the madding crowd at San Marco behind, and you'll soon come across superb pictures in obscure churches: glowing altarpieces and pulsating canvas *laterali* (paintings for side walls of chapels). Seeing these pictures in their original sites reveals how aware painters were of the relation of their works to the surrounding architecture, light and existing artwork.

Yet, exceptionally, the paintings also relate to the physical context of Venice itself. What makes Venetian painting distinctive – the decorated surfaces, asymmetry, shimmering light effects and, above all, warm tonalities – can also be found in the lagoon environment. Renaissance Venice's visual culture encompassed the richness of Islamic art and Byzantine mosaics, the haphazard arrangement of streets and canals with their strong shadows, and light experienced through haze or reflected off moving water.

THE END OF ANONYMITY

Venetian church interiors were once covered with frescoes; the damp climate means that very few of these earliest works survive today. The official history of Venetian painting begins in the 1320s with the first painter to emerge

Giovanni Bellini's **Madonna with Child**.

from medieval anonymity, **Paolo Veneziano** (c1290-1362), who worked in egg tempera and gold leaf on wood panel. He championed the composite altarpiece, which would become one of the key formats of Venetian painting. His polyptychs, such as *The Coronation of the Virgin* in the Accademia gallery (*see p145*), were ornately framed, compartmentalised works featuring sumptuous fabrics, a preference for surface decoration and pattern over depth, and a stiffness derived from Byzantine icons. A love of drapery and textile patterns proved to be a Venetian constant, still visible in Veronese's paintings in the 16th century and even beyond that in Tiepolo's 18th-century works.

Although many painters worked in Venice in the century after Paolo Veneziano, the next major legacy was that of a team, **Giovanni d'Alemagna** (John of Germany) and his brother-in-law **Antonio Vivarini**, active in the mid 15th century. Their three altarpieces in San Zaccaria (dated 1443, *see p80*), one in San Pantalon (*see p139*) and an imposing canvas triptych in the Accademia demonstrate the transition from Gothic to Renaissance.

Although Italian art historians give precedence to Antonio, the sudden decline in the quality of his works after Giovanni's death in 1450 suggests that his partner was the brains behind the operation. Antonio's younger brother, **Bartolomeo Vivarini**, who ran the family workshop from the 1470s until about 1491, learned Renaissance style from both painting and sculpture, as seen in the lapidary figures in the altarpiece (1474) in the Cappella Corner of the Frari (*see p126*).

By the next generation, the main players had become more clearly defined. From around 1480, **Giovanni Bellini** directed the dominant workshop in Venice. Most of Bellini's sizeable output, stretching from the late 1450s until his death in 1516, was painted on wood panel rather than the newer canvas. The important group of early Bellini devotional pictures in the Museo Correr (*see p55*) and the many variations on the Madonna and Child theme in the Accademia show how varied and moving these subjects could be.

Equally impressive is Bellini's magnificent series of altarpieces. In these he perfected the subject of the *Sacra conversazione*

(Sacred Conversation), where standing saints flank a seated figure, usually the Virgin Mary, within a setting that evokes the gold mosaics and costly marbles of the Basilica di San Marco (*see p50*). The inner glow afforded by the new medium of oil paint allowed Bellini to model his figures with an astonishing delicacy of light and shadow. One can follow his progress through a series of altarpieces that remain *in situ*: in Santi Giovanni e Paolo (*see p79*), the Frari, San Zaccaria and San Giovanni Crisostomo (*see p98*).

Giovanni's elder brother, **Gentile Bellini**, enjoyed even greater official success: from 1474 until his death in 1507 he directed the decoration of the Palazzo Ducale (*see p98*), replacing crumbling frescoes with huge canvases. He also performed a diplomatic role for the Venetian government, travelling to Constantinople in 1479 to paint for the

---

JACOPO, GIOVANNI & GENTILE
The Bellinis and the Venetian Renaissance.

Jacopo Bellini (1400-1470) had good reason to be proud of his sons: **Gentile** (1429-1507) and **Giovanni** (1430-1516) are synonymous with Venetian Renaissance art. But their father also played a crucial role. A pupil of Gentile da Fabriano, and familiar with the most prominent artists of the very early Italian Renaissance, Jacopo brought back to his native Venice styles and techniques (including the use of oil paint rather than tempera) that would determine the development of art at this remarkable period for the city.

In a flourishing workshop that would also include Andrea Mantegna, who married a Bellini daughter, Jacopo and his acolytes broke away from the art of the late Middle Ages, gradually exchanging the stiff style adopted from Byzantine icons for a softer, more natural one.

If Giovanni is the Bellini brother considered more highly today, Gentile was perhaps more successful during his lifetime, appointed as the official portrait painter to the doges and given key diplomatic tasks too. In 1479 he was sent to Constantinople as Venice's cultural representative to the court of Sultan Mehmed II, whose portrait he painted. But it is as a chronicler of life in Venice that Gentile fascinates most today. Immense canvases painted for the Doge's Palace have been destroyed by fire. But his two scenes from the *Miracle of the Relic of the Holy Cross* (1496-1500), now in the Accademia (*see p246*) are packed with minute, charming details – each

Gentile Bellini's **Doge Giovanni Mocenigo**.

of which tells its own particular story about life in 15th-century Venice.

Giovanni Bellini's lasting appeal is due, arguably, to his extraordinary way with colour. Using oils in a way no one before him had mastered so well, he created hues and moods that broke the mould of Italian painting. The 1505 altarpiece of San Zaccaria church (*see p80*) is a case in point. The warmth and the contrasts, the delicacy and humanity of the subjects in this *Sacra conversazione* are a total break with the past.

Giovanni's novel approach set off ripples that would continue to widen through the Venetian Renaissance and beyond: through pupils such as Sebastiano del Piombo, the enigmatic Giorgione and the great colourist Titian, Giovanni's influence was lasting and profound.

Ottoman sultan. Although his Palazzo Ducale canvases were destroyed by fire in 1577, his *Procession in Piazza San Marco* (1496), now in the Accademia, shows his ability to depict sumptuous public spectacle with choreographic verve.

Three painters born in the second half of the 15th century, and who were active in the 16th, are worth seeking out. **Cima da Conegliano** (c1459-1517) offers a stiffer style than Bellini, depicting figures standing in dignified repose against crisp landscapes. Cima's best altarpieces, in the Accademia, and at San Giovanni in Bragora (*see p87*), the Madonna dell'Orto (*see p104*) and the Carmini (*see p141*), all demonstrate a mastery of light.

Vittore Carpaccio (c1465-1525) specialised in narrative works for the *scuole* (*see p129* **School Stories**). Two intact cycles from around 1500 are among the treasures of Venetian painting: the grand St Ursula cycle in the Accademia and that of St George and St Jerome in the intimate Scuola di San Giorgio degli Schiavoni (*see p88*).

Lorenzo Lotto (c1480-1556) spent much of his career outside Venice. His best altarpieces in the city, in the Carmini and Santi Giovanni e Paolo, combine an uncanny accuracy – in rendering landscape or cloth, for example – with a deeply felt spirituality. His impressive portraits, such as the *Portrait of a Youth*, in the Accademia, employ an unusual horizontal format.

SECULAR SUBJECTS

At the beginning of the 16th century, Venetian painting took a dramatic turn. Three of Bellini's pupils – Giorgione, Sebastiano del Piombo and Titian – experimented with new secular subject matter and new ways of handling paint. **Giorgione** (c1477-1510) remains one of the great enigmas of art. No other reputation rests on so few surviving pictures. The hard contours and emphasis on surface pattern seen in earlier Venetian painting have softened in his work, and for the first time the atmosphere becomes palpable, like damp lagoon air. Two haunting pictures in the Accademia, *La Tempesta* (*pictured pp244-245*) and *La Vecchia*, may be deliberately enigmatic, more concerned with mood than story. It can be argued that the modern concept of the painting was born

in Venice soon after 1500. For the first time, three conditions that we now take for granted were met: these works were all oil on canvas, painted at the artist's initiative, and not intended for a specific location.

Sebastiano del Piombo (c1485-1547) left his mark with a similar emphasis on softened contour and tangible atmosphere. His major altarpiece, which was painted around 1507 and can still be seen in San Giovanni Crisostomo, shows a *Sacra conversazione* in which some of the figures are seen in profile, rather than head on, and hidden in shadow. Even more exciting is a set of standing saints painted as organ shutters, now in the Accademia, which show an unprecedented application of thick paint (*impasto*).

TITIAN AND TINTORETTO

Events conspired to boost the early career of **Titian** (Tiziano Vecellio, c1488-1576) when, in the space of only six years (1510-16), Giorgione fell victim to the plague, Sebastiano del Piombo moved to Rome and Giovanni Bellini passed away. Titian soon staked his claim with a dynamic *Assumption of the Virgin* (1518) for the high altar of the Frari. There he dominated the enormous space by creating the largest panel painting in the world.

The lagoon city is the place to appreciate *in situ* the nearly 70-year span of the master's religious work. These include a second, glorious altarpiece in the Frari (the *Madonna di Ca' Pesaro*), the virile St Christopher fresco in the Palazzo Ducale and the ceiling paintings in the sacristy of the Salute (*see p148*).

For a decade (c1527-39), Titian had a true rival in **Pordenone** (c1483-1539), a painter of muscular figures engaged in violent action. Now, for the first time in decades, Pordenone's work can be appreciated in Venice. The recently restored *Saints Christopher & Martin* in the church of San Rocco (*see p128*) shows an urgent style that had great appeal. Even more interesting is the confrontation in the church of San Giovanni Elemosinario (*see p119*), where Pordenone's bulging figures on the right altar square off against the soft contours of Titian's high altar. Yet, once again, Titian found his road cleared of obstacles when his adversary suddenly died.

Pordenone's **Saints Christopher & Martin**.

By the 1560s, in works such as the extraordinary *Annunciation* in San Salvador (*see p62*), Titian's handling of paint had become so loose that his forms were not so much defined by contours as caressed into being. Line was replaced by quivering patches of warm colouring.

Contemporaries swore that the old artist painted as often with his fingers as with the brush. Nowhere is this tactile quality more apparent than in Titian's final painting, a *Pietà* originally intended for his tomb, and now in the Accademia. Left unfinished at his death during the plague of 1576, this picture summarises the Venetian artistic tradition, with its glittering mosaic dome and forms so dissolved as to challenge the very conventions of painting.

Instead of mourning Titian's death, Jacopo Robusti (c1518-94) – better known as **Tintoretto** – probably breathed a sigh of relief. Though he rose to fame in the late 1540s, he had to wait until he was 58 years old before he could claim the title of Venice's greatest living painter. Yet Tintoretto was

canny enough to learn from his rival. He supposedly inscribed the motto 'The drawing of Michelangelo and the colouring of Titian' on the wall of his studio.

Tintoretto's breakthrough work, *The Miracle of the Slave* (1548), now in the Accademia, offered a brash attempt at this synthesis, combining Michelangelo's confident muscular anatomies with Titian's glistening paint surface. Borrowing the figure types and violent compositions of Pordenone, Tintoretto's aggressive and tumultuous canvases marked the end of the decorative narrative painting tradition perfected by Carpaccio.

As Ruskin noted in *The Stones of Venice* (1851), Tintoretto, unlike Titian, is an artist who can be appreciated only in Venice. Among the dozens of works in his home town, the soaring choir paintings in the Madonna dell'Orto (c1560) or the many canvases at the Scuola Grande di San Rocco (*see p128*), executed in 1564-87, amaze in their scale and complexity, notably his wall-sized *Crucifixion* (1565). His many workshop assistants, including two sons and a daughter, allowed him to increase production to unprecedented levels. Tintoretto went even further than Titian in the liberation of the brush stroke. The tradition of bravura handling that goes from Rubens to Delacroix to De Kooning begins with the action painters of 16th-century Venice.

Paolo Veronese (1528-88) made his impact in Venice with a love of rich fabrics and elegant poses that contrasts with Tintoretto's agitated figures. Veronese's savoir faire is best seen in the overpopulated feasts he painted for monastery refectories, such as the *Feast in the House of Levi*, now in the Accademia. His wit can be seen in one of the few great 16th-century mythological paintings remaining in Venice: *The Rape of Europa*, in the Palazzo Ducale, with its leering, slightly comical bull. His supreme ensemble piece is in San Sebastiano (*see p135*), a church that features altars, ceilings, frescoes and organ shutters all painted by Veronese, as well as the artist's tomb.

Venetian painting was also practised outside Venice: **Jacopo Bassano** (c1510-92) was an artist based in a provincial centre who kept pace with the latest innovations. Alhough his work is best seen in his home town, Bassano del Grappa (*see p227*), a number of canvases in the Accademia and an altarpiece in San Giorgio Maggiore (*see p159*) display characteristic Venetian flickering brush work and dramatic chiaroscuro.

With the following generation, the golden age of Venetian painting drew to a close. The prolific **Palma il Giovane** (c1548-1628) created works loosely in the style of Tintoretto. His finest pictures, such as the *Crucifixion* in the Madonna dell'Orto or those in San Giacomo dell'Orio (*see p123*) or the Oratorio dei Crociferi (*see p107*), all date from the 1580s.

After the deaths of Veronese and Tintoretto, the pressure was gone and the quality of Venetian art took a nosedive, as can be seen at San Giovanni Elemosinario, now open after decades *in restauro*.

IN CONTEXT

RIVALS: BELLINI AND DEL PIOMBO

Showdown at the altars.

A fascinating showdown can be seen in San Giovanni Crisostomo (*see p98*), where the elderly **Giovanni Bellini** outshone his former pupil **Sebastiano del Piombo**, some 50 years his junior. Sebastiano struck first, around 1507, with the high altarpiece, boldly setting the central figure of St John Chrysostom in profile and immersed in shadow. He contrasted the saint with a particularly lyrical John the Baptist (note how the scroll winding around his staff mimics the turning of the saint's body and the drapery swirls). Not to be outdone, Bellini's 1513 altarpiece in the right chapel includes similar chessboard paving and a twisting St Christopher, clearly critiquing Sebastiano's Baptist. The central figure is presented as a seated geriatric holding a tome, literally facing off against his rival's prototype. Bellini made sure viewers knew that this was not the work of a young trendy: he signed and dated the painting prominently near Christopher's knee.

San Giovanni Crisostomo: high altarpiece by **Sebastiano del Piombo**.

Outsized canvases by painters active at the end of the 16th century crowd the church's walls but the aforementioned small altarpieces by Titian and Pordenone, executed more than half a century earlier, dominate the space.

BAROQUE AND ROCOCO

In the following years, Baroque in Venice was represented largely by out-of-towners (**Luca Giordano**, whose restored altarpieces adorn the Salute) or by bizarre posturing (**Gian Antonio Fumiani**'s stupefying canvas ceiling in San Pantalon). Exaggerated light effects ruled the day. It was only at the beginning of the 18th century that Venetian painting experienced a resurgence. **Giambattista Piazzetta** (1683-1754) produced a ceiling painting in Santi Giovanni e Paolo and a sequence of altarpieces – particularly those in Santa Maria della Fava (*see p80*), the Gesuati (*see p146*) and San Salvador – all demonstrating restrained elegance and a muted palette.

    Giambattista Tiepolo (1696-1770), the greatest painter of the Venetian rococo, adapted the zigzag scheme introduced by Piazzetta for use with warm pastel colours. In his monumental ceilings in the Gesuati, the Pietà (*see p87*) and Ca' Rezzonico (*see p139*), Tiepolo reintroduced frescoes on a large scale after more than two centuries of canvas ceilings. Perhaps the most satisfying place in which to view his work is the upper room of the Scuola Grande dei Carmini (*see p141*), where the disproportionately low ceiling provides a close-up view of his technique. The dazzling Tiepolo was only one of a number of important artists at work in 18th-century Venice, including his own son, **Giandomenico Tiepolo** (1727-1804).

    Though frequently his father's assistant, Giandomenico can be seen at his independent best in an eerie cycle of 14 *Stations of the Cross* in San Polo (*see p119*). **Gaspare Diziani** (1689-1767) deserves credit for three gorgeous ceiling canvases on the life of St Helen in the former meeting room of the Scuola del Vin (wine merchants' confraternity), entered through the church of San Silvestro (*see p119*). Above all, the essence of the Venetian rococo is to be found in the sites where architecture, sculpture and painting were employed to form a unified whole: the Gesuati, Santa Maria della Fava, San Stae (*see p124*) and the furnished rooms of Ca' Rezzonico.

    In the 18th century, collectors provided a constant demand for portraits and city views. A female artist, **Rosalba Carriera** (1675-1757), developed a refined portrait style using pastels. **Canaletto** (1697-1768) and **Guardi** (1712-93) offered views of Venice. The popularity of these landscape paintings as Grand Tour souvenirs means that although examples exist in the Accademia and Ca' Rezzonico, both artists are seen at their best in Britain. A different aspect of 18th-century painting, and perhaps Guardi's masterpiece, can be seen in the astonishingly delicate *Stories of Tobias* (1750-53) decorating the organ loft in the church of Angelo Raffaele (*see p134*). **Pietro Longhi** (1702-85) created amusing genre scenes that gently satirised the social life of his day; they can be enjoyed in the Museo della Fondazione Querini Stampalia (*see p75*).

PATRONS, NOT PRODUCERS

By the time of Napoleon's conquest in 1797, Venetian painting, like Venetian military power, was a spent force. Over the following 200 years, however, Venice's unique setting and lavish collections have been a magnet for foreign visitors, including artists.

    Venice now exhibits painters, rather than producing them. The city's contemporary art scene is increasingly vibrant, with a handful of smaller players and three major institutions: the prestigious Biennale (*see p31*); the Peggy Guggenheim Collection (*see p147*), which has expanded and is flourishing; and the extraordinary Palazzo Grassi–Punta della Dogana nexus (*see p65 and p147*).

    Although attention is currently focused on the contemporary, Venice's incomparable artistic heritage has had a boost recently too: after ten years' work, to a design by Tobia Scarpa (son of Carlo, *see p260*), the Grandi Gallerie dell'Accademia finally saw the light of day in December 2013. The ground floor of the present Accademia building – used by the city's fine arts school from 1807 to 2003 – has been converted into additional galleries so that nearly 650 works (instead of the previous 400) can be displayed, many of them specially restored for the opening.

IN CONTEXT

Architecture

Competitive construction against the odds.

TEXT: ANNE HANLEY

Think of the least likely place to build a successful city and Venice ticks all the boxes: marshy islands in a salt lagoon, buffeted by winds and at the mercy of tides, with no fresh water and only the most difficult means of communication. The earliest structures, set on wooden piles driven deep into the mud and created by nameless local master-masons, were things of elegance and grace. Later, the technical challenges – and of course a surplus of fabulously wealthy patrons in this trade-and-art superpower – drew the greatest architects from elsewhere too: early Renaissance master Mauro Codussi from Bergamo; Vicenza-based Andrea Palladio; Tuscan-born Jacopo Sansovino. A sense of practicality mixed with a love of extravagant, competitive show led to the construction of family *palazzi* that were a perfect mix of business hub and desirable residence. When decline set in, former glories flaked, chipped, peeled and began subsiding into the muddy lagoon. But even in its decay Venice remained peerlessly beautiful – a unique gem to be cherished and preserved in its watery setting.

San Giacomo di Rialto.

MEDIEVAL AND BYZANTINE

Venetian architecture began in Torcello, where the cathedral of **Santa Maria Assunta** (*see p174*), founded in 639, is the oldest surviving building on the lagoon. It has been remodelled since then – notably in the ninth and 11th centuries – but still retains the simple form of an early Christian basilica. Next door, the 11th-century church of **Santa Fosca** (*see p173*) has a Greek cross plan – also found in **San Giacomo di Rialto** (*see p112*), considered to be the earliest church in Venice proper. The portico of Santa Fosca exhibits a feature that recurs in the first-floor windows of 12th-century townhouses on the Grand Canal: stilted arches, with horseshoe-shaped arches atop slender columns.

That the history of Venetian architecture can be charted by following the development of the arch is understandable in a city built on mud, where load-bearing capabilities were a prime consideration. In the latter part of the 13th century, the pure, curved Byzantine arch began to sport a point at the top, under the influence of Islamic models. An early example of this can be seen in the heavily restored **Albergo del Selvadego** in calle dell'Ascensione (San Marco). Soon this point developed into a fully fledged ogee arch – a northern Gothic trait.

Meanwhile, the **Basilica di San Marco** (St Mark's basilica; *see p50*) was continuing to evolve. A makeshift chapel for holding St Mark's relics was replaced in 832 by a church modelled on the Church of the Apostles in Constantinople; that burnt down, to be replaced with the one we see today. The main body of the current church, with its Greek cross plan surmounted by five domes, dates from the 11th century; but it was embellished extensively over the next four centuries. Two humbler 12th-century churches, **San Giacomo dell'Orio** (*see p123*) and **San Nicolò dei Mendicoli** (*see p135*), both feature squat, detached bell towers – a key feature of the Veneto-Byzantine style.

GOTHIC AND LATE GOTHIC

In the 14th and 15th centuries, Venetian architecture developed an individual character unmatched before or since. It was at this time that the city's own Arab-tinged version of Gothic came into its own. By the mid 14th century, the ogee arch (two concave-convex curves meeting at the top) had sprouted a point on the inside of its concave edge – producing the cusped arch, which distributes the forces pressing down on it so efficiently that the Victorian art critic John Ruskin decreed that 'all are imperfect except these.'

By the beginning of the 15th century, this basic shape had been hedged around with elaborate tracery and trefoils (clover-shaped openings) and topped with Moorish-looking pinnacles in a peculiarly Venetian take on the flamboyant Gothic style, which reached its apotheosis in the façades of the **Palazzo Ducale** (*see p56*) and the **Ca' d'Oro** (*see p100*) – both completed by 1440.

CHURCHES AND SCUOLE

Outside of St Mark's, church architecture reflected the traditional building styles of the large religious orders that commissioned the work: the cavernous brick monuments of **Santi Giovanni e Paolo** (1430; *see p79* and the **Frari** (1433; *see p126*) are classic examples of, respectively, the Dominican and Franciscan approaches. Both have a Latin cross plan, a large rose window and a generous sprinkling of pinnacles.

More individual are churches such as **Santo Stefano** (*see p65*), with its wooden ship's-keel roof, and the **Scuola Vecchia della Misericordia** (*see p104*), with its ogee windows and Flemish-style roof gable. Both involved the collaboration of Giovanni and Bartolomeo Bon, who also worked on the Ca' d'Oro.

THE VENETIAN PALAZZO

Majestic Grand Canal palaces (*see also pp38-47*) continued to indulge the yen for elaborate tracery windows, but behind the façade the structure went back centuries. The Venetian palazzo was not only a place of residence; it was also the family business headquarters; the internal division of space reflects this, with loading and storage space below a magnificent first-floor *piano nobile*. On the roof there was often a raised wooden balcony or *altana*: in a city where space was always at a premium, private courtyards were the preserve of the very wealthy indeed.

EARLY RENAISSANCE

Venetians were so fond of their own gracefully oriental version of Gothic that they held on to it long after the new classicist orthodoxy had taken over central Italy. For the second half of the 15th century, emergent Renaissance forms existed alongside the Gothic swansong. Sometimes they merged or clashed in the same building, as in the church of **San Zaccaria** (*see p80*), which was begun by Antonio Gambello in 1458 in the pure northern Gothic style but completed by Mauro Codussi in the Renaissance idiom he was then elaborating.

Next to nothing is known about Codussi's background, save that he may have trained under Giovanni Bon. In 1469, he was appointed *protomagister* (works manager) for the church of **San Michele** (*see p164*).

Within ten years he had completed the first truly Renaissance building in the city. The austere Istrian marble façade with its classical elements has something Palladian about it, though the curves of the pediment and buttresses are pure Codussi, adapted from a late Gothic model.

LOMBARDESQUE STYLE

Codussi took over a number of projects begun by Pietro Lombardo, who represents the other strand of early Renaissance architecture in northern Italy. This was based on the extensive use of inlaid polychrome marble, Corinthian columns and decorated friezes. Lombardo's masterpiece is **Santa Maria dei Miracoli** (*see p107*), but he also designed – with his sons – the lower part of the façade of the **Scuola Grande di San Marco** (*see p81*), with its trompe l'oeil relief. The Lombardesque style was all the rage for a while, producing such charmers as tiny, lopsided **Ca' Dario** (1487-92) on the Grand Canal.

HIGH RENAISSANCE

Codussi's influence lingered into the 16th century in the work of architects such as Guglielmo dei Grigi and Scarpagnino, both

Santi Giovanni e Paolo.

VENETIAN PEOPLE ANDREA PALLADIO

Classical motifs for an influential new style.

Arguably the most influential figure in Western architecture, Andrea Palladio had an unremarkable start. He was born in Padua on 30 November 1508 and baptised Andrea di Pietro della Gondola. His father apprenticed him at the age of 13 to Giovanni da Porlezza, a stonecarver in Vicenza. Recognising his talent, the workshop put up the money for Andrea's guild entrance fee. He learned to design and carve church altars, tombs and architectural elements, many commissioned by local nobility.

While working on a villa on the outskirts of Vicenza between 1530 and 1538, he met its owner, Count Giangiorgio Trissino, the wealthy leader of a group of Humanist intellectuals dedicated to reviving classical culture. This chance meeting was to change the course of Western architecture.

Trissino set about turning Andrea into a worthy heir to Vitruvius, the ancient architect whose treatise De Architectura underpinned the return to classical models in the Italian Renaissance. He also gave Andrea a more suitable name: 'Palladio' resonated with classical associations, and was the name of a helpful angel in Trissino's epic poem *Italia liberata dai goti* ('Italy Liberated from the Goths'). Trissino also gave Palladio time off and funds to study Roman antiquities in Verona and Padua, and took him to Rome three times between 1540 and 1550. Palladio studied, measured and sketched all the major classical remains, as well as the buildings and plans of Renaissance greats throughout Italy. In 1554, he published *Le antichità di Roma* (*The Antiquities of Rome*), a sort of proto-guidebook.

Palladio's early patrons were part of the Trissino circle, who provided both work and intellectual stimulation after Trissino died in 1550. Among these enlightened Vicentine nobles were Pietro Godi, whose Villa Godi Valmarana ora Malinverni (*see p220*) was Palladio's first independent commission, completed by 1542 and one of his most radical, pared-back designs. The Barbaro brothers encouraged Palladio to create one of his masterpieces, the Villa Barbaro a Maser (1550-57; *see p221*). Another patron, Girolamo Chiericati helped give the architect his first big break, in 1549: restructuring Vicenza's town hall (the Basilica Palladiana; *see p219*), which established Palladio as one of the leading architects of his day.

Palladio also benefited from good timing. In the 16th century, the Venetian government insisted that nobles build villas on the *terra ferma* (mainland) in order to boost agricultural production and increase *La Serenissima*'s control over the countryside. Commissions for villas were thus plentiful throughout the Veneto. In 1570, Palladio moved to Venice, to become unofficial chief architect, with prominent churches such as **San Giorgio Maggiore** (*see p159*) and the **Redentore** (*see p156*) reinforcing his fame. His influential treatise, *I quattro libri dell'architettura* (*The Four Books of Architecture*, 1570), spread his name further.

The pared-back design for which Palladio became so famous was certainly inspired by Roman and Greek architecture, but was never copied from it; Palladio used classical motifs, creating a style that defined elegance. The most recognisable feature of his buildings is the use of the

Redentore.

Greco-Roman temple front as a portico; equally innovative were the dramatic high-relief effects on façades. The floor plans usually emphasised a strong central axis and symmetrical wings, with room proportions determined mathematically to create harmonic spaces, typically with high ceilings. Though always unmistakeably his, each of Palladio's buildings is startlingly different – from the stark simplicity of **Villa Pisani** (1540; *see p220*) at Bagnolo di Lonigo to the vast complexity of the statue-crowned Palazzo Chiericati (now the **Museo Civico**; *see p222*) in Vicenza.

In his day, Palladio's domestic villa architecture largely overshadowed his other accomplishments. His country residences uniquely combined both a working farmhouse and elegant country retreat, with much of the decoration serving a function: the gracious entrance ramp at the **Villa Emo** (*see p221*) was also intended as a platform for threshing grain.

Palladio's designs also encompassed other practical functions: stables, cellars, granaries and dovecotes were located within the compounds and were intrinsic to the villa as a whole. Never ostentatious, overbearing in size or using costly materials, they make subtle statements through a dignified classical vocabulary, harmony of proportions both external and internal, and a human scale. Palladio's inventiveness and sensitivity extended to the aspect and location of villas, which he regarded as highly important in their function as an antidote to the stresses of urban life. Building near a river or canal was recommended; as well as allowing easy access by boat, water guaranteed cool breezes during the hot summer months, irrigated the gardens and, not incidentally, 'will afford a beautiful prospect'.

Palladio's style would be copied throughout Europe for centuries.

Biblioteca Marciana.

of whom have been credited with the design of the **Palazzo dei Camerlenghi** (1525-28; *see p112*). Around this time, the construction in piazza San Marco of the **Procuratie Vecchie** and the **Torre dell'Orologio** (for both, *see p50*), both to designs by Codussi, demonstrated that in the centre of civic power, loyalty to the myth of Venice tended to override architectural fashions.

It was not until the late 1520s that something really new turned up, courtesy of Jacopo Sansovino, a Tuscan sculptor. Perhaps it was the influence of his new-found friends Titian and the poet Pietro Aretino that secured him the prestigious position of *protomagister* of St Mark's only two years after his arrival, despite his lack of experience; Sansovino went on to create a series of buildings that changed the face of the city. He began to refine his rational, harmonious Renaissance style in designs for the church of **San Francesco della Vigna** (begun in 1532; *see p78*) and **Palazzo Corner della Ca' Grande** (*see p46*), Venice's first Roman-style palazzo.

But it was in piazza San Marco that Sansovino surpassed himself. **La Zecca** (*see p60*) – the state mint – with its heavy rustication and four-square solidity, is a perfect financial fortress. The **Biblioteca Marciana** (completed in 1554, also known as the Libreria Sansoviniana; *see p286*) is his masterpiece, disguising its classical regularity beneath a typically Venetian wealth of surface detail. The little **Loggetta** at the base of the

Campanile (*see p55*) showed that Sansovino was capable of a lightness of touch.

PALLADIAN PRE-EMINENCE
Michele Sanmicheli built the imposing sea defences on the island of Le Vignole, and two hefty Venetian *palazzi*, the **Palazzo Corner Mocenigo** (1559-64) in campo San Polo and the **Palazzo Grimani di San Luca** (1556-75) on the Grand Canal.

But it was another out-of-towner, Andrea Palladio (*see p256* **Venetian People**), who would set the agenda for what was left of the 16th century. The man who invented the post-Renaissance found it difficult to get a foothold in a city that valued flexibility above critical rigour. But he did design two influential churches: **San Giorgio Maggiore** (begun in 1562; *see p159*) and the **Redentore** (1577-92; *see p156*). The church of **Le Zitelle** (*see p154*) was built to Palladio's plans after the architect's death.

Palladio's disciple, Vincenzo Scamozzi, designed the **Procuratie Nuove** (*see p50*. At the same time, Antonio Da Ponte was commissioned to design a stone bridge at the **Rialto**, in 1588, after designs by Michelangelo and Palladio had been rejected.

BAROQUE
The examples of Sansovino and Palladio continued to be felt well into the 17th century. It wasn't until the arrival of Baldassare Longhena in the 1620s that Venice got twirly bits in any abundance. Longhena was a local

boy who first made his mark with the Duomo in Chioggia. But it was with the church of **Santa Maria della Salute** (*see p148* that he pulled out all the stops. Commissioned in 1632, and 50 years in the making, this highly theatrical church dominates the southern reaches of the Grand Canal.

Longhena was also busy designing a series of impressive *palazzi*, including the huge Grand Canal hulk of **Ca' Pesaro** (1652; *see p122*). He also designed the façade of the **Ospedaletto** (1667-74; *see p80*), with its grotesque telamons. It was a taste of things to come: the overwrought façade continued to develop in the 1670s, extending from the exuberance of the **Scalzi** (*see p98*) and **Santa Maria del Giglio** (*see p69*) – both by Longhena's follower Giuseppe Scalzi – to the bombast of **San Moisè** (*see p68*, a kitsch collaboration between Alessandro Tremignon and sculptor Heinrich Meyring.

NEOCLASSICISM

During the 18th-century decline, limp variations on Palladio and Longhena dominated the scene. Domenico Rossi adorned Palladian orders with swags and statuary in the façades he designed for the churches of **San Stae** (1709-10; *see p124*) and the **Gesuiti** (1715-28; *see p107*).

Sumptuous palaces continued to go up along the Grand Canal; one of the last was the solid **Palazzo Grassi** (*see p65*), built between 1748 and 1772. It was designed by Giorgio Massari, who was also responsible for **La Pietà** (*see p87*) – the Vivaldi church – the oval floorplan of which strikes a rare note of originality. The **Palazzo Venier dei Leoni** – now home to the Peggy Guggenheim Collection (*see p147*) – also dates from the mid 18th century. Funds ran out after the first storey, giving Venice one of its most bizarrely endearing landmarks.

Giannantonio Selva's **La Fenice** opera house (1790-92; *see p69*) was one of the Serene Republic's last building projects. Napoleon's arrival in 1797 marked the destruction of many churches and convents, but also began a series of clearances that allowed for the creation of the city's first public park, the **Giardini pubblici** (*see p85*), and the nearby thoroughfare now known as **via Garibaldi**. Piazza San Marco took on its present-day appearance at this time too, when the Procuratie Vecchie and Nuove were united by the neoclassical **Ala Napoleonica**.

Under the Austrian occupation (1815-66), restoration replaced construction, and a railway bridge linking Venice to Mestre (1841-42) was built, ending the city's isolation.

La Fenice.

SCARPA IN VENICE

A true Venetian architect.

A Venetian born and bred (save for a few years spent in his youth in nearby Vicenza, Carlo Scarpa (1906-78) was one of Italy's most highly regarded architects – without even qualifying as an architect until just before his death.

Utterly imbued with the textures of the lagoon city, he worked with wood and glass (he was creative director of the Venini glassmaker from 1933 to 1947), stone and concrete to blend his very modern designs into the context of his native city. The results are dotted all around Venice.

With the restoration and reopening of the **Negozio Olivetti** (Olivetti showroom, 1957-58; see *p56*) in piazza San Marco, one of Scarpa's most remarkable gems has been returned to the city, thanks to the FAI (www.fondoambiente.org), Italy's equivalent of Britain's National Trust.

In his restyling (1961-63) of the ground floor of the **Fondazione Querini Stampalia** (*see p75*), Scarpa ran water from the canal outside, bringing it into an indoor space of travertine and games with levels, then through a garden courtyard of deceptive simplicity. His too is the wooden bridge leading across to one of the Foundation's entrances.

Despite his lack of academic qualifications, Scarpa had a close relationship with Venice's universities, teaching interior design at the IUAV (the architecture & design university) from the late 1940s until his death. For IUAV he designed the main entrance (Santa Croce 191, campazzo dei Tolentini), and comprehensively overhauled the IUAV Fondazione Masieri annexe (Dorsoduro 3900, calle del Remer). For **Ca' Foscari**, Venice's other university, he designed the entrance to the Arts faculty (Dorsoduro 1686, campo San Sebastiano); and revamped (1935-37) the ground floor of the main university premises (Dorsoduro 3246, calle Foscari; you can take a good look over coffee or a meal at the university's

Negozio Olivetti.

VENICEAT@CaFoscari canteen, open 8am-7pm Mon-Fri, 8am-1pm Sat during term time). His wooden Baratto lecture theatre there (1955-56) burnt down but was rebuilt in 1979 to his specifications.

The architect left his mark on the **Biennale gardens** (*see p85*), designing what was once the main ticket booth (1952), the Venezuelan pavilion (1956) and a sculpture garden (1952). He was also responsible for the plinth (1968) for Augusto Murer's *Partigiana* sculpture by the Giardini vaporetto stop.

Between 1945 and 1959, he pottered away at the **Gallerie dell'Accademia** (*see p145*), modernising and upgrading in a series of interventions of such delicacy that you'll need to look closely to notice them. (The gallery's new rooms, designed by his son Tobia and opened to the public in 2014, are far less subtle.)

There's more of Scarpa's work to be seen around the Veneto region, including the dramatic **Castelvecchio** (*see p215*) makeover in Verona and the Antonio Canova sculpture museum in Possagno. Scarpa died after falling down a flight of stairs in Japan, but was buried – according to his wishes – standing, wrapped in winding sheets like a medieval knight, in a corner of his extraordinary Brion-Vega tomb in San Vito d'Altivole, near Treviso.

In his influential book the *Stones of Venice* (1853), John Ruskin set out to discredit 'the pestilent art of the Renaissance' in favour of 'healthy and beautiful' Gothic. Such was his clout that the city became an architectural sacred cow, untouchable by the unclean hand of innovation. Instead, Venice began to recreate its Gothic and Byzantine past, with exercises such as the **Palazzo Franchetti**, a 15th-century edifice at the north-eastern foot of the Ponte dell'Accademia that was redesigned in neo-medieval style (1878-82).

One of the city's most elegant neo-Gothic works is the **cemetery of San Michele** (1872-81). Another landmark from the period is the **Molino Stucky** (1897-1920; *see p154*), a flour mill on the Giudecca designed in Hanseatic Gothic style by Ernest Wullekopf. The turn of the 20th-century was also a boom time for hotels, with the **Excelsior** on the Lido (1898-1908) setting the eclectic, Moorish-Byzantine agenda.

MODERNITY CATCHES UP

Venice's modern architecture is limited. To date, only locally born modernist Carlo Scarpa (1906-78; *see p260* **Scarpa in Venice**) has created a body of work: the entrance and garden patio ofthe **Biennale gardens** (1952; *see p85*), the **Olivetti showroom** (1957-58; *see p56*) in piazza San Marco, the entrance lobby of the IUAV architecture faculty near piazzale Roma and the ground-floor reorganisation of the **Museo Querini Stampalia** (1961-63; *see p75*). Scarpa's student, Mario Botta, has recently overhauled the top-floor exhibition rooms of this last establishment.

The 1970s and '80s brought one or two adventurous public housing projects around outlying areas of the city or lagoon, such as Giancarlo De Carlo's low-income housing on the island of Mazzorbo (1979-86). A new high-tech airport terminal by local architect Giampaolo Mar was inaugurated in summer 2002 and the 70-hectare (170 acres) **Parco di San Giuliano**, designed by Boston-based urban planner Antonio Di Mambro, opened on the mainland by Mestre in 2004. Vittorio Gregotti and others worked on the revamp of industrial areas in north-western Cannaregio, including a former slaughterhouse that now houses the university's economics faculty. Milan's Cino Zucchi reworked the Venetian idiom in housing built around the former Junghans factory on the Giudecca. Japanese superstar Tadao Ando refurbished **Palazzo Grassi** (*see p65*) and the **Punta della Dogana** (*see p147*.

After years of controversy, delays, staggering over-spending and a long litany of other woes, the **Ponte della Costituzione** – by Spain's Santiago Calatrava and known invariably to locals as the ponte di Calatrava – was inaugurated in 2008, *sans* the requisite disabled access (since added, in the shape of a strange bubble that crosses the canal on the outside of the structure). But this fourth bridge over the Grand Canal, linking the railway station and the key road transport hub at piazzale Roma, continues to bring more troubles in its wake: in 2013 city hall announced that it was sueing the Calatrava studio for the extra cost of its various shortcomings.

A deafening silence hangs about projects long in the pipeline, including an extension of the **cemetery at San Michele** by London-based architect David Chipperfield, and the **Venice Gateway** hotel and convention complex by Frank Gehry: the former is struggling to get past its first stage, with deadlines for stage two slipping inexorably backwards; the latter is drowning (has drowned?) beneath a sea of red tape.

Museo Querini Stampalia.

Essential Information

Hotels

A day-trip to Venice just won't do. To appreciate the city's 24-hour magic, you have to fall asleep to the sound of gondoliers crooning and awake to the very particular bouncing echo of footsteps rushing along a narrow *calle*.

If horror tales of hair-raising prices are a deterrent, remember, this is a Jekyll and Hyde city: even the most expensive places will slash prices in the low season. Of course, peak times still pull in visitors in their thronging millions. As well as summer, Carnevale, big regattas, Biennale events and important religious festivities including Christmas and Easter will push up prices. Outside of these times, you'll find that the Lagoon City is refreshingly quiet and relatively cheap – to sleep in, at least.

THE SCENE

Venice's accommodation sector continues to change and expand. Some of this is retrenching: at the **Gritti Palace** (*see p265*), a massive revamp has reduced the number of rooms, but ramped up the luxury quotient still further. Across on the Lido, the historic **Excelsior** (*see p278*) has done some serious tweaking, and in 2014 inaugurated the lagoon's largest suite.

Small continues to be beautiful, and the march of the chic B&B shows no signs of slowing (*see p272* **Bed & Breakfast**). But off-piste locations are also proving popular, with some of the most uncharacteristic out on the islands of the lagoon (*see p278-79*).

OUR CATEGORIES

Because Venice is a city of immense accommodation price swings (*see p268* **Seasonal Variations**), placing hotels under category headings is as difficult as it is misleading.

As a general rule of thumb, 'Deluxe' means a double room in mid-season will start at €500 and stop at nothing; 'Expensive' means it will cost from €300 up to €500 per night; 'Moderate' means €150-€300, and 'Budget' will come in at below €150.

However, it really does pay to check hotel websites carefully, especially at peak times, and to book directly with the selected establishment. A room that costs €500 in high season might plummet to €150 in late November; and even mid-range options at around €200 will be on offer at €75 a night or less in the dog days.

ENQUIRE BEFORE YOU BOOK

In general room prices include breakfast, of wildly varying freshness and generosity. We have tried to indicate cases where it is not, as a rule, included, but if you want to avoid surprises, you are advised to ask when booking.

Reaching your hotel in this labyrinthine city can be a challenge. Ask for very clear directions, including the nearest vaporetto (ferry) stop or church, or GPS coordinates. If you have mobility problems and/or don't fancy dragging your suitcase over too many bridges with steps, ask whether your hotel of choice has a *porta d'acqua* (canal-side entrance) where a water taxi can pull right up to reception.

Facilities for the disabled are scarce in Venetian hotels, partly due to the nature of the buildings. Many establishments spread over several floors but do not have lifts; always check first. *See p283* for information on disabled travel in Venice.

Most hotels will charge more for rooms with canal or lagoon views. As some canals are muddy backwaters, and others are major highways with a constant procession of bellowing gondoliers (not good for light sleepers), it pays to ask exactly what this water view consists of.

SAN MARCO
Deluxe

Bauers Hotels
San Marco 1459, campo San Moisè (041 520 7022, www.bauerhotels.com). Vaporetto San Marco Vallaresso. **Rooms** 210. **Map** p309 H8.
This is a hotel of many parts. The main block – Bauers L'Hotel – occupies a 1940s extension of the original 18th-century hotel building; though the place is brutal outside, the vast hall inside with its marble, gold and black looks like a grand old ocean liner. Luxurious, antique Il Palazzo is housed in an older building and has Grand Canal frontage. Adjacent to the L'Hotel, Casanova has a series of comfortable, sunny serviced apartments. Though the whole place oozes pampered luxury in a grand, Grand Canal style, Il Palazzo's discreet opulence is perhaps the best bet. The Bauers empire extends across the water to the Giudecca, where accommodation options back on to a gorgeous garden (*see p278* Palladio Spa & Villa F).

Gritti Palace
San Marco 2467, campo Santa Maria del Giglio (041 794 611, www.thegrittipalace.com). Vaporetto Giglio. **Rooms** 82. **Map** p309 G8.
With much fanfare, the Gritti Palace reopened in 2013 after a massive makeover that reduced the number of rooms and suites but upped the already considerable luxury quotient, while adding some handy 21st-century conveniences such as a state-of-the-art concrete lining for the ground floor, so that guests checking in during *acqua alta* (high water) will no longer have to do so with the lagoon lapping around their knees. The air of old-world charm and nobility about this 15th-century palazzo now feels fresher, with superb Rubelli fabrics (*see also p57* **Material Makers**) replacing fittings that had become frayed over the decades, and every piece of antique furniture restored and polished. Refined and opulent, adorned with luscious bathroom treats and fresh flowers, each room is uniquely decorated; one is lined with antique floor-to-ceiling mirrors. If you want a canal or campo view, specify when booking: some rooms overlook a dingy courtyard. Breakfast, or just an aperitivo on the vast canal terrace, is an experience in itself.

Luna Hotel Baglioni
San Marco 1243, calle larga dell'Ascensione (041 528 9840, www.baglionihotels.com).

TAXING TOURISTS
Where does the money go?

In 2011 Venice's council decided to inject a little more cash into city coffers by imposing an *imposta di soggiorno* – a levy on tourists visiting *La Serenissima*. If the imposition seemed harsh, the aim appeared noble: the income, it was said, would be used to maintain and restore monuments and sights, and improve the quality of services for the tourist trade.

The tax varies according to a hotel's star rating and the time of year. As this guide went to press, the February-November rate ranged from €1 to €5 per person per night; in December and January it fell to 70c-€3.50.

For travellers who are unaware of the levy, checkout can come as an unpleasant shock: the tax is payable at your hotel, at the end of your stay, over and above your hotel fees, in cash. It is levied for a maximum five days, however long your visit; under-tens visit free.

In 2013 the *imposta di soggiorno* netted Venice around €24 million. But city hall's interpretation of 'upkeep and services' was loose, to say the least. Under the heading 'Tourism' came €8 million for the municipal police, for patrolling areas frequented by tourists – arguably, the whole city; and €1.35 million for improving Wi-Fi services. Under the heading 'Upkeep of cultural and environmental heritage' was €4.6 million for cinema productions and €5.8 million for maintenance of parks and gardens... in a city where visitors struggle to find a single tree for a little summer shade.

ESSENTIAL INFORMATION

Police on patrol.

Vaporetto San Marco Vallaresso. **Rooms** 104.
Breakfast €40. **Map** p309 H8.

In a 15th-century palazzo, this hotel has little remaining period decor, with the exception of the original frescoes and stucco decorations in the conference room. Elsewhere, kilometres of shiny marble, swathes of rich fabric and lots of Murano glass provide the backdrop for luxurious bedrooms and communal areas. Views from the rooms are of the Giardinetti Reali, the lagoon and San Giorgio Maggiore.

Expensive

AD Place

*San Marco 2557A, fondamenta della Fenice
(041 241 3234, www.adplacevenice.con).
Vaporetto Giglio.* **Rooms** 12 + 1 loft apartment.
Map p309 G8.

Tucked away on a quiet canal behind the La Fenice opera house, AD Place mixes a friendly atmosphere with great service in bedrooms and public spaces which revel in a wild combination of candy-stripe colours and baroque touches. Rooms (spread over four floors with no lift) vary in size: some of the standard rooms are fairly small but the top floor suite with its canopied bed in the master bedroom is suitable for families, as is a ground-floor room that is wheelchair-adapted. The hotel's private water entrance means you can get straight here by water taxi. The glorious roof terrace is a great place to watch the sun set. AD Place has recently added a similarly multicoloured self-catering loft apartment in a nearby palazzo to its repertoire. In low season, the hotel slips into the moderate category.

Corte di Gabriela

San Marco 3836, calle degli Avvocati (041 523 5077, www.cortedigabriela.com). Vaporetto Sant'Angelo. **Rooms** 10. **Map** p309 F7.

This recent addition to the Venetian hotel scene marries classic Venetian frescoes and stucco with some *molto*-mod design details to produce a very stylish four-star boutique handily placed in a quiet street near campo Santo Stefano (*see p65*). Obliging, well informed staff preside over a pretty courtyard and a warmly red living room complete with grand piano and a little bar. Spacious bedrooms come with iPads and kettles; the bathrooms are large and chic. The breakfast is a rich feast of home-baked goodies. This hotel is towards the lower end of this price range.

Hotel Monaco & Grand Canal

San Marco 1332, calle Vallaresso (041 520 0211, www.hotelmonaco.it). Vaporetto San Marco Vallaresso. **Rooms** 100. **Map** p309 H8.

This Grand Canal classic is a curious hybrid. The lobby and bar area is a fussy mix of classic and modern, the rooms in the main building are untouched by the design revolution, while those on the Grand Canal are ultra-traditional Venetian. More *charmant* is the Palazzo Selvadego residence: no lagoon views, but

Ca' del Nobile.

its rooms are done out in a modern Mediterranean style. Even if you're not staying here, pop in for a look at the extraordinary Teatro Ridotto, a 17th-century jewel that was Venice's first gambling hall.

Palazzo Sant'Angelo sul Canal Grande
San Marco 3878B, fondamenta del Teatro a Sant'Angelo (041 241 1452, www.palazzosant angelo.com). Vaporetto Sant'Angelo. **Rooms** 26. **Map** p309 F7.
While it enjoys a superb location on the Grand Canal and luxurious facilities, Palazzo Sant'Angelo is rather lacking in soul. The red and gold bedrooms are traditional in style; all have whirlpool baths, fine bed linen, fluffy robes and slippers. Rooms overlooking the Grand Canal cost extra; instead, watch the gondolas drift by from the sitting room and bar area.

Saturnia & International
San Marco 2398, via XXII Marzo (041 520 8377, www.hotelsaturnia.it). Vaporetto San Marco Vallaresso. **Rooms** 93. **Map** p309 G8
An old-fashioned, friendly air pervades this bustling hotel. The 14th-century building's interior has been done up in a delightfully eclectic faux-Renaissance style. The bedrooms vary considerably: most are in traditional Venetian style, but a handful have been given a more contemporary makeover in the retro style of sister hotel Ca' Pisani (*see p276*). The roof terrace has a view of Santa Maria della Salute.

Moderate

★ Ca' del Nobile
San Marco 987, rio terà delle Colonne (041 528 3473, www.cadelnobile.com). Vaporetto Rialto. **Rooms** 6. **Map** p309 H7.
The last five years have seen a rash of six-room locandas with near-identical websites opening in Venice, but this compact charmer has an edge on the competition. It's two minutes' walk from piazza San Marco, service is spot-on, there's free Wi-Fi and the warm classic-contemporary decor is a cut above the usual cookie-cutter Casanova look.

Do Pozzi
San Marco 2373, via XXII Marzo (041 520 7855, www.hoteldopozzi.it). Vaporetto Giglio. **Rooms** 29. **Map** p309 G8.
This hotel has a homely, friendly feeling and is very appealing in spite of some rather cramped rooms and tiny bathrooms. Although it's situated very near piazza San Marco, it's down a little alleyway and off the main tourist track. In front of the hotel is a lovely courtyard with an ancient well in the middle where guests can eat breakfast or relax.

Flora
San Marco 2283A, calle Bergamaschi (041 520 5844, www.hotelflora.it). Vaporetto San Marco Vallaresso. **Rooms** 43. **Map** p309 G8.

> ### IN THE KNOW
> ## WHAT YOU WON'T GET
>
> By law Italian hotels cannot provide irons in rooms, though some will have an ironing room for guests' use, or will press clothes on request. The electric kettle is not a piece of equipment considered vital by Italians, and so won't feature in most hotel rooms. Except in more upmarket hotels, 'breakfast included' means a continental breakfast of tea/coffee, pastries and, if you're lucky, yoghurt and/or fruit: don't expect a full cooked meal.

Book well in advance if you want to stay at the perennially popular Flora. Situated at the bottom of a cul-de-sac near piazza San Marco, it offers a dreamy, tranquil stay in the palazzo adjacent to what's known as Desdemona's house. The decor in the bedrooms is classic Venetian, varying significantly from quite opulent to relatively spartan; some are tiny. There's a cosy bar and a delightful garden with wrought-iron tables and a fountain. The Flora prides itself on its child-friendly features, which include children's tea served daily, family rooms, babysitting on request and provision of all the paraphenalia – cots, pushchairs, changing tables and so on – that you might need if you're travelling with little ones.

Locanda Art Deco
San Marco 2966, calle delle Botteghe (041 277 0558, www.locandaartdeco.com). Vaporetto San Samuele or Sant'Angelo. **Rooms** 10. **Map** p309 F7.
This little hotel is situated off relaxed campo Santo Stefano. The welcoming entrance hall and the simple but stylish bedrooms are dotted with pieces of 1930s and '40s furniture, and other deco details. There's a tiny breakfast area tucked away on a mezzanine floor, and a second property – the Art Deco B&B – located nearby. The range of prices here is huge: in low season, this hotel is a good budget option.

★ Locanda Novecento
San Marco 2683-4, calle del Dose (041 241 3765, www.novecento.biz). Vaporetto Giglio. **Rooms** 9. **Map** p309 F8.
This home-from-home is a real pleasure to come back to after a hard day's sightseeing, especially when it's warm enough to relax in the delightful little garden. With its friendly, helpful staff, and reading and sitting rooms, Novecento is a very special place to stay. Wooden floors, ethnic textiles, oriental rugs, Indonesian furniture and individually decorated rooms make a refreshing change from the ubiquitous pan-Venetian style. Art shows are regularly mounted in the public rooms.

★ Locanda Orseolo

San Marco 1083, corte Zorzi (041 520 4827, www.locandaorseolo.com). Vaporetto Rialto or San Marco Vallaresso. **Rooms** 15. **Map** p309 H7.
This wonderfully welcoming *locanda* has beamed ceilings, painted wood panelling, leaded windows and rich colours; there's even a tiny water entrance. The immaculate bedrooms are ranged over three floors (there's no lift) and are furnished in a fairly restrained Venetian style. Choose between a canal view (which can be noisy) or quieter rooms overlooking the square. Breakfast is exceptionally generous. The team who run the place bend over backwards to ensure their guests are happy. This delightful hotel is fiendishly difficult to find: go through the iron gate almost opposite the church in campo San Gallo, bear left into a smaller campo and you'll see the sign.

Budget

San Samuele

San Marco 3358, salizada San Samuele (041 522 8045, www.hotelsansamuele.it). Vaporetto San Samuele or Sant'Angelo. **Rooms** 10. **Map** p309 E7.
Flowers cascade from the window boxes of this delightful, friendly little hotel in an excellent loca-

tion. The spotlessly clean rooms have a simple, sunny aspect and the welcome from manager Judith is always warm. The San Samuele is several notches above most of its fellow one-star establishments, although both the single rooms and one of the doubles have bathrooms in the corridor, and walls are rather thin. There's free Wi-Fi throughout and Judith and her staff are always ready with well informed advice and recommendations. Plans are afoot to add further 'superior' rooms upstairs, all with air-con. San Samuele is very popular, so book well in advance. Breakfast is not included, though there's a coffee machine in reception for guests, and a fridge to keep your supplies in.

CASTELLO

Deluxe

★ Danieli

Castello 4196, riva degli Schiavoni (041 522 6480, www.danielihotelvenice.com). Vaporetto San Zaccaria. **Rooms** 215. **Map** p310 K8.
Whether or not you're staying at this Venetian classic, twirl through the revolving door for a look at the magnificent reception hall. The Danieli is split between an unprepossessing 1940s building and

---

SEASONAL VARIATIONS

Grab a bargain by visiting in low season.

Venice is expensive, there's no doubt about that. The exception – and at times it's a startling exception – to this rule is accommodation: flick through hotel websites for off-season rooms and you'll be amazed at the prices. Even the most expensive hotels will slash their prices to a small fraction of their high-season rates. The reason? There are simply too many beds in Venice for the city's winter doldrums.

For many decades, Venice was a sellers' market, a place where too many visitors fought over too few rooms, with the result that hoteliers could charge more or less what they wanted for accommodation – which ranged, in many cases, from plain shabby to unsalubrious in the extreme. Even the luxe end of the market wasn't forced to put on a particularly good show, and a trend was set for Venice charging much more for much less – a trend that extended well beyond hotels and, in other fields, continues to this day. Nowadays, however, Venice's accommodation scene is looking like a victim of its own success.

A desperate shortage of beds coupled with a desperate desire to cash in on mass tourism meant that the B&B revolution at the turn of the millennium was hailed as the only way forward. Between 2000 and 2007, the number of non-hotels with beds for hire rose an astonishing 890 per cent, though the small dimensions of most establishments (an average across this sector of 6.4 beds each) meant that pillows on which to rest your head had increased by a relatively 'modest' 251 per cent.

Not to be outdone, hotels were increasing and expanding too, with 20 per cent more hotels offering 26.5 per cent more beds over the same period. At the same time, many were revamping and upgrading, alarmed at the sudden surge in visitor interest for the cute and chic, the homely and welcoming, the touches of style and idiosyncracy.

The result for the visitor has been more choice, higher standards and a very noticeable drop in room prices, especially in low season when even top-rank hotels slash their prices.

the 14th-century Palazzo Dandolo: the former, however, has benefited from a makeover by designer Jacques Garcia. Ten rooms have terraces with lagoon views; all are sumptuously decorated with Rubelli and Fortuny fabrics, antiques and marble bathrooms. The renovation never progressed to the older building, where rooms are not always what you would expect from a hotel of this quality/price range. Views from the newly revamped rooftop restaurant – where chef Gian Nicola Colussi, formerly of London's Canary Wharf Hotel, now presides – are spectacular.

Londra Palace
Castello 4171, riva degli Schiavoni (041 520 0533, www.hotelondra.it). Vaporetto San Zaccaria. **Rooms** 53. **Map** p310 K7.
It's no wonder that Tchaikovsky found this hotel – with no fewer than 100 of its bedroom windows facing San Giorgio Maggiore across the lagoon – a congenial spot in which to write his fourth symphony in 1877. Today, the Londra Palace is elegant but restrained, offering traditional-style rooms furnished with antiques and paintings. You can sunbathe on the roof terrace or enjoy a romantic dinner at the restaurant where, in good weather, tables are laid out on the *riva*.

Metropole
Castello 4149, riva degli Schiavoni (041 520 5044, www.hotelmetropole.com). Vaporetto San Zaccaria. **Rooms** 67. **Map** p310 L8.
Of all the grand hotels that crowd this part of the *riva*, the Metropole is arguably the most characterful. Owner-manager Pierluigi Beggiato is a passionate collector, and his antiques and curios are dotted in the elegant and varied bedrooms and the sumptuous, spacious public rooms. In winter, tea and cakes are served in the velvet-draped *salone*; in summer, guests relax in the pretty garden to the sound of water trickling in the fountain. There are views over the lagoon (for a hefty supplement), the canal, or on to the garden. The hotel's Met restaurant, with a slew of young chefs boasting illustrious CVs in its kitchen, has one Michelin star and prices to match. Breakfast is not always included in the room rates: check your booking.

Expensive

Charming House i Qs
Castello 4425, campiello Querini Stampalia (041 241 0062, www.thecharminghouse.com). Vaporetto San Zaccaria. **Rooms** 4. **Map** p310 J6.
The latest addition to the Charming House boutique hotel group is as radical a design statement as you'll find in play-safe Venice. If it weren't for the charming, chandeliered *porta d'acqua* gondola entrance and the overhead beams, i Qs' four accommodation options (including a two-bedroom, self-catering apartment) could almost be in Milan or New York

Ca' Sagredo. *See p271.*

– though architect Mauro Mazzolini's warm but serious minimalism works well as an antidote to the city's frills and frippery. Be warned that the dark colours can make for a gloomy ambience; but in summer, this is a classy, cool refuge. Service is impeccable too.

Locanda Vivaldi
Castello 4150-2, riva degli Schiavoni (041 277 0477, www.locandavivaldi.it). Vaporetto San Zaccaria. **Rooms** 27. **Map** p310 L8
This luxurious hotel offers tasteful rooms with lashings of modern comforts. Located partly in the house where composer Antonio Vivaldi lived, and next to the church where he taught music (La Pietà; *see p87*), the Vivaldi offers views of the island of San Giorgio from the magnificent roof terrace – where breakfast is served in summer – and from the front bedrooms.

Savoia & Jolanda
Castello 4187, riva degli Schiavoni (041 520 6644, 041 522 4130, www.hotelsavoiajolanda. com). Vaporetto San Zaccaria. **Rooms** 51. **Map** p310 K7.
A hotel of two different but lovely halves, the Savoia offers rooms with balconies and views across the Bacino di San Marco to San Giorgio Maggiore in one direction, or facing back over Castello towards the glorious façade of San Zaccaria. The decor manages to be pleasantly luxurious without going over the top, and breakfast is a sumptuous spread.

Moderate

Casa Querini

Castello 4388, campo San Giovanni Novo (041 241 1294, www.locandaquerini.com). Vaporetto San Zaccaria. **Closed** Jan. **Rooms** 6. **Map** p310 J7.
This friendly hotel has a pretty little terrace area shaded by big umbrellas on a quiet square between bustling campo Santa Maria Formosa and St Mark's; breakfast is served here when the weather is fine. From a tiny reception area, stairs lead up to bedrooms pleasantly decorated in sober Venetian style; all are spacious, but try to secure one with a view of the square rather than the side alley.

Casa Verardo

Castello 4765, calle della Sacrestia (041 528 6138, www.casaverardo.it). Vaporetto San Zaccaria. **Rooms** 25. **Map** p310 K7.
Tucked away as it is at the end of a narrow *calle*, and across its own little bridge only a few minutes from piazza San Marco, the first impression of Casa Verardo is of cool and calm. Walls in the public areas are white and pale lemon while bedrooms are decorated in elegant, tasteful fabrics. There's a pretty courtyard at the back of the building and a terrace off the elegant salon where tables are laid for breakfast. The level of comfort and facilities is above what you might expect at these prices.

Locanda La Corte

Castello 6317, calle Bressana (041 241 1300, www.locandalacorte.it). Vaporetto Fondamente Nove. **Rooms** 16. **Map** p310 K5.
Housed by a narrow canal in a small 16th-century palazzo down the side of the church of Santi Giovanni e Paolo, La Corte is far from the noisy tourist trails. Bedrooms are decorated in restful greens or striking russets and there is a lovely little

courtyard where breakfast is served in summer. There's a bar, too, so you can wind down after a hard day's sightseeing with an *aperitivo*.

La Residenza

Castello 3608, campo Bandiera e Moro (041 528 5315, www.venicelaresidenza.com). Vaporetto Arsenale. **Rooms** 14. **Map** p310 L7
Occupying the first and second floors of a grand if rather faded Gothic palazzo, La Residenza possesses a genteel old-fashioned air and offers good value for money. Though there's a slightly frayed feeling to the reasonably large bedrooms, the vast salon is rather fine, with splendid stucco decoration. Bedrooms 221 and 228 overlook the pretty *campo*. The hotel has the feeling of being far from the crowds, but it is actually within easy walking distance of San Marco.

Budget

B&B San Marco

Castello 3385L, fondamenta San Giorgio degli Schiavoni (041 522 7589, 335 756 6555, www.realvenice.it/smarco). Vaporetto San Zaccaria. **Closed** Jan; 2wks Aug. **Rooms** 3. **Map** p310 L7.
One of the few Venetian B&Bs that come close to the British concept of the genre, Marco Scurati's homely apartment lies just behind San Giorgio degli Schiavoni. Two of the three cosy, antique-filled bedrooms share a bathroom; the other is en-suite. There's also an apartment that sleeps four. Marco and his wife Alice serve breakfast in their own kitchen and guests are treated as part of the family.

Bed & Venice – Casa per Ferie

Castello 3701, calle della Pietà (041 244 3639, www.bedandvenice.it). Vaporetto San Zaccaria. **Rooms** 15. **No credit cards. Map** p310 L7.
The building that houses this clean, bright hostel is part of the sprawling Pietà complex, which once housed the part of the girls' school where Vivaldi taught. It's spacious, sunny and spotlessly clean, with around 40 beds; there are a couple of singles and six doubles, while the rest are dormitory rooms sleeping up to six. None have private baths. Families with children are particularly welcome, and the hostel can provide cots and other baby equipment. The rooms occupy the top two floors of the building, so there are some great views, especially from the terrace at the top.

Ca' del Dose

Castello 3801, calle del Dose (041 520 9887, www.cadeldose.com). Vaporetto Arsenale or San Zaccaria. **Rooms** 6. **Map** p310 L7.
This friendly guesthouse, on a quiet *calle* off the busy riva degli Schiavoni, has simple rooms on three floors (without a lift). If you book ahead, you may be able to secure the one at the top with a fabulous little

roof terrace; there is no extra charge. In the morning, the means for a simple breakfast are supplied in the rooms and you can order fresh croissants. Note that the hotel also offers accommodation – rooms and apartments – off the main premises: some of these are of very dubious quality. This is one of the few hotels in Venice that still charges for Wi-Fi.

CANNAREGIO

Deluxe

Ca' Sagredo
Cannaregio 4198, campo Santa Sofia (041 241 3111, www.casagredohotel.com). Vaporetto Ca' d'Oro. **Rooms** 42. **Map** p307 G4.
This Grand Canal palazzo dating from the 15th century is as much a museum as a hotel, with a magnificent double staircase, a huge rococo ballroom and frescoes by Giambattista Tiepolo among its many treasures. There are six stunning historic suites (including one inside a library where Galileo once worked), and rooms in which decor is standard luxe-Venetian, albeit of the bright, light-filled sort. Service is mostly charming, especially at breakfast, where there's an impressive spread. *Photo p269.*

Expensive

★ Al Ponte Antico
Cannaregio 5768, calle dell'Aseo (041 241 1944, www.alponteantico.com). Vaporetto Rialto. **Rooms** 7. **Map** p310 H5.

With its padded reception desk, festooned curtains and lashings of brocade in public spaces and most of the bedrooms, the family-run Al Ponte Antico takes the traditional Venetian hotel decor idiom and turns it into something over-the-top, Louis Quinze-ish and faintly decadent: a pleasant change from the prudish norm. In a 16th-century palazzo on the Grand Canal, with views over the Rialto bridge, Al Ponte Antico's exquisite little balcony overlooks the water, as do some doubles and suites. Owner-manager Matteo Peruch will make you feel totally at home from the moment you arrive; the breakfasts here are famous and feted.

★ Palazzo Abadessa
Cannaregio 4011, calle Priuli (041 241 3784, www.abadessa.com). Vaporetto Ca' d'Oro. **Rooms** 15. **Map** p307 H4.
A beautiful shady walled garden is laid out in front of this 16th-century palazzo, which is filled with antiques, paintings and silver and where the prevailing atmosphere is that of an aristocratic private home (which it is), restored and opened to guests. Service is charming but discreet. A magnificent double stone staircase leads to the impressive bedrooms, all of which are beautifully appointed with richly coloured brocade-covered walls, and some of which are truly vast. Beware, however: the three low-ceilinged doubles on the mezzanine floor are rather cramped. Bathrooms tend to be on the cramped side. In low season, prices at this lovely place fall into the affordable end of the 'moderate' category, especially if you book ahead.

Palazzo Abadessa.

BED & BREAKFAST
The best B&B options.

Residenza de l'Osmarin.

Venice's huge supply of B&Bs varies from spartan squats to rooms in glorious antiques-filled *palazzi*, with an equally wide range of prices reflecting location and facilities.

In addition to the cosy **B&B San Marco** (*see p270*) and the charming **Campiello Zen** (*see p274*), a few other places are worth considering. A pretty plant-filled courtyard with a well is the main draw of **Corte 1321** (San Polo 1321, campiello Ca' Bernardi, 041 522 4923, www.corte 1321.com), a three-room ethno-chic B&B. The welcome from hosts Maria and Rodolfo makes **Residenza de l'Osmarin** (Castello 4960, calle Rota, 347 450 1440, www.residenzadelosmarin.com) a hit, and you'll need to book well in advance to bag one of the pretty airy rooms – especially the huge top-floor suite. Similarly, it's Lorenzo's personal touch that gives **B&B Ai Tagliapietra** (Castello 4943, salizada Zorzi, 347 323 3166, www.aitagliapietra.com) its edge: but the three comfortable rooms also come with all the advice and help you need, at a reasonable price.

The handy www.bed-and-breakfast.it website has many more Venice options.

B&B Ai Tagliapietra.

Moderate

Ca' Dogaressa
Cannaregio 1018, calle del Sotoportego Scuro (041 275 9441, www.cadogaressa.com). Vaporetto Guglie or Tre Archi. **Rooms** 9. **Map** p306 C2.
This wonderfully welcoming, family-run hotel overlooking the Cannaregio canal offers a modern take on 'traditional' Venetian accommodation decor: the Murano glass light fittings and brocade-covered walls are there, but so are neat marble bathrooms, very comfortable beds and air-con. Breakfast is served at tables along the canalside on fine days. There's also a roof terrace with fantastic views.

Domus Orsoni
Cannaregio 1045, sottoportego dei Vedei (041 275 9538, www.domusorsoni.it). Vaporetto Guglie or Crea. **Rooms** 5. **Map** p306 C2.
The Orsoni dynasty has been producing glass in its foundry attached to this charming B&B for generations, and their magnificent wares decorate floors and walls here in richly coloured mosaics. Many guests stay here while attending mosaic-making courses at the foundry. The five rooms (including one single) are large, airy and uncluttered, with great bathrooms; some look out over the property's beautiful garden. Breakfast is served on a pleasant terrace in fine weather. Hosts Valentina and Flavio are always on hand with help and advice, and on request will take you on a tour of the fascinating foundry – the only one allowed to remain in Venice after 1291 when the others were dismissed to Murano as a precaution against devastating fires. At quieter times of year, this is a budget option.

Giorgione
Cannaregio 4587, calle larga dei Proverbi (041 522 5810, www.hotelgiorgione.com). Vaporetto Ca' d'Oro. **Rooms** 76. **Map** p307 H4.
Just off the busy campo Santi Apostoli, the Giorgione exudes warmth. A 15th-century palazzo joins the newer extension around a flower-filled courtyard with a lily pond (a rather less picturesque salt-water whirlpool tub was also planned for this space). Some split-level rooms have terraces overlooking the rooftops.

Locanda del Ghetto
Cannaregio 2892-3, campo del Ghetto Nuovo (041 275 9292, www.locandadelghetto.net). Vaporetto Guglie or San Marcuola. **Rooms** 6. **Map** p307 E2.
The building that houses this guesthouse dates from the 15th century, and several rooms still retain the original decorated wooden ceilings. Upstairs, the light and airy bedrooms are all done out with pale cream walls, honey-coloured parquet floors and pale gold bedcovers; two of them have small terraces on the campo side. A rather sparse kosher breakfast is served in the ground-floor dining room, which overlooks a canal.

Ca' Nigra Lagoon Resort.

Locanda ai Santi Apostoli

Cannaregio 4391A, strada Nuova (041 521 2612, www.locandasantiapostoli.com). Vaporetto Ca' d'Oro. **Rooms** 11. **Map** p307 H5.

A pair of handsome dark green doors lead through the courtyard of this palazzo facing on to the Grand Canal, where a lift sweeps you up to the third floor. The hotel feels like a genteel private apartment and the bedrooms are individually decorated. The two best rooms overlook the canal; book well ahead and be prepared to pay extra. A comfortable sitting room, filled with antiques and books, overlooks the water. A very good-value family suite sleeps four.

Budget

Rossi

Cannaregio 262, calle delle Procuratie (041 715 164, www.hotelrossi.ve.it). Vaporetto Ferrovia. **Rooms** 14. **Map** p306 D3.

Located at the end of a quiet alley, this cheap one-star is quite a find for the area around the railway station (which, as a rule, is best avoided), with no bridges to cross between station and hotel. The very basic rooms are acceptably clean and all have air-con. Five rooms have shared bathrooms.

SAN POLO & SANTA CROCE

Deluxe

Aman Grand Canal Venice

Santa Polo 1364, calle Tiepolo Baiamonte (041 270 7333, www.amanresorts.com). Vaporetto San Silvestro. **Rooms** 24. **Map** p307 F6.

Aman's Venetian outpost – opened in 2013 – is exactly what you'd expect of this Far Eastern hotel group: utter luxury, immaculate service and

exceptional style. The hotel is housed in palazzo Papadopoli (not to be confused with Sofitel's Papadopoli hotel, *see below*), the only building on the Grand Canal with two private gardens; the count-owner of the palazzo still lives on the top floor and often sweeps in to lend an aristocratic Venetian air – which is just as well because one complaint that could be levelled at the hotel is that it's much like any Aman hostelry anywhere in the world. The restaurant serves Italian and Asian cuisine. The bedrooms and suites are exercises in pared-back luxury: one has frescoes by GB Tiepolo; another has a magnificent fireplace designed by Sansovino.

Expensive

Ca' Nigra Lagoon Resort

Santa Croce 927, campo San Simeon Grande (041 275 0047, www.hotelcanigra.com). **Rooms** 22. **Map** p306 D4.

Ca' Nigra is a classy little hotel with a fantastic position on the Grand Canal, in a 17th-century villa painted deep red and set in a beautiful waterside garden. Public spaces and the spacious junior suites are done out with interesting antique oriental pieces; the reception area is all glass, chrome and down lighting, while the *piano nobile* has partially retained the period decor. Ultra-contemporary bathrooms are particularly impressive. Pick of the bedrooms is the Loggia Suite with its private terrace; light sleepers should avoid ground-floor rooms close to the breakfast room. Guests arriving by water disembark at the hotel's private dock.

MGallery Papadopoli

Santa Croce 245, Giardini Papadopoli (041 710 4004, www.mgallery.com). Vaporetto Piazzale Roma. **Rooms** 96. **Map** p306 C5.

Well placed for piazzale Roma and the railway station, this hotel somehow avoids the total anonymity that chains such as owners Accor-Sofitel often serve up. Rooms at the front of the modern building overlook a canal and bustling campo Tolentini; those on the top floors have stunning views. There is an elegant cocktail bar, and a restaurant housed in a plant-lined winter garden where breakfast is also served.

San Cassiano – Ca' Favretto

Santa Croce 2232, calle de la Rosa (041 524 1768, www.sancassiano.it). Vaporetto San Stae. **Rooms** 35. **Map** p307 G4.
In a 14th-century Gothic building on the Grand Canal, the San Cassiano has its own private jetty, but if you're arriving on foot, get good directions as the hotel is difficult to find. Rooms are, on the whole, quite elegant, though some are showing their age. The airy breakfast room has huge windows overlooking the canal and there is a tiny but charming veranda right on the water – a great spot for an early evening *spritz*. Staff are friendly and welcoming, but there's a charge for Wi-Fi and the three flights of steps (no lift) can be daunting for some.

Moderate

Ai Due Fanali

Santa Croce 946, campo San Simeon Grande (041 718 490, www.aiduefanali.com). Vaporetto Riva di Biasio or Ferrovia. **Rooms** 16. **Map** p306 D4.
Housed in what was once the annexe of the church of San Simeon Grande, this neat little hotel faces the Grand Canal across a pretty, quiet campo. On a terrace at the front, tables are set out under big white umbrellas; there's also a rooftop breakfast room and *altana* (roof terrace). The reception area has antiques, oriental rugs and fresh flowers, and the 16 smallish bedrooms have painted bedheads, a refreshing lack of brocade and good modern bathrooms.

★ Al Ponte Mocenigo

Santa Croce 2063, fondamenta Rimpetto Mocenigo (041 524 4797, www.alpontemocenigo.com). Vaporetto San Stae. **Rooms** 18. **Map** p307 F4.
A delightful hotel across its own little bridge on a quiet canal near campo San Stae, this has to be one of Venice's best-value accommodation options. It has tastefully decorated mod-Venetian rooms – some in a luscious shade of deep red, others in rich gold – and well-appointed bathrooms, not to mention Wi-Fi access throughout, a bar, a Turkish bath, a pretty courtyard garden and genuinely charming owners – Walter and Sandro – who manage to be warm and laid-back in just the right ratio. Just round the corner, the eight-room annexe has similarly decorated accommodation – many regulars love this, though it does not have the advantage of a lovely courtyard and other amenities right downstairs. This hotel is at the less expensive end of the moderate price range, becoming remarkably budget in low season.

Campiello Zen

Santa Croce 1285, rio terà di Biasio (041 710 431, www.campiellozen.com). Vaporetto Riva di Biasio. **Rooms** 3. **Map** p306 D4.
This three-room charmer is in a quiet, untouristy spot but handy for the Riva San Biasio vaporetto stop, for some very good restaurants and for the railway station. More importantly, it offers a welcome that will make you feel like part of the family and endless excellent advice from host Andrea who will plot itineraries and organise restaurant bookings and generally make sure that your Venice experience is a special one. The rooms are carefully and tastefully decorated: one is on the ground floor and the others are up two flights of stairs (no lift). Breakfast is a sumptuous spread.

Locanda Marinella

Santa Croce 345, rio terà dei Pensieri (041 275 9457, www.locandamarinella.com). Vaporetto Piazzale Roma. **Rooms** 6. **Map** p306 B6.
On a tree-lined street near piazzale Roma, the Locanda Marinella offers stylish, comfortable rooms done out in pale yellow and blue. A tiny garden at the back is shaded by white umbrellas. This is a good choice for those with late arrivals or early departures, and is much favoured by people overnighting in the city before or after cruises. Two smart little apartments sleep four to five people.

La Villeggiatura.

ESSENTIAL INFORMATION

Locanda Sturion
San Polo 679, calle dello Sturion (041 523 6243, www.locandasturion.com). Vaporetto Rialto Mercato or San Silvestro. **Rooms** 11. **Map** p307 G6.
Established in the late 13th century by the doge as an inn for visiting merchants, this hotel is still thriving – not surprising, given its Grand Canal location. Only two of the rooms overlook the canal (rooms one and two; the others give on to a quiet *calle*), but even if you decide you can't afford the view, you can enjoy it from the breakfast room. It's a long haul up steep stairs, and there's no lift. Staff can be terse.

★ Oltre il Giardino
San Polo 2542, fondamenta Contarini (041 275 0015, www.oltreilgiardino-venezia.com). Vaporetto San Tomà. **Rooms** 6 + 2. **Map** p307 E6.
Tucked away at the end of a fondamenta and accessed through a *giardino* (garden), this attractive villa was once owned by Alma Mahler, widow of the composer Gustav. Today host Lorenzo Muner welcomes guests to this stylish yet homely hotel. Going against the deep-hued, brocaded Venetian grain, Oltre il Giardino's neutral shades and wood floors provide the backdrop for a mix of antique furniture, contemporary objets and unexpected splashes. Subtly colour-themed bedrooms vary considerably in size. All are equipped with LCD TVs, robes, slippers and luxurious bath goodies. In the palazzo next door, two large suites offer the same stylish amenities and are great for groups or families.

★ La Villeggiatura
San Polo 1569, calle dei Botteri (338 853 1264 mobile/041 524 4673, www.lavilleggiatura.it). Vaporetto Rialto Mercato or San Silvestro. **Rooms** 6. **Map** p307 G5.
A scruffy entranceway and a steep climb (there's no lift) lead to Francesca Adilardi's charming third-floor apartment, which has six tastefully decorated bedrooms, each with its own character and all spacious and bright. Thai silks are draped over the generous-sized beds and at the windows of the subtly themed rooms, two of which have lovely old parquet floors. Windows in the two loft rooms are ceiling lights: bright, but offering views of nothing but the sky. There are electric kettles with tea and infusions in each room. Breakfast is served around a big table in the sunny dining area.

Budget

★ Casa Peron
Santa Croce 84, salizada San Pantalon (041 710 021, www.casaperon.com). Vaporetto San Tomà. **Closed** Jan. **Rooms** 11. **Map** p306 D6.
Casa Peron is an excellent budget choice. The friendly Scarpa family and their parrot Pierino preside over the very simple, very clean hotel. It's located in the bustling university area, with the

IN THE KNOW
LOCATING LOCATING

Even old Venice hands get lost in the city. Make sure you obtain very detailed directions before you arrive: ask your hotel for the nearest vaporetto stop, easily identifiable campo (square) and/or landmark (such as a church). Alternatively, you'll need an excellent map and a fiendishly good sense of direction.

shops, restaurants and bars of campo Santa Margherita nearby. Two rooms at the top of the house have private terraces; all have showers, though four are without toilets.

Salieri
Santa Croce 160, fondamenta Minotto (041 710 035, www.hotelsalieri.com). Vaporetto Ferrovia or Piazzale Roma. **Rooms** 10. **Map** p306 C6.
This simple one-star located between the railway station and piazzale Roma offers ten smartish bedrooms on three floors. Unusually for a hotel of this category, all have bathrooms, air-con, TV and free Wi-Fi. Some rooms look over a canal; others have garden or rooftop views.

DORSODURO
Expensive

Accademia – Villa Maravege
Dorsoduro 1058, fondamenta Bollani (041 521 0188, www.pensioneaccademia.it). Vaporetto Accademia. **Rooms** 27. **Map** p308 D8.
This wonderful secluded 17th-century villa used to be the Russian embassy; it's perennially popular with visitors seeking comfortable pensione-style accommodation within easy reach of Dorsoduro's galleries but also handy for more central sights. Located at the junction of the Toletta and Trovaso canals with the Canal Grande, it has a wonderful waterside patio where a generous breakfast buffet is served, as well as a grassy rear garden. The rooms are stylish, if fairly traditional, with antiques and marble or wood floors.

American – Dinesen
Dorsoduro 628, fondamenta Bragadin (041 520 4733, www.hotelamerican.com). Vaporetto Accademia. **Rooms** 30. **Map** p309 E9.
The pleasant American is a well-run and popular hotel with friendly service. Set on the delightful rio di San Vio, its generally spacious rooms are decorated in antique Venetian style; some have balconies with bright geraniums and look over the canal. Try to secure one of the corner rooms where multiple French windows make for wonderful light. There's a tiny

La Calcina.

terrace where breakfast is served under a pergola. In low season, rooms here are remarkably inexpensive.

Ca' Maria Adele
Dorsoduro 111, rio terà dei Catecumeni (041 520 3078, www.camariaadele.it). Vaporetto Salute. **Rooms** 12. **Map** p309 G9.

Situated in the shadow of the basilica of Santa Maria della Salute, Ca' Maria Adele marries sumptuous 18th-century Venetian decadence to modern design with some Moorish elements and a host of quirky tongue-in-cheek details thrown in. Brothers Alessio and Nicola Campa preside attentively over 12 luxurious bedrooms, five of which are themed; the red and gold Doge's Room is voluptuous, the Sala Noire ultra-sexy. There's an intimate sitting room on the ground floor with chocolate brown faux-fur on the walls and black pony-skin sofas, plus a Moroccan-style roof terrace for sultry evenings. Breakfast can be consumed in bed or in any of the hotel's public spaces. Service is deft but discreet.

Ca' Pisani
Dorsoduro 979A, rio Terà Foscarini (041 277 1478, www.capisanihotel.it). Vaporetto Accademia. **Rooms** 29. **Map** p309 E9.

Ca' Pisani's luxurious, designer-chic rooms done out in art deco style make a refreshing change from the usual fare of brocade, gilt and Murano glass; this was the first hotel to throw off the yawn-making pan-Venetian style, and though it's no longer the only one, it's still one of the most effective. Bedrooms are all generously sized and there's a restaurant with tables outside in the summer, a sauna and a roof terrace. The hotel is conveniently located right behind the Accademia gallery (*see p145*).

DD 724
Dorsoduro 724, ramo da Mula (041 277 0262, www.dd724.com). Vaporetto Accademia. **Rooms** 7. **Map** p309 F9.

Off a gated cul-de-sac (there is a sign, but it's easy to miss), DD 724 is a design hotel in miniature. The bedrooms are stylishly understated in pale shades and dark wood, with contemporary artworks from the owner's collection dotted around; one has a little terrace. Bathrooms in pale travertine are tiny but super-modern with walk-in showers. Public spaces (and some bedrooms) are cramped, though, and the atmosphere isn't exactly warm. A recent annexe, DD 694, is located two minutes' walk away at Dorsoduro 694 and has three similarly stylish rooms.

Palazzo Stern
Dorsoduro 2792, calle del Traghetto (041 277 0869, www.palazzostern.com). Vaporetto Ca' Rezzonico. **Rooms** 24. **Map** p308 D8.

Built in the early 20th century in eclectic pastiche style, Palazzo Stern is now home to this elegant hotel. A magnificent wooden staircase leads up to rooms done out in classic Venetian style in pale shades. Pricier rooms have views over the Grand Canal but the standard doubles at the back overlook a lovely garden. On the rooftop terrace is a jacuzzi. A wonderful breakfast terrace overlooks the canal.

Moderate

Agli Alboretti
Dorsoduro 884, rio terà Foscarini (041 523 0058, www.aglialboretti.com). Vaporetto Accademia. **Closed** 3wks Jan. **Rooms** 23. **Map** p309 E9.

The model ship in the window of the tiny, wood-panelled reception area of this friendly hotel lends a nautical air to the place. The simply decorated rooms are comfortable and well equipped, though some are truly tiny. Each has an electric kettle for tea and coffee. There is a pretty, pergola-covered terrace at the back of the hotel where meals are served in summer. The staff are exceptionally helpful. A fully equipped three-bed apartment is also available.

La Calcina

Dorsoduro 780, fondamenta delle Zattere (041 520 6466, www.lacalcina.com). Vaporetto Accademia or Zattere. **Rooms** 29. **Map** p309 E9.

La Calcina is a perennial favourite – Victorian critic John Ruskin opted to stay here – but remains great value at quieter moments. The open vistas of the Giudecca canal provide the backdrop for meals taken on the terrace of this hotel, a view shared by the bedrooms at the front of the building. With an air of civilised calm, La Calcina is one of the best value hotels in its category. Rooms have parquet floors, 19th-century furniture and a refreshingly uncluttered feel; one single is without private bath. There is an *altana* (suspended roof terrace), and a number of suites and self-catering apartments are available in adjacent buildings.

★ Ca' Zose

Dorsoduro 193B, calle del Bastion (041 522 6635, www.hotelcazose.com). Vaporetto Salute. **Rooms** 12. **Map** p309 F9.

The enthusiastic Campanati sisters run this immaculate little guesthouse. There's a tiny, neat breakfast room off the cool white reception area; upstairs, the dozen bedrooms are done out in a fairly restrained traditional Venetian style with painted furniture.

Locanda San Barnaba

Dorsoduro 2785-6, calle del Traghetto (041 241 1233, www.locanda-sanbarnaba.com). Vaporetto Ca' Rezzonico. **Rooms** 13. **Map** p308 D8.

Situated at the end of a quiet alleyway, the friendly San Barnaba has 13 comfortable, individually decorated rooms featuring a mix of antique furniture and elegant fabrics, and extremely helpful staff. There's a pretty little courtyard and a roof terrace, and no bridges to cross to get to the nearest vaporetto. Besides the regular boat services, the airport boats also stop here. Note though that there's no lift in the hotel.

Palazzetto da Schio

Dorsoduro 316B, fondamenta Soranzo (041 523 7937, www.palazzettodaschio.it). Vaporetto Salute or Zattere. **Apartments** 4. **No credit cards**. **Map** p309 F9.

The gracious antique-packed family home of Contessa Anna da Schio has been divided into four superb apartments, sleeping between two and six people. The *contessa* is absolutely hands-on, helping all her guests to get the very best out of her city. All the apartments have been restored recently, and fitted out with smart modern fully equipped kitchens, and well appointed bathrooms. Two look over the little canal out front, the others over the little garden and the rooftops of Dorsoduro. The Peggy Guggenheim Collection and Accademia gallery are a short stroll away.

Budget

Antica Locanda Montin

Dorsoduro 1147, fondamenta di Borgo (041 522 7151, www.locandamontin.com). Vaporetto Accademia or Zattere. **Rooms** 12. **Map** p308 D8.

It's difficult to get a booking in this funny little *locanda*, which overlooks a delightful canal. It owes its popularity to the fact that it is also home to one of Venice's most famous – though very overrated – restaurants. Rooms house an eccentric mix of old and new furniture, but the overall feeling is homely and cosy. Only half have private bathrooms.

★ Ca' Foscari

Dorsoduro 3887B, calle della Frescada (041 710 401, www.locandacafoscari.com). Vaporetto San Tomà. **Rooms** 11. **Map** p308 D7.

The Scarpa family has been offering a friendly welcome to guests at this *locanda* since the 1960s. The rooms – some of which could do with a makeover – are on the second and third floors of the building (no lift); they are spotlessly clean. The quietest of them have views over neighbouring gardens while others face the street; not all have private bathrooms.

Silk Road

Dorsoduro 1420E, calle Cortelogo (388 119 6816, www.silkroadhostel.com). Vaporetto San Basilio. **Rooms** 3 (2 dorms, 1 double). **Map** p308 C9.

Sparse, basic but well placed and extremely clean, Silk Road offers six beds in a women's dorm, six in a mixed dorm and one double room. There are lockers for all in the dorms, and the kitchen – where owner Alex will spontaneously cook up meals for guests from time to time – is equipped with a big fridge and other facilities. The vibe is convivial, and lone women travellers will feel totally safe.

IN THE KNOW SELF-CATERING

If you're travelling as a family or group, or staying for an extended period, an apartment with kitchen facilities might prove a sensible option. Some of the hotels listed in this chapter offer self-catering accommodation. These include **La Calcina** (see above), **Locanda Marinella** (see p274), **Bauer Casanova** (see p265 **Bauers Hotels**, **AD Place** (see p266), **Charming House i Qs** (see p269), **Agli Alboretti** (see p276), **Palazzetto da Schio** (see above) and **Villa F** (see p278).

The websites www.aplaceinvenice.com, www.viewsonvenice.com and www.veniceapartment.com are also good resources for finding an apartment.

ESSENTIAL INFORMATION

ESSENTIAL INFORMATION

LA GIUDECCA
Deluxe

Belmond Hotel Cipriani
Giudecca 10, fondamenta San Giovanni (041 520 7744, www.hotelcipriani.com). Hotel launch from San Marco Vallaresso vaporetto stop, or Vaporetto Zitelle. **Rooms** 95. **Map** p157 G2.
Set amidst verdant gardens, the Cipriani has great facilities as well as a private harbour for your yacht and a better-than-average chance of rubbing shoulders with an A-list film star, especially during the film festival (*see p184*) when many make this their base. Rooms are as luxurious and well-appointed as you'd expect in this category. If this seems too humdrum, take an apartment in the neighbouring 15th-century Palazzo Vendramin, with butler service and private garden. Facilities include tennis courts, a pool, a sauna, a spa and a gym. There's a motorboat to San Marco, but many guests never even leave the premises.

Palladio Spa & Villa F
Giudecca 33, fondamenta Zitelle (041 270 3806, www.bauerhotels.com). Vaporetto Zitelle. **Rooms** *Palladio* 50; *Villa F* 11 apartments. **Map** p157 F2.
Venice's Bauers luxury hotel group (*see also p265*) has expanded across the lagoon on to the Giudecca, where the Palladio Hotel & Spa and the super-elegant self-catering accommodation in Villa F look over the Giudecca canal towards San Marco out front and over Bauer's own lush gardens – one of the city's largest – at the back. Rooms at Palladio are all that you would expect at this level: large, with beautiful fabrics, a modern-classic feel, lashings of marble in the large bathrooms and superb views. The spa offers a host of wonderful treatments to guests of all the Bauer properties. At Villa F, apartments full of heirloom antiques have huge windows making the most of those views. There are fully fitted kitchens, and large reception rooms. But though it's all phenomenally stylish, with efficient, discreet staff on hand, the decor remains just slightly frosty.

Budget

Generator
Giudecca 86, fondamenta delle Zitelle (041 523 8211, http://generatorhostels.com). Vaporetto Zitelle. **Beds** 240. **Map** p157 F2.
Venice's once-dowdy youth hostel has undergone the Generator treatment, emerging with some hip decor, infinitely more inviting public spaces, a lively nightlife scene and a restaurant which is rather less like a sad canteen. There are double, triple and quad rooms suitable for families, and dorms sleeping up to 16 people, some of which are women-only. Though prices are low when the city's quiet, they do follow the trend elsewhere and go up at busy times; breakfast and other meals are extra.

And of course people travelling on a tight budget should factor in the cost of a vaporetto pass, because most of what you'll be wanting to visit is over the water.

LIDO & LAGOON
Deluxe

Hotel Excelsior
Lungomare Marconi 41, Lido (041 526 0201, www.excelsiorvenezia.com). Vaporetto Lido. **Rooms** 197. **Map** p163 B5.
This Moorish extravaganza overlooking the serried ranks of candy-striped bathing huts on the Lido's long strip of sand has been catering to the luxe hotel trade since early in the 20th century. Come during the film festival (*see p184*) and luvvies galore will be mixing with A-list celebrities and caffeine-fuelled journalists on the Excelsior's spreading terraces. There's a hotel boat shuttle service across to Venice proper, and the friendly, well-informed staff can arrange trips and reservations. New for 2014 is the San Marco Suite – at 2,260 sq ft the largest on the lagoon – with massive windows giving a 360° view.

San Clemente Palace
Isola di San Clemente (041 244 5001, www.san clementepalacevenice.com). Hotel launch from jetty at piazza San Marco. **Rooms** 200.
Over time, the island of San Clemente has hosted a hospice for pilgrims, a powder store, an ecclesiastical prison for unruly priests and, more recently, a mental hospital. Today, the restored buildings house this luxurious hotel set in extensive, landscaped grounds with rooms done out in traditional Venetian style, restaurants, a business centre, a beauty farm, tennis courts and all the attendant facilities; there's even a three-hole practice golf course. Children are made particularly welcome. And if you can tear yourself away, a hotel launch shuttles back and forth to central Venice several times an hour.

Expensive

Locanda Cipriani
Torcello, piazza Santa Fosca (041 730 150, www.locandacipriani.com). Vaporetto Torcello. **Rooms** 5.
Some people might argue that there's no point in going to Venice and staying on the island of Torcello, but this famous green-shuttered inn is special enough to justify the remoteness of the setting, at least for a couple of nights. Some of the five rooms (done out in understated, elegant country style) look over the hotel's gorgeous garden; you might end up in the one where Ernest Hemingway wrote *Across the River and into the Trees*, apparently standing up because of haemorrhoids. You can opt to limit yourself to the locanda's wonderful breakfast, or go for half-board

Generator.

(from €150 per person per day), giving you a chance to sample the fare at one of Venice's dining classics (*see p174*).

Moderate

Venice Certosa Hotel

Isola della Certosa (041 277 8632, http://hotel. ventodivenezia.it). Vaporetto Certosa. **Rooms** 18.
Facing across the lagoon towards the eastern end of Castello (*see p84*) and a short hop from Venice proper on the 4.1/4.2 vaporetto, this bright, modern hostel/hotel on the quiet island of Certosa has a pine forest on one side and a forest of masts on the other – and a large percentage of yachties from the neighbouring marina occupying its clean, simple rooms. Packages include sailing and kayaking trips around the lagoon, as well as cooking classes in the hotel's kitchen. There's a night shuttle service from the city centre, and a restaurant for those times when you can't face another lagoon crossing. The hotel lies somewhere between the budget and moderate range.

Venissa

Mazzorbo, fondamenta Santa Caterina 3 (041 527 2281, www.venissa.it). Vaporetto Mazzorbo. **Rooms** 6. **Map** p171 A1.

Many visitors to Venice make the trip to multi-hued Burano. Few alight at the stop just before – Mazzorbo. It is on this picturesquely rural island (linked to Burano by a footbridge) that the prosecco producer Bisol has taken over an ancient walled vineyard, cajoled a long-forgotten grape variety (Dorona) back to life and created a Michelin-starred restaurant (*see p172*) with hotel attached. To fulfil the terms of a deal struck with local authorities, Venissa's attractive minimal-chic boutique rooms can be taken with a host of plush amenities (linen sheets, gorgeous bathroom products) at a higher price, or with not much more than a bed at budget rates for cash-strapped travellers. In both cases, breakfast is extra, and à la carte.

Budget

Il Lato Azzurro

Via Forti 13, Sant'Erasmo (041 523 0642, www.latoazzurro.it). Vaporetto 13 to Sant' Erasmo-Capannone.
This friendly guesthouse on the vegetable-garden island of Sant'Erasmo is the ideal place to stay if you want a really quiet retreat. Colourful triple and quad rooms come with a balcony. There is a restaurant, and you can hire bikes to explore the island.

Getting Around

ARRIVING & LEAVING

By air

Low-cost carriers fly visitors to Venice through Venice, Treviso and Verona airports. National carriers fly principally to Venice, although some have services to Verona.

Venice Marco Polo Airport

Switchboard 041 260 6111, flight & airport information 041 260 9260, www.veniceairport.it.
You can get a bus or taxi (*see below*) to piazzale Roma, but you may find that the **Alilaguna boat service** (041 240 1701, www.alilaguna.it) drops you nearer your hotel. The dock is seven minutes' walk from arrivals; porter service costs €5 per bag. Various Alilaguna services call at San Marco, Rialto, Fondamenta Nove, Guglie, Zattere, Ca' Rezzonico, Sant'Angelo, San Stae, Zitelle, San Zaccaria, Arsenale, Lido, Bacini, Ospedale, Murano Colonna and Madonna dell'Orto vaporetto stops, as well as the Mulino Stucky Hilton on the Giudecca island, and at the Stazione Marittima cruise ship terminal: check which is handiest for your final destination. Main services are hourly, others less frequent. Tickets (€15 to Venice, the Lido or the Stazione Marittima) can be purchased at Alilaguna's counter in the arrivals hall or on board. Allow 70mins from or to San Marco.

Two **bus** companies operate services from the airport. The slower bus 5, run by **ACTV** (041 272 2111, timetable information 041 24 24, www.actv.it), travels between the airport and piazzale Roma, leaving every 15mins; journey time 25-30mins. Tickets (€6) can be purchased at the machine next to the bus stop at the airport, or at any ACTV/Hellovenezia ticket office; discounted fares are available when purchased together with tourist transport passes; *see p289*.

The quicker, non-stop bus service (20mins) between the airport and piazzale Roma is run by **ATVO** (0421 594 671, www.atvo.it). Buy tickets (€6; €11 return) from the ATVO counter at the airport, or at their piazzale Roma office. You may also be able to just pay the driver directly if you have exact change.

A regular **taxi** from the airport to piazzale Roma costs €40 and takes about 20mins. You can pay in advance by credit card in the arrivals hall or from the **Cooperativa Artigiana Radio Taxi** desk (041 59 64, information 041 936 222).

The most luxurious way to reach the centre is by **water taxi**. **Consorzio Motoscafi Venezia** (041 522 2303) charges from €100 for the half-hour crossing. *See also p282* **Water Taxis**.

Sant'Angelo Airport (Treviso)

0422 315 111, www.trevisoairport.it.
ATVO (0422 315 381, www.atvo.it) bus services run from Venice's piazzale Roma and back to coincide with flights – if the flight arrives late, the bus will wait. The journey takes about 70mins, and costs €11 one way, €18 return (valid for ten days). Buses from piazzale Roma leave ridiculously early, so ensure your timely arrival.

Alternatively, take a **train** from Venice to Treviso (35mins) and then a bus or taxi (**Taxi Padova**, 049 651 333) to the airport. **ACTT** (0422 32 71) bus 6 does the 20-minute trip from in front of Treviso train station to the airport at frequent intervals throughout the day, and costs €1.30.

Valerio Catullo Airport (Verona)

045 809 5666, www.aeroportoverona.it.
A **bus** (0458 057911) runs every 20mins to Verona train station, from 5.35am to 11.35pm. The 20-minute journey costs €6 (pay on board).

Major airlines

Alitalia *89 20 10, www.alitalia.com.*
British Airways *199 712 266, www.britishairways.com.*
Easyjet *199 201 840, www.easyjet.com.*
Ryanair (Treviso Airport) *895 895 8989, premium-rate booking line 895 969 7900, www.ryanair.com.*

By train

Most trains arrive at **Santa Lucia** station in Venice (map p306 C4), though a few will only take you as far as Mestre on the mainland;

if so, change to a local train (every ten minutes or less during the day) for the short hop across the lagoon. *See also p282.*

The **Trenitalia** website (www.trenitalia.com) gives exhaustive information on timetables, in English as well as Italian. Tickets can be booked through the website with a credit card; you'll receive an email with a barcode and a booking code, either of which should be presented (on your smartphone, tablet, computer and so on, or in a print-out) to inspectors on board the train.

Trenitalia's national rail information and booking number is 892 021 (24 hours daily). Press 1 after the recorded message, then say '*altro*' to speak to an operator (who may not speak English).

The information office in the main hall of the station is open 7am-9pm daily. Buy tickets from the ticket windows (open 6am-9pm daily, all major credit cards accepted), vending machines in the station, travel agents around the city bearing the Trenitalia logo or online at www.trenitalia.com.

The slowest trains are prefixed R (Regionale) or RV (Regionale Veloce) and are remarkably cheap; Intercity (IC) trains are slightly faster and cost a little more. Frecce high-speed trains are more expensive still, though there are large discounts to be had if you book online and well in advance: you will be given a reserved seat number when you book on Frecciarossa and Frecciargento trains.

If you have a regular railways-issued ticket, **you must stamp it** in the machines on the platform before boarding or face a fine. If you forget to stamp your ticket, locate the inspector as soon as possible to waive the fine.

The private train operator **Italo** (www.italotreno.it) also runs high-speed services from Venice's Santa Lucia to Rome, Florence, Bologna, Naples, Padua and Salerno. It's worth checking the website, as prices can be competitive.

By bus

Buses to Venice all arrive at piazzale Roma.

By car

Prohibitive parking fees make cars one of the least practical modes of arrival. Many Venetian hotels offer their guests discounts at car parks, and VeneziaUnica (see p289) has special offers too. Main car parks (all open 24 hours) are listed below.

Autorimessa Comunale

Santa Croce 496, piazzale Roma (041 272 7211; ticket office 041 272 7307, www.asmvenezia.it). Vaporetto Piazzale Roma. **Rates** €26 per 24hrs or part thereof. **Map** p306 A5.

Marco Polo Park Venice

Marco Polo Airport (041 260 3060, www.veniceairport.it). Bus 5 from piazzale Roma, or free shuttle bus from main entrance of Venice airport. **Rates** from €5.50/day (discounts for longer periods).

Parking Stazione

Viale Stazione 10, Mestre (041 938 021). Bus 2 from piazzale Roma or train to Mestre station. **Rates** €16/day.

Venezia Tronchetto Parking

Isola Nuova del Tronchetto 1 (041 520 7555, www.venice parking.it). Vaporetto Tronchetto. **Rates** €3/hr; €21/day. **Map** off p306 A4.

PUBLIC TRANSPORT

Public transport – including *vaporetti* (water buses) and local buses – in Venice itself and in some mainland areas is run by **ACTV** (www.actv.it). **ATVO** (0421 594 671, www.atvo.it) runs more extensive bus services to numerous destinations on the mainland.

Information

Hellovenezia (see also p289) is ACTV's ticketing, information and merchandising wing. Its extremely helpful call centre (041 2424) provides information on vaporetto and bus schedules. Its outlets at many vaporetto stops sell tickets and VeneziaUnica passes (see p289) which allow users to buy multiple services and access them all through one ticket. If you're lucky, you can also pick up one of the free transport timetable booklets, but these are published at the start of the season and tend to run out swiftly; timetables are posted at all vaporetto stops.

The free VeneziaUnica app has real-time transport information and can be downloaded from Google Play or the iTunes store.

Fares & tickets

Vaporetto tickets and passes can be purchased at *tabacchi* (see p288) and at Hellovenezia counters (see p289) at many vaporetto stops. Stops without ticket counters have automatic ticket-dispensing machines. Passes can be purchased as part of a VeneziaUnica (see p289) package. On board *vaporetti*, you can only buy single tickets.

Ticket costs are:

Single trip €7 (valid 60mins on multiple boats)

12hrs	€18
24hrs	€20
36hrs	€25
48hrs	€30
72hrs	€35
1 week	€50

A **shuttle journey** (ie one stop across the Grand Canal, the hop across to the Giudecca, or from Sant'Elena to the Lido) is €4.

Tickets must be validated prior to boarding the vaporetto, by swiping them in front of the machines at the entrance to the jetty. Note that for multiple journey tickets you need only stamp your ticket once, at the start of the first journey.

Vaporetti

Venice's *vaporetti* (water buses) run to a very tight schedule, with sailing times for each line marked clearly at stops. Strikes sometimes occur, but are always announced in advance; look out for notices posted inside vaporetto stops bearing the title *sciopero* (strike). Services are also curtailed and rerouted for Venice's many rowing regattas; these disruptions are also announced with posters in vaporetto stops.

Regular services run from about 5am to around midnight, after which a frequent night service (N) operates.

Taking a boat in the wrong direction is all too easy. Remember: if you're standing with your back to the station and want to head down the Grand Canal, take Line 1 (slow) or Line 2 (faster) heading left.

Not all passenger ferries are, strictly speaking, *vaporetti*. A **vaporetto** is larger, slower and more rounded in shape, and has room for 230 passsengers; older boats have outside seats at the front that are much sought after.

These vessels follow routes along the Grand Canal.

The **motoscafo** is sleeker, smaller (160 passengers) and has outside seats only at the back. It runs on routes encircling the island. **Motonave** are large double-decker steamers, taking 600-1,200 passengers, and cross the lagoon to the Lido.

Traghetti

The best way to cross the Grand Canal when you're far from a bridge is to hop on a *traghetto*. These unadorned *gondole* are rowed back and forth at fixed points along the canal. At €2 (70c for resident travel card holders), this is the cheapest gondola ride in the city – Venetians make the short hop standing up.

Traghetti ply between the following points:

Santa Sofia–Pescheria

7.30am-8pm Mon-Sat; 8.45am-7pm Sun. **Map** p307 G4-5.

Riva del Carbon–riva del Vin

8am-12.30pm Mon-Sat. **Map** p307 G6.

Ca' Garzoni–San Tomà

7.30am-8pm Mon-Sat; 8.30am-7.30pm Sun. **Map** p309 E7.

San Samuele–Ca' Rezzonico

7.45am-12.30pm Mon-Sat. **Map** p309 E7.

Santa Maria del Giglio–Santa Maria della Salute

9am-6pm daily. **Map** p309 F8-9.

Punta della Dogana–Vallaresso

9am-2pm daily. **Map** p309 G9.

Buses

ACTV buses operate to both Mestre and Marghera on the mainland, as well as serving the Lido, Pellestrina and Chioggia. Services for the mainland depart from piazzale Roma (map p306 B5). From midnight until 5am, buses N1 (leaving every 30mins) and N2 (leaving every hour) depart from Mestre for piazzale Roma, and vice versa. There are also regular night buses from the Lido (departing at least hourly) to Malamocco, Alberoni and Pellestrina.

Bus tickets, costing €1.30 (also available in blocks of ten tickets for €12), are valid for 75mins, during which you may use several buses, though you can't make a return journey on the same ticket. They

ESSENTIAL INFORMATION

can be purchased from ACTV/ Hellovenezia ticket booths (*see p289*) or from *tabacchi* (*see p288*) anywhere in the city. They should be bought before boarding the bus and then stamped on board.

Trains

Santa Lucia (map p306 C4) is Venice's main station. Most long-distance trains stop here, though some only go as far as Mestre on the mainland. Local trains leave Mestre for Santa Lucia every ten minutes or so. For information on rail travel in Italy, *see p280*.

WATER TAXIS

Water taxis are hugely expensive: expect to pay €100 from the airport (*see p280*) directly to any single destination in Venice, and more for multiple stops. The minimum possible cost for a 15-minute trip from hotel to restaurant is €60, with most journeys averaging €110 once numbers of passengers and baggage have been taken into account. In all cases, tariffs are for five people or less, with each extra passenger charged €10 up to a maximum of ten people. Between the hours of 10pm and 7am, there is a surcharge of €10.

Taxi pick-up points can be found at piazzale Roma, outside the train station, next to the Rialto vaporetto stop, and next to San Marco-Vallaresso vaporetto stop, but it's more reliable to call and order yourself. Pre-booking through the Motoscafi Venezia website can give discounts on some routes. Avoid asking your hotel to book a taxi for you, as they frequently add a 10% mark-up. Beware of unlicensed taxis, which charge even more than authorised ones. The latter have a black number on a yellow background.

Consorzio Motoscafi Venezia *041 522 2303, www.motoscafi venezia.it.* **Open** 24hrs daily.

GONDOLAS

Official gondola stops can be found at (or near) the following locations:

Fondamenta Bacino Orseolo **Map** p310 H7.

Riva degli Schiavoni in front of the Hotel Danieli. **Map** p310 K8.

San Marco Vallaresso vaporetto stop. **Map** p309 H8.

Santa Lucia railway station. **Map** p306 C4.

Piazzale Roma bus terminus. **Map** p306 C5.

Santa Maria del Giglio vaporetto stop. **Map** p309 F8.

Piazzetta San Marco jetty. **Map** p310 J8.

Campo Santa Sofia near Ca' d'Oro vaporetto stop. **Map** p307 G4.

San Tomà vaporetto stop. **Map** p309 E7.

Campo San Moisè by the Hotel Bauer. **Map** p309 G8.

Riva del Carbon at the southern end of the Rialto bridge, near the vaporetto stop. **Map** p309 G6.

Fares

These are set by the Istituzione per la Conservazione della Gondola e Tutela del Gondoliere (Gondola Board; 041 528 5075, www.gondolavenezia.it); in the event that a gondolier tries to overcharge you – and it does happen: be prepared to stick to your guns – complain to the Gondola Board. Prices below are for the hire of the gondola, for six passengers or fewer. Having your own personal crooner will push the fare up.

8am-7pm €80 for 40mins; €40 for each additional 20mins. **7pm-8am** €100 for 40mins; €50 for each additional 20mins.

DRIVING

Driving is an impossibility in Venice: even if your vehicle was capable of going up and down stairs and squeezing through the narrowest of alleyways, it wouldn't be legal for you to do so. Instead, you'll need to park on the outskirts and walk or use alternative means of transport.

You can, on the other hand, drive on the Lido but there aren't many places to go. A car ferry (route 17) leaves from the Tronchetto–Ferry Boat stop for Lido–San Niccolò every 50mins and the cost is determined by the size of your car, starting at €21 per car, plus a regular vaporetto ticket (*see p281*) per person.

It's certainly worth hiring a car, however, if you are planning to visit the Veneto countryside and its fine

villas. For route information, see the relevant chapters, which start on p202. If you decide to rent a car, motorcycle or moped while in Italy, make sure you pay the extra charge to upgrade to comprehensive insurance cover.

Car breakdowns (Automobile Club d'Italia) *803 116.* **CCISS traffic news** *1518.*

Car hire

Avis *041 523 7377, www.avisautonoleggio.it.*

Europcar *041 523 8616, www.europcar.it.*

Hertz *041 528 4091, www.hertz.it.*

Maggiore National *041 935 300, www.maggiore.it.*

Mattiazzo *041 522 0884, www.mattiazzo.it.* Chauffeur-driven limousine hire.

Parking

For a list of car parks, *see p281*.

CYCLING

Bicycles are banned – and otiose – in Venice itself. One of the best ways to explore the Lido, however, is by bike, but be prepared to fight off hordes of journalists and film critics during the Film Festival (*see p184*) in early September.

Cycle hire

Lido on Bike *Gran Viale 21B, Lido (041 526 8019, www.lidoonbike.it).* **Open** *Mar-Sept* 9am-7pm daily. **Rates** €5/1.5hr; €9/day.

Venice Bike Rental *Gran viale Santa Maria Elisabetta 79A, Lido (041 526 1490, www. venicebikerental.com).* **Open** *Mar-Oct* 8.30am-8pm daily. **Rates** €4/hr; €9/day. **No credit cards**.

WALKING

Much of your Venetian sightseeing will be done on foot. Be aware that there are over 400 bridges, all with steps. For etiquette tips and how to traverse Venice when it floods, *see p108* **Walk Like a Venetian**. For getting around with children, *see p182*. For tour guides, *see p289*.

Resources A-Z

ADDRESSES

Postal addresses in Venice consist of the name of the *sestiere* (district) plus the house number. With only this information, you will likely never reach your destination. For convenience, we have also given the name of the *calle* (street) or *campo* (square) etc, where each place is located. But finding your way around remains a challenge, especially as matters are sometimes complicated by there being an official Italian and several unofficial Venetian dialect names in use for the same location. When asking for directions, make sure you ascertain the nearest vaporetto stop, church, large square or other easily identifiable local landmark.

AGE RESTRICTIONS

Buying/drinking alcohol 18.
Driving 18.
Sex (hetero- & homosexual) 14.
Smoking 16.

ATTITUDE & ETIQUETTE

For advice on navigating Venice's pedestrian-clogged streets, *see p108* **Walk Like a Venetian**.

BUSINESS

If you are planning to do business in Venice, a call to your embassy's commercial sector in Rome (*see p284*) is always a good idea.

Conventions & conferences

Venice has plenty of conference facilities. Palladian villas and other historic landmarks in the surrounding areas also make great venues for all sorts of events. For information on trade fairs in Venice,

contact Venezia Fiere (041 714 066, www.veneziafiere.it).

Most of the organisers listed below are able to book hotels, transport and other facilities, and provide interpreters.

Endar *Castello 4966, fondamenta de l'Osmarin (041 523 8440, www.endar.it).* **Map** p310 K7.
Nexa *San Marco 4571/C, campo San Luca (041 521 0255, www.nexaweb.it).* **Map** p309 G7.
Venezia Congressi *San Marco 4606, calle del Teatro Goldoni (041 522 8400, www.venezia congressi.com).* **Map** p309 G6.

Couriers & shippers

BRT *041 531 8944, www.brt.it.*
DHL *199 199 345, www.dhl.it.*
FedEx *199 151 119, www.fedex.com/it.*
TNT *199 803 868, www.tnt.it.*
UPS *02 30 30 30 39, www.ups.com.*

Translators & interpreters

Lexicon Translations *Via A Moro 47B, Quarto d'Altino (0422 828 193, www.lexiconline.it).*
TER Centro Traduzioni *Cannaregio 1076C, ramo San Giovanni (041 524 2538, www.ter-traduzioni.com).* **Map** p306 D2.

CONSUMER

Tourism-related complaints are handled by the **APT's** (*see p289*) Tourist Mediation Counter (phone 041 529 8700 or send an email to complaint.apt@turismovenezia.it).

CUSTOMS

If you arrive from an EU country you are not required to declare goods imported into or exported

from Italy as long as they are for personal use.

For people arriving from non-EU countries the following limits apply:
● 200 cigarettes or 100 cigarillos or 50 cigars or 250 grams of tobacco.
● one litre of spirits or two litres of wine.
● one bottle of perfume (50 ml/ 1.76 oz), 250ml of eau de toilette.
● gift items not exceeding €430 (€150 for children under 15)

Anything above these limits will be subject to taxation at the port of entry. For more information, call customs (*dogana*) at Marco Polo Airport on 041 269 9311 or consult www.agenziadogane monopoli.gov.it.

If you are not an EU citizen, remember to keep your official receipt (*scontrino*) as you are entitled to a rebate on IVA (sales tax) paid on purchases of personal goods costing more than €155, as long as they leave the country unused and are bought from a shop that provides this service. Make sure there's a sign displayed in the window, and also ask for the form that you'll need to show at customs on departure. For more information about customs, see the Italian government website, **www. agenziadoganemonopoli.gov.it**, which has a section in English.

DISABLED

With its narrow streets, 400-plus stepped bridges and lack of barriers between canals and pavements, this city is no easy task for anyone with impaired mobility or vision to negotiate. But with determination and forward planning, Venice is far from impossible, and recent efforts to make the city more negotiable for disabled travellers have helped.

ESSENTIAL INFORMATION

ESSENTIAL INFORMATION

Start your research on the city council website, **www.comune. venezia.com**. Type '*Venezia accessibile*' into the search box; once you reach the page, you'll find the English option button. Here you'll find itineraries and a useful map of barrier-free zones; at time of writing, the map still showed long-removed stairlifts previously installed on some bridges.

VeniceConnected (041 2424, www.veniceconnected.com) also provides information and shows itineraries without barriers, as well as hosting a helpful FAQ section on its 'Accessible Venice' pages.

Alilaguna (www.alilaguna.it) services between the airport and Venice proper can carry wheelchairs, as can most *vaporetti*: these will move you between bridge-free areas of the city in an enjoyable fashion. Staff will help you on and off the boats, and ensure that assigned areas are available; if they're short-tempered at peak times, don't take offence – they're like that with everyone. Tickets for wheelchair users cost €1.30 for 75 minutes; if you have an *accompagnatore*, s/he travels free.

Transport

Public transport is one area where Venice scores higher than many other destinations, as standard *vaporetti* and *motonavi* have a reasonably large, flat deck area and there are no steps or steep inclines on the route between quayside and boat, enabling easy travel along the Grand Canal, on lines 1 and 2. Lines that circle the city use *motoscafi*; some of their older models have not yet been adapted to accommodate wheelchairs, although the onboard ACTV personnel are unerringly helpful. The vaporetto lines that currently guarantee disabled access (though peak times should be avoided if possible) are 1, 2, LN and N. Some of the buses that run between Mestre and Venice also have wheelchair access.

For further information, consult the Accessible Venice site or phone:

Trains Trenitalia *199 303 060*
Planes Marco Polo Airport *041 260 9260*

DRUGS

Anyone caught in possession of any quantity of drugs of any kind will be taken before a magistrate. There is no distinction between possession for personal use and intent to supply. All offenders are therefore subject to stiff penalties, including lengthy prison sentences. Foreigners can expect to be swiftly deported. Couriering or dealing can land you in prison for up to 20 years.

ELECTRICITY

Italy's electricity system runs on 220/230V. To use British or US appliances, you will need two-pin adaptor plugs: these are best bought before leaving home, as they tend to be expensive in Italy and are not always easy to find. If you do need to buy one here, try any electrical retailer (look for *Casalinghi*, *Elettrodomestici* or *Ferramenta* in the yellow pages).

EMBASSIES & CONSULATES

There are a handful of diplomatic missions in Venice. But for most information, and in emergencies, you will probably have to contact offices in Rome or Milan. The British Consulate in Venice has closed. For assistance, refer to the duty officer at the Milan consulate.

Consulates in Milan

Australia *02 7767 4200.*
Ireland *02 5518 7569.*
New Zealand *02 7217 0001.*
South Africa *02 885 8581.*
United Kingdom *06 4220 2431.*
United States *02 290 351.*
There is a US Consular Agency in Venice, open by appointment only (041 541 5944).

Embassies in Rome

Australia *06 852 721.*
Canada *06 85444 2911.*
Ireland *06 585 2381.*
New Zealand *06 853 7501.*
South Africa *06 8525 4262.*
United Kingdom *06 4220 0001.*
United States *06 46741.*

EMERGENCIES

See also p288 **Safety & security**. For hospitals, *see right* **Accident & emergency**.

Thefts or losses should be reported immediately at the nearest police station (either the Polizia di Stato or Carabinieri; *see p287*). Report the loss of your passport to the nearest consulate or embassy (*see above*). Report the loss of credit cards or travellers' cheques to your credit card company (*see p287*).

Ambulance *118.*
Coastguard *1530* or *041 240 5711.*
Fire *115* or *041 257 4700.*
Infant emergency *114.*
Police – Carabinieri *112.*
Police – Polizia di Stato *113.*

GAY & LESBIAN

For information, *see pp185-186.*

HEALTH

The *pronto soccorso* (casualty department) of public hospitals provide free emergency treatment for travellers of any nationality. EU citizens are entitled to reciprocal medical care if they have an EHIC (European Health Insurance Card) card, which, in the UK, can be applied for online (www.dh.gov.uk) or by post using forms that you can pick up at any post office. For minor treatments, take your EHIC card with you to any doctor for a free consultation. Drugs they prescribe can be bought at chemists at prices set by the health ministry. Tests or appointments with specialists in the public system (*Sistema sanità nazionale*, SSN) are charged at fixed rates (*il ticket*) and a receipt issued.

Non-EU citizens should review their private health insurance plans to see if expenses incurred while travelling are covered. If not, some form of health insurance is advisable.

Accident & emergency

For urgent medical advice from local health authority doctors during the night, call 041 238 5648 in Venice, 041 238 5668 on the Lido and 041 238 5631 in Mestre (8pm-8am Mon-Fri; 10pm Sat-8am Mon). The public relations department of Venice's **Ospedale Civile** (041 529 4588) can provide general information on being hospitalised in Venice.

The hospitals below all have 24-hour casualty facilities. For an ambulance boat, telephone 118.

Ospedale dell'Angelo *Via Tosatto, Mestre (041 965 7111).* A huge hospital in the outskirts of Mestre.
Ospedale Civile *Castello 6777, campo Santi Giovanni e Paolo (041 529 4111, casualty 041 529 4516). Vaporetto Ospedale.* **Map** p310 K5.
Housed in the 15th-century Scuola di San Marco (*see p81*), Venice's main civic hospital has helpful staff and doctors who are quite likely to speak English.

Ospedale di Padova *Via Giustiniani 2, Padua (049 821 1111).*
Ospedale di Verona *Piazzale Stefani 1, Verona (045 812 1111).*

Contraception & abortion

Condoms are on sale near the checkout in supermarkets, or over the counter at chemists. The contraceptive pill is freely available with a prescription at any pharmacy.

Consultori familiari (family-planning clinics) are run by the local health authority; EU citizens with an EHIC card (*see p284*) are entitled to use them, paying the same low charges for services and prescriptions as locals. Non-EU citizens may use the service and, depending on their insurance plan, claim refunds. The *consultori* are staffed by good gynaecologists – book ahead for a visit. Abortions are legal when performed in public hospitals.

Dentists

Dental treatment in Italy is expensive; your insurance may not cover it. For urgent dental issues, go to the **Ambulatorio Odontostomatologico** at the **Ospedale Civile** (*see p284*).

Hospitals

See p284 **Accident & emergency.**

Opticians

Most opticians will do emergency repairs on the spot.

Punto Vista (Elvio Carraro)
Cannaregio 1982, campiello Anconeta (041 720 453). Vaporetto San Marcuola. **Open** 9am-7.30pm Mon-Sat. **Map** p307 F3.

Pharmacies

Pharmacies (*farmacie*), identified by a green or red cross above the door, are run by qualified chemists who will dispense informal advice on, and assistance for, minor ailments, as well as filling prescriptions. Over-the-counter drugs are much more expensive in Italy than in the UK or US. They can be purchased in some larger supermarkets.

Most chemists are open 9am-12.30pm, 3.45-7.30pm Mon-Fri and 9am-12.45pm Sat. A small number remain open on Saturday afternoon, Sunday and at night on a duty rota

system, details of which are posted outside every pharmacy.

Most pharmacies carry homeopathic medicines, and will check your blood pressure. If you require regular medication, bring adequate supplies with you. Ask your GP for the generic rather than the brand name of your medicine: it may only be available in Italy under a different name.

ID

You are legally obliged to carry photo-ID with you at all times. Hotels will ask for a document when you check in. They should take your details and return it to you immediately.

INSURANCE

For information on car insurance, *see p282* **Driving.** For health insurance, *see p284* **Health.**

INTERNET & EMAIL

For useful websites, *see p295.* Most hotels, of all standards, offer Wi-Fi. Very few now charge for it, but to avoid surprises, it's best to enquire before you use.

City-wide Wi-Fi service is accessible for a fee, through VeneziaUnica (*see p289*). However, you will find no shortage of cafés and bars offering free Wi-Fi. If you opt to use an internet café, you will be asked to present ID to conform with anti-terrorism laws.

LEFT LUGGAGE

Marco Polo Airport *Arrivals hall, ground floor, behind the bar (041 260 5043).* **Open** 5am-9pm daily. **Rates** €6 per item per day. **No credit cards.**
Piazzale Roma bus terminus *041 523 1107.* **Open** 6am-9pm daily. **Rates** €7 per item per day. **No credit cards. Map** p306 B5.
Santa Lucia railway station *041 785 670.* **Open** 6am-11pm daily. **Rates** €6 per item for 5hrs; 90¢ every additional hour from 6am-midnight, 40¢ every additional hour after midnight. **No credit cards. Map** p306 C4.

Legal help

If you are in need of legal advice, your first stop should always be your consulate or embassy (*see p284*). For diplomatic missions not listed here, check online or look for *Ambasciate* in the phone book.

LIBRARIES

Most of the libraries listed below have online catalogues. For assistance with in-depth research at the national level consult the **Servizio bibliotecario nazionale** website (www.sbn.it). In most cases, you will need ID and/or a letter of presentation to use these libraries; they do not lend books to non-members.

Archivio di Stato *San Polo 3002, campo dei Frari (041 522 2281, www.archiviodistatovenezia.it).* *Vaporetto San Tomà.* **Open** 8.10am-5:50pm Mon-Thur; 8.10am-1:50pm Fri, Sat. **Map** p306 D6.
The state archives house all official documents relating to the administration of the Venetian Republic, and a host of other historic manuscripts. Material must be requested between 8.10am and 1pm Mon-Fri.
Archivio Storico delle Arti Contemporanee (ASAC)
Padiglione Centrale ai Giardini di Castello, calle Paludo Sant'Antonio (041 521 8939, www.labiennale.org/it/asac). *Vaporetto Giardini.* **Open** 10am-5pm Tue-Fri. **Map** p312 P10.
Located inside the Biennale gardens, at the eastern end of Castello, this is the archive of the Venice Biennale contemporary art festival (*see p31*).
Biblioteca Centrale IUAV *Santa Croce 191, fondamenta Tolentini (041 257 1106, www.iuav.it).* *Vaporetto Piazzale Roma.* **Open** 9am-midnight Mon-Fri (from 2pm 1st Mon of mth). **Map** p308 C6.
The library of one of Italy's top architecture faculties has a vast collection of works on the history of architecture, town planning, art, engineering and social sciences.
Biblioteca Fondazione Giorgio Cini *Isola di San Giorgio Maggiore (041 271 0255, www.cini.it).* *Vaporetto San Giorgio.* **Open** 9am-4.30pm Mon-Fri. **Map** p157 G1.
The Giorgio Cini Foundation houses libraries that are dedicated to art history, Venetian history, literature, theatre and music.
Biblioteca Fondazione Scientifica Querini Stampalia
Castello 5252, campo Santa Maria Formosa (041 271 1411, www.querinistampalia.org). *Vaporetto Rialto or San Zaccaria.* **Open** 10am-midnight Tue-Sat; 10am-7pm Sun. **Map** p310 J6.
A collection with an emphasis on all things Venetian. *See also p75.*

ESSENTIAL INFORMATION

Ca' Foscari Cultural Flow Zone
Dorsoduro 1392, Zattere (041 234 5811, www.unive.it/cfz). Vaporetto Zattere. **Open** 9am-midnight Mon-Fri; 9am-8pm Sat; 2pm-midnight Sun. **Map** p308 D9.
This newly designed modern space functions as a cultural centre dedicated to promoting exchange amongst students.

Biblioteca Museo Correr
San Marco 52, piazza San Marco (041 240 5211, www.visitmuve.it). Vaporetto San Marco Vallaresso. **Open** 8.30am-1.30pm Mon, Wed, Fri; 8.30am-5pm Tue, Thur. **Map** p310 H8.
This small library contains prints, manuscripts and books about Venetian history and art history.

Biblioteca Nazionale Marciana
San Marco 7, piazzetta San Marco (041 240 7211, www.marciana. venezia.sbn.it). Vaporetto San Marco Vallaresso. **Open** 8am-7pm Mon-Fri; 8am-1.30pm Sat. **Map** p310 J8.
The city's main public library has medieval manuscripts and editions of the classics dating from the 15th century.

LOST PROPERTY

Your mislaid belongings may end up at one of the *uffici oggetti smarriti* listed below. You could also try the police (*see p287*), or get in touch with Veritas, the city's rubbish collection department (041 729 1111).

ACTV *Santa Croce, piazzale Roma (041 272 2179). Vaporetto Piazzale Roma.* **Open** 7am-7.30pm daily. **Map** p306 B5.
Items found on *vaporetti* or buses.
Comune (City Council) *San Marco 4136, riva del Carbon (041 274 8225). Vaporetto Rialto.* **Open** 9am-1pm Mon-Fri. **Map** p307 G6.
FS/Stazione Santa Lucia
(041 78 55 31). Staff hand over all lost and found items to the Comune of Venice (*see above*).
Marco Polo Airport *Arrivals Hall (ATA Italia 041 260 9226; GH Venezia 041 260 9228; AVIA Partner 041 260 9227, lost objects 041 260 9260). Bus 5 to Aeroporto.* **Open** *ATA Italia* 9am-1pm; 5-8pm. *GH Venezia* 10am-1pm; 3-6pm. *AVIA Partner* 10am-1pm; 3-6pm.

MEDIA

Daily newspapers (national)

Sometimes lengthy, turgid and featuring indigestible political stories, Italian newspapers can be a frustrating read. On the plus side, papers are delightfully unpretentious and happily blend serious news, leaders by globally known commentators, and well-written, often surreal, crime and human-interest stories.

Sports coverage in the dailies is extensive and thorough. There are also the mass-circulation sports papers *Corriere dello Sport*, *La Gazzetta dello Sport* and *Tuttosport*.

Corriere della Sera
www.corriere.it.
To the centre of centre-left, this solid, serious but often dull Milan-based daily is good on crime and foreign news.
La Repubblica *www.repubblica.it.*
Centre-ish, left-ish *La Repubblica* is good on the Mafia and the Vatican, and comes up with the occasional scoop on its business pages.
Il Sole-24 Ore
www.ilsole24ore.com.
This business, finance and economics daily has a great arts supplement on Sunday.

Daily newspapers (local)

Il Gazzettino *www.gazzettino.it.*
Il Gazzettino is one of Italy's most successful local papers. It provides national and international news on the front pages and local news inside, with different editions for towns around the Veneto region.
La Nuova Venezia
http://nuovavenezia.gelocal.it.
This popular, small-circulation daily – known to Venetians as *La Nuova* – contains lively editorials, crime stories, local news and event listings.

Foreign press

The *Financial Times*, *Wall Street Journal*, *USA Today*, *Herald Tribune* and most European and (usually) UK dailies can be found on the day of issue at news-stands around town – especially those at the station, within striking distance of St Mark's and the Rialto, and at the large *edicole* (newsagent) at the Lido and Accademia vaporetto stops. US publications sometimes take a day or two to appear.

Magazines

News weeklies *Panorama* (roughly centre right) and *L'Espresso* (centre left-ish) provide a general round-up of the week's events, while *Sette* and *Venerdì* – respectively the colour supplements of *Corriere della Sera* (Thursday) and *La Repubblica* (Friday) – have nice photos, though the quality of the journalism often leaves much to be desired.

For *Hello!*-style scandal, try *Gente* and *Oggi* with their weird mix of sex, glamour and religion, or the generally execrable scandal sheets *Eva 3000*, *Novella 2000* and *Cronaca Vera*. *Internazionale* (www.internazionale.it) provides an excellent digest of interesting bits and pieces gleaned from around the world the previous week.

But the biggest-selling magazine of them all is *Famiglia Cristiana*, which alternates Vatican line-toeing with Vatican baiting, depending on the state of relations between the Holy See and the idiosyncratic Paoline monks who produce it. It's available from news-stands or in most churches.

Other publications

Aladino *www.aladinoannunci.com.*
Weekly classified ads for everything from flats for rent to *gondole* for sale, available in *edicole*, their website offers free ads.
Il Boom *www.nuovoboom.com.*
A weekly small-ads paper that's delivered free through letterboxes or available at street dispensers. *Boom* is the place to look for flats, jobs and lonely hearts.
Gente Veneta
This weekly broadsheet, produced by the local branch of the Catholic church, blends cultural and religious listings with reports on Venetian social problems.
Venews *www.venezianews.it.*
This information-packed magazine, which comes out on the first of each month, encompasses music, film, theatre, art and sports listings, plus interviews and features, in both Italian and English.

Radio

Radio Venezia FM 92.4
Pop music, pop music, pop music. Did we mention pop music?
Radio Capital FM 98.5
Heavy on advertising, but generous with information on city events and news. 1980s and '90s classics with a sprinkling of current hits.
Radio Padova FM 103.9 & 88.4
Popular chart music and concert information for the Veneto area.

Television

Italy has six major networks (three are owned by the state broadcaster

RAI, the other three belong to Silvio Berlusconi's **Mediaset** group). Dancing girls, variety shows, music and beauty competitions predominate. The standard of news and current affairs programmes varies. Television in the Veneto is now digital.

MONEY

Italy's currency is the euro (€). There are euro banknotes of €5, €10, €20, €100, €200 and €500, and coins worth €1 and €2 as well as 1¢ (*centesimo*), 2¢, 5¢, 10¢, 20¢ and 50¢. Notes and coins from any euro-zone country are valid.

Banks & ATMs

Most banks have cash dispensers and the vast majority of these accept cards with the Maestro, Cirrus or Visa Electron symbols. Most cashpoint machines dispense cash to a daily limit of €250.

Most banks are open 8.20am-1.20pm and 2.45-3.45pm Mon-Fri. All banks are closed on public holidays and work reduced hours the day before a holiday, usually closing at 11am. Banks are listed under *Banche ed istituti di credito* in the yellow pages.

Changing money

The best exchange rates are to be had by withdrawing cash from ATMs. The exchange rates and commissions for currency transactions at banks vary greatly, but most offer more generous rates than bureaux de change (*cambio*). Travellers' cheques are almost a thing of the past: many banks no longer accept them and those that do charge large commissions.

Note that anywhere with a 'no commission' sign will probably offer dire exchange rates. There is no longer an American Express office in Venice.

Travelex *San Marco 5126, riva del Ferro (041 528 7358, www.travelex.it). Vaporetto Rialto.* **Open** 9.30am-6.45pm Mon-Sat; 9am-5pm Sun. **Map** p307 H6. Cash and travellers' cheques exchanged. MasterCard and Visa cardholders can also withdraw cash – but note that you will need your passport or other valid photo ID. **Other locations** San Marco 142, piazza San Marco (041 277 5057); Marco Polo Airport arrivals (041 269 8271).

Lost or stolen credit cards

Report lost credit or charge cards to your issuing bank.

Tax

For information on reclaiming IVA (VAT or sales tax), *see p283.*

OPENING HOURS

Banks *See left.*
Pharmacies *See p285.*
Post offices *See right.*
Shops Food shops traditionally close on Wednesday afternoon; non-food shops on Monday morning. In practice, larger shops open six or even seven days a week, as do smaller ones at busier times of the year.

Opening times given in the Explore chapters in this guide are the venues' winter hours; they may be open slightly later or longer in summer months. Ticket offices often shut an hour (or even more) before closing time. *See also p290* **Public holidays**.

POLICE

For emergencies, *see p284.*
Both the (nominally military) **Carabinieri** and the **Polizia di Stato** deal with crimes and emergencies of any kind. If you have your bag or wallet stolen, or are otherwise made a victim of crime, go as soon as possible to either force to report a *scippo* ('bagsnatching'). A *denuncia* (written statement) of the incident will be made for you.

Give police as much information as possible, including your passport number, holiday address and flight numbers. The *denuncia* will be signed, dated and stamped with an official police seal. It is unlikely that your things will be found, but you will need the *denuncia* for making an insurance claim.

Carabinieri *Castello 4693A, campo San Zaccaria (041 27411). Vaporetto San Zaccaria.* **Map** p310 K7.
Polizia di Stato *Questura Santa Croce 500, piazzale Roma (041 271 5586, www.questura.poliziadistato. it). Vaporetto Piazzale Roma.* **Map** p306 B5.

POSTAL SERVICES

Italy's postal service (www.poste.it) is generally reliable. Postage supplies – such as large mailing boxes and packing tape – are available at most post offices.

Italy's standard postal service, *posta prioritaria*, gets letters to their destination within 48 hours in Italy, three days for EU countries and four or five for the rest of the world. A letter of 20g or less in Italy costs: 70¢ within the EU 85¢, and to the rest of the world €2 or €2.50 (Oceania); stamps can be bought at post offices and *tabacchi* (*see p288*).

Express and parcel post are also available; for other couriers and shippers, *see p283*.

Letterboxes are red and have two slots: *Per la città* (for Venezia, Mestre and Marghera), and *Tutte le altre destinazioni* (all other destinations).

Each district has its own sub-post office, open 8.20am-1.45pm Mon-Fri, 8.20am-12.45pm Sat.

Posta Piazzale Roma *Santa Croce 511, fondamenta Santa Chiara (041 244 6811). Vaporetto Piazzale Roma.* **Open** 8.20am-7.05pm Mon-Fri; 8.20am-12.35pm Sat. **Map** p306 B5.

RELIGION

Mass (*messa*) times vary from church to church and are posted by front doors. Services are usually held between 9am and 11am and again at 6.30pm on Sundays (6.45pm in St Mark's basilica; *see p50*); most churches have Mass on Saturdays at 6pm. *Un'ospite di Venezia*, a free brochure, has Mass times. The church of San Zulian (*see p62*) has Mass in English at 11.30am on Sundays throughout the year.

Listed below are the non-Catholic denominations in the city.

Anglican

St George's *Dorsoduro 729A, campo San Vio (041 520 0571). Vaporetto Accademia.* **Services** Holy Eucharist 10.30am Sun. **Map** p309 E9.

Greek Orthodox

San Giorgio dei Greci *Castello 3412, ponte dei Greci (041 522 5446). Vaporetto San Zaccaria.* **Services** 9.30am, 10.30am Sun. **Map** p310 L7.

Jewish

Synagogue *Cannaregio, campo del Ghetto Vecchio (041 715 012, www.jvenice.org). Vaporetto Guglie.*

Services after sunset Fri; Sat am. **Map** p307 E2.

For security reasons, those wishing to attend services at the synagogue must present themselves, with ID, to the main office of the Jewish Community (at the synagogue) or call them on 041 715 012.

Lutheran

Chiesa Evangelica Luterana
Cannaregio 4443, campo Santi Apostoli (041 524 2040). Vaporetto Ca' D'Oro. **Services** 10.30am 2nd & 4th Sun of mth. **Map** p307 H5.

Methodist & Waldensian

Chiesa Valdese *Castello 5170, fondamenta Cavagnis (041 522 7549, www.chiesavaldese.org). Vaporetto Rialto or San Zaccaria.* **Services** 11am Sun. **Map** p310 K6.

SAFETY & SECURITY

Venice is, on the whole, an exceptionally safe place at any time of day or night, and violent crime is almost unknown. Lone women would be advised to steer clear of dark alleyways (as far as is possible in labyrinthine Venice) late at night, though even there they are more likely to be harassed than attacked (*see also p290* **Women**).

Bag-snatchers are a rarity, mostly because of the logistical difficulties Venice presents for making a quick getaway. However, pickpockets operate in crowded thoroughfares, especially around San Marco and the Rialto, and on public transport, so make sure you leave passports, plane/train tickets and at least one means of getting hold of money in your hotel room safe.

If you are the victim of theft or other serious crime, contact the police (*see p287*).

SMOKING

Smoking is banned anywhere with public access – including bars, restaurants, stations, offices and on all public transport – except in clearly designated smoking rooms.

Tabacchi

Tabacchi or *tabaccherie* (identified by a white T on a black or blue background) are the only places in Italy where you can legally buy tobacco products. They also sell stamps, telephone cards, individual or season tickets for public transport, lottery tickets and the

stationery required when dealing with bureaucracy.

Most of Venice's *tabacchi* pull their shutters down by 7.30pm. If you're gasping for nicotine late in the evening or on Sunday, you will have to try one of the automatic cigarette vending machines in campo Santa Margherita, piazzale Roma, next to the train station, on strada Nuova near Ponte della Guglie and near Santi Apostoli, fondamenta della Misericordia, calle dei Fabbri and via XXII Marzo, although these only 'open' at 9pm to prevent sales to minors.

STUDY

Studying at either of Venice's two main universities is likely to involve lectures and exams in Italian, making a good knowledge of the Italian language a prerequisite. However, there are some exceptions, especially at the more international IUAV. To find out about entrance requirements, consult the faculty websites of the **Istituto Universitario di Architettura di Venezia** (IUAV; www.iuav.it) or the **Università degli Studi di Venezia Ca' Foscari** (www.unive.it), both in English.

EU citizens have the same right to study at Italian universities as Italian nationals. You'll need to have your school diplomas translated and authenticated at the Italian consulate in your own country before presenting them to the *ufficio studenti stranieri* (foreign students' department) of any university.

Both universities run exchange programmes and participate in the EU's Erasmus scheme. The **Venice International University** (041 271 9511, www.univiu.org) is a consortium of 15 universities and agencies. Students registered at one of the member universities (see the website for a list) are eligible to apply for VIU undergraduate activities. There are also masters and PhD programmes available for foreign students.

TELEPHONES

Dialling & codes

Italian landline numbers must be dialled with their prefixes, even if you're phoning within the local area. Numbers in Venice and its province begin **041**; numbers in Padua province begin **049**; in Vicenza they begin **0444**; in Verona **045**.

Numbers generally have seven or eight digits after the prefix;

some older ones have six, and some switchboards five. If you try a number and can't get through, it may have been changed to an eight-digit number. Check the directory (*elenco telefonico*) or with directory enquiries (*see below*).

Numeri verdi ('green numbers') are free and start 800 or 147. Numbers beginning 840 and 848 are charged at a nominal rate. These numbers can be called from within Italy only, and some are available only within certain regions. Mobile phone numbers always begin with a 3.

When calling an Italian landline from abroad, the whole prefix, including the 0, must be dialled, so dial 00 39 041… for Venice from the UK. To make an **international call** from Venice dial 00, then the country code (for common country codes, *see below*), then the area code (usually without the initial 0) and the number.

Australia 61
Canada 1
Ireland 353
New Zealand 64
South Africa 27
UK 44
USA 1

Mobile phones

Standard European handsets will work in Italy, but your service provider may need to activate international roaming before you leave; beware of extortionate roaming charges. Tri-band US handsets should also work; check with the manufacturer.

If your phone is not locked to your home SIM card/service provider, you can buy an Italian pay-as-you-go SIM card available from mobile phone shops for around €10, allowing you to make cheaper calls within Italy. In theory you have to provide an Italian tax code to purchase one of these; in practice, many vendors will waive this requirement.

Operator services

Directory enquiries is a jungle, and charges for information given over the phone are steep. The major services are: **1254** (Italian and international numbers); **892 412** (international numbers, in English and Italian, from mobile phones); Italian directory information can be had for free on **http://mobile1254.virgilio.it** or **www.paginebianche.it**.

Public phones

There are some public phones in Venice along the tourist routes, but many are out of service. Most public phones operate only with phone cards (*schede telefoniche*). Newer models take major credit cards. Phonecards costing €2.50, €5 and €7.50 can be bought at post offices, *tabacchi* (*see p288*) and some newsstands.

TIME

Italy is one hour ahead of London, six ahead of New York, eight behind Sydney and 12 hours behind Wellington.

TIPPING

There are no hard and fast rules on tipping in Italy, though Venetians know that foreigners tip generously back home, and expect them to be liberal. Some upmarket restaurants (and a growing number of cheaper ones) will add a service charge to your bill: ask *il servizio è incluso?* If not, leave whatever you think the service merited (Italians leave 5%-10%). Bear in mind that all restaurants charge a cover charge (*coperto*) – a quasi-tip in itself.

TOILETS

Public toilets (*servizi igienici pubblici*) are numerous and relatively clean in Venice, but you have to pay (€1) to use them, unless you have invested in the appropriate VeneziaUnica package (*see below*). Follow blue and green signs marked WC. By law, all cafés and bars should allow anyone to use their facilities; however, many Venetian bar owners don't.

TOURIST INFORMATION

Cards & passes

See also p89 **Chorus**. For transport-only passes, *see p281*.

The museums around piazza San Marco (but not the paying parts of the basilica) can only be visited on one of these museum passes:

Musei di Piazza San Marco
Valid for three months, with one visit to each of the sights covered; costs €16 (€10 reductions, under-5s free). Covers Doge's Palace, Museo Correr, Museo Nazionale Archeologico and Biblioteca Marciana.

Museum Pass Valid six months with one visit to each museum covered; costs €24 (€18 reductions, under-5s free). Covers the sights listed above plus Ca' Rezzonico (p139), Casa di Carlo Goldoni (p118), Ca' Pesaro (p122), Museo dell'Arte Vetraria (*p166*), Museo dei Merletti (p172), Museo di Storia Naturale (p122) and Palazzo Mocenigo (p122) .

Passes can be bought at the sights themselves (not all accept credit cards), by phone (041 4273 0892) or online (www.visitmuve.it). Alternatively they can be booked through the city council's **VeneziaUnica** website, **www.veneziaunica.it**, where they can be purchased as part of a sightseeing + transport deal that may bring costs down.

Visitors can get a top-upable VeneziaUnica swipe card, permitting them to add events and services at prices that – for some things – come in at slightly less inflated levels than purchasing directly and/or individually.

The card can be ordered and paid for online through the website (not easy to navigate but worth the struggle) or purchased in the city. In both cases, it can be picked up at offices of Hellovenezia – the sales outlet of the ACTV transit company, generally open 8am-8pm daily – at points of entry to the city (railway station, piazzale Roma, Marco Polo airport, Tronchetto cruise ship terminal) and at those vaporetto stops where Hellovenezia has its larger sales counters (Rialto, San Marco-Vallaresso, San Zaccaria).

In addition to the two museum passes, the extensive menu of goodies on offer with VeneziaUnica includes city-wide Wi-Fi, use of public toilets, transport to and from the airport, the **Chorus** church pass (*see p89*), tours of the La Fenice opera house (*see p69*), car parks (*see p281*) and audio-guides.

Travellers aged between 14 and 29 should consider buying the **Rolling Venice** card (€4), which allows you to purchase a three-day travel pass for €20 instead of the usual €25, and gives discounts at many sights, shops and restaurants.

For further information, see www.hellovenezia.it.

Information

Before you arrive...
The APT tourist board's website, **www.turismovenezia.it**, has

useful information for visitors. The free VeneziaUnica application (downloadable from the usual outlets) provides transport timetables, events listings and a host of other information, in English and Italian.

Once you're in town...
There are several free publications – available at **APT** and **Hellovenezia** offices, (for both, (*see below*) and in some bars – which provide comprehensive tourist information in Venice. Most hotels will provide you with a copy of the bi-weekly (monthly in winter) *Un'ospite di Venezia (A Guest in Venice)*, a bilingual booklet compiled by hoteliers, which contains useful addresses, night pharmacies, Mass times and transport timetables. The Giardinetti branch of APT has a selection of books and sells concert tickets. In high season, supplementary kiosks are set up around the city.

Hellovenezia's extremely helpful call centre (041 2424) provides information on sights, events, and vaporetto and bus timetables, in English. Hellovenezia offices dispense tourist information, and issue and add services to the VeneziaUnica card (*see left*); outlets at the railway station, Tronchetto and piazzale Roma also sell tickets for events.

Branches can be found at the following vaporetto stops: Tronchetto, Piazzale Roma, Ferrovia, Rialto, San Marco-Vallaresso, San Marco-San Zaccaria, Fondamenta Nove, Lido. These offices are generally open 8am-8pm.

The local press (*see p286*) is another source of useful information on events, as are posters plastered on walls across the city.

Azienda di Promozione Turistica (APT) *San Marco 71F, piazza San Marco (041 529 8711, www.turismovenezia.it). Vaporetto San Marco-Vallaresso.* **Open** 9am-7pm daily. **Map** p310 H8.
APT offices provide information on sights and events, a list of hotels, and walking itineraries with maps for sale. Staff will also put you in touch with registered guides and give details of official fees for guided tours (also available on the website).

Other APT locations
Venice Pavilion *San Marco 2, Giardinetti Reali (041 529 8711).* **Open** 9am-7pm daily. **Map** p310 H8.

Venice-Santa Lucia railway station *(041 529 8711).* **Open** 9am-7pm daily. **Map** p306 C4.
Marco Polo Airport arrivals hall *(041 529 8711).* **Open** 9am-8pm daily.
Piazzale Roma Garage ASM *Santa Croce, piazzale Roma (041 529 8711).* **Open** 9am-2.30pm daily. **Map** p306 B5.

Guided tours

The APT tourist office website *(see p289)* provides information on guides by language and area, or try the following. *See also p186* **Venice à la Carte**.

Context
www.contexttravel.com/venice.
Rates vary according to length and number of participants. The university professors and experts at Context take groups of visitors (maximum six) on customised and/or themed tours.

Cooperativa Guide Turistiche
041 520 9038, www.guide venezia.it. **Rates** €115 for half-day tour, for groups of up to 30 people; €4 for every extra person. **No credit cards**.
This cooperative offers made-to-measure tours in English and other languages. In high season, book at least a week in advance.

See Venice *349 084 8303, www. seevenice.it.* **Rates** from €70/hr.
Luisella Romeo organises tours of sights, a range of interesting themed visits and shopping tours.

Guide to Venice *328 948 5671 mobile, www.guidetovenice.it.*
Rates €50-€70 per person.

Historian Martino Rizzo specialises in tours of the islands, including cruises on traditional boats such as the *Nuovo Trionfo (see p166).* He also runs tours of Venice itself.

Venice with a Guide
www.venicewithaguide.com.
Rates €146 2hrs.
Ten qualified multilingual guides.

VISAS

For EU citizens, a passport or a national identity card valid for travel abroad is sufficient. Non-EU citizens must have full passports. Citizens of the US, Canada, Australia and New Zealand do not need visas for stays of up to 90 days. In theory, visitors are required to declare their presence to the local police within a few days of arrival, where this will be done for them. In practice, you will not need to report to the police station unless you decide to extend your stay and you apply for a *permesso di soggiorno* (permit to stay).

WATER

Forget *Death in Venice*-style cholera scares: tap water here is regularly checked, safe to drink and tastes good. Fountains throughout the city provide a constant source of free tap water. For information, visit www.gruppoveritas.it.

WHEN TO GO

Climate

Venice's unique position gives the city a bizarre mix of weather conditions. During the winter, high levels of humidity often make winter days seem colder than their average few degrees above zero, and summer days become humid as soon as the thermometer rises above 25°C (77°F).

Strong north-easterlies in winter, coming off the snow-covered Alps (snow in the city is rare) have bone-chilling effects but make the weather crisp and clear, with blue skies and great views. In the still summer months, high humidity can make it stiflingly hot; a warm southerly wind called the *scirocco* makes the heat more intense.

Autumn and spring are generally mild, with occasional pea-soup fog. August and November are the rainiest months, while *acqua alta (see p108* **Walk Like a Venetian**) is mainly an autumn and winter event.

Public holidays

On official public holidays (*giorni festivi*), public offices, banks and post offices are closed. So, in theory, are shops – but in tourism-oriented Venice, this rule is often waived. Some bars and restaurants may observe holidays: if in doubt, call ahead. You won't find much open on Christmas Day and New Year's Day.

Public transport is reduced to a skeleton service on 1 May, Christmas Day and New Year's Day, and may be rerouted or curtailed for local festivities, especially those including regattas (*see pp26-31*); details are posted at vaporetto stops and at the bus terminus in piazzale Roma.

Holidays falling on a Saturday or Sunday are not celebrated on the following Monday. By popular tradition, if a public holiday falls on a Tuesday or Thursday, many people will also take the Monday or Friday off as well, a practice known as *fare il ponte* ('doing a bridge').

The public holidays are:
New Year's Day (Capodanno) 1 Jan
Epiphany (Befana) 6 Jan
Easter Monday (Pasquetta)
Liberation Day (Festa della Liberazione) and patron saint's day (San Marco) 25 Apr
Labour Day (Festa del Lavoro) 1 May
Assumption (Ferragosto) 15 Aug
All Saints' Day (Ognissanti) 1 Nov
Festa della Salute (Venice only) 21 Nov
Immaculate Conception (L'Immacolata) 8 Dec
Christmas Day (Natale) 25 Dec
Boxing Day (Santo Stefano) 26 Dec

ESSENTIAL INFORMATION

THE LOCAL CLIMATE

Average temperatures and monthly rainfall in Venice.

	High (°C/°F)	Low (°C/°F)	Rainfall (mm/in)
Jan	6 / 42	-1 / 30	58 / 2.3
Feb	8 / 47	1 / 33	54 / 2.1
Mar	12 / 54	4 / 39	57 / 2.2
Apr	16 / 61	8 / 46	64 / 2.5
May	21 / 70	12 / 54	69 / 2.7
June	25 / 77	16 / 61	76 / 3.0
July	28 / 82	18 / 64	63 / 2.5
Aug	27 / 81	17 / 63	83 / 3.3
Sept	24 / 75	14 / 58	66 / 2.6
Oct	18 / 65	9 / 49	69 / 2.7
Nov	12 / 53	4 / 40	87 / 3.4
Dec	7 / 44	0 / 32	54 / 2.1

Glossary

A

amphitheatre (*ancient*) an oval open-air theatre.
apse large recess at the high-altar end of a church.

B

baldachin canopy supported by columns.
barrel vault a ceiling with arches shaped like half-barrels.
Baroque artistic period from the 17th-18th centuries, in which the decorative element became increasingly florid, culminating in the rococo (*qv*).
basilica ancient Roman rectangular public building; rectangular Christian church.
Byzantine Christian artistic and architectural style drawing on ancient models developed in the fourth century in the Eastern empire and through the Middle Ages.

C

campanile bell tower.
campo Venetian for piazza or square.
capital head of a column, generally decorated according to classical orders (*qv*).
caryatid column carved in the shape of a female.
chiaroscuro from Italian *chiaro* (light) and *scuro* (dark); juxtaposition of light and shade to bring out relief and volume.
cloister courtyard surrounded on all sides by a covered walkway.
coffered ceiling decorated with sunken square or polygonal panels.
cupola dome-shaped roof or ceiling.

E

ex-voto an offering given to fulfil a vow; often a small model in silver of the limb/organ/loved one cured as a result of prayer.

F

fan vault vault formed of concave semi-cones, meeting at the apex; it has the appearance of four backwards-leaning fans meeting.
festoon painted or carved swag or swathe decorated with fruit and/or flowers.

fresco painting technique in which pigment is applied to wet plaster.

G

Gothic architectural and artistic style of the late Middle Ages (from the 12th century), of soaring, pointed arches.
Greek cross (church) in the shape of a cross with arms of equal length.
grisailles painting in shades of grey to mimic sculpture.

I

iconostasis rood screen; screen in Eastern-rite churches separating nave from the sanctuary.
intarsia form of mosaic made from pieces of different-coloured wood; also know as **intaglio**.

L

Latin cross (church) in the shape of a cross with one arm longer than the other.
loggia gallery open on one side.
lunette semi-circular surface, usually above window or door.

M

Mannerism post-High Renaissance style of the later 16th century; characterised in painting by elongated, contorted human figures.
monoforate with one opening (cf biforate, triforate, polyforate *qv*), usually used of windows.

N

narthex enclosed porch in front of a church.
nave main body of a church; the longest section of a Latin cross church (*qv*).

O

ogival (arches, windows etc) curving in to a point at the top.
opus sectile pavement made of (usually) geometrically shaped marble slabs.
orders classical rules governing the proportions of columns, their entablatures and their capitals (*qv*), the most common being the less ornate Doric, the curlicue Ionic

and the Corinthian order, in which capitals are decorated with stylised acanthus leaves.

P

palazzo large and/or important building (not necessarily a palace).
pendentives four concave triangular sections on top of piers supporting a dome.
piano nobile showiest floor of a palazzo (*qv*), containing mainly reception rooms with very high ceilings.
pilaster column-shaped projection from a wall.
polyforate with more than one opening (cf monoforate).
polyptych painting composed of several panels (cf dyptych with two panels, triptych with three).
porphyry hard igneous rock ranging from dark green to dark purple; this latter was most commonly used, and known as *rosso antico*.
presbytery the part of a church containing the high altar.

R

reredos decorated wall or screen behind an altar.
rococo highly decorative style fashionable in the 18th century.
Romanesque architectural style of the early Middle Ages (c500 to 1200), drawing on Roman and Byzantine (*qv*) influences.
rusticated large masonry blocks with deep joints between them used to face buildings or monuments.

S

sarcophagus (*ancient*) stone or marble coffin.
stele upright slab of stone with decorative relief sculpture and/or commemorative inscription.

T

transept shorter arms of a Latin cross church (*qv*).
trilobate with three arches.
triumphal arch arch in front of an apse (*qv*), usually over the high altar.
trompe l'œil decorative painting effect to make surface appear three-dimensional.

Menu

ANTIPASTI (STARTERS)

The dozens of *cicheti* – tapas-style snacks – that are served from the counters of the city's traditional *bacaro* (trattorias) are essentially antipasti; the choice may include: **baccalà mantecato** stockfish beaten into a cream with oil and milk, often served on grilled polenta; **bovoleti** tiny snails cooked in olive oil, parsley and garlic; **carciofi** artichokes, even better if they are **castrauri** – baby artichokes; **canoce** (or **cicale di mare**) mantis shrimps; **folpi/folpeti** baby octopus; **garusoli** sea snails; **moleche** soft-shelled crabs, usually deep-fried; **museto** a boiled pork brawn sausage, generally served on a slice of bread with mustard; **nervetti** boiled veal cartilage; **polpetta** deep-fried spicy meatball; **polenta** yellow or white cornmeal mush, served either runny or in firm sliceable slabs; **sarde in saor** sardines marinated in onion, vinegar, pine nuts and raisins; **schie** tiny grey shrimps, usually served on a bed of soft white polenta; **seppie in nero** cuttlefish in its own ink; **spienza** veal spleen, usually served on a skewer; **trippa e rissa** tripe cooked in broth.

PRIMI (FIRST COURSES)

Bigoli in salsa fat spaghetti in an anchovy and onion sauce; **gnocchi... con granseola** potato gnocchi in spider-crab sauce; **pasta... e ceci** pasta and chickpea soup; **...e fagioli** pasta and borlotti bean soup; **spaghetti... alla busara** in anchovy sauce; **...al nero di seppia** in squid-ink sauce; **...con caparossoli/vongole** veraci with clams; **risotto... di zucca** pumpkin risotto.

SECONDI (MAIN COURSES)

In addition to the antipasti mentioned above, you may find: **anguilla** eel; **aragosta/astice** spiny lobster/lobster; **branzino** sea bass; **cape longhe** razor clams; **cape sante** scallops; **cernia** grouper; **coda di rospo** anglerfish; **cozze** mussels; **granchio** crab; **granseola** spider crab; **orata** gilt-headed bream; **rombo** turbot; **pesce San Pietro** John Dory; **pesce spada** swordfish; **sogliola** sole; **tonno** tuna; **vongole/caparossoli** clams.

Meat eaters are less well catered for in Venice; local specialities include: **fegato alla veneziana** veal liver cooked in onions; **castradina** a lamb and cabbage broth.

DOLCI

Venice's restaurants are not the best place to feed a sweet habit – with a few exceptions, there are far more tempting pastries to be found on the shelves of the city's pasticcerie. The classic end to a meal here is a plate of **buranei** – sweet egg biscuits – served with a dessert wine such as Fragolino. Then it's quickly on to the more important matter of which grappa to order.

Vocabulary

Italian is pronounced as spelled. Stresses usually fall on the second-last syllable; a stress on the final syllable is indicated by an accent.

There are three 'you' forms: the formal singular *lei*, the informal singular *tu*, and the plural *voi*. Masculine nouns and accompanying adjectives generally end in 'o' (plural 'i'), female nouns and their adjectives end in 'a' (plural 'e').

VENETIAN

The distinctive nasal Venetian drawl is more than just an accent: locals have their own vocabulary too. Venetians tend to ignore consonants, running vowels together in long diphthongs (explaining how *vostro schiavo* – 'your servant' – became *ciao*.) *Xè* is pronounced 'zay'; *gò* sounds like 'go' in 'got.' For more, visit www.veneto.org/language.

PRONUNCIATION

Vowels
a – as in ask
e – like a in age (closed e) or e in sell (open e)
i – like ea in east
o – as in hotel (closed o) or in hot (open o)
u – as in boot
Consonants
c before a, o or u – like c in cat
c before an e or an i – like the ch in check (sh as in ship in Venetian)
ch – like c in cat
g before a, o or u – like g in get
g before an e or an i – like the j in jig
gh – like the g in get
gl followed by an i – like lli in million
gn – like ny in canyon
qu – as in quick
r – always rolled
s – two sounds, as in soap or rose
sc before an e or an i – like the sh in shame
sch – like the sc in scout
z – two different sounds, like ts or dz

USEFUL PHRASES

(**English** – Italian/*Venetian*)

● **hello and goodbye** – ciao (used informally in other parts of Italy; in all social situations in Venice); **good morning, hello** – buongiorno; **good afternoon, good evening** – buonasera

● **please** – per favore, per piacere; **thank you** – grazie; **you're welcome** – prego; **excuse me** – mi scusi (polite), scusami (informal) *scusìme*/*me scusa*
● **I'm sorry** – mi dispiace/*me dispiaxe*; **I don't understand** – non capisco, non ho capito/*no gò capìo*; **do you speak English?** – parla inglese?
● **open** – aperto/*verto*; **closed** – chiuso; **when does it open?** – quando apre?; **it's closed** – è chiuso/*xè serà*; **what's the time?** – che ore sono?
● **do you have a light?** – hai d'accendere?/*ti gà da accender, ti gà fógo?*

TRANSPORT

● **car** – macchina; **bus** – autobus; **taxi** – tassi, taxi; **train** – treno; **plane** – aereo; **stop** (bus/vaporetto) – fermata; **station** – stazione; **platform** – binario
● **ticket/s** – biglietto, biglietti; **one way** – solo andata; **return** – andata e ritorno; **I'd like a ticket to...** – Vorrei un biglietto per...

COMMUNICATIONS

phone – telefono; **mobile phone** – cellulare; **postcard** – cartolina; **stamp** – francobollo; **email** – (messaggio di) posta elettronica

DIRECTIONS

entrance – entrata; **exit** – uscita; **where is...?** – dov'è...?/*dove xè?*; **(turn) left** – (gira a) sinistra; **(it's on the) right** – (è sulla/a) destra; **straight on** – sempre dritto; **could you tell me the way to...?** – mi può indicare la strada per...?; **is it near/far?** – è vicino/lontano?

EATING & DRINKING

See also p169 **The Menu.**
● **I'd like to book a table for four at eight** – vorrei prenotare una tavola per quattro alle otto; **that was poor/good/delicious** – era mediocre/buono/ottimo
● **the bill** – il conto; **I think there's a mistake in this bill** – credo che il conto sia sbagliato; **is service included?** – è incluso il servizio?

ACCOMMODATION

I'd like to book a single/ twin/double bedroom – vorrei prenotare una camera singola/doppia/matrimoniale; **I'd prefer a room with a bath/shower/window over the courtyard/canal** – preferirei una camera con vasca da bagno/doccia/finestra sul cortile/canale

SHOPPING

● **shop** – negozio/*botega*; **how much does it cost/is it?** – quanto costa?, quant'è?/*quanto xè?* **do you accept credit cards?** – si accettano le carte di credito? **do you have small change?** – ha delle monete?
● **I'd like to try on the blue sandals/black shoes/brown boots** – vorrei provare i sandali blu/le scarpe nere/gli stivali marroni; **I take (shoe) size** – porto il numero...; **I take (dress) size** – porto la taglia...; **it's too loose/ too tight/just right** – mi sta largo/ stretto/bene
● **a litre** – un litro; **100 grams of** – un etto di; **200 grams of** – due etti di; **one kilo of** – un kilo di

DAYS & TIMES

● **Monday** – lunedì; **Tuesday** – martedì; **Wednesday** – mercoledì; **Thursday** – giovedì; **Friday** – venerdì; **Saturday** – sabato; **Sunday** – domenica
● **yesterday** – ieri; **today** – oggi/*ancùo*; **tomorrow** – domani; **morning** – mattina; **afternoon** – pomeriggio; **evening** – sera; **this evening** – stasera; **night** – notte; **tonight** – stanotte

NUMBERS

0 zero; **1** uno; **2** due; **3** tre; **4** quattro; **5** cinque; **6** sei; **7** sette; **8** otto; **9** nove; **10** dieci; **11** undici; **12** dodici; **13** tredici; **14** quattordici; **15** quindici; **16** sedici; **17** diciassette; **18** diciotto; **19** diciannove; **20** venti; **21** ventuno; **22** ventidue; **30** trenta; **40** quaranta; **50** cinquanta; **60** sessanta; **70** settanta; **80** ottanta; **90** novanta; **100** cento; **1,000** mille; **2,000** duemila

Further Reference

ESSENTIAL INFORMATION

BOOKS

Non-fiction

Paolo Barbaro *Venice Revealed: an Intimate Portrait*
Fascinating facts on the city's physical structure.
Robert Davis & Garry Marvin
Venice: the Tourist Maze
A well-documented study of Venice's role as a tourist mecca.
Deborah Howard
The Architecture of Venice
Howard's *Architecture* is the definitive account.
WD Howells *Venetian Life*
US consul's (1861-65) account of Venetian life before mass tourism.
Peter Humfrey
Painting in Renaissance Venice
Informative and compact enough to carry with you.
Frederick C Lane
Venice: a Maritime Republic
The best single-volume scholarly history of Venice.
Mary Laven *Virgins of Venice: Broken Vows and Cloistered Lives in the Renaissance Convent*
The title says it all.
Michelle Lovric
Venice: Tales of the City
Compendium of writers on Venice.
Mary McCarthy
Venice Observed
Witty account of Venetian art.
Damiano Martin
The Da Fiore Cookbook
How to cook like they do at Da Fiore (*see p175*).
Francesco Da Mosto
Francesco's Venice
Coffee-table guide by a scion of an aristocratic Venetian family.
Jan Morris *Venice*
Impressionistic history.
John Julius Norwich *A History of Venice; Paradise of Cities*
Engagingly rambling.
John Pemble
Venice Rediscovered
On the 19th-century obsession with things Venetian.
David Rosand
Painting in 16th-Century Venice
Read before your trip.
John Ruskin
The Stones of Venice
Ruskin's hymn to the Gothic.
Gary Wills *Venice: Lion City*
Fascinating blend of history and art criticism.

Fiction & literature

Lord Byron
Childe Harold's Pilgrimage; Beppo
Venice as a dream (*Harold*) and at Carnevale (*Beppo*).
Giacomo Casanova *My Life*
The great seducer's escapades in mid 18th-century Venice.
Michael Dibdin *Dead Lagoon*
Aurelio Zen returns to Venice.
Ernest Hemingway
Across the River and into the Trees
Could have been titled 'Across the Canal and into the Bar'.
Henry James
The Wings of the Dove
Melodrama couched in elegant prose.
Donna Leon
Acqua Alta (and many others)
Series featuring detective *commissario* Guido Brunetti.
Thomas Mann
Death in Venice
Disease, decadence, indecision, voyeurism.
Ezra Pound *The Cantos*
Full of abstruse Venetian details.
William Rivière
A Venetian Theory of Heaven
Novel set among the English community in Venice.
William Shakespeare
The Merchant of Venice; Othello
The bard's Venetian offerings.
Sally Vickers
Miss Garnett's Angel
Elderly English lady's staid life is overturned by angelic encounters.

FILM

Casanova (Lasse Halstrom, 2005)
Heath Ledger plays a sugary no-sex-please version of the legendary lover.
The Comfort of Strangers
(Paul Schrader, 1990)
Based on an Ian McEwan novel.
Death in Venice
(Luchino Visconti, 1971)
Dirk Bogarde chases boy around cholera-plagued Venice.
Don't Look Now
(Nicholas Roeg, 1973)
Chilling tale of a couple in Venice after the death of their daughter.
Eve (Joseph Losey, 1962)
Budding novelist meets temptress.
The Merchant of Venice
(Michael Radford, 2004)
Al Pacino is Shylock in this star-studded adaptation.

Senso (Luchino Visconti, 1954)
Tale of sadism and passion.
The Tourist
(Florian Henckel, 2010)
Jolie and Depp in schlocky thriller-comedy.

MUSIC

Lorenzo Da Ponte (1749-1838)
Penned *libretti* for Mozart's *Marriage of Figaro, Don Giovanni* and *Cosi fan tutte*.
Andrea Gabrieli (c1510-1586)
Organist of St Mark's basilica, Gabrieli senior's madrigals were Venetian favourites.
Giovanni Gabrieli (c1556-1612)
composed sacred and choral music, particularly motets; *In ecclesiis* is perhaps his masterpiece.
Antonio Vivaldi (1678-1741)
There's no escaping his *Four Seasons* in Venice.

WEBSITES

www.veneziaunica.it Essential site for pre-booking transport and services (English; *see also p289*).
www.venezia.net Apartment rentals to information on hiring a carnevale costume (English).
www.venetia.it History, useful phone numbers and links (English).
http://english.comune.venezia.it City council's site with useful practical information (English).
www.turismovenezia.it Cultural offerings around the province of Venice. Museum info in English.
www.meetingvenice.it
Hotel booking service for city and surrounds, plus news on events and tourist attractions (English).
www.agendavenezia.org
Comprehensive cultural events listings for the city. (English)

APPS

Tap Venice Eating Essential guide to snacking and dining (English).
Eat Venice Good tips for foodies (English).
hi!tide Venice Instant info on tides and acqua alta (English).
Venezia Unica real-time vaporetto and events info (English).
Telegraph Travel Guide-Venice Handy maps and tips (English).

Death in Venice.

Index

INDEX

INDEX

Maps

Bags packed, milk cancelled, house raised on stilts.

You've packed the suntan lotion, the snorkel set, the stay-pressed shirts. Just one more thing left to do – your bit for climate change. In some of the world's poorest countries, changing weather patterns are destroying lives.

You can help people to deal with the extreme effects of climate change. Raising houses in flood-prone regions is just one life-saving solution.

Climate change costs lives.
Give £5 and let's sort it *Here & Now*

www.oxfam.org.uk/climate-change

Oxfam is a registered charity in England and Wales (No.202918) and Scotland (SCO039042). Oxfam GB is a member of Oxfam International.

Be Humankind (X) Oxfam

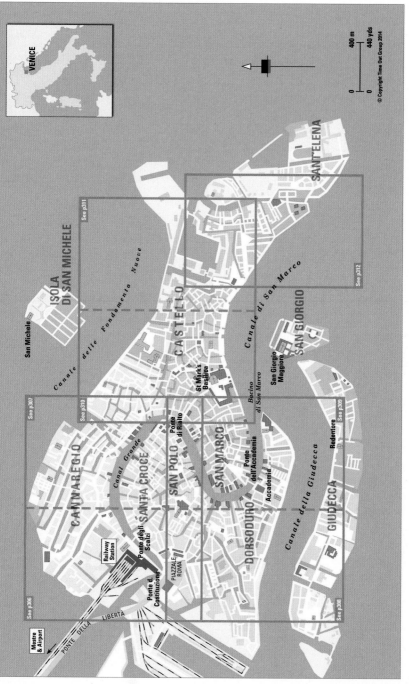

MAPS

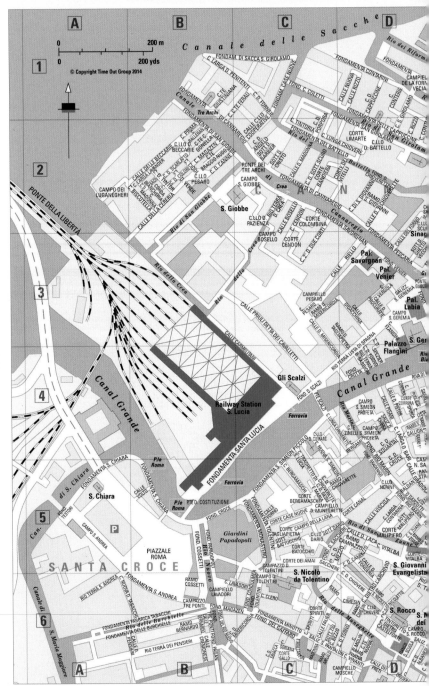

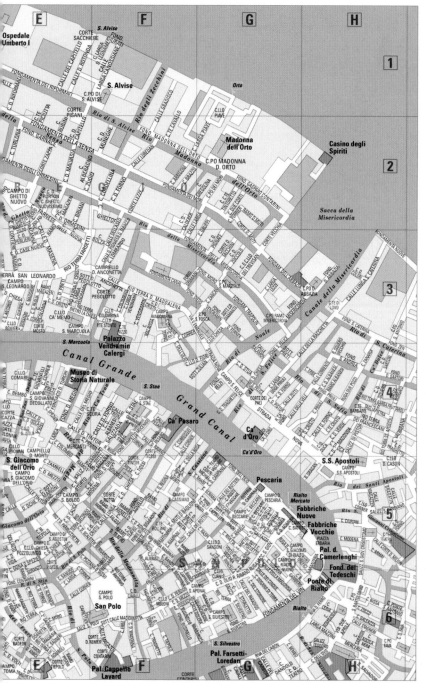

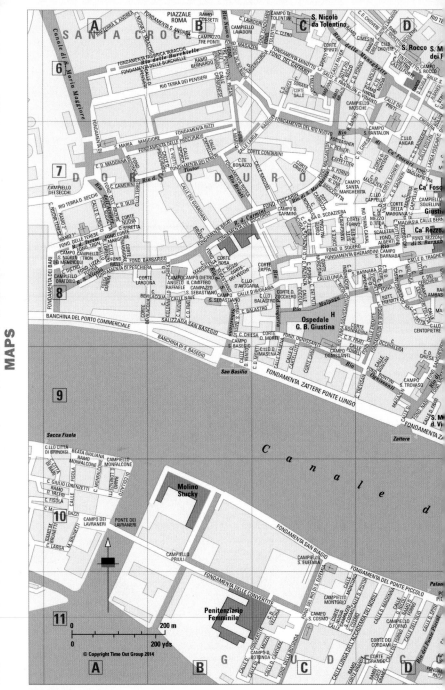

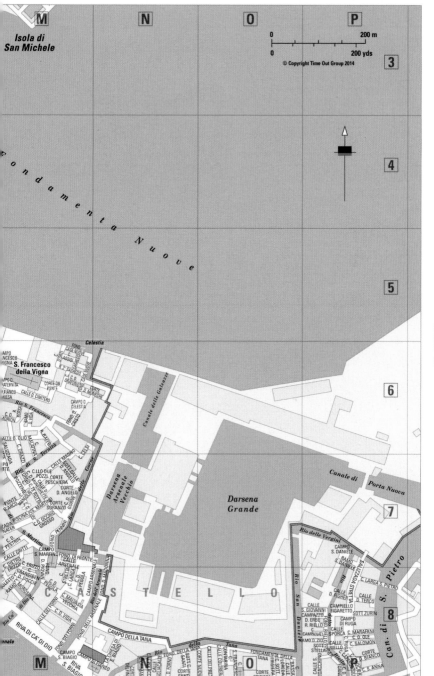

Isola di
San Michele

0 ⊢————————————┤ 200 m
0 ⊢————————————┤ 200 yds
© Copyright Time Out Group 2014

3

4

5

Celestia

S. Francesco
della Vigna

Canale delle Galeazze

6

Canale di Porta Nuova

Darsena
Arsenale
Vecchio

Darsena
Grande

7

Rio delle Vergini

CAMPO
S. DANIELE

CAMPO
S. DANIELE

CALLE LARGA S. PIETRO

S. Martino

S. Martino

CAMPO
S. MARTINO FOND. DI FRONTE

CALLE
ARSENALE

CAMPO ARSENALE

C A S T E L L O

CALLE
D. FIGHER

CAMPIELLO
FIGARETTO

CALLE
D. TERCO

SOTT. ZURLIN

CAMPO
DI RUGA

C. MARAFANI

C. D. OLE

CORTE
BIANCO

Cald' S. Pietro

CAMPO DELLA TANA

CAMPO
S. BIAGIO

RIVA
S. BIAGIO

CAMPO DELLA TANA

Rio della Tana

FONDAMENTA DELLA TANA

CORTE NUOVA

CALLE DEI PRETI

CORTE
FRISIERA

8

M   **N**   **O**   **P**

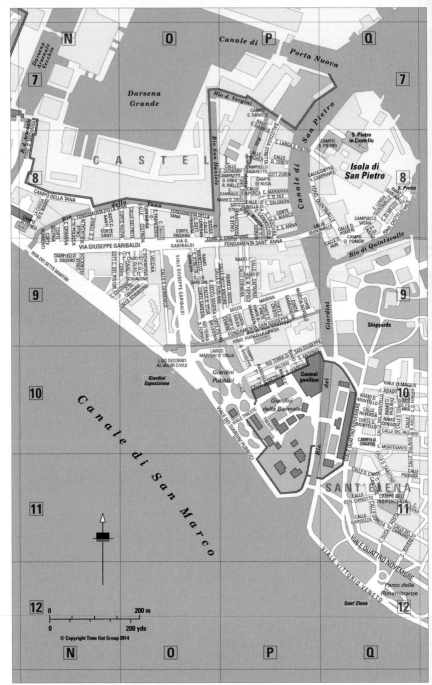

Linee di navigazione \ waterborne routes

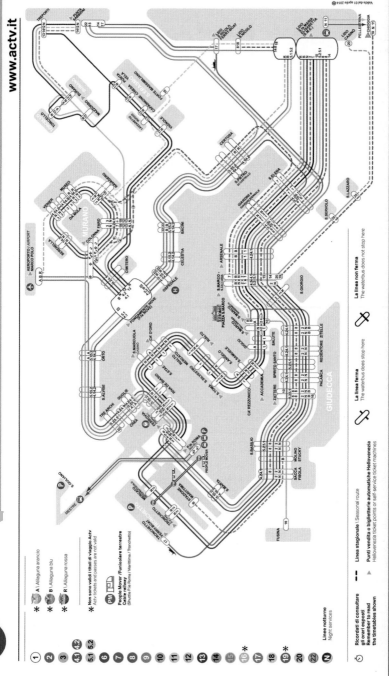

Actv

www.actv.it

①
②
③
④ 4.2
5.1 5.2
⑥
⑦
⑧
⑨
⑩
⑪
⑫
⑬ ⑭
⑯ *
⑰
⑱
⑲ *
⑳
㉒
Ⓝ

* A \ Alilaguna arancio
* B \ Alilaguna blu
* R \ Alilaguna rossa

* Non sono validi i titoli di viaggio Actv
Actv tickets and passes are not valid

People Mover /Funicolare terrestre
Cable railway
(Shuttle P.le Roma / Marittima / Tronchetto)

Ⓧ La linea ferma
The waterbus does stop here

Ⓧ La linea non ferma
The waterbus does not stop here

Linee notturne
Night services

Ⓘ Ricordati di consultare
gli orari esposti
Remember to read
the timetables shown

‒ Linea stagionale \ Seasonal route

▲ Punti vendita o biglietterie automatiche Hellovenezia
Hellovenezia ticket points or self-service ticket machines

Presso i punti vendita Hellovenezia puoi trovare anche: biglietti per eventi, musei, mostre e teatri // guide e mappe // tour // Venezia Unica // merchandising
At the Hellovenezia ticket points you can also find: tickets for events, museums, exhibitions and theaters // guides and maps // tours // Venezia Unica // merchandising

Info call center Hellovenezia +39 0412424 \ www.hellovenezia.com

HELLOVENEZIA

Street Index

STREET INDEX

STREET INDEX

STREET INDEX

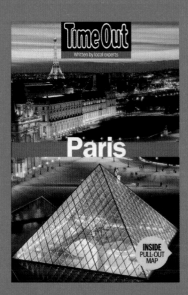